Women and the Anglican Church Congress 1861–1938

Bloomsbury Studies in Religion, Gender and Sexuality

Series Editors: Dawn Llewellyn, Sonya Sharma and Sîan Hawthorne

This interdisciplinary series explores the intersections of religions, genders and sexualities. It promotes the dynamic connections between gender and sexuality across a diverse range of religious and spiritual lives, cultures, histories and geographical locations, as well as contemporary discourses around secularism and non-religion. The series publishes cutting-edge research that considers religious experiences, communities, institutions and discourses in global and transnational contexts, and examines the fluid and intersecting features of identity and social positioning.

Using theoretical and methodological approaches from inter/transdisciplinary perspectives, *Bloomsbury Studies in Religion, Gender, and Sexuality* addresses the neglect of religious studies perspectives in gender, queer and feminist studies. It offers a space where gender can critically engage with religion, and for exploring questions of intersectionality, particularly with respect to critical race, disability, post-colonial and decolonial theories.

Becoming Queer and Religious in Malaysia and Singapore, Sharon A. Bong
Beyond Religion in India and Pakistan, Navtej K. Purewal and Virinder S. Kalra
Experience, Identity & Epistemic Injustice within Ireland's Magdalene Laundries, Chloë K. Gott
Narrative, Identity and Ethics in Postcolonial Kenya, Eleanor Tiplady Higgs
Street Football, Gender, and Muslim Youth in the Netherlands, Kathrine van den Bogert

Women and the Anglican Church Congress 1861–1938

Space, Place and Agency

Sue Anderson-Faithful and Catherine Holloway

BLOOMSBURY ACADEMIC
LONDON • NEW YORK • OXFORD • NEW DELHI • SYDNEY

BLOOMSBURY ACADEMIC
Bloomsbury Publishing Plc
50 Bedford Square, London, WC1B 3DP, UK
1385 Broadway, New York, NY 10018, USA
29 Earlsfort Terrace, Dublin 2, Ireland

BLOOMSBURY, BLOOMSBURY ACADEMIC and the Diana logo
are trademarks of Bloomsbury Publishing Plc

First published in Great Britain 2023
This paperback edition published in 2025.

Copyright © Sue Anderson-Faithful and Catherine Holloway, 2023

Sue Anderson-Faithful and Catherine Holloway have asserted their rights under the Copyright, Designs and Patents Act, 1988, to be identified as Authors of this work.

For legal purposes the Acknowledgements on p. x constitute
an extension of this copyright page.

Cover image: Church League for Women's Suffrage procession, c.1909-1914
© LSE Library, No restrictions, via Wikimedia Commons

All rights reserved. No part of this publication may be reproduced or transmitted in any form or by any means, electronic or mechanical, including photocopying, recording, or any information storage or retrieval system, without prior permission in writing from the publishers.

Bloomsbury Publishing Plc does not have any control over, or responsibility for, any third-party websites referred to or in this book. All internet addresses given in this book were correct at the time of going to press. The author and publisher regret any inconvenience caused if addresses have changed or sites have ceased to exist, but can accept no responsibility for any such changes.

A catalogue record for this book is available from the British Library.

Library of Congress Control Number: 2022950925

ISBN: HB: 978-1-3503-2418-3
       PB: 978-1-3503-2422-0
       ePDF: 978-1-3503-2419-0
       eBook: 978-1-3503-2420-6

Series: Bloomsbury Studies in Religion, Gender, and Sexuality

Typeset by Integra Software Services Pvt. Ltd.

To find out more about our authors and books visit www.bloomsbury.com
and sign up for our newsletters.

For my mother Anne Steel Anderson 1927–1999 SAF
For my father Edward Charles Henning 1938–2012 CH

Contents

List of figures	viii
List of tables	ix
Acknowledgements	x
Archives and abbreviations	xi
Introduction – Congress a space for women	1
1 Visiting the Church congress	9
2 Women in the Church – Deaconesses, Sisters, Missionaries and Spiritual Aspirations	47
3 The Mothers' Union and the Girls' Friendly Society	75
4 Networks – Organizations, Politics, Empire and Suffrage	97
5 Widening Horizons – Education and Leisure	123
6 Public Service and the World of Work	153
7 The Legacy of Congress – Women, Space and Place	179
Notes	192
Bibliography	236
Index	249

Figures

1.1	Louise Creighton by Walter Stoneman, *c.* 1916. Source: By permission National Portrait Gallery	35
2.1	Agnes Maude Royden by Underwood and Underwood, *c.* 1928. Source: By permission National Portrait Gallery	66
3.1	Mary Sumner, *c.* 1910. Source: By permission Hampshire Record Office	80
4.1	Lady Laura Elizabeth Ridding and George Ridding by Schemboche, after 1876. Source: By permission National Portrait Gallery	103
5.1	Lilian Mary Faithfull by Eliot and Fry. Source: By permission National Portrait Gallery	137
6.1	Gertrude Mary Tuckwell by Bassano Ltd. Source: By permission National Portrait Gallery	170

Tables

1	Frequent contributors to congress	21
2	Congress ticket sales from official reports 1882–1924	28

Acknowledgements

This book is result of a collaboration engendered through participation in the Centre for the History of Women's Education at the University of Winchester, a forum that enables scholarly network connections and fosters enduring friendship.

We would like to thank the helpful staff of the Maughan Library, King's College London, who ventured into the basement on our behalf. We would also like to express our gratitude to all those who have worked to assemble the treasure trove that is the British Newspaper Archive.

Archives and abbreviations

Archives

British Newspaper Archive
Church of England Record Centre
Hampshire Record Office
King's College London Maughan Library
Lambeth Palace Library Mothers' Union Collection

List of Abbreviations

ARCC	*Authorized Record of the Church Congress*
BWES	British Women's Emigration Society
COS	Charity Organization Society
CT	*Church Times*
GDA	Girls' Diocesan Association
GFS	Girls' Friendly Society
HRO	Hampshire Record Office
IGCC	*Illustrated Guide to the Church Congress*
MIC	*Mothers' in Council*
MU	Mothers' Union
NUWW	National Union of Women Workers
ODNB	*Oxford Dictionary of National Biography*
ORCC	*Official Record of the Church Congress*
SACS	South African Colonization Society
SPG	Society for the Propagation of the Gospel

Introduction – Congress a space for women

The Church congress was instigated in 1861 by Archbishop of Canterbury, John Bird Sumner. His aim was to strengthen the Anglican Church at a time of social change, developments in education and an ongoing context of contested authority in matters of religion.[1] The congress was intended to foster relations between clergy and lay people, educate the populace in Church views and in so doing promote both Anglican unity and social cohesion.[2] The week-long congresses, which were held annually in different locations, proclaimed the established Church as part of the social and political fabric of the nation with parades, services addressed by prominent churchmen and civic receptions hosted by the Mayor and Mayoress of the host town. Fringe meetings and exhibitions provided additional attractions to the official programme of papers and discussion. Topics tabled for consideration demonstrated the engagement of 'church people' with issues of the day such as poverty, education, industrial relations and the position of women. At the second meeting of congress the issue of women's work for the Church was on the agenda, and women spectators were allowed to watch the proceedings from a segregated section of the gallery in Oxford's Sheldonian Theatre.[3] This modest concession opened the way for women's participation in congress initially as members of the audience and hostesses.

From 1862 onwards, the annual congresses attracted substantial numbers of attendees both male and female. Despite the disapproval articulated by a disgruntled clerical correspondent in the *Yorkshire Post and Leeds Intelligencer* in 1872, who complained of 'ladies crowding the platform' and observed with disapproval that 'three fifths of the audience were ladies' women were there to stay.[4] The following year, at the Bath congress, the topic of women recurred as an agenda item, and *The Hampshire Advertiser* reported 'a goodly number of ladies' present.[5] However, it was not until 1875 that a female perspective, but not physical voice, was heard when novelist Charlotte Yonge had her paper on 'Women's Work in the Church' read from the platform by the Rev. C. W. Bond.[6] The 1881 Newcastle congress saw two new developments: the first meeting dedicated to an audience of women, and the first women speakers on the platform.[7] The following year at the Derby congress, purity campaigner Jane Ellice Hopkins became the first woman to address an audience of men.[8] The years between 1882 and 1913 were the heyday for women's meetings when special sections of the congress programme directed at a female audience, provided an opening for women to speak on a range of topics. Meetings targeted a widening audience representing various categories such as mothers, working women and later, girl students and school girls. Although the number of women speakers who addressed mixed audiences on topics featured in main congress agendas increased over time, they remained a small minority. By the final congress of 1938 a total of 294 speeches had been given by women.

Every congress had its proceedings published in book form. The official reports of congress included verbatim transcripts of the papers given by all platform speakers. So congress voices were captured for posterity and could reach audiences beyond those present in the congress venue. Congress was also well publicized. Regional and national newspapers and magazines gave considerable and consistent coverage of congress and recorded a range of perspectives on its proceedings and its female participants, and a visual record is evident in photographs and latterly in newsreel footage. Diaries and correspondence from congress contributors add another dimension to the archive. This provides a rich source of data to inform an exploration of the topics, themes and voices at congress with an emphasis on the hitherto unexplored experience of women.

The congress years coincide with a dynamic period for women in the negotiation of citizenship and the enlargement of horizons of possibility in education, work and leisure. Religion has been identified as a significant mediator of constructions of gender and contingent interpretations of the 'nature' and role of women.[9] It was a period in which relations between the sexes, marriage and the role and status of women were topical both within the Church and in wider society. Religion was a mediating factor here, and also permeated the proliferation of philanthropic activity. A field in which women found opportunities for self-realization pursued aspirations towards the alleviation of social problems and in some cases found a pathway to employment.[10] This book adds to existing scholarship by highlighting congress as a long-standing forum where these themes come together.

The two main Anglican organizations run by women, the Girls' Friendly Society and Mothers' Union dating from 1875 and 1876, respectively, exemplify the role of religion in framing and legitimizing women's activism both 'at home' and overseas in colonies and contact zones, and congress provided a launch pad for the latter organization's official sanction by the Church.[11] Louise Creighton, one of the most active and well-connected women within the Anglican communion at the time, was active in both organizations, and served as the first president of the National Union of Women Workers, a forum for women's philanthropic groups in which 'congress women' were well represented.[12] Creighton, who went on to achieve distinction through other contributions to public service, spoke at ten Church congresses between 1894 and 1924. In her debut speech, which took the theme 'What women can do to raise the standard of moral life', she stated that: 'We do not wish to be sofa cushions, or even props to men, but we wish to work by their side'.[13] Her assertion encapsulated the aspiration of 'churchwomen' to participate alongside their male counterparts in initiatives directed towards the improvement of society.[14] It was also a plea that women should have their intellect, capacity for action and their contribution as citizens acknowledged.

Women's aspirations to pursue a religious life were expressed in missionary activity, both at home and overseas, and through the establishment of Anglican sisterhoods.[15] The Deaconess movement and university settlements also provided opportunities to pursue a vocation.[16] All these categories found a voice on the congress platform. So too did women aspiring to equality of spiritual authority within the ministry of the Church. In the period after the First World War Edith Picton-Turbervill and notable evangelist Maude Royden used congress to promote their views, and meetings organized by groups such as the League of Church Militant were scheduled to coincide with congress.[17]

Education, both informal and formal, was evolving; printed material proliferated, and educational opportunities and curricula for girls and young women were enlarged and negotiated against a context of gendered social practice and religious involvement in schooling.[18] Here, and in other fields such as medicine, and later the law, women were working towards the achievement of professional status. Legislative reform engaged with women's rights to property and access to local government.[19] Aspirations for female suffrage and political engagement were articulated in the formation of organized bodies such as the 1889 Women's Franchise League, the 1897 National Union of Women's Suffrage Societies and the Conservative Primrose League.[20] At a time of imperial expansion women were also looking overseas and engaging with emigration, race and the exercise of colonial power.[21] Travel writing and missionary intelligence from the British imperial periphery and beyond informed identities 'at home' and were embodied at congress by celebrated traveller Isabella Bird Bishop.[22]

Congress brings together women activists networked by philanthropic, political and religious orientation, those with emergent careers both paid and unpaid in public service, and professionals in education, health, journalism and law. It exemplifies what Martha Vicinus designated a widening sphere of opportunity in work and community.[23] Speakers between 1881 and 1938, some of whom are noted below, include a roll call of women distinguished as pioneers for their contribution to public service, several have the distinction of entries in the *Dictionary of National Biography* and attention in scholarly works. The overlapping category of philanthropists and wives of distinguished clergy is represented amongst others by Laura Ridding, who, like Louise Creighton, was active in the National Union of Women Workers, and Mary Sumner, GFS activist and founder of the MU.[24]

At a time when the discourse of motherhood was moving from a moral and religious emphasis to include interest in the physical aspects of women's reproductive function, medical and scientific authority was drawn on to legitimize assertions towards the regulation of women's conduct.[25] Engagement with temperance, a recurrent topic at congress, similarly drew together the association of morality and self-restraint with medical perspectives. Anxieties were not just about personal well-being but the heath of 'race' and nation. At congress, this topical interest in heath and eugenics was articulated by (amongst others) medically qualified experts Mary Scharlieb, whose publications included *Womanhood and Race Regeneration*, and *Youth and Sex*. Kate Mitchell, the author of *The Drink Question: Its Social and Medical Aspects*, and Ellen Pinsent of the National Association for the Care and Protection of the Feeble Minded, both served on both the 1904 and 1908 Royal Commissions into the subject.[26]

Katherine Gleadle, Sarah Richardson and Krista Cowman have drawn attention to the political activism of women before enfranchisement, and the entanglement of kinship networks and sites of power.[27] At congress, women connected to the political world are represented, among others, by Laura Ridding, daughter of Lord Chancellor Roundell Palmer, first Earl of Selborne, Lucy, Lady Frederick Cavendish and her sister-in-law, the journalist Kathleen Lyttelton, and Helen Gladstone, the daughter of Prime Minister William Ewart Gladstone.[28] Women with an imperialist outlook, a category that overlaps with political positioning, views on 'race' and religious orientation, and membership of the patriotic MU and GFS, are exemplified by the Hon. Ellen Joyce of the British Women's Emigration Society and Louisa Knightly, the editor of its magazine *The Imperial Colonist*.[29] Trade Union activist Clementina Black and employment law expert Gertrude Tuckwell, contributors to the 1908 volume *Women in Industry from Seven Points of View*, reflect both increasing professionalism and the involvement of women (and the congress) with social justice and the world of work.[30] In the field of education Headmistresses Lilian Faithfull and Sara Burstall, and Elizabeth Wordsworth, the first principal of the Oxford women's college Lady Margaret Hall, represent the emerging professional elite.[31] Literature and leisure were also represented by novelists including Mrs Leith Adams and Christabel Coleridge; perhaps more unexpectedly distinguished actress Sybil Thorndike used the congress platform to assert the respectability and cultural value of her profession.[32]

The diverse themes noted above, from philanthropy, politics, empire, education, motherhood and medicine, have drawn a substantial body of work from scholars interested in women's agency and activism, and the congress has been referenced by Brian Heeney in his investigation into the aspirations of women for spiritual authority in the Church of England. This book covers new ground by focusing on congress as a public participatory space for women and a location for the negotiation of women's place. It aims to recover the hitherto under-explored presence of women at the congresses and acknowledge the contribution made by significant women, to public life and discourse on womanhood, via the platforms of the Church congresses. In addition, the book seeks to commemorate the unvoiced presence of the large numbers of women including those from the working class, who engaged with the congresses as members of the audience.

Women associated with congress demonstrate allegiance to over fifty organizations. A feature of congress that this book examines is the intricacy and reach of kinship, friendship and what Margaret Keck and Katheryn A. Sikkink have designated as advocacy networks.[33] The analysis of networks which have a spatial dimension as affirmative and communicative structures in relation to the realization of women's individual aims and collective activism is an appropriate lens for the exploration of congress as an associative space and node of connection between individuals, groups, organizations and topical developments relevant to women's lives.[34] There is resonance too, with Linda Eisenmann's analysis of female institution building both within and in addition to existing structures.[35]

An exploration of women negotiating agency,[36] in relation to a space demarcated by an institution which prioritized male authority, must engage with socially constructed notions of femininity and masculinity.[37] As Sue Morgan has noted, 'the lens of gender is a tool in an analysis of experience that looks beyond categorizations of oppression to consider the negotiation, replication and transference of power within the fluidities of public and private space'.[38] The unequal relationships of power signified as class must also be acknowledged.[39] Although the notion of separate spheres has been proven to be much more nuanced and complex than a simple binary,[40] women's access to the public world remains of interest, and this book draws on the spatial turn in scholarship marked by Lefebvre's landmark *Production of Space*, and the work of feminist geographers Linda McDowell and Doreen Massey.[41] In the field of religion the spatial turn in scholarship is exemplified by the work of Kim Knott who advocates attention to the significance of place in religious practice.[42] As with separate spheres, private and public are not a binary absolute for there are varieties of public space and degrees of public exposure according to context but gender remains a mediating factor in access to space and performance within it.[43]

In addition to officially designated spaces and places for women as in the women's section meetings, congress provided opportunities for sociability as in the congress 'conversatzione'. The congress exhibition, and fringe meetings which addressed a diversity of topics including suffrage, gave further opportunities for the exchange of ideas. Lyn H. Lofland conceives of space divided into the public realm and the parochial realm, and Jane Rendall thinks in terms of a variety of publics and advocates alertness to the different possibilities and gendered codes and nuanced behaviours that might apply to spaces involving degrees of public exposure and contingent inclusion or restriction.[44] Linda Kerber's observation that women may work both within and beyond existing institutional spaces to forward their aspirations may also apply to women participants at congress who were operating within the official institutional space at 'the Church Congress' and also negotiating authority in diverse fields such as education, medicine and local government.[45] How women achieve access to space, both individually and collectively, and what attributes and strategies they draw upon to cross boundaries and improve their position is a theme of this book.

The chapters in this book are organized to reflect how the key themes pertinent to women's opportunities and horizons of possibility relating to religion, philanthropy, work, education, leisure and political engagement were evident at congress. The analytical stance underpinning investigation of the congress as a space for women rests on Massey's notion that place is not static and that spaces/places are the product of interrelations constituted through interaction in what may be a theatre of conflict.[46] To unpick women finding space and making 'their place', that is, negotiating constraint and agency within, through and beyond the space of the congress, analysis draws on the concepts and categories proposed by Pierre Bourdieu. His 'thinking tools' of habitus, field and capital accommodate the significance of networks, the mediating factors of class and gender, the prioritization of various forms of knowledge and the authority accorded to individuals or groups. In using the term field to conceptualize political, economic or cultural arenas such as religion, in which identity is established, agency is enacted, Bourdieu uses a spatial metaphor. The notion of fields as locations for the production of value, knowledge or symbolic goods in which competition for ascendant position, based on the recognition of desirable capital attributes, takes place accords with Massey's notion of a theatre of conflict.[47] However, the first priority is to tell the story of women's diverse engagement with congress.

We begin by building a picture of the civic, social and cultural character of the congress and its organization and evoke women's experience of congress. Next, women's official roles in the Church as deaconesses, sisters and missionaries are the focus, and the chapter reviews the claims for greater spiritual authority asserted by women after 1918. Chapter 3 relates dominant discourses of purity, motherhood, patriotism, mission and the imperial project to the Mothers' Union and Girls' Friendly Society, organizations endorsed by the Anglican hierarchy. Chapter 4 locates congress women in organizational and political networks beyond the MU and GFS, notably the National Union of Women Workers, recognizing their diverse positions in relation to politics, imperialism and suffrage. Chapter 5 uses congress as a lens for examining initiatives in educational provision for girls and women, noting the emergence of elite institutions and changing perceptions relating to women and leisure. Chapter 6 picks up the theme of public service and the world of work. We note the presence of professional women at congress and explore the trajectories of women moving from traditions of philanthropy to positions of authority in local welfare admiration and thence to service in government and the judiciary. The concluding chapter returns to the lens of feminist geography, the spatial turn in scholarship and the concepts and categories suggested by Bourdieu, to reflect on the legacy of congress as a transactional space for women both intimate and public in which the negotiation of agency, authority and autonomy place played out.

1

Visiting the Church congress

Congress comes to town: Pomp and pageantry

The Church congress was held in the autumn, usually in October and was an annual event between 1861 and 1913. After being suspended for the duration of the First World War it resumed in 1919 and continued on an annual basis until 1928. Congress was not held in 1929 as no host venue could be found.[1] The last three congresses were held in 1930, 1935 and 1938, respectively. According to the Reverend Lamplugh's 1935 retrospective reflection on the Church congresses, 'One of the strongest points of congress is its mobility.'[2] Congress took place in a different location each year in England and Wales with the exception of 1868, when congress was held in Dublin. Host towns were located within the diocese that had assumed congress organizing duties for the year in question, and varied from coastal resorts to industrial cities. Venues were dispersed across the country from Newcastle in the north, Plymouth in the south west, Wolverhampton in the midlands and from Rhyl in Wales across to Great Yarmouth in the east. Bristol provided the location for congress three times, and Birmingham, Cambridge, Manchester and Newcastle-upon-Tyne hosted the congress twice.

The objective of congress was to promote more active lay participation in religious activity, if not church governance, and to make the Church visible as part of the political and social fabric of the nation.[3] *The Quarterly Review* of January 1864, which regarded the congress as an 'awakening', endorsed this intention and pointed to the usefulness of a forum that brought Church of England clergy and laymen together as a means of countering adherence to rival denominations, at a time when in the words of their reporter: 'Other shepherds have been appointed, and have done a great deal for the flock.'[4] Congress was also intended to draw together factions within Anglicanism at a time when differences between High Church Tractarians and Low Church evangelicals on the literal or symbolic significance of the Eucharist, 'correct' forms of worship, and appropriate Church adornment had threatened Church unity. In his report on the Bournemouth Church congress of 1935 the Rev. K. E. N. Lamplugh, vicar of Hartley Wintney, writing in the *Church Monthly Parish Magazine*, looked back at the history of congress and referred to its introduction as a 'breath of fresh air' after the controversy of the Gorham Case and the prosecution of Bishop Colenso for heresy.[5] In referring to these painful incidents, one a protracted legal wrangle over doctrine, and the other a dispute over uniformity of worship, he was highlighting the congress as an inclusive and conciliatory initiative which sought to bring Anglicans, clergy and lay people, together in a sociable and celebratory forum.[6] In 1867 sectional meetings exclusively for clergy were abandoned, a move considered a 'great improvement' by *The Cardiff Times*, and the congress programme was extended from three to four days.[7] In 1878, sixteen years after women had first been admitted to congress as members of the audience, *The Examiner*, with its tongue in its cheek, evoked congress as a social event in which women were included:

> For fun of a mild kind this annual meeting of clergy affords fair scope. There is a certain amount of eating and drinking and flirtation – all of course kept within very careful bounds … mixed up with a certain amount of church going, and an attendance at meetings half religious, half humorous which combine to provide at Church congress, attractions not without their value to the male or female mind.[8]

The 1851 census which elicited information on religious affiliation had revealed the popularity of rival denominations. Congress can be seen as an attempt to raise the profile and popularity of the Anglican Church.[9] The issue of disestablishment and the claims of rival denominations to civic inclusion were reflected at congress, particularly when the venue was located in a region in which nonconformists were well represented. At Shrewsbury in 1896 'The Idea of a National Church' was on the agenda and three years later at the London congress 'the Church in Wales' was addressed, and by 1909, at the Swansea congress, an entire section of the agenda was devoted to the topic. The Swansea congress also reflects the acknowledgement accorded to nonconformist denominations as fellow Christians. The programme featured a message from the Methodist Assembly by the Rev W. Talbot Rice and an address of welcome from the Free Churches. The recognition of nonconformist allegiances became a regular feature of congress. In 1910, Cambridge followed Swansea by including a 'Free Church Welcome' to members of congress, and a nonconformist greeting was given at Middlesbrough in 1912. The following year Southampton continued the trend.[10] Despite these ecumenical courtesies congress was focused on promoting the Anglican Church as the Church of the nation.

The presence of congress was welcomed by host towns and was endorsed by the provision of mayoral hospitality.[11] Congress not only gave the town the symbolic endorsement of the established Church but also, with its influx of visitors, who required accommodation, meals and entertainment, was a stimulus to the local economy. In its coverage of the 1891 congress *The North Wales Chronicle* observed that: 'In many of the shops at Rhyl during the week were to be seen the words "Success to the Congress."' The *Yorkshire Post and Leeds Intelligencer*, in its coverage of the same congress, noted with amusement the less-than-subtle publicity for local business and the attractions of the town, given by a local councillor in the opening speeches.[12] However, there were times when congress had to accommodate local circumstances. Laura Ridding noted that despite the enthusiasm for the Nottingham congress shown by the 'Churchpeople of Notts and Derbyshire', the congress had to be 'held at an unusually early week in the autumn on account of the unchangeable date of the historic Goose Fair. I learned that no Mayor or Council, or Home Secretary, or "all the Queen's horses and all the Queen's men", could disturb the sacred birds from our Capitol for an hour without an Act of Parliament'.[13]

There were other logistic challenges, the concentration of large numbers of visitors in the host town centre could cause congestion, and the *Norfolk Chronicle* of Saturday, 30 September 1865, published the detailed and extensive 'POLICE REGULATIONS' for managing traffic flow at the congress venue, which, according to their author Robert Hitchman, the Chief Constable of Norwich, would be 'strictly enforced'.[14] Transport by rail was less problematic. Those seeking to attend were well served by the railway network and the willingness of railway companies to offer advantageous ticket prices for conference goers. An article promoting the 1885 congress in the *Morning Post* reminded readers of the 'large concessions made by the South Western and Brighton Railway companies in allowing return tickets at single fares from any station on their system, if ten miles from Portsmouth' that were available to those in possession of a congress ticket.[15] *The Times* in 1891 made a point of noting that Rhyl, the chosen destination for the congress that year, was 'almost at the junction of the railways' and a 'package tour' for travel from Dublin to the congress was advertised in the *Irish Times*.[16]

Congress began with the pageantry of a ceremonial parade of robed clergy and civic dignitaries through the streets of the host town. At Great Yarmouth the town band and fire brigade joined the procession.[17] Nottingham boasted the presence of twenty one 'Transmarine brothers' as the President [George Ridding] called the visitor bishops from colonies and contact zones overseas who added colour to the procession.[18] The parades were well documented by photographs and later newsreels, which record crowds of spectators and confirm public interest in the spectacle. *The Times*, reporting on the Southampton congress of 1913, noted the large number of spectators who lined the High Street as the procession marched past singing hymns including 'The Church's One Foundation'.[19] The procession was seen by its organizers as an integral part of congress. Canon Charles Earle Raven, the author of the 1926 Southport congress official report, thought that there were: 'Few pageants of the Church more dignified, more inspiring, or more impressive than the great procession from the Town Hall to the several churches in which the congress sermons were to be preached … the onlookers were silenced and awed'. He continued: 'a procession can not only be an allegory and a witness, but a real act of worship'.[20]

This large-scale pageantry required a great deal of coordination. The congress route was planned meticulously and the positioning of those taking part took a great deal of organization. At the Southport congress the parade that so impressed Charles Raven was under the direction of Canon Dwelly. The Bournemouth congress of 1935 employed a Congress Marshall, the Rev. Eric Southam, to coordinate three processions, comprising choirs and robed clergy that were to take place at three different churches. Instructions for those participating and contingency plans for wet weather were published in the conference handbook to ensure that those taking part were aware of the plans.[21]

Pathé News reels were taken of the congress opening from 1920 and give an impression of the impressive scale of the procession. They also illustrate that the parades, which consisted largely of clergy and civic dignitaries, were very much dominated by men. It was not until the twentieth century that women, albeit still in a minority, appeared in the procession. The 1923 film shows a handful of women in the procession whose 'ordinary' feminine dress is outdone by the opulent robes and mortar boards, denoting academic status and affiliation to institutions of power, worn by the male participants.[22] One of the two archived Pathé films of the 1926 congress procession includes material that was omitted from the version released to cinema audiences. These outtakes provide a visual record of women in the procession who were edited from the final cut. They also show the antics of a small stray dog who runs in and out of shot, an irritant to film-makers and procession participants alike, proof that the procession did not always achieve the gravitas and spiritual solemnity claimed by Charles Raven.[23]

There were other incidents that threatened to disrupt the dignity of the procession. Whilst congress was intended to promote lay participation in religious activity, theological topics liable to divide opinion were avoided. The *Bury Free Press* noted that 'Subjects of a practical rather than polemical nature' would be on the agenda at the Norwich congress of 1865.[24] However, the sense that feelings were still running high amongst adherents of Low and High Church views on matters of religious observance is suggested by the preface of the 1881 congress report which reminded readers that the congress 'Objects' were to foster harmonious discussion of topical issues of interest to church people. The preface went on to spell out that there was to be no voting on motions or theological debate, and that speakers, who should be communicants of the Church, should keep to both the allotted subject and to the time allowed.[25] Despite these exhortations congress provided a focus for protests from John Kensit, a vehement campaigner against ritual within Anglicanism, and founder in 1889, of the 'Protestant Truth Society'. His accusations of a Roman Catholic conspiracy among members of the Anglican clergy and uninhibited courting of publicity provided 'good copy' and photographic opportunities for newspapers. Kensit, described by *The Daily Mail* as 'an individual of peculiar prominence', protested at Bradford in 1898, and his appearance on the platform at Newcastle in 1900 caused what the *Cheltenham Examiner*, in an article whose subheading was 'A Kensit Scene', described as an 'extraordinary uproar' amongst the audience.[26] For Kensit, the parade offered a good opportunity to attract attention. *The Times* reported that the 'long line of surpliced clergy had to run the gauntlet of a disturbance led by Mr John Kensit'.[27] The 'Wycliffe Crusaders', as they were referred to by the *London Daily News*, targeted the congress procession on more than one occasion. Kensit died in 1902, after being injured in an incident of sectarian violence at Birkenhead.[28] His supporters continued his crusade and provocative tactics at Barrow. *The Leeds Mercury* noted:

> As the Bishops and members left the hall, they were met by the Kensit crusaders, who held aloft placards protesting against Ritualism. An indignant Churchwoman knocked a Kensitite's top hat off, and he asked the police to take her in charge. This they refused to do.[29]

At Swansea, they walked ahead of the parade 'holding aloft their "No Popery" banners' whilst 'uttering their war cry "Down with the Romanisers"'. For some spectators this added to the entertainment: *The Daily News* correspondent commented that the crowds cheered them 'good humouredly'.[30] This contrasted with the previous year's attempt at disruption in Manchester when the protest was 'nipped in the bud by the strong force of the police who lined the route'.[31]

Divine, rather than human, interference disrupted the procession at Rhyl where, according to the *Yorkshire Post and Leeds Intelligencer*: 'in consequence of the rain, the procession [had to be] abandoned. The clergy had to disrobe somewhat unceremoniously, and there were many complaints that they had not been given longer notice'.[32] Five years later rain also spoiled the Shrewsbury parade and the demeanour of its participants: 'The vested clergy looked unhappy, for who could help it considering the splashed cassocks and drenched surplices. Further umbrellas do not add dignity to a function of this kind.'[33] The 1899 procession in London was also spoiled by bad weather. Heavy fog had descended, and the congress committee decided that under these circumstances it would be particularly disruptive to traffic if the procession 'marched in a body' to the cathedral from the Guildhall.[34]

It was a time when banners were a popular visual symbol of group identity. The spectacle of the congress procession was enhanced by numerous banners that represented the various organizations associated with congress.[35] The pride of place in each congress procession was given to the specially commissioned congress banner. The banner provided a point of visual interest for illustrated publications but text was also used to describe colour, design and texture. According to the women's magazine *The Queen* of Saturday, 9 October 1897: 'The banner appears as the visible symbol of the diocese to which it belongs. Displayed high above the chair of the president during the days which succeed the opening ceremony it marks the dignity of his position.'[36] The banner was also a way to showcase the contribution of women both collectively and individually to congress.[37] This might be through labour or subscriptions, such as the donations solicited from the ladies of Yarmouth, by Mayoress Edith Worlledge, towards the £50 needed for materials.[38] The London Women's Diocesan Association supplied the banner for the 1899 congress, and the following year *The Times* report of the Newcastle congress parade of 1900 observed that: 'in the middle of the procession was borne aloft a handsome banner, provided by the ladies of the diocese, the main design of which was the white ensign, which is in general use as the customary flag of the Church of England, the whole being enriched by embroidery of gold'.[39] The following year Brighton's banner featured a red cross with a central 'figure of Our Lord and at the sides are St Peter, St Nicholas, St Wilfred and St Richard'.[40] The Cambridge congress banner pictured in *The Graphic* of Saturday, October 1910, was also noted as being a gift from the churchwomen of the diocese.[41] The production of banners could involve qualified labour. The Swansea banner was worked at the Welsh School of Art Needlework at Cardiff, and the 1923 banner for the

Plymouth congress was listed as being designed by Mr W. D. Snell, but the needlework was acknowledged in a local newspaper as the work of Miss Mabel Keighly of Plymouth a 'gold medallist in needlework of the Royal College of Art'.[42] The efforts of Mrs T. Patterson Develin, who, over a period of seven months, both designed and executed 'in floss silk satin stitch' on cloth of gold, watered silk and velvet, the seven by four foot Yarmouth banner, drew fulsome praise from the *Eastern Daily Press*. In part of an extensive description of the banner it noted:

> The central figure, that of St. Nicholas, the patron saint sailors, after whom the historic mother church at Yarmouth is named, has the verisimilitude of life about it. and is complete to the smallest detail of jewelling. There is no stiffness or angularity, the face full expression, and the folds of mantle have been wrought with charming effect in lovely shades ... At the base are our own borough arms with the civic mace, sword, and oar. It is triumph for a Yarmouth lady to have produced so fine a piece of work, numbers of congress visitors will compliment Mrs. Devlin on her wonderful talents that been devoted to so praiseworthy purpose.[43]

However, not all banners were so well received, the *Cambridge Independent* of 26 September 1902, after noting that the banner for the Northampton congress had been organized by the bishop's wife Lady Mary Glyn, designed by Mr G. F. Bodley RA, and 'worked by the Ladies of the Guild of Church Embroiderers, which Miss Ingram, sister of the late Dean of Peterborough, originated', expressed some reservations as to the quality of the work: 'Without being ungallant to these artistic ladies, there will be those who will question whether their taste and energies might not have been even better spent'.[44]

The congress programme and women participants

After the opening procession there was an inaugural service presided over by the bishop of the host diocese. Other services featuring distinguished preachers were scheduled during the four-day congress period: the Wolverhampton congress of 1887 opened with a sermon by the Bishop of Durham, and the 1920 Southend congress featured sermons from the Archbishop Canterbury, and to reflect the worldwide nature of the Anglican communion, the Bishops of Brisbane and Sydney. Congress usually ran from Tuesday to Friday and the topics and key speakers were announced in advance and a detailed programme of events was available for attendees.

At a time of rapid urbanization and population growth, working conditions, social cohesion and the negotiation of class were topical. The 1862 Oxford congress agenda's inclusion of a section 'on the means of recovering the alienated classes to the Church' reflected concern that that the working classes (particularly men) were being drawn to rival denominations which were perceived as being less aligned with the interests of the ruling classes.[45] The *Saturday Review* of October 1875 commented that the job of congress was 'to work a wholesome influence in the places which they visit as much as to entertain or edify the strangers who throng to them', a comment that summed up the view held amongst 'Church people' that acting in accordance with religiously authorized codes of behaviour was a force towards social cohesion and the alleviation of social ills such as poverty and drunkenness.[46] As congress speaker Archdeacon George Sumner put it to an audience of Girls' Friendly Society organizers: 'Anything that tends to unite the classes together should certainly be welcomed by us who have the interests of society at stake'.[47]

Recurrent themes at congress such as the poor, leisure, education, temperance and employment conditions signalled the attempt of the Church to engage with matters featuring on the government's legislative agenda and position itself in relation to current issues. These themes can be seen in parallel to the resolutions passed by the Lambeth Conferences of Bishops, such as those of 1908, which asserted that greater attention be paid to social justice, and pointed to the moral duties of property owners and capitalists towards humane treatment of workers.[48] The creation of new dioceses such as Manchester (1847), Liverpool (1880), Newcastle (1882) and Southwell, Nottinghamshire (1884), was another means of addressing the need for increased ministry as a result of rapid urban expansion. Existing dioceses were reconfigured into smaller administrative units under the authority of Suffragan bishops, a trend that was reflected at the Church congresses. *The Penny Illustrated Paper* accompanied its photographic record of the 1906 congress with the caption: 'Bishops were as plentiful as blackberries at Barrow last week.'[49]

The *Exeter and Plymouth Gazette* of 3 October 1887, in its overview of the forthcoming congress programme at Wolverhampton, provides an example of this engagement with social affairs. Amongst the promised papers were 'Socialism and Christianity', 'Rapid Growth and Movements in Population' and 'Child Life in Our Cities'. The more traditional themes of 'The Church and History', and 'The Church in Africa' were also covered, and the *Gazette* noted 'a special meeting for women members of the congress: speakers The Hon. Mrs Maclagan, Lady Laura Riding, Mrs Frank Bevan and Miss Mason'.[50]

Wolverhampton was continuing the practice of holding meetings directed at women that had been introduced six years earlier. In his inaugural address to the 1881 Newcastle congress, the president, Bishop Lightfoot of Durham, spoke of the introduction of the first women's meeting alongside the existing working men's meetings reasoning that: 'in a society which is "neither male nor female" we are bound to provide for the wants of the wives and sisters'.[51] Agnes Weston, who campaigned against alcohol abuse amongst sailors and was due to speak in the main session, and vicar's wife Mrs Philip Papillon, who advocated the Church of England Young Women's Help Society in a meeting for women, were the pioneer speakers. The Newcastle innovation of having women speakers and formally recording their contributions in the congress programme and report of proceedings was noted in the press. The *North Devon Journal* noted that: 'At the Church Congress women this year are for the first time admitted upon the platform and formally recognized in the programme'.[52] The *London Evening Standard* referred to the contribution of Mrs Papillon as 'the first time in the history of the Congress' that a paper was read by its female writer but also noted that her paper 'found great favour with the audience' and was 'warmly applauded'.[53] Another first was achieved the following year when purity campaigner Jane Ellice Hopkins addressed an audience of men at the Derby congress on the sensitive subject of prostitution. Women addressing men remained a rare occurrence: other women speakers at Derby, who were drawn from a clerical milieu, spoke only in the meeting dedicated to women. The next two years record no women speakers, but 1885 included contributions from Girls' Friendly Society founder Mary Townsend and GFS Associate Mrs Grant, Mothers' Union founder Mary Sumner, and imperialist Ellen Joyce, in what, according to the *Church Times*, was: 'A meeting for women only at Ginets Circus at which it was calculated that at least fourteen hundred were present'.[54] The women's meetings continued to be well attended, the following year at Wakefield, an overflow meeting had to be organized to accommodate the large number of women wanting to attend. There were similar accommodation problems at the Nottingham congress. Laura Ridding noted in her diary that: 'Congress began with a huge meeting for mothers it overflowed to the tune of 600 into Crocus Street Hall then I had to take the chair'.[55]

Once women's meetings were established as a regular congress feature, further categories of female audience were targeted: in 1887 the first meeting for 'working girls and young women' was held. 1896 offered both a mothers' meeting and a 'young women's meeting', and two years later Bradford offered a meeting for girls over sixteen.[56] The targeted audience expanded further in the early twentieth century to include separate meetings for 'girls at secondary schools'.[57] After the First World War the separate meetings for women continued even though an increasing number of women were presenting in the main agenda sessions. A 'new venture' was instigated at the 1921 congress with a meeting for an even younger female audience, for girls over the age of fourteen.[58] The inclusion of these various separate meetings continued until 1928; the last three congresses held in 1930, 1935 and 1938 did not have separate sessions for women.

Congresses largely tackled similar themes to those on the programme at Wolverhampton, and contributions on topics such as missions, the poor and temperance tended to predominate. As the *Saturday Review* noted in its feature on the forthcoming congress of 1898 'subjects ... vary little from year to year. Several hardy annuals appear upon the Bradford programme; and it is scarcely likely that anything fresh will be said in regard to such well-worn matters as Sunday observance or Church music'.[59] At Weymouth in 1905, there were sixty-six papers delivered in the main congress programme, and in addition there were further talks targeted at specific categories of audience such as a 'Working Men', 'Lads' and 'Working Women' in outreach meetings in surrounding districts, a typical congress practice. The opening day began with a municipal welcome and then had sessions on 'The Permanent Value of the Old Testament', 'Christianity and Wealth' and 'Temperance'. The next day offered audiences the opportunity to hear speakers on 'Revivals', 'Lay Workers' and 'Education'. The topic of 'Christian Marriage' was also addressed but only by male contributors, and the theological topic of 'Apologetics' was confined to clerical speakers.[60] Later congresses were advertised under an overarching heading. Southampton in 1913 linked congress contributions under the theme of 'The Kingdom of God', the 1924 and 1926 congress titles were 'The Church of Tomorrow' and the 'Eternal Spirit', respectively, and the congress of 1935 was billed as 'Christianity and The Modern State'.[61] Each day during congress was timetabled into three or four sessions in which different themes were addressed. Following introductory remarks from the session chair, the invited speakers, who numbered between two and five, the usual average being four, gave their views on aspects of the chosen theme. Then followed a discussion forum to which those wishing to contribute were required to submit their question or point to the chair in writing, and not to exceed the allotted time.[62] The Southend congress section on 'Christ and Recreation' provides an example: under the chairmanship of the Bishop of Colchester, papers were contributed by four clergymen and actress Sybil Thorndyke. There were eleven contributors to the discussion, eight were clergymen, two laymen and a woman's perspective was represented by the contribution of Madame Isabelle Beresford, who had a reputation both as a player in pantomime and the 'straight' theatre, having appeared in the title role as Aladdin opposite Mrs Patrick Campbell as the princess, and as Joan of Arc and Lady Macbeth.[63]

Each congress programme involved a large number of speakers who gave papers related to scheduled topics or what were recorded as 'addresses'. At Weymouth, out of the sixty-six speakers in the main agenda sessions, twenty-three were laymen and four were women. Miss Strachan spoke in the section on Missions, Mrs Carter Sturge and Amy Hughes in the section on the 'Church and the Sick' and Alice Ravenhill, a representative of the National Health Society, in the section on Temperance. Weymouth also featured four outreach meetings aimed at women that were held either as parallel sessions or on additional days, at which sixteen speeches, but not sixteen different contributors were heard, for Bishop's wife Louise Creighton and 'Greylady' Emma Yeatman did double duty, and the hard-working Mary Clifford, a Poor Law guardian, spoke to three different audiences.[64]

At Southampton in 1913 there were thirty-one papers and twenty-six addresses, not counting remarks from the chair, making a total of fifty-seven speeches. Nineteen were from laymen and six from women; however, two non-official meetings for women each featured three speakers, and evangelist Maude Royden, a contributor to one of these, also spoke to a men-only audience. The Leicester congress of 1919 offered forty-nine papers and addresses, plus twenty more speakers in what were recorded in the congress report as non-official meetings, that is, meetings aimed at specific categories in this case 'Lads', 'Young Women and Girls', 'Demobilized Men' and a less targeted 'Public Meeting'. Out of the forty-nine contributions delivered in the main session nine were given by laymen and four by women. The non-official meeting for girls and young women featured three women speakers. Mrs Nina Theodore Woods, the wife of the incumbent Bishop, and GFS president for Peterborough, represented the diocese in which Leicester was located. Augusta Dean OBE, of the Ministry of Labour, and Lilian C. Barker CBE, the former Lady Superintendent of women workers at Woolwich Arsenal, provided models of distinguished public service. The Southend congress the following year included forty-six papers delivered in main sessions and an additional seventeen speeches in non-official meetings. Unusually the nine women's contributions outnumbered the eight contributions of laymen. Two additional women's meetings were each addressed by two women speakers. In addition to the giving of talks and addresses, women's voices could be heard contributing to the discussions that followed each paper. Leicester recorded seven women's contributions and Southampton and Southend both listed nine.[65]

Over the entire congress period between 1861 and 1938 there were sixty-six congresses. If a rough conservative estimate of fifty speeches per congress is assumed based on the numbers of papers and addresses at Weymouth, Bristol, Southampton and Southend, this gives a figure of 3,300. Whilst this does not pretend to be accurate it does give an indication of the scale of congress and the proportion of women speakers. Out of sixty-six congresses there were a total of 294 papers or addresses contributed by women. An additional point to consider is the section headings under which women were speaking. Some papers were given to mixed audiences in the main agenda sessions of congress and some, and these tended to be categorized as 'addresses', were given in additional meetings that did not engage with the congress programme topics, to specific categories of audience such as working women and girls. Laura Ridding felt it worthwhile to note the innovations instigated at the Nottingham congress when meetings for business men, and teachers, a category in which women were well represented, were included.[66] Of the 294 speeches given by women throughout the congress period, 164 were to women and girls, 3 were delivered to audiences consisting of men only by purity campaigner Jane Ellice Hopkins and Maude Royden, respectively, and 127 were given in main agenda sessions. Broadly more speeches from women were delivered in main sections towards the latter decades of congress; however, this also coincided with a diminution in the provision of targeted special meetings. *The Saturday Review* of 24 September 1898 commented that: 'We notice that the Bradford Committee have very sensibly given up the sectional meetings, except in the evenings, when there are to be separate gatherings for women.'[67] Women's meetings tended to be addressed by representatives of women's organizations such as the Mothers' Union or Girls' Friendly Society, which as national Anglican organizations provided a substantial cohort of potential speakers across the country. However, women identified with particular expertise in areas such as social welfare tended to contribute papers in main sessions. Philanthropist and housing reformer Henrietta Barnett of Toynbee Hall University Settlement and Hampstead Garden Suburb, who delivered all her congress papers as main agenda items in the years between 1906 and 1919, provides a distinguished example amongst others in this category.

The figure of 294 does not represent the number of women speakers who total 178. Forty-five of these women spoke at more than one congress or contributed more than once during congress week. Amongst this number are a several women who stand out for multiple contributions (see **Table 1**). Louise Creighton, after her first congress attendance as a member of the audience in

Table 1 Frequent contributors to congress.

Contributors	Affiliation/expertise	Years between	Speeches	Congresses	Main Congresses	Men	Women or girls
Mrs Louise Creighton	BW, GFS, MU, GDA	1894, 95, 96, 97, 99, 1903, 05, 06, 13, 24, 26	14	10+1	3		11
Miss Mary Clifford	Poor Law Guardian	1896, 97, 99, 1903, 05	10	5	2		8
Miss Elizabeth Wordsworth	BS, BD Head Lady Margaret Hall	1894, 1895, 1898, 1904, 05, 08	6 (5=+1)	4			6
Miss Gertrude Tuckwell	CD Employment Law expert JP	1902, 06, 08, 11, 20, 21	8	5	6		2
Lady Frederick (Lucy) Cavendish	Education and Temperance advocate	1892, 97, 98, 1900, 04	5	5	1		4
Mrs Mary Sumner	BW MU GFS	1895, 90, 1904.13	7	5			5
Miss Agnes Weston	Naval welfare and temperance philanthropist	1881, 85, 1901, 02	5	5	5		
Miss Maude Royden	Religious evangelist advocate of women's ministry	1913, 20, 22, 27	5	4	3	2	
Mrs Henrietta (Samuel) Barnett	CW Housing Reformer Toynbee Hall	1906, 07, 10, 19	4	4	4		
Lady Laura Ridding	BW GFS MU	1883, 1895, 90, 93 97 1904, 13	4+ chair	7			
Miss Lucy Soulsby	Headmistress MU Associate	1894, 98, 1904, 13	4	4			4

Contributors	Affiliation/expertise	Years between	Speeches	Congresses	Main	Men	Women or girls
Miss Emma Yeatman	BS Greyladies Religious community for women(B)	1895, 1902, 1905	4	3			4
Mrs Emma Paget	BW advocate of women's ministry	1911, 1913, 1921, 1927	4	4			
Mrs Arthur Phillp	MU Central organizer	1896, 1903. 1911, 1912	4	7 inc. discussion	1		3
Mrs (Edith Noel) Hubert Barclay	MU Central president	1921, 22, 27, 28	4	4	2		2
Alice Dowager Countess of Chichester formerly Hon Mrs Francis E Pelham	CW MU Central president	1910, 12 1896, 1899	4	4			4
Mrs Louisa Knight Bruce	BW – GFS MU	1903, 1920, 22, 23	4	4	1		3

BW, wife of bishop; BD BDS, daughter and sibling; CW, clergy wife; CD, clergy daughter.

1893, gave fourteen speeches at ten congresses between 1889 and 1926. Mary Clifford, whose contribution to the Weymouth congress has been noted above, delivered ten speeches at five congresses between 1896 and 1905. Amongst other top contributors were employment expert Gertrude Tuckwell who delivered eight speeches between 1902 and 1921. Mothers' Union founder Mary Sumner gave seven speeches and educationalist Elizabeth Wordsworth contributed six papers and addresses.

Twenty-three women in addition to those who delivered papers or addresses are recorded as contributors to the discussion section that followed the delivery of papers. The Southampton congress of 1913 stands out for the most recorded contributions made by women to discussions. Unsurprisingly there were six contributions relating to the congress theme of 'The Kingdom of God and the Sexes', which included papers on 'Marriage', and 'Ideals of Womanhood and Manhood'. Helen Sprott, a member of Emmeline Pankhurst's Women's Social and Political Union (WSPU), contributed her views in this section and claimed that women were being unfairly criticized for taking up the Suffrage cause. She also emphasized her view that God created men and women equal.[68] However there were also two contributions to discussion on 'The Kingdom of God and the Races' from Lucy Phillimore who spoke out against racism in South Africa and Mrs A. Little who said 'She would cry if told "You are a member of a backward race"- How would this assembly like it if she addressed them as "natives"'.[69]

At Cambridge in 1910, Mrs Rackham contributed to discussion on the Poor Law, and Miss James contributed to discussion in the 'Science' section following a paper presented by eugenicist and founder of the 1899 National Association for the Care and Protection of the Feeble Minded, Ellen Pinsent. Stoke on Trent in 1911 attracted four contributions in the discussion sections from women not otherwise recorded as speakers. Mrs John Jones shared her views on 'The Mission Field' and 'Sunday Schools', a topic to which Mrs Comber also contributed. Miss E. G. Bennitt engaged with the topic of the Poor law and the Feeble minded, following a paper presented by Ellen Pinsent on her second congress appearance, and Miss Phillips joined the discussion following a paper on working conditions by Gertrude Tuckwell. At Leicester in 1919, Mrs Gilchrist engaged with Church Finance. The papers on 'The Ministry of Women' at the same congress drew contributions from Miss Streeter and Helen Ward. The following year at Southend, the topic of 'the Ministry of Women' attracted two women contributors to recorded discussion whilst Mrs Grubbe commented on 'the Presentation of Christ to Young people'.

These numbers do not constitute all the voices heard in scheduled sessions at congress. A handful of women distinguished by social position and/or public service contributed as chairs only, in congress sessions directed at female audiences. Lady Harlech was in the chair at Rhyl at 1891.[70] The Hon. Mrs Legge, the wife of the Bishop of Lichfield, who later served as GFS Diocesan President between 1902 and 1906, undertook double duties in 1896 at Shrewsbury where she chaired the Young Women's meeting on 'Work and Recreation' and another session on 'Women as Poor Law Guardians'. Imperialist and political activist Lady Louisa Knightley, who took the chair at Nottingham in 1902, was distinguished for her local service as a GFS diocesan president. She also served as the first president of both the Conservative and Unionist Women's Franchise Association and the South African Colonisation Society, and editor of the British Women's Emigration Association magazine the *Imperial Colonist*.[71] Lady Beatrice Kemp, later Lady Rochdale, who presided in the Women's Meeting at Manchester in 1908, was, like Louisa Knightley, the wife of an MP and had an interest in South Africa, having accompanied her husband whilst on military service there in 1900. They also shared a commitment to suffrage; Lady Beatrice was the president of the Manchester Federation of Women's Suffrage Societies and was later a participant in the Suffrage Pilgrimage of 1913.[72]

The constituency of platform speakers also included women of social distinction. Congress documentation records twenty women styled as the Honourable, Lady or another title but this does not provide a full picture of social status as women may have had possible connections to titled relatives not revealed in the congress record, as in the case of baronet's niece Mary Sumner, Mrs Legge, who as a peer's daughter was entitled to the honorific The Hon., and Lavinia Talbot, one of the daughters of George, 4th Baron Lyttelton. The majority of contributors were very largely drawn from women with middle- or upper middle-class backgrounds. The women noted in **Table 1** as frequent contributors to congress represent the spectrum of speakers who were broadly divided between those from a clerical milieu, and those representing women's church organizations, often an overlapping category, or women of distinction or acknowledged expertise in a diversity of fields including public service and local government, law, education, health, culture and religious service as missionaries or deaconesses. Amongst the frequent congress contributors Louise Creighton, Laura Ridding and Mary Sumner are amongst several women who fit the categories of wives of bishops and activists in church organizations. Marianne Mason, Gertrude Tuckwell, Lucy Soulsby and Elizabeth Wordsworth are women with 'professional' credentials, who tended to be unmarried. Emma

Yeatman and Maude Royden stand out for activism in the religious field. These categories can be broadly aligned with the trajectory of women's access to the congress as speakers. The earlier platform speakers were largely associated with clerical networks or notable activism in the causes of morality or temperance, as exemplified by Mary Sumner and Agnes Weston, whilst professionals and women from the world of work were later arrivals. Author Mrs Leith Adams, who took the subject of literature at Cardiff in 1889, was the first of her profession to speak directly to a congress audience. The following year, Marianne Mason, who was employed as HM Inspector of Boarded out Pauper Children, made her debut. 1891 was significant for having a qualified medical practitioner, Dr Kate Mitchell, on the platform, and the next year Amie Hicks Secretary of the London Rope Makers Union addressed the women's meeting and Miss Stuart Snell a teacher of gymnastics gave a paper in the main congress session.

Congress members and audiences

The preoccupation of congress with the negotiation of class is evident in the attention given to social issues on congress agendas throughout its history, and is a theme picked up in a later chapter on public service and work. Despite the standing ovation given by the working-class audience to Bishop Fraser at the Leeds congress of 1872 when he, untypically for a churchman, defended the right of agricultural workers to their union,[73] the engagement with working-class perspectives is more evident in congresses in the last decade of the nineteenth and early twentieth centuries, when speakers such as the Rev. Goodwin spoke on the hardship experienced by shop girls, Amie Hicks represented the views of rope makers, and Gertrude Tuckwell took the platform to engage with legislation on employment[74]. However, congress organizers did attempt to reach out and engage working-class audiences, albeit in a way that, particularly in its earlier years, evoked missionary enterprise rather than inclusive partnership. At Newcastle in 1881 evening meetings to coincide with congress were organized in the industrial districts of Jarrow, South Shields and Sunderland. The report of the 1895 congress noted that: 'The Norwich Committee, with praiseworthy zeal, endeavoured to make congress useful to all classes of the community.' It noted that: 'Working men's meetings formed an integral part of the congress programme and were held every night in large halls'. A meeting for working women and meetings in satellite towns were also detailed, and the commentary on these outreach meetings concluded that: 'the mission aspect of congress was well brought out'.[75] The following year, in an attempt to encourage working-class inclusion 1,750 free tickets for main congress sessions were distributed to working men.[76] The congress approach to class was criticized by the *Saturday Review*. In its discussion of the forthcoming Bradford congress, referring to a separate meeting for women, it commented that: 'In one programme before us those invited are classified as "married women", *"young ladies"*, and *"young women"*, a vulgar and snobbish distinction' [italics in source]. The article went on to approve a revised version of the programme that referred to a 'men's meeting' rather than a 'working men's meeting', and to commend both the introduction of a working men's committee and the appearance of local trade union leader George Hawkins amongst the speakers. This, according to the *Review*, was 'sufficient to show how immensely the Church of England is advancing in the great towns, where she was supposed to be weakest thirty years ago,' a vindication of the missionary approach and the aim of congress to widen Church participation.[77]

Clearly congress had an appeal for clergy and their friends and families. The clerical speakers who formed the majority of speakers at congress were likely to be accompanied by relations and possibly friends. Congress was also attractive to middle-class and upper middle-class laymen and women who identified as 'Church people'. Attendees were drawn from those living locally or those who travelled for further afield. The 1865 Norwich congress report included a list of all the attending members, families were listed with the male head of the house first, then his wife and other relatives were noted. A large percentage of these attendees were resident in Norfolk, the county in which the congress was located.[78] The same is true for the 1879 Swansea congress in which Welsh addresses predominate amongst the attendees. *The South Wales Daily* published a full list of these 'visitors and their entertainers' that covered almost two pages. This, in addition to revealing the home location of visitors, shows that married couples were well represented amongst them. It also records several family parties, as well as sisters and single ladies.[79]

Publicity for the congress in the form of advertisements and articles in the national and local press informed potential attendees of the programme, the price of the various categories of ticket and where to obtain them in advance of the congress. Those who purchased a ticket for entry to congress events for the entire week were categorized as 'members'. Day tickets and tickets for evening sessions could also be purchased. Two congresses in the 1920s sold tickets for single sessions. Examples from the press illustrate not only the cost of the various categories of tickets but a striking consistency in pricing over time. In 1865 tickets for the three-day congress were 'Five shillings each, admitting either a Lady or

Gentleman to all the Meetings', day tickets were half a crown [two shillings and sixpence]. The organizers were keen that tickets should be purchased in advance and they could be obtained by post from a local book seller as 'NO MONEY WILL BE TAKEN AT THE DOORS'.[80] For the 1905 Weymouth congress weekly tickets were seven shillings and sixpence; a family ticket for three, one guinea; day tickets were two shillings and sixpence; tickets for a women's meeting were two shillings. Advanced publicity for the Eastbourne congress of 1925 in the *Hastings and St Leonards Observer* read:

> Members tickets to admit to all Official Sessions, 7/8 [seven shilling and eightpence]each. Day tickets 2/6 each. Reserved Seats 1/- for each Session. One copy of Official Programme Free to Holders of Members' Tickets. Reduced Railway Fares to Members. Tickets and Information from:-THE CONGRESS SECRETARIES, TOWN HALL, EASTBOURNE[81]

Ten years later for the Bournemouth Congress of 1935, prices for members' tickets had reduced back to the 1905 rate of 7/6 each. Day tickets remained at 2/6. Single sessions were 1/- and Family Double tickets 12/- whilst a reduction was offered for 'Parochial parties'.[82] Some indication of the popularity of congress can be gleaned from references in the press and from the records of ticket sales that were included in the official congress reports between 1882 and 1924. These do not represent a full data set because congress organizers did not always record the numbers of day and evening tickets. Despite these omissions the data in **Table 2** give an indication of the numbers of people who engaged with congress events and the patterns of attendance over thirty-seven years. What is consistent throughout is that sales of membership tickets always exceeded other categories, usually by a considerable amount, which suggests that congress was the destination for a predominantly middle-class audience intent on using it as the focus for a full week of religious edification and recreation. For some congress members attendance could be influenced by offers of hospitality from the presence of family or friends in the vicinity. It is unlikely that Ellen Joyce's presence at the 1891 congress in Rhyl was unrelated to the fact that her relative, Lady Dynevor, lived nearby. Similarly Mary Sumner's presence at the 1904 Liverpool congress is likely to have been encouraged by having relatives in the vicinity. Her nephew Sir Arthur Percival Heywood, who was also the husband of Sumner's daughter Margaret Effie, had his seat at Claremont near Manchester which was also the home to Sumner's nieces Monica, Ethelred and Isobel, who was to be honoured with an OBE for her work for the Manchester and Salford Blind Aid Society.[83]

Table 2 Congress ticket sales from official reports 1882–1924.

Congress	Date	Members	Day	Single session	Evening	Total
Derby	1882	3,219	779			
Reading	1883	3,640				
Carlisle	1884	1,967	793		137	
Portsmouth	1885	2,141	1,493			
Wakefield	1886	1,999	1,254			
Wolverhampton	1887	2,567	614		474	
Manchester	1888	4,450	1,531		411	
Cardiff	1889	2,248	691		54	
Hull	1890	2,303	1,023		574	
Rhyl	1891	3,225	37			
Folkestone	1892	3,343	87		361	
Birmingham	1893	4,396	2,082		914	
Exeter	1894	3,302	1,402		1,018	
Norwich	1895	2,525	c. 1,000		229	
Shrewsbury [+1750 free distribution]	1896	2,601	1,678		441	
Nottingham	1897	2,544	1,240		139	
Bradford	1898	2,753	1,096		640	
London	1899	8,000				
Newcastle	1900	2,024				
Brighton	1901	2,856	542		606	
Northampton	1902	1,506	1,098		102	
Bristol	1903	2,957	1,345		195	
Liverpool	1904	4,182	756		423	
Weymouth	1905	2,322	292		684	
Barrow in Furness	1906	1,454	91		601	
Great Yarmouth	1907	2,239	441		308	
Manchester	1908	3,481	956		1,384	
Swansea	1909	2,915	774		282	
Cambridge	1910	3,597	333			
Stoke on Trent	1911	1,534	278		341	
Middlesbrough	1912	1,718	229		589	

Congress	Date	Members	Day	Single session	Evening	Total
Southampton	1913	2,494	580		780	
Leicester	1919	1,780	'Numerous'			
Southend	1920	1,972	761	1,446	585	
Birmingham	1921	2,370	507		499	
Sheffield	1922	2,452	'Numerous'			
Plymouth	1923	1,614	557		565	
Oxford	1924	2,279	803	1,490	None	

Some locations proved more popular than others, perhaps for reasons of accessibility, or cultural and recreational appeal. The lower numbers at Plymouth, Barrow-in-Furness and Carlisle may be accounted for by their location at the further branches of the railway network, whilst Stoke on Trent, although easily accessible, may have been perceived as lacking cultural attraction. With the exception of Southend, the seaside resorts reported robust attendance figures, with Rhyl and Folkestone prominent with 3,225 and 3,343 members, respectively. Unsurprisingly the large urban centres Manchester, Birmingham, London and Liverpool attracted the highest numbers. Birmingham in 1893 recorded the sale of 4,366 members tickets and 2,082 day tickets. Although day ticket sales tended to be greatest in urban centres, the Liverpool congress of 1904, despite attracting over 4,000 members, reported day ticket sales of only 756 although evening ticket sales were a robust 423.

Congress organization and committees

The complexity and scale of congress required a substantial amount of forward planning and coordination during the week that it was in session. A permanent Church of England congress standing committee had been established following the 1861 initiative by Bishop of Oxford Samuel Wilberforce. The *Quarterly Review* of January 1864 confirmed that the Church congress had 'boldly come out into public life'. William Emery, a participant in the 1861 assembly, was to become a key figure in the establishment of congress, first as a member of the standing committee and later as the Permanent Secretary of congress, a position he held from 1869 to 1907. The duration and scope of congress can be attributed in part to the ambition, enthusiasm and application of Emery, the Archdeacon of Ely from 1864, who attended all of the first forty-seven congresses, a feat which earned him the title of 'Father of Church Congress'.[84] Emery was recognized for his organizational ability. Commenting on this to the 1869 congress, he said that it was his role to 'set a committee to work' maintaining that 'generally some good' came from doing so.[85] He continued to serve as permanent secretary until the fortieth congress at Newcastle when he was offered a public vote of thanks for his dedication by the organizing committee.[86] The main role of the standing committee was to obtain and coordinate diocesan offers to host congress to secure the continuity of congress year by year. Although the standing committee was prepared to act in an advisory capacity, the arrangements for each congress were the remit of the host diocese. An executive committee of clergy and prominent laymen such as the Earl of Dartmouth and Lord Lyttelton who served on the 1867 Wolverhampton executive gave social and political endorsement to the congress organization and took overall responsibility for the success of congress, notably in ensuring its financial viability and keeping a permanent record of congress proceedings.[87]

The earliest congress of 1861 had the agenda, speakers and the content of their papers published in book form. For most of the period between 1865 and 1913 the production of the *Authorised* or *Official Report of the Church Congress* was under the jurisdiction of Charles Dunkley. Like Archdeacon Emery, Dunkley was a loyal and long-standing servant of congress, which showed its appreciation for his work with a presentation to mark his '30 years' work' in 1911.[88] The book length reports were a detailed documentation of the minutiae of congress. Published with hard covers, they were also a substantial and handsome artefact as the Weymouth report of 1905, which features gold lettering and decoration on its spine and cover, demonstrates. The *Official Reports* included an introductory preface which usually alluded to the hospitality of the host town and highlighted some notable features of congress. In the preface to the 1895 *Official Report of the Church Congress Held at Norwich*, Dunkley drew attention to the reports as a means of augmenting the function of congress as an exercise in Church outreach: not only had the report been 'prepared with great care' it was 'sent forth in the earnest hope that it may contribute to the greater glory of God, and the extension of Christ's Kingdom in the world'.[89]

The main body of the report consisted of a day-by-day record of the topics on the congress agenda. The contribution of every speaker was recorded verbatim and usually ran to several pages. Those giving papers were asked to submit a copy in advance to aid with record keeping. Contributors to discussion sessions following the delivery of papers also had their views published in the *Official Report* so that all speakers, including those in women's sections, had their views included in a permanent Church-endorsed publication that could be retained for future reference and disseminated to audience beyond those attending congress.

After the retirement of Charles Dunkley and the interruption of the 1914–18 war, the congress official report lost momentum and editorial consistency. There were official reports published in 1919, 1920 and 1921 by Nisbet that did not credit any individuals in an editorial capacity. The 1924 report published by Maltravers under the title *The Church of Tomorrow* also fails to name an editor. The character of the report changed too and became less exhaustive in documenting proceedings and attendance. The report on the Southport congress of 1926 by the Rev. Charles E. Raven moved to a synthesis and commentary on the congress theme titled '*The Eternal Spirit*', rather than a verbatim account. Raven, who also contributed to the congress as a speaker, reflected his concerns about discussing his own paper in the preface to his report and also noted the pressure of writing the account in a short time. However, he claimed it was 'a joy and privilege to have had a share in making some part of what we received at Southport available to a wider public'.[90] His efforts were appreciated by the *Dundee Courier* which described the publication as reading 'like a personal letter, written by the most engaging and delightful of correspondents'.[91] Two years later the publication edited by Canon H. A. Wilson reflected the small-scale and rather introspective character of congress that year, and focused on '*The Anglican Communion, Past Present and Future*' and did not mention the Special Meeting for Young Women and Girls with Beatrice M. Sparks MA, principal of Cheltenham Ladies' College in the chair, or the meeting for women addressed by Noel Hubert Barclay of the MU. Fuller treatment of congress was given in the official reports of the last two congresses. The 1935 volume *Christianity in the Modern State. A Report of the Proceedings of the Sixty-Fifth Church Congress* edited by Maxwell Studdy Leigh ran to 300 pages and could be obtained 'cloth bound, price five shillings, post free from the publisher'. Three years later M. H. Fitzgerald took charge of *The Gospel to This Generation. A Report of the Proceedings of the Sixty-Sixth Church Congress, 1938.*

In case the financial outgoings exceeded income the support of patrons or guarantors who were financially liable in the event of the congress making a loss was secured by the executive committee. Women as well as men were welcome to undertake the risk. The report of the 1893 congress at Birmingham lists amongst a majority of male guarantors seven women guarantors; Mrs P. D. Bennett and Mrs Isaac pledged £10 and Mrs Edith Flavel, Mary Ellen Archer,

Mrs Eliza Avins, Annette E. Couchman and Jane E. Barber promised lesser amounts.[92] In the interests of transparency the congress accounts were noted in the official report and also publicized in the press. The intention was that revenue from ticket sales should cover congress expenses, but this was not always the case. Mr W. Letitbridge, the Mayor of Exeter and Chairman of the Finance Committee for the 1894 Congress hosted in his city, was 'exceedingly pleased' to report a profitable congress ... 'because it was very unusual'. He contrasted Exeter's success with the previous year: 'At Birmingham, the guarantors were asked to pay 7s 6d in the £', and the financial burden could be even heavier for 'at Croydon, the guarantors were, he believed, asked to pay 17 s 6d in the £. Therefore, it would a relief to the guarantors for the Exeter Congress to know that it was not proposed to ask them to pay anything'.[93] The Swansea executive committee was also able to report a successful financial outcome, and advertised their income and expenditure in the *Western Mail* of Thursday, 28 October 1909. Receipts totalled £1,058 which comprised £875 from full members tickers, £110 from day tickets and £71 from day tickets. Expenditure included £89 on the hire of halls and a substantial investment of £170 on the congress banner. Printing and stationery were £149; postage £76 and insurance and carriage for the banner were £6. A £15 contribution towards extra policing and a £90 subsidy for the official report left a credit balance of £448.[94] The Weymouth Congress balance sheet reported additional sources of income of £161 from the sale of official programmes at 6d. each 18/- from the sale of congress postcards £71 17/3 from Offertories and £3 4/8 proceeds from 'band entertainments in Alexandra gardens'.[95]

The variety of tasks involved in organizing and coordinating congress resulted in a diversification of committees, whereas the Norwich congress of 1865 required only a general committee under the executive to deal with business; the breakdown of expenditure at the Swansea congress indicates that the congress included a committee for organizing the hire of venues and advance publicity. The Hull congress of 1890 had committees for finance and for building, as well as a Subjects Committee that decided topics and speakers, and a Reception committee that dealt with hospitality.[96] Finding accommodation for visitors was a perennial challenge for congress organizers. In 1922 *The Sheffield Daily Telegraph* noted: 'There has been a good response to the appeal in this column last week for Sheffield hostesses, and most of the guests for the Church Congress have been allocated, but there is almost sure to be a last minute rush, and it is this that the Reception Committee are trying their best to meet smoothly'.[97] A letter written on behalf of congress organizers published in the *Western Morning News* in June 1923 appealed to readers for 'offers of hospitality for the members of the Church Congress', and requested the local clergy to canvass their congregations for hostesses. By way of encouragement and reassurance to perspective offers, the following was added: 'It may be worthwhile to state that the limit of necessary entertainment is bed and breakfast as our guests will probably be away all day'.[98]

Whilst women were clearly contributors to the success of congress through informal channels as providers of hospitality or embroiderers of the banner, and even as members of the audience from the earliest years, their official participation as committee members, and formal recognition of it, was a later development. Louise Creighton noted in her memoir that there was no need for a special women's committee to organize women's meetings at the London Congress of 1899 because her own Women's Diocesan organization was already constituted and available for just such a task.[99] The 1905 Weymouth Congress, which was notable for its provision of outreach meetings aimed at women, provides evidence of changing practice. The congress report gave details of a Women's Executive committee presided over by Mary Wordsworth, the second wife of the Bishop of Salisbury, and sister-in-law to Elizabeth Wordsworth, a regular speaker at congress. The Women's Executive Committee also included Mrs Leonard Burrows of the GFS and Alice Carr-Glynn, the wife of the Bishop of Peterborough, and Mrs Whytehead, Mrs Williams and Emma Yeatman who also contributed to the congress as speakers. In addition to the Women's Executive Committee, there was a Ladies' Committee which had five members listed: Mrs Akers, Miss Barnes, Mrs Boulter, Mrs Bromley and Miss Clapcott and a Reception Committee which noted that ladies formed part of the Reception Committees for Weymouth and Dorchester.[100] In 1921, there were fifty-one women listed as members of what was now referred to as the Women's Committee.[101] Six years later there was no longer a dedicated women's committee, and Mrs W. E. Fletcher was the only woman listed as a member of the Ipswich Executive Committee, which oversaw all aspects of congress. Further down the congress committee hierarchy the General Committee which involved itself in more practical administrative duties included twenty-eight women members. The Subjects Committee, amongst its twenty-seven members, included two women, Lady Cranworth and Mrs J. W. Greene, a member of the prominent Suffolk brewery family, who added social cachet to the proceedings. The committee for non-official meetings had five women members. The Hospitality Committee as in previous years consisted mostly of women, whereas the Banner Committee had only one man, H. E. Singleton Cooper, the designer of the banner.[102] This situation was not unconditionally accepted, and the *Church*

League for Women's Suffrage raised the issue of the representation of women within congress committees in its coverage of the Southport congress of the previous year. It asked:

> Has one to be a mayoress or the wife of the presiding bishop before one can aspire to the honour of being a Vice-President of a Church Congress? A number of women were invited to serve on the Devotional and General committees, while on the Hospitality Committee they outnumbered the men. No woman was serving on the Subjects Committee, but as the choice of subjects could not have been bettered one will not cavil at that, but merely ask "Does the Subjects Committee choose the speakers also?" If so, there are women one would desire to hear address Church Congresses.[103]

Sociability, fringe events and the congress exhibition

Louise Creighton enjoyed the congresses because they helped her to 'get in touch with church people generally, and to understand more about church affairs'.[104] However, congress had a lighter side, entertainments and fringe events added to its appeal, and provided opportunities for socializing. The Rev. Charles Dunkley, in his preface to the official report of the 1890 Hull congress, noted the 'completeness of hospitality and bountiful provision made for the physical wellbeing and social happiness of the visitors'.[105] It was customary for congresses to include receptions hosted by the mayor and mayoress of the host town supported by civic dignitaries, which at Ipswich in 1927 included the Borough Coroner, Surveyor and Veterinary Inspector.[106] These were, however, largely for invited guests from amongst ticket-holding congress members, and the practice of a social 'conversatzione' to conclude the proceedings was established by 1879. Despite the lack of enthusiasm demonstrated by the *Church Times* correspondent of October 1883, who considered that 'no one with anything else to do need waste much time on the conversatzione', it proved popular with other congress goers.[107] Laura Ridding, wife of the presiding bishop, was responsible for the tea and cheesecake supplied at the Nottingham 'conversatzione' and noted with relief in her diary: 'it is all going very well'.[108] Recalling the London Congress of 1899, Louise Creighton wrote: 'Fulham [the Bishop's place} was crowded to its utmost capacity with guests who stayed through the congress, and each day we had lunch prepared in a large room in the Albert Hall'.[109] A reception and conversatzione held by the Bishop of St Asaph and Mrs Edwards at the Rhyl congress in 1891, catered for over 3,000 people, a figure representing the entire

Figure 1.1 Louise Creighton by Walter Stoneman, c. 1916. Source: By permission National Portrait Gallery.

congress membership. Amongst the invited guests were 'principal notabilities of the Congress and influential people of the diocese'. The event was held in the Congress Hall which provided sufficient space for the visitors to 'promenade' whilst listening to a small orchestra perform works by Gilbert and Sullivan.[110] Musical entertainment was also provided for the 1,500 guests who attended the mayor's reception for the Newcastle-upon-Tyne congress in 1900.[111] In 1921, Quaker philanthropists and prominent citizens Mr and Mrs George Cadbury arranged a garden party at Bourneville, the model village associated with their chocolate manufactory, to which 'around two thousand members of the Birmingham Congress' attended.[112] However, it was only committee members for the Bournemouth congress of 1935 who were invited to attend a reception held by the president of the congress, Cyril Garbett. Guests were asked to RSVP to Miss Garbett, the bishop's sister, who was to act as hostess for the occasion.[113] Three years later corporate hospitality at Bristol was once again on an impressive scale. The welcome to congress from the Mayor and Mayoress was held in the city art gallery and included various entertainments:

> The City of Bristol Police Light Orchestra, directed by Captain F. W. Wood, provided an attractive programme of music. The Bristol film was shown and attention was drawn to Museum items of interest to the Congress members. The Lord Mayor in his official welcome expressed the hope that the Congress would result in the Church of England becoming an ever-increasing power'.[114]

The social side of the Bristol congress also made the women's pages in the local paper. As well as noting the mayor's civic reception the author of the society column 'Barbara's Budget' went on to note that:

> The Archdeacon of Bristol and Mrs Alford are inviting members to attend the Great Hall, University of Bristol, when talks will be given by the Bishop of Tewkesbury, Lady Apsley and Mr W. R. Vaughan on the work done by the Waifs and Strays Society Tea will be at 4.30, and the talks will follow.[115]

In addition to the more exclusive social events there were other attractions and excursions on offer. The *Illustrated London News* of Saturday, 14 October 1899, noted that: 'the meeting of the Church congress in London will bring many sightseers to the palaces of Lambeth and Fulham ... for not even the most inveterate sightseers have the faintest idea of the real beauties that lie behind the high dull red wall'.[116] *The Times*, drawing its readers' attention to the forthcoming congress of 1900, agreed: 'Every Church Congress has its sightseeing and pleasure-seeking side' and averred that Newcastle offered 'great attractions for those who would relieve the discussion of present-day Church questions by excursions into history and antiquity and the relics of remote past'.[117] At Weymouth in 1905, band entertainments in the public gardens were an attraction for many attendees.[118] To mark the Cambridge Congress of 1910 *The Church Times* introduced a congress supplement, which under a pictorial heading included historical and topographical information. The following year, the supplement for the Stoke-on-Trent congress was subtitled 'In and around the Potteries'. The Southampton supplement although headed 'Industrial Development and Church Life' gave attention to the historical and cultural institutions of the town. The Ipswich and Cheltenham supplements featured particularly attractive illustrations. The 1919 supplement with the heading 'Peterborough – the Diocese of Varied Life' was rather different in character, being less focused on cultural attractions, although it did regard the 'magnificent physique' of the Bishop [Theodore Woods] as noteworthy. The supplement was discontinued after 1935, but *The Church Times* did give alternative coverage to the Bristol Congress of 1938 that included an article by the bishop and a guide to the ecclesiastical exhibition in addition to reports of congress day by day.[119] The *Illustrated Guide* for the 1913 Southampton congress advertised excursions by train to Southampton Docks, Romsey Abbey, Beaulieu Abbey, Lyndhurst, the New Forest, Winchester Cathedral and the elite public school Winchester College. For physically active members of the congress the New Forest could also be visited by bicycle, excursions were advertised 'for ladies and gents, cycles may be hired'.[120] There were also exhibitions some of which were aimed at a female audience. The exhibition of 'Painted Fabrics' produced by wartime veterans at the 1922 Sheffield congress was advertized in the *Sheffield Daily Telegraph*:

> Lady Bewicke Copley, perhaps better known in Sheffield than some of the other ladies, is to open the Exhibition of Painted Fabrics at Messrs. Cockayne's on Wednesday. This exhibition, by the way, will remain open all week and it is hoped in this way that everyone will have time to see some of the lovely things on view which include the latest in evening cloaks and wraps, as well as many other delightfully dainty stencilled garments so dear to the feminine heart.[121]

From 1879 the Church congress featured an Ecclesiastical Art Exhibition which was open to members of the congress, and the public who paid a modest entrance fee. In 1913 at Southampton, charges for admission were a shilling between 11 am and 6 pm, and in the evening it cost 6d, although the exhibitions were free to the clergy.[122] The exhibitions consisted of pictures, sculpture and objects of ecclesiastical or historical interest that were loaned for the occasion. Cheltenham in 1928 secured support from the British Museum, which loaned a sculpture of the *Madonna and Child* by Bozzetto dating from 1670. However, support for the exhibition tended to be drawn from the congress locality: The *Tewkesbury Register* reminded its readers that the 1903 Bristol exhibition of ecclesiastical art was not without local interest, for the 'Ancient silver sacramental plate of the abbey' had been loaned by the vicar.[123] The *Church Times* devoted an entire article to the 1938 exhibition, where once again the venue was Bristol. Under the heading 'Some treasures of a By Gone Age' the article gave details of some of the most striking exhibits that included ancient manuscripts, a religious painting 'after Hogarth' and a thirteenth-century 'head of a pastoral staff' studied with turquoises, rubies and emeralds loaned by Wells

Cathedral. The article went on to observe that the purpose of the exhibition was 'to remind members of the congress that the Church has been the patron and, in some ages, the chief guardian of the arts'.[124] A catalogue of the exhibition and acknowledgement to those individuals and institutions who loaned the exhibits was recorded in the *Illustrated Guides to the Church Congress and Church Congress Exhibitions*. As the title suggests pictures of some of the exhibits were included. The 1897 Nottingham edition, a hardback with a gothic-style black and red cover, provided a handsome example and set a design style copied by guides into the twentieth century, exemplified by the 1922 and 1928 guides to Plymouth and Cheltenham, respectively.[125]

The guides, which were also in some cases referred to as handbooks, were more than just a catalogue for the art exhibition. They also served as the congress programme and a guidebook to the congress personnel. A contents page at the beginning of each publication listed all the speakers in each session and short biographies of speakers were included. In the Southampton guide's 'Who's who at congress,' amongst several women speakers introduced to readers were 'Miss Lucy Soulsby Head of the Manor House School Brondesbury a well-known authority on Educational matters and in connection with the GFS and the MU'; 'Miss Ruth Rouse Travelling Secretary of the World's Student Christian Federation' and 'Miss A. Maude Royden ed. Cheltenham and Lady Margaret Hall worked at Victoria Women's Settlement Liverpool 3 years [has] taken Classes for the WEA for factory girls, member of the executive committee of the National Union of Women's Suffrage Societies, editor of the Common Cause'.[126] The Newport guide had even more to say about the impressive record of public service demonstrated by Mrs Carruthers JP (formerly Miss Violet Markham). She was a 'Member of the Executive Committee National Relief Fund, and Central Committee Women's Employment 1914. Deputy Director Women's Section National Service Department, 1917: Member of Lord Chancellor's Advisory Committee for Women Justices, 1919-20; Member of Industrial Court: Author of *South Africa Past and Present, The New Era in South Africa, The South African Scene, A Woman's Watch in the Rhine*, etc.' Despite being known for having taken an anti-suffrage stance the guide also noted that she stood for parliament as an Independent Liberal in Mansfield in 1918 and served as Mayor of Chesterfield in 1927.[127] These were not the only guides to note the achievements of congress speakers of distinction both women and men. The 1927 programme for the Ipswich congress included short biographies of notable speakers including Mothers' Union president Noel Hubert Barclay and Phyllis Dent but also gave recognition to the committee members involved in organizing the congress.[128]

The guides also acted as aids for the tourist and included topographical information about the local area.[129] Maps within the guides enabled the reader to orientate themselves to places of interest. The 1930 *Illustrated Guide to Congress* map of Newport included captioned pointers to the churches and congress venues.[130] The Rev. W. L. Martin, the vicar of Bettisfield and the Hon. Secretary of the 1891 congress committee, contributed a 'descriptive sketch of Rhyl and its neighbourhood' to the *Illustrated Church Congress Handbook* edited by the Rev. Charles Mackeson which, according to *The Times'* reviewer, formed 'a useful work of reference and supplementary record'.[131] The tradition continued, and Rev. Canon Deedes supplied notes on the churches in the Brighton and Hove for readers of the 1901 *Illustrated Guide*.[132]

The guide also included a list of the exhibitors and organizations and a plan of the numbered stands that made up the section of the ecclesiastical exhibition devoted to commercial interests and voluntary organizations rather than artistic and historical content. It is unsurprising that the suppliers of church furniture, stained glass and heating apparatus were well represented and also amplified their impact by taking space in the pages of the guides devoted to advertisements. The guide also provides an insight into congress fringe events and the activities of groups who used congress as a focus for publicity. Amongst numerous charities several women's organizations were represented. The Mothers' Union and the Girls' Friendly Society were regular stall holders.[133] The 1913 congress guide listed the GFS, the Church of England Temperance Society, Church Nursing, the Ambulance Brigade for Women and Girls, the British League for Women's Suffrage and the Church of England Women's Help Society as all being in attendance. The GFS was still a presence at congress in 1935 and took space in the *Illustrated Guide* to advertise their objective: 'To unite for the Glory of God in one fellowship of Prayer and Service, the Girls and Women of the Empire, to uphold Purity in thought, word and deed'. The guide also represented a less traditional women's organization and a perspective that will be explored in a later chapter that engages with congress as a focus for the articulation of women's aspirations for spiritual authority. The advertisement for 'The Anglican Group for the Ordination of Women to the Historic Orders of the Church's Ministry' asked the reader: 'Should WOMEN be ORDAINED? What is YOUR answer? NO? – come and tell us why. YES – come and join us. Block W Avenue 12' [capitals as source].[134]

Publicity and the press

Congress, and those with an interest in its affairs, benefited from it taking place against a context of growth in communications. This was manifest in the opportunity for physical movement facilitated by the railway and also in the accessibility of print associated with increasing literacy and the speed of communication enabled by the telegraph. The numerous anecdotes relating to congress drawn from the press that illustrate this chapter reflect the widespread and ongoing coverage given to congress in national dailies, regional and local newspapers and special interest magazines.[135] A striking aspect of this vibrant print culture is the attention given to national events in local papers, which gave coverage to the congress, even if it was located in a distant part of the country.[136] Journalists evidently considered congress of interest to their readers, and congress organizers made efforts to cultivate their attention and exploit the publicity that coverage in the press could bring. In 1876 at Plymouth the subject of 'Periodical Literature and the Press' was covered by Godfrey Thring BA, and The 'Church and the Press' featured at the 1893 Birmingham congress.[137] Extensive use was made of the media to alert potential attendees to congress dates and content; this was in the form of advertisements but also through press releases that assumed congress as a newsworthy event. Congress organizers were also keen to get the press engaged with reporting from congress on a daily basis, and the Weymouth organizers felt it worthwhile to spend £15 on a dinner for members of the press.[138] Other efforts were made to encourage press coverage. During the 1927 Ipswich congress 'The Magistrates Room' at the Town Hall' was 'fitted up as a writing room for members of the London and Provincial Press'.[139] The Executive Committee minutes for the 1935 Bournemouth congress dealing with publicity noted the need to approach national dailies and Sunday and local newspapers. Other strategies for publicizing congress included the use of diocesan machinery, bill posting and the exploitation of 'Bournemouth Corporation publicity machinery'. The committee were also alert to the audience that could be reached by radio and had successfully approached the British Broadcasting Corporation (BBC). The committee heard that 'the director of religious broadcasting is prepared to help as far as he is able'. The director enabled a radio broadcast by the Bishop of Winchester Cyril Garbett, on the Sunday before congress, in which he spoke about the forthcoming congress and its history, and the opening service presided over by the Archbishop of York was also given coverage.[140] This was not the first time modern communication methods had been used to disseminate congress voices. Reporting on the

1893 congress at Birmingham, *The Times* noted 'upon the rail in front of the chairman's seat a telephone has been fixed, and it is understood that subscribers in London, Birmingham and other large centres will be allowed the privilege of listening to the speeches'.[141] It was not just the committee that made use of the media. In 1938 Dame Christabel Pankhurst used the telephone to alert the press to her presence at congress.[142]

The press provides a window into debate and perspectives that complements and enriches the official congress record. The coverage given to what the *Exeter and Plymouth Gazette* recorded in its report on the 1921 Birmingham congress as 'considerable debate' and 'the sharp division of opinion' on the contested issues of women's roles and specifically their authority in the church, is embedded in later chapters.[143] Here the focus is on the representation of, and attitudes to, the presence of women at congress and their visibility. Women did attract the attention of print journalists and photographers. Press coverage recorded the increasing participation of women and changing attitudes to them, as female speakers, and women with acknowledged expertise in public service or professions became less novel. It also helps to document the presence of women, both middle and working class, whose voices were not heard in the formal proceedings of congress.

Pictorial coverage also indicates the presence of 'non speaking' women although those features are mostly women of social status. The unnamed Mayoress of Yarmouth pictured in the *Daily Mirror* behind a large bouquet, and Lady Llewellyn, Mrs Talbot Rice and Mrs Davidson who were featured in a group photograph with their husbands in *The Tatler's* coverage of the Swansea congress of 1909 provide typical examples.[144] *The Western Daily Press* commented on the arrival by train of congress attendees to the Birmingham Congress in 1893: 'Every train thither yesterday took a crowd of clergymen and influential laymen, accompanied by their lady friends'.[145]

In addition to recording the content of speeches, newspapers added colour to their reports by noting reactions to particular women speakers, describing the average age of the gathering, the number of listeners and the composition of the audience in regard to men and women. Newspapers also commented of the appearance of speakers: The *Daily News* reporter described traveller Isabella Bird Bishop as 'grey haired and sweet voiced', whilst Augusta Maclagan of the Girls' Friendly Society and Mothers' Union was 'tall, handsome, and clear-voiced, – as almost all women speakers are'.[146] Congress was clearly attractive to women, commenting on the composition of the audience at Hull, the *Sheffield Daily Telegraph* noted that: 'the fair sex formed the greater proportion of the audience'.[147] Working-class women were well represented. Reporting on the 1884 Carlisle congress, *The Church Times* noted that:

> The Congress Hall was crowded on Saturday night with an audience of women. Addresses were delivered specially adapted to women in regard to their social relations and domestic duties. It was the first meeting of the kind in connection with a Church Congress and was probably one of the largest meetings of women ever held ... There must have been 2,500 women present, a fair proportion of whom were from the working class.[148]

At the 1899 London Congress the women's meeting was 'representative of all classes', an assertion substantiated by the presence of 'a crying babe at the back whose voice was heard even above the singing'.[149] At Newcastle the following year, Isabella Bird Bishop addressed her remarks to 'wives of working men who constitute the majority of this gathering'.[150] At another Newcastle meeting there was 'an enormous hall crammed' with 3,000 young women.[151]

Initially there was resistance to women in the congress space. The 'John Bull' column in the *Yorkshire Post and Leeds Intelligencer* considered the arrangements for the Leeds Congress of 1872 'admirable' but objected to 'the admission of ladies on the platform', presumably because they were taking space from (in the columnist's view) better qualified audience members such as clergy or laymen.[152] Despite this curmudgeonly response the advent of women as platform speakers almost a decade later received positive coverage. Temperance campaigner and 'Sailors' Friend' Agnes Weston had been due to speak at Newcastle:

> Miss Weston's name stood for the first paper [on seaports], but owing to unavoidable absence, Commander Dawson undertook to read. The expected reading by a lady appeared to have been looked forward to with great interest by many there, and not a little disappointment therefore was manifested when it was discovered that Miss Weston was not present.[153]

The following year, according to *The Derbyshire Advertiser and Journal*:

> Although was scarcely in accordance with the traditions the Church Congress, it had been thought right to invite gifted woman to tell the tale of misery and shame which largely upon the Church to uplift her voice defence of her tempted and unprotected children. The audience almost exclusively consisted clergymen; there were no ladies present except Miss Ellice Hopkins, whose courage in coming forward at such a meeting met with most hearty rounds of cheers.[154]

Three years later The *Church Times* recorded its approval of the 'several ladies' who were among the speakers at Portsmouth in a meeting for women which the reporter judged 'a good idea and no doubt will do good'.[155] However, the *Church Times* had a tendency to adopt a patronizing tone towards women. Coverage of the Folkestone congress included a disparaging remark on the 'ladies in the audience knitting'.[156] Five years later the *Church Times* correspondent was again unimpressed; covering the Young Women's Meeting addressed by Louise Creighton, noting that:

> Her theme was the old womanly theme of self-denial and self-sacrifice applied in daily work- But [asked the reporter, whose identity is not revealed] is it heresy to say so? ... I could not help wondering whether the effect of men speakers would have gone straighter to the hearts of the audience.

However, despite these reservations the reporter did concede that Lady Sophia Palmer, who also spoke in this meeting 'found great favour with the girls'.[157] Two years later, possibly the same journalist noted that: 'Knowing from experience precisely what the women speakers would say, and how charmingly they would say it, I stayed away'.[158]

Overall the press were supportive of women's inclusion in congress. *The Huddersfield Chronicle* challenged and poked fun at what it saw as (in 1892) the 'mediaeval' attitude of Rev. Husband, the Vicar of Folkestone, who had had threatened to resign over the inclusion of a woman speaker on the programme.

> It is a good thing that the incumbent of St. Michael's, Folkestone, is a Husband already: he might never have become one after his latest utterances on "the women question!" The next meeting of the Church Congress is to take place at Folkestone, and among the "fixtures" on that occasion is an address by a Churchwoman. It is this that has drawn from Mr. Husband his anti-feminine protest. This good cleric scents danger in the choice of a female speaker at the congress. He thinks it will encourage those women of our time who desire to assume offices and undertake duties hitherto assumed and undertaken by men. In this, we think, he is mistaken ... Mr. Husband, surely, would not argue seriously that there is no point on which a Churchwoman could enlighten other Church people. As the spiritual director of a congregation, he must know that women are of the greatest service in Church work, on which they have an undoubted right, as well as capacity, to express opinions.[159]

By 1894 the *Illustrated London News*, which accompanied its coverage with an engraving of Laura Ridding who spoke on The *Guardianship of Working Girls*, was able to report that: 'at Exeter there was an increasing tendency to recognize the value of women's opinion and the wisdom of allowing women to state them'.[160] Two years later, in its coverage of the Shrewsbury congress, Laura Ridding was again pictured alongside 'Mrs. Creighton another bishop's wife', and 'the changed views of church people towards women speakers' were still regarded as worthy of comment which paradoxically suggests that women on the platform were still regarded as a relative novelty. *The Sphere* coverage of the 1905 Weymouth congress included photographs of Elizabeth Wordsworth, Mary Sumner, Emma Yeatman and Mary Clifford who were amongst other women speakers.[161] The *Church Family Newspaper* 'Special Report' for the Southampton congress of 1913 also included photographs of some of the women presenters including Mary Sumner and Louise Creighton, alongside its commentary on the large number of women speakers.[162]

Women platform speakers were recorded particularly when they were innovators, such as Mrs Papillon, the first woman to directly address an audience, or speakers who tackled sensitive issues such as Jane Ellice Hopkins or Maude Royden. Even *The Church Times* approved of Royden as 'the Prophetess of Purity'; its reporter noted: 'I should think that so plain spoken a speech by a woman to a vast assembly of men has never before been delivered ... I think it was largely the calm, deliberate and earnest language in which modestly but unflinchingly, she handled so delicate a subject, and some appalling details that created a profound impression'.[163] Women of distinction in other fields also received press attention. Coverage of educationalist Lilian Faithfull's speeches evokes their entertaining content and favourable reception by the audience, whilst the traveller, writer and missionary sympathizer Isabella Bird Bishop drew the following comment from *The Barnsley Chronicle*: 'From her quiet, self-possessed manner and look no one would suppose that this is the bold woman who has penetrated into unknown Chinese wilds, led adventurous existence in the Rocky Mountains, and explored Japan from end to end'.[164] Like the reporters of the papers and periodicals that covered congress this book sees women at congress worthy of attention and seeks to give the reader some sense of their interests, achievement and views.

Conclusion

The Church Congress ran between 1861 until 1938, and apart from a hiatus during the years of the First World War was an annual event until 1928. Then followed three final congresses in 1930, 1935 and 1938. It was an exercise in Church outreach that was intended to promote Anglican unity and raise the profile of the established Church at a time of denominational rivalry. From 1862 women had access to the congress as members of the audience. Thereafter women were a regular feature in audiences, either as the companions to their male friends and kin, or as attendees in special meetings targeted at categories of women, including those from the working class which attracted women in their hundreds.

Women first gained access to congress as platform speakers in 1881 but it was not until 1885 that women speakers became a regular feature at congress. Whilst the majority of women speakers contributed to the women's sections of congress, several, notably those with particular expertise, such as Gertrude Tuckwell, the employment law expert, spoke in main agenda sessions that covered a variety of topics both religious and secular. Whilst women constituted a small proportion (about 10 per cent at a rough approximation) of the total number of congress speakers, those who did speak were distinguished for church work, social and public service or professional expertise. Some of these women made repeated contributions to congress. The publication of an official congress record, which contained verbatim reports of speeches, ensured the capture of women contributors voices alongside those of men and distribution to an audience of clergy and 'church people'. The extensive press coverage of congress and the interest shown by reporters to women at congress, both in the audience and on the platform, further advertised their contribution to congress and disseminated a synthesis of their views to a geographically remote audience.

The reach of congress, particularly to those not likely to read the official report, was also facilitated by its movement to different locations and its street presence in the form of the congress parade. This spectacle announced the presence of congress to members of the public who were not congress members. The congress banner, a key feature of congress pageantry, offered an opportunity for women to contribute, as designer or embroiderers. Women also offered financial support for the banner and also in some case pledged to underwrite congress and financial guarantors. Over time women participated increasingly in congress organization as members of committees other than those sole concerned with the women's programme of events and from the first made an informal but essential contribution to congress as landladies and hostess. Moreover, it could be argued that without the presence of women, social events, particularly those of a civic character, would not have taken place.

The significance of congress goes beyond the official programme and its topical content. Congress offered cultural diversion thorough the curation of artworks and historical artefacts. In addition the congress exhibition offered a showcase for diverse women's organizations, philanthropic, religious and political. The provision of the printed guides to that included topographical information on the congress locality and possibilities for recreation locates congress as an event that offered recreational possibilities. The attendance of families and the frequent documenting of the provision of hospitality further emphasize the social dimension of congress and its possibilities for informal networking. With its family orientation, opportunities for social contact, provision of safe and respectable public venues, dedicated meetings for women, representation of women's organizations, women speakers of distinction, opportunities to contribute to organization and the possibility for engagement with topical social issues, the Church congress was indeed a space for women.

2

Women in the Church – Deaconesses, Sisters, Missionaries and Spiritual Aspirations

'Her true strength is loyal submission': The Anglican doctrine of subordination

Women seeking to participate in the work of the Church did so against a context of assumptions concerning the nature of 'woman' that encompassed intellect and emotion, and which were embedded in social practice and codified in their legal status. Religion was drawn on to inform and legitimize these assumptions of gendered difference. Women with a religious vocation needed to accommodate and negotiate these circumstances either by arguing for space within existing institutions of the Church or through the establishment of separate spaces.[1] Denominational rivalry and contested views on observance within Anglicanism also mediated women's participation in Anglican religious life. The expansion of imperial horizons stimulated Church growth overseas, offered opportunities for individuals including women to pursue a vocation and prompted 'church people' to consider the position of the Church in relation to the exercise of colonial power and the negotiation of race. At home, access to education, the opening of civic roles and increased access to professional space by women raised questions concerning their authority both secular and spiritual. This chapter explores the roles achieved by women in the church against this context. The chapter begins by considering the participation of women in the Church, as deaconesses, sisters and missionary workers as it was reflected at congress, with an emphasis on the period before the First World War. The latter part of the chapter focuses on the articulation of women's spiritual aspirations towards priesthood in the context of the post-war congresses from 1919.

    The notion that religious authority was unwomanly was drawn from scripture and the interpretation of St Paul.[2] The Pauline position derived from Genesis and woman's secondary creation from Adam's rib as his companion. Biblical authority was drawn on to assert that women and men had been endowed by the Creator with different but complementary characteristics, not only biologically but emotionally, intellectually and even spiritually, which suited them for the performance of different roles.[3] Christopher Wordsworth, Bishop of Lincoln and the father of congress contributor Elizabeth, the principal of Lady Margaret Hall, Oxford's first college for women, encapsulated the doctrine of subordination in a sermon on 'Christian womanhood'. According to the bishop, woman was subsequent to man and derived from him, 'anything that disturbs that subordination weakens her authority and mars her beauty. Her true strength is loyal submission'.[4] Moreover, according to scripture, woman was responsible for loss of innocence and sin because of her susceptibility to temptation. Novelist and 'churchwoman' Charlotte Yonge wrote in her 1878 publication *Womankind*: 'I have no hesitation in declaring my full belief in the inferiority of woman nor that she brought it on herself'.[5] It was considered appropriate that woman should be subordinate to masculine authority and her dangerous sexuality should be contained within the family. Canon Sparrow Simpson was unequivocal in his assertion before the Birmingham congress of 1921 'that the principle of subordination exists in the Church as well as the home, and there also the man is the head of the woman'.[6] The Dowager Countess of Chichester, in her capacity as president of the Mothers' Union, speaking to congress in 1910, summed up:

> There were two types of woman from the first; the Eve type through which the race fell. And through which it is falling still, the type which shifted the centre of life from God to self: the other type was that of Mary, the blessed handmaid of the Lord, humble and devout, the prepared instrument for the incarnation, to which they allowed their elevation.[7]

So esteemed attributes of 'good' women accrued around self-restraint (notably chastity), domesticity and service.

The term 'spiritual womanhood' used by Jenny Daggers encapsulates the supposed superior religious 'sensibility' of good women as asserted by evangelical enthusiast William Wilberforce, and endorsed in the work of influential critic John Ruskin, a theme explored in Julie Melnyk's 'Theological Approaches to Women in the Age of Empire'.[8] Notions of women's supposed maternal qualities, and contingent assumptions on nurturing roles, were applicable to unmarried as well as married women.[9] Once family duties were discharged, the improving moral 'mission' of the 'spiritual woman' could, and according to a number of congress speakers, should, extend beyond the home. Philanthropic service was a social and religious expectation. The chapter 'Charity' in Charlotte Yonge's *Womankind* asserted alms giving as a religious duty and provided examples of how young ladies may discharge the obligation of charitable service through the support of missions 'at home' or overseas even if parents forbade direct contact with the poor.[10] Archdeacon R. F. L. Blunt, speaking at the Hull Congress of 1890, after repeating conventional tropes concerning women's weakness and susceptibility to temptation, went on to assert the greater religious instinct of women which suited them for caring service.[11] Eleven years later, Canon Denton Thompson's advocacy for women's work in the Church also emphasized the idea of womanly caring qualities.[12]

Women seeking access to the congress forum and concessionary authority within the Church did so in the context of this discourse of gendered difference and contingent indices of religious capital. The notion of spiritual womanhood accommodates those identifying as 'churchwomen' who, motivated by religious belief, sought vocations in Church work, or were committed to activism towards the reform of society. Activism was permissible in the role of what Archdeacon George Sumner called 'handmaids of the Church'.[13] It was not just men who deployed these arguments. Charlotte Yonge's paper 'Woman's work in the Church' in the church congress report read by Rev CW Bond starts 'Behold the handmaid of the lord should be the spirit of Christian Women'.[14] Miss E. J. Whatley, an author of religious works and sister of a female missionary, in a paper read on her behalf by a gentleman friend at the 1878 congress, justified a role for women in Church work by asserting 'as woman was appointed the helpmate of man in the family so she is in the Church'.[15] Later, distinguished congress contributor Elizabeth Wordsworth used the idea of helpmate in the context of advocacy for higher education.[16] Congress participants, both men and women, were interested in the implications that biblically informed notions of womanhood had for women in relation to citizenship and roles within the Church, and the doctrine of difference was drawn on to support varying interpretations of what was deemed appropriate in relation to women's activity.[17] Whilst interpretations of appropriate roles, scope for action and spiritual authority might differ, biblically endorsed notions of good womanhood and the nature of woman could not be ignored, and congress is a forum in which these themes were represented and the negotiation of them played out.

Women on the congress agenda: Official employment in the Church, sisterhoods and deaconesses

The exploration of and negotiation of women's work for the Church and the ministry of women proved to be a durable theme at congress. The second congress at Oxford in 1862, which admitted women as members of the audience in the secluded space of the Sheldonian Theatre gallery, had the role of women in the Church or church work on the agenda. A paper on workhouse visiting was read by Captain Burrows on behalf on an author whose identity is not revealed. This, and the tone and content, suggests the paper may have been written by a woman. It articulated the aspiration of women for useful 'work' and evoked the popular trope of the supposed spiritual elevation and caring nature of the domesticated Christian woman.

> Oh, that the hundreds, we might say thousands of our country women who sit at ease, many of them longing for work, for interests, for some object to 'kill time', would come forward and taste the pleasure of ministering to others, nay, to Christ himself in the persons of his sick, His afflicted, His wandering children. Oh! That every workhouse in the land were purified and hallowed by the labours of those who by their very presence be a check to sin and iniquity ...[18]

The paper also pragmatically noted that 'educated' women volunteers would save on expenditure from the rates. It also added a disclaimer that women would not be asserting any inappropriate authority; their work would 'not be superseding but cooperating with the Guardians'.[19] The same congress also featured addresses on more formalized women's service in what the *Birmingham Daily Post* described as 'works of piety and charity' that had arisen out of, and sought to extend, the philanthropic initiatives of middle and upper middle-class women.[20] Discussion covered the appointment of what were known as 'parochial mission women', a new organization for the employment of poorer women who would undertake home visiting. As these women were drawn from the lower end of the social spectrum they provoked less interest and debate than middle-class women seeking roles in Church work. The aims of the Parochial Mission Society, which had been instigated by Caroline Jane Talbot, were explained to the audience by the Reverent C. Wellington Furze.[21] The following year The *London Quarterly Review*, which devoted pages to the discussion of sisterhoods and deaconesses in its coverage of women's Church work at the Reading congress, dealt with them in just one line, noting that: Mr J.G Talbot M.P. [Caroline's son] 'described and commended the work of "Mission Women".[22] Mission women were to undertake bible reading and foster self-help by initiating savings schemes and thrift clubs. Following the example of the Charity Organisation Society (COS) the giving of handouts of charitable relief was not encouraged.[23] Another overlapping category, paid 'Bible women', who were also from less socially distinguished backgrounds, would advocate Church views amongst members of their own class. By 1884 there were 187 parochial mission women but neither category attracted controversy, because their activities were subject to parochial authority; moreover, women from less socially advantaged backgrounds, under the supervision of a middle-class 'lady superintendent', posed no challenge to either the temporal or spiritual authority of middle-class male clergy.[24]

Formal service for middle-class women fell into two broad categories, Deaconesses and Sisterhoods, and both were represented at congress. The instigation of these categories prompted anxiety over the bounds of their spiritual authority. Anglican women seeking to live in religious communities which implied segregated space and exclusion from family divided opinion.[25] Controversy over 'sisterhoods' as they were known, for the term 'nun' was avoided, reflected the sometimes bitter division within Anglicanism between the Low Church party and High Church Tractarians over the 'correct' interpretation of doctrine and form of worship that had been playing out in the Church since the spiritual wakeup call represented by the publications issued between 1833 and 1841, known collectively as the *Tracts for the Times*. Adherents of the Low Church position were, in general, strongly committed to upholding the Protestant Reformation, saw the Eucharist as a symbolic commemorative rite and emphasized preaching and more austere forms in worship. The High Church view aligned with the Tractarian movement (also known as the Oxford movement on account of the academic location of its contributing authors) which favoured priestly authority, and sought revival and beautification of worship. Tractarian belief in transubstantiation, that is, the 'actual' mystical presence in the Eucharist was characteristic of Roman Catholic faith and this, combined with reintroduction of Roman Catholic hierarchy to England in 1851, and the defection of high-status Anglicans to the Roman Church, provoked concern that the established Anglican Church was under attack.[26] Roman Catholicism was also a focus for concern because it was seen to undermine family life. Bishop Charles Sumner, who, like his brother of congress instigator John Bird Sumner, aligned with the Lower Church evangelical party, articulated the anxiety that Roman Catholic priests might undermine paternal authority exercised over wives and daughters in the family:

> The system of the confessional is foreign to the spirit of the gospel [...] Englishmen will never endure to see the weaker members of their families subjected to an authority which, if it does not taint and confuse the moral sense, will subdue the mind to the extinction of all independent volition and chains it captive with passive submission to the will of a spiritual director.[27]

The revival of sisterhoods was one aspect of the aspiration for spiritual revival articulated through the Tractarian movement and supported by those aligning with High Church views. The first Anglican sisterhoods to be established were the Park Village West community in 1845 and Lydia Sellon's community at Devonport in 1848.[28] The establishment of such communities required and secured the support of sympathetic men. The Reverend Dr Pusey, one of the contributing authors to the 'Tracts for the Times', read a paper at the 1862 Oxford congress commending the community of the Sisters of Mercy. However, support for sisterhoods was by no means universal. Clergy and lay response reflected anxieties that accrued not just about women's segregation away from the paternal authority of the family but also around women's autonomy and spiritual authority.[29] Susan Mumm's observation that anti-Roman Catholic suspicion extended to the segregation of women in religious communities is substantiated by congress proceedings.[30] In the session on sisterhoods to which Dr Pusey contributed, despite his emphasis on the important practical contribution made to parochial work by the sisters, there were mixed feelings amongst the speakers and the audience. According to a report in *John Bull*:

> Had it not been for the tact of the President, a difference of opinion would undoubtedly have been manifested. The able papers by Dr Pusey, Dr Howson, Mr Carter, and Mr W. Ellington Forse, all bearing more or less on this question, undoubtedly excited greater enthusiasm among some, and fear among others, than any others that were read.

The report went on to note that:

> Some little time back, Sisters of Mercy could not walk in our streets without attracting rude observation. Although there are still vulgar and ignorant persons who do their best to prove their ill breeding by staring a Sister out of countenance, and even following her in the streets ... they are getting, we are glad to think, scarce animals.[31]

Despite the optimism expressed by *John Bull*, at future congresses and in the press, sisterhoods continued to be the focus of controversy, and a stimulus for vehemently expressed opinions that reflected the suspicion of any system that suggested 'Roman practice'.[32] However, the number of Anglican Sisterhoods did increase, and by 1875 there were eighteen communities. Father T. T. Carter, who was in favour of these communities, reported to the Stoke-on-Trent congress audience and, like Pusey, possibly mindful of the concerns over seclusion and autonomy, emphasized the practical contribution made by the sisters to nursing, visiting and rescue work, rather than their spiritual engagement in prayer and contemplation.[33] Canon Clewer's advocacy for sisterhoods at the Reading congress in 1883, although commended by the *Church Times* as 'an admirable paper', was condemned by the *London Quarterly Review* for promoting what was 'virtually a counterpart of the system of the Church of Rome'. Its report continued in vehement tones: 'A fuller acquaintance with all the facts respecting the obedience, chastity, and poverty avowed by members of the "Sisterhoods" would probably intensify into disgust, the healthy repugnance of the English to these communities.'[34]

The official view on Anglican religious communities became more relaxed as time passed and defections from Anglicanism to Roman Catholicism became less topical. The 1897 Lambeth Congress articulated in Resolution 11, 'thankfulness for the revival alike of brotherhoods and sisterhoods' but sounded a cautious note in Resolution 12, by stating that: 'In view of the importance of the further development and wise direction of such communities, the Conference requests the Committee to continue its labours, and to present a further Report to His Grace the Archbishop of Canterbury in July 1898'.[35] By 1900 the number of recognized sisterhoods in the Church had increased to ninety. Despite this numerical increase, perhaps as a result of the antipathy to sisterhoods expressed in the press,[36] the voices of individual sisters had not yet been heard at congress. However, there were women engaged at congress who were sympathetic to sisterhoods. Charlotte Yonge, whose spiritual mentor was prominent Tractarian John Keble, was a supporter of the movement, and from 1868 was associated with the community of St Mary's Wantage as an 'Exterior Sister'.[37] In 1899 at the London congress, Yonge's friend and protégé through the Gosling essay society, Miss Anderson Morshead, herself an author, gave an address in which she stressed not just the practical work done by sisterhoods, but their aspiration towards a spiritual, rather than pastoral identity.[38] However, suspicion still lingered, and in 1921 at Birmingham, Mrs Emma Paget, wife of the Bishop of Stepney, and an advocate for the recognition of women's spiritual authority, asserted the popularity of sisterhoods, but pointed out that, despite this, they remained the branch of organized women's church work 'least encouraged' by authority.[39]

For women seeking to realize a religious vocation, the role of deaconess offered an alternative to entering a sisterhood. Deaconesses, who were likely to work as individuals, were directly subject to parochial and episcopal authority, and were less identified with collective and segregated communities. So, becoming a deaconess was less controversial and more easily accessible than joining a sisterhood. Moreover, the role of deaconess chimed with the recognition amongst clergy that women were valuable assets in practical aspects of ministry.[40] Dean Howson, the author of the 1862 publication *Deaconesses or, the Official Help of Women in Parochial Work and in Charitable Institutions,* looked back to historical precedents in the early Church, and to the New Testament for examples of women's ministry.[41] In his congress paper delivered the same year, according to the report in the *Birmingham Daily Post*, he also cited current social need as a rationale for appointing deaconesses, when he advocated the introduction of a carefully selected body of women, trained to work in institutions and in urban areas 'where the largest mass of the poor are congregated'. He continued:

> With regard to dress ... when a system matured – whatever was the case in experimental stages – a distinctive though not peculiar dress would be found important. It settled what often occupied a great deal of time and thought [laughter and cheers] It promoted economy, it was a bond of union, it was a great protection and secured immediate recognition ... among those among whom the ministrations took place.[42]

The reference to avoiding 'peculiar dress' hints at a concern that deaconesses' costumes should not be confused with the habits of Roman Catholic nuns. Deaconesses, trained to do pastoral work and teaching, without what Bishop Harold Browne referred to as 'unwomanly usurpation of authority in the church',[43] were again on the agenda at Stoke on Trent in 1857 when the Reverend Arthur Gore reiterated the idea that deaconesses were not an autonomous group when he insisted that: 'A Deaconess is the servant of the Church, and she is nothing else'.[44] At the 1883 Reading congress, Dean Howson once took the platform to advocate an authorized and official diaconate of women, and echoed the sentiments of Browne and Gore when he insisted that deaconesses 'did not constitute a sisterhood'.[45] Whilst his assertion of the need for a distinct identity for deaconesses, and his advocacy for their induction 'to be a distinctly religious act', acknowledged women's seriousness in seeking religious service and the biblical legitimacy of their ministry, his advocacy for the deaconess was also located, possibly with the avoidance of controversy in mind, in the acceptable tradition of women's philanthropic service, and was envisaged to be under parochial direction.[46] A point stressed by clergy who advocated deaconesses, yet were cautious of aligning them with sisterhoods. Deaconesses did not take vows, and thus by implication, were not accountable to an external extra parochial or diocesan authority, a notion of concern because of the supranational nature of Roman Catholic hierarchy. As with sisterhoods, attitudes towards deaconesses changed over time. Resolution 11 of the 1897 Lambeth Conference stated: 'That this Conference recognizes with thankfulness the revival alike of brotherhoods and sisterhoods and of the office of deaconess in our branch of the Church, and commends to the attention of the Church the Report of the Committee appointed to consider the Relation of Religious Communities to the Episcopate.'[47] However, despite this tentative acceptance of deaconesses, they were relatively few in number and their status continued to be ambivalent until the resolutions passed by the Lambeth Conference of 1920. Resolution 47 stated that: 'the diaconate of women should be restored formally and canonically, and should be recognized throughout the Anglican Communion.' However, Resolution 48 cautioned that: 'The order of deaconesses is for women the one and only order of the ministry', and Resolution 49 noted that:

> The office of deaconess is primarily a ministry of succour, bodily and spiritual, especially to women, and should follow the lines of the primitive rather than of the modern diaconate of men. It should be understood that the deaconess dedicates herself to a life-long service, but that no vow or implied promise of celibacy should be required as necessary for admission to the order. Nevertheless, deaconesses who desire to do so may legitimately pledge themselves either as members of a community, or as individuals, to a celibate life.[48]

As the Dean of Wells noted in his preface to a 1924 memoir of Head Deaconess Isabella Gilmore:

> At one time there was some fear lest the revival of a true Diaconate for women would be hampered by a confusion with the parallel movement of organised sisterhoods, the members of which were also engaged in the activities of parish life. It was indeed natural that some women should wish to combine the function of a parish deaconess with the strength and sympathy provided by the life of a community. On the other hand, it was most important to assert the normal independence of the deaconess who was bound only to obedience to her bishop and to the parish priest under whose directions she ministered.[49]

From the last decade of the nineteenth century distinguished deaconesses began to make personal appearances on the congress platform to assert their vocation. At the Folkestone congress of 1892 Isabella Gilmore, at that point Head Deaconess of the Diocese of Rochester, insisted that training for the role should be hard work.[50] In 1894 at Exeter, in a similar advocacy for professionalism, Emily Cheveley, known as 'Sister Emily', the Head of the Diocesan Institution for the Work and Training of Deaconeses, speaking to an audience of women, was scathing in refuting the assumption that the role was suitable for candidates seeking a genteel occupation:

> First there is the feeble "goody – goody" candidate. She is obliged to earn her living – has tried teaching, and failed. We are at once struck with the fact that the main thought in her mind is, whether in the future she can support not only herself, but, it may be, an aged mother: in other words what the profit or loss will be in Church work *versus* teaching. She *thinks* she can do most things required …[51]

Sister Emily was equally dismissive of 'the self confident, opinionated candidate' who:

> when told of of the difficulties we have to encounter: how some will not listen, and most are hardened; how some pretend to be religious for the loaves and fishes, but by far the majority never attend any place of worship; how difficult it is to bring young people to Confirmation, and still harder to get them to be Communicants, the only reply is "*I never had any difficulties of this kind*".[52]

Her point was to emphasize the sense of vocation and commitment to discipline required to be a deaconess. Her assertion that candidates needed to demonstrate 'oblation; i.e. entire surrender, self – abandonment, utter relinquishmnet of selfish desires … surrendering to God the spirit, and aim and purpose of life' was as much a profession of vocation as that undertaken by sisters both Anglican and Roman Catholic.[53] She went on to elaborate at some length on the spiritual, intellectual and personal training of the worker, which should involve bible study, prayer, meditation, attention to Church history and the exercise of personal self-restraint.[54]

In 1908, Gilmore spoke to an audience at the Pan Anglican Congress of bishops representing the worldwide Anglican communion, to advocate official endorsement and clarification of the spiritual status and responsibilities of the deaconess throughout the Church. As part of her assertion of the commitment of deaconesses to lifelong religious vocation, she pointed out that marriage was incompatible with the role.[55] 1908 was also the year in which the Head Deaconesses' Association was established with the patronage of Archbishop Randall Davidson. The following year Gilmore took the platform at the Swansea Church congress in the section on 'Women's Work in the Church'. The substance of her talk was similar in content, if not tone to the paper delivered by Sister Emily. Gilmore laid out the curriculum undertaken by candidates in their two-year period of training. She described academic study of the Bible and Prayer book, Church history and 'Dogmatics' being taken alongside practical skills such as nursing, sewing, cooking and bookkeeping, in addition to experience in how to undertake pastoral visiting. She also made sure to signal the religious dignity of the deaconess by noting that she: 'is a woman who has been set apart by the bishop with the laying on of hands, and a permanent ministry bestowed upon her'.[56]

Isabella Gilmore was recognized as a pioneer of the deaconess movement, but she was not the only prominent deaconess to contribute to congress. With the ministry of women identified as an agenda item for the 1920 Lambeth Conference the subject was of topical interest. Head Deaconess Mary Siddall and Head Deaconess Edith Banks, who both made appearances at congress, also served on the committee of enquiry into women's ministry established by Archbishop Randall Davison in 1917.[57] Siddall, like Gilmore, had a long and illustrious career as a deaconess. A former headmistress, she had served as Head Deaconess of the Newcastle Diocese between 1905 and 1911, before taking over from Mother Emma Marrat Day as Head Deaconess for the Winchester Diocese. By the time of the 1919 Leicester congress, where she contributed to the section on 'The Church's Equipment for Corporate Life and Witness', to a debate on the topical issue of 'the ministry of Women', she was Head Deaconess of Rochester and Southwark.[58] It is unsurprising that the Southend congress, which followed the Lambeth conference, featured papers and discussion on 'Christ and womanhood' to which Head Deaconess Banks, Siddal's successor first at Newcastle in 1911, and then at Winchester in 1918, contributed. Head Deaconess Siddall also made an appearance and contributed a paper to the meeting for women.[59]

One solution to the aspiration of women seeking religious service in a community, which circumvented the anti-Tractarian and anti-Roman Catholic antipathy accruing to sisterhoods, and the confrontation of questions over vows and training relating to the status of deaconesses, was provided by the Greyladies. Greyladies College, as it was uncontroversially but somewhat misleadingly styled, aimed to 'provide a body of ladies, living a common life, who should carry on diocesan work in the parishes of South London'.[60] The college, which had been set up under the auspices of Bishop Yeatman, the Suffragan Bishop of Southwark, in 1893, was under the direction of his sister Miss Emma Yeatman, who spoke at congresses in 1895, 1902 and 1905. It remained an independent institution, initially at Blackheath, then another outpost in Coventry was established. The Blackheath branch evolved into the Southwark Diocesan Training School for Deaconesses with Susan Wordsworth, the sister of distinguished educationalist and congress speaker Elizabeth, as its head between 1900 and 1911. Greyladies

College targeted single women of means who possessed religious enthusiasm and an aptitude for philanthropy, according to *Everywoman's Encyclopaedia*.

> The college is described as a society of ladies living together for the purpose of helping in the work of the Church of England under the incumbents of the diocese. The bishop of the diocese has ultimate control over all its affairs. The Greyladies work in twenty-two parishes in South London ... Many women emerge through such association from a life of narrowness and emptiness into one of breadth and satisfaction.[61]

The article went on to describe the appeal of the establishment. For 50 guineas a year 'lonely genteel women of means' could enjoy their own room and sitting room in the elegant surroundings of a country house on the breezy heights of Black Heath [sic], in exchange for the opportunity to venture out in pairs to do parochial work according to the methods of the incumbent, 'there was no asceticism' – and members were encouraged to cultivate artistic talents and enjoy cultural events or visit friends or go to the country on their guaranteed days off.[62] Although the genteel surroundings were emphasized, the article also elaborated on the 'work' undertaken:

> They do every kind of parish work, except sick nursing. Some do district visiting, others provident collecting, while others hold mothers' meetings, classes, and clubs, Bands of Hope, and Sunday-schools. Others act as school managers, or serve on C.O.S. [Charity Organisation Society] committees; some help to prepare the less instructed women and girls for confirmation and communion, and hold a Saturday Church Catechism school for the little ones. Others, again, give short addresses during the dinner-hour in some factory or woodyard where women are employed, or direct a school for mothers.[63]

Miss Emily Yeatman, who was head of Greyladies until 1900, when Wordsworth took over and the 'college' moved towards alignment with deaconess service, did not use the opportunity of her congress appearances to advocate communal living, nor did she emphasize philanthropic outreach. Her speech to an audience of women at the Norwich congress of 1895 prioritized women's work in the home, 'cheap homely work that does not show', should not be despised: 'Surely a woman's best place is at home. This is where she can do most, for the race, keeping a home pure, true and happy: teaching boys and men to admire truth, honour and virtue, Surely that is the highest woman's work.' She went on to assert that 'clever' educated women were needed to accomplish it.[64]

In 1902, at Northampton, she urged her audience of girls to guard their reputations, and counselled them on the avoidance of gossip and frivolous pursuits.⁶⁵ Three years later, Yeatman made a significant contribution to the Weymouth congress. In an outreach meeting to women in Bridport, her focus was on self-culture and the use of talents, and she appeared on the platform again at the central women's meeting. She also served as a member of the women's organizing committee.⁶⁶ Her contribution was publicly celebrated in a photographic feature in *The Sphere*, in which she is pictured wearing a head dress with a veil falling over the back of the head that references the traditional costume of women religious. It is a matter of speculation whether it conformed to what Dean Howson had in mind when he called for dress that was 'distinctive but not outlandish'⁶⁷.

Missionaries

The congress period, from its inception up until the First World War, coincided with geographical exploration, an appetite for travel, notably amongst women, and rapid and competitive colonial expansion. Popular interest in overseas was reflected in a proliferation of travel diaries, a genre contributed to by congress speaker Mary Sumner whose *Our Holiday in the East* of 1881 described a family journey through Egypt, Syria and the Holy Land.⁶⁸ Charlotte Yonge, also a congress contributor, was the biographer of the martyred Bishop Patterson of Melanesia, and missionary themes and characters feature in her novels.⁶⁹ The Established Anglican Church was by definition bound up with imperial expansion, and was a presence in regions in which the British government sought to extend its influence. In 1891 there were a total of seventy-five overseas bishops collectively organized in administrative units known as Provinces. They represented Anglican organization in Canada, Australia, South Africa (including St Helena) and the West Indies. Fifteen dioceses under the province of the Archbishop of Canterbury included Central Africa, Eastern Equatorial Africa, Corea [sic], North China, Japan and Honolulu and Jerusalem. The Church provided a conduit for information from the imperial periphery to its congregations.⁷⁰ Missionary endeavour in distant lands was regularly reported to congress audiences, and there are over twenty references to missionary subjects on congress agendas in the period between 1863 and 1910. Congress contributors included overseas and 'missionary bishops' whose jurisdiction might be in territory beyond the British empire or its colonies. At the 1871 Nottingham congress the section on 'Foreign Missions' included 'a paper by the late [former] Bishop of Mauritius on the Slave trade still in existence on the west coast of Africa'. In 1873 at the Bath congress, the topic of foreign missions was taken by British Colonial Administrator Sir Bartle Frere, the president of the Royal Geographical Society and former Governor of Bombay. Frere, an 'ardent' supporter of missionary societies, published *Eastern Africa as a Field for Missionary Labour Four Letters to the Archbishop of Canterbury* the following year.[71] In the context of colonial wars, notably the Zulu war in which Frere was a protagonist, and the later Boer war, the exercise of Imperial power prompted reflections on its legitimacy and the appropriate stance of the Church towards subject peoples and non-believers, both within and beyond the dominion of the British empire.[72] Towards the end of the nineteenth and early twentieth century congress agendas reflected an increased attention to the negotiation of race. The 1897 Nottingham congress discussed 'aboriginal races', 'mixed races' in India and 'Native' Churches, amongst other topics relating to missions and the colonies. At Bristol in 1903, Henry Montgomery, the Secretary of the Society for the Propagation of the Gospel and former Bishop of Tasmania, reflected on 'Racial Characteristics affecting Missionary Work'. According to the *Derbyshire Advertiser and Journal*: 'Bishop Montgomery urged that when converting the Asiatic and the African they should keep him Asiatic and African.' It also reported views expressed in the following discussion. Rev. Dr. Tidsall encapsulated the notion the white Christians should set an example, an idea present in the writing of Mothers' Union founder Mary Sumner, which will be given attention in the following chapter. He said: 'that one difficulty confronting them was that other races believed that Englishmen were irreligious and immoral.' The Earl of Stamford, however, revealed some assumptions about race and 'idleness', and saw the way to redemption though instilling a protestant work ethic. According to the Earl 'industrial missions were most essential for Africa. To teach its natives manual labour was honourable.'[73] Bishop Montgomery was an enthusiastic advocate of an imperial Church, and the driving force behind the 1908 Pan Anglican Congress which drew in bishops accompanied by their wives, and others from the worldwide Anglican Communion, an event that was publicized through agenda item at the Norwich congress the preceding year.[74]

Women were participants in the evangelization of potential converts in colonies and contact zones, and this activity was recognized at congress.[75] If sisterhoods raised anti-Tractarian and anti-Roman Catholic hackles, and deaconesses also created anxiety over women exceeding the bounds of gendered spiritual authority, women who sought to realize a religious vocation through missionary work provoked less controversy. The 'lady missionary' embodied not only the conspicuous witness of faith, but valorous travail for Christianity, and in her association with distant 'exotic' locations was a figure of interest whose exploits featured in published stories and non-fiction.[76] Missionary work was also drawn on to inspire and validate philanthropy, a theme that will be addressed in following chapter.

The first congress contribution by a woman on a missionary theme was at the 1889 Cardiff congress when a paper by Mrs Francis Petrie was read on her behalf by the Rev. Kingsbury. Mrs Petrie's subject was the missionary achievements of the Rev. A. R. M. Wilshere, a 'son of the Church of England' who had worked in a leper colony for many years.[77] At the 1890 Hull congress, Miss Editha Mulvany of the Church of England Zenana Mission Society (CEZMS), which, by focusing on ministry to women in seclusion, allowed an exclusive role and contingent authority for its lady missionaries, evoked a well-worn trope when she contrasted the privileged status of white Christian women with the degraded status of women 'in the East'.[78] Miss Mulvaney, who was 'just on the eve of going out for the third time to do God's work in India', was entirely convinced of the legitimacy of her mission and painted a dramatic picture of the need for missionary endeavour:

> The women of the East-what a panorama passes before the mind's eye! The millions of China Japan, India, and Africa. Scenes representing cruelty, oppression and wrong; womanhood degraded and debased in some of these countries, and in all held in low estimation. Oh, my dear Christian sisters, we who have been highly blessed above all the women of the earth, shall we turn away without a throb for their woe, without a stretched out hand to show them practical and helpful sympathy.[79]

She was honoured to speak to congress as the representative of 'all those bands of Christian women who have devoted their lives to the moral, spiritual and intellectual elevation of the women in foreign mission fields'. She 'also sought to represent the millions of the daughters of the East to plead their needs'.[80] Editha Mulvaney went on to catalogue the work done towards conversion in villages, zenanas and through the education of girls. She went on to condemn the 'debasing and cruel' practices of child marriage and enforced widowhood. It was her view that, although enlightened Indian gentlemen were against these customs, they were trapped by tradition and so were 'only too glad for the subject to be agitated by outsiders'.[81] Miss Mulvaney then noted the urgent need for more female medical missionaries, and she urged her audience to respond to the call. Her talk concluded with a rhetorical flourish that was intended to encourage support for missionary endeavour: 'We favoured Christians, what are we doing for the millions and millions, who know not, who have never heard of the Saviour who died for the whole world?' She continued with a call to conscience that was evangelical in tone and emphasis: 'What shall we each individually be able to say to our Lord on his return about these millions?'[82]

Seven years later, Miss Mulvaney, still a representative of the CEZMS, returned to the platform at Nottingham, where the main congress focus on colonies and race was reflected in a section of the programme for women dedicated to 'Foreign Missions'.[83] Mary Clifford, although identified in the congress report as a Guardian of the Barton Regis Union Redlands Bristol, also focused on 'Women in the Indian Zenana' as the subject of her first address, and chose 'Women's Work for Missions' in a second platform appearance.[84] Also present at Nottingham was Miss Patteson, a figure who attracted sympathy as the sister of John Coleridge Patteson, the martyred missionary Bishop of Melanesia. Bishop Patteson, who died in 1870, was a relative of his biographer Charlotte Yonge, also an enthusiast for missionary work, who funded the Melanesian Mission ship *Southern Cross*, from the proceeds of her bestselling novel *The Heir of Redcliffe*.[85]

The 'Women's Work for Missions' section of the London Congress in 1899 featured the celebrated traveller and advocate of missionary work, Mrs John (Isabella Bird) Bishop, currently of Tobermory Argyllshire. Mrs Bishop, the author amongst other publications of the travel diary *A Ladies Life in the Rocky Mountains*, educated the audience with a glimpse of exotic destinations on the imperial periphery and beyond.[86] She, like Editha Mulvaney and Mary Clifford, affirmed the worth of the Christian doxa in relation to the position of women, when she asserted that women abroad enclosed in harems were uneducated and ignorant.[87] The following year at Newcastle, where she made two platform appearances, she pursued a similar theme: according to the *Manchester Courier and Lancashire General Advertiser*, she 'caused some excitement and enthusiasm as she stepped on the platform'. Her speech condemned polyandry and noted that despite 'dazzling progress in Japan', in Korea and China the lack of Christian influence meant that women remained a despised category.[88] Her second speech was before a working-class audience. She expressed sympathy for the hardships experienced by the wives of working men, who constituted the majority of the gathering, yet she contrasted their circumstances with the plight of eastern women, and urged them as mothers to act as exemplars of Christian life to their girls.[89] Foreign missions were again on the agenda in 1905 and 1911, tackled by Miss Strahan and Mrs John Jones, respectively.[90]

The issue of religious inclusion in relation to those in colonies and the imperial periphery returned to the agenda at Southampton in 1913. Under the programme section titled 'The Kingdom of God and the Races', The Earl of Selborne, Laura Ridding's brother, and former colonial governor of South Africa, was the keynote speaker. According to the *Belfast Newsletter*, the Earl, 'who had very cordial reception from a crowded audience', opened the discussion on 'The Kingdom of God and the Races' by contributing a short address on the relation between 'civilized' and 'backward races'. The main thrust of his argument was that it was the duty of the 'civilized' nation to act as peacekeeper and guardian to the subject race by preventing their exploitation by whites, and through fostering education towards participation in 'civilized' institutions. In the discussion following the address the topic of mixed congregations of the indigenous inhabitants of a colony and settlers was debated. Miss Lucy Phillimore and Mrs A. Little, who both contributed to the discussion, were in accord with the opinion that to exclude worshipers on the grounds of colour was 'intrinsically contemptuous and intrinsically unchristian'.[91] In 1925 'Race Problems' were on the agenda; E Louie Acres, writing in the *Church League for Women's Suffrage*, noted that Miss Ruth Rouse, one of the speakers, was 'well qualified to speak' on the subject. Mentioned also was Miss Monica Storrs, who 'captured everyone's interest' with her paper on 'Our Trusteeship for Other Races'.[92]

From Mission at home to aspirations for greater spiritual authority

It was clear to congress participants and their contemporaries that, against a background of industrialization, urban expansion and population growth which posed challenges to the physical, and it was thought, the moral welfare of society, reform was needed as much at home as overseas. The term 'Mission', with its connotation of virtuous travail for God, provided a useful label that could be applied to legitimize the application of power relations in the assignation of roles or status, or to dignify philanthropic activism and Church outreach initiatives. The report of the 1898 Bradford congress noted that the 'missionary aspects' of congress were prominent in 'meetings for men, women, young women, girls and lads – also in mills and workshops and for the police at their own request'.[93]

Just as the trope of the 'Angel in the House' served to encapsulate religious and societal approval of women as providers of physical and spiritual home comforts, the notion of women's mission evoked the legitimate extension of women's supposed aptitude for caring into the public sphere. Philanthropist Angela Burdett Coutts' 1898 publication, which documented the breadth of philanthropic activity undertaken by women, was titled *Woman's Mission: A Series of Congress Papers on the Philanthropic Work of Women by Eminent Writers*. The topics ranged from emigration and the employment of women to agricultural entomology, but Church work, childcare and social reform, exemplified by papers on poor law guardianship, and work amongst navvies were also well represented.[94] The book included contributions from congress speakers Mary Sumner and Agnes Weston, who wrote on 'The Responsibilities of Mothers' and 'Work Amongst Sailors', respectively.[95] Miss Violet Brooke-Hunt, who addressed the Brighton congress of 1901 on her work among troops in the South African war, maintaining that the British soldier was neither 'dear Tommy' nor a 'drunken brute' and asserting the need for good army chaplains, contributed a chapter on 'Clubs for Boys and Young Men'.[96] The theme of philanthropic 'work' as an extension of women's supposed caring qualities is embedded in the diverse aspects of activity represented at congress and will be returned to in following chapters that address the Mothers' Union and Girls' Friendly Society, congress women's engagement with other organizations, education and the emergence of access to professionals and politics.

Notable women congress speakers who had achieved distinction in the field of 'mission at home' were purity campaigner Jane Ellice Hopkins and later the prominent evangelist Maude Royden, both of whom were regarded as exceptional, and whose access to the platform was mediated by the patronage of churchmen. Hopkins's reputation as a published advocate of purity and protégée of Bishop George Wilkinson, and as a campaigner for moral reform, enabled her to speak to an audience of men at the Derby congress in 1882. Prior to her platform appearance at Derby, she had a record of philanthropic activism as the founder of the 1876 'Ladies' Association for the Care of Friendless Girls', and author of *A Plea for the Wider Action of the Church of England in the Prevention of the Degradation of Women*, an essay submitted to the Church of England Convocation of Bishops in 1879. Not only was she the first woman to address men directly, but her engagement with prostitution was also controversial for one of her sex and class.[97] Hopkins challenged the Church to engage with sexual double standards and to turn 'the full force of our education and compulsory reformation machinery against the 80,000 women on the streets'.[98] However, she prefaced her talk with a disclaimer that sought to excuse her engagement with a subject considered unsuitable for a lady, according to gendered assumptions accruing around the presumed 'innocence' of the 'pure' woman: 'I am sure I may ask the sympathy of my audience in the terrible effort they must be aware it costs a woman to speak on this subject'.[99] The year following the Derby congress, she founded the 'White Cross Army', an organization that challenged prevailing sexual double standards by asserting men's responsibility for morality. With the motto 'My strength is as the strength of ten because my heart is pure', it encouraged working men to honour women, avoid blasphemy and pledge themselves to chastity.[100] Hopkins was supported in this endeavour by Bishop of Durham Joseph Lightfoot who, the same year, had affirmed his advocacy for women's church work by endorsing the biblical legitimacy of a women's diaconate in his Primary Charge of the Clergy of the diocese of Durham.[101]

Evangelist Maude Royden, notable as a preacher, suffragist and campaigner for the ordination of women, was active a generation later than Hopkins, but shares characteristics with her congress predecessor.[102] Royden's debut at the Southampton congress under the patronage of Bishop of Winchester, Alfred Lyttelton, where she addressed both a women's meeting and a meeting for men echoes Hopkins appearance at Derby and its treatment in the press as exceptional.[103] *The Manchester Courier and Lancashire General Advertiser* reported on the meeting for men, and, having noted that the audience numbered 2,000, commented: 'Curiously enough, one of the speakers was a lady, Miss Maude Royden the only representative of her sex in the hall. She occupied a seat of honour, on the right of the president, the Bishop of Winchester, "one little woman," as his lordship said, "among all us rough men".'[104] Royden, the author of the 1921 volume *Sex and Common Sense*, also shared advocacy for parity in sexual moral standards with Hopkins, and both appear to have been compelling speakers.[105]

Hopkins and Royden are distinguished examples of women moved by evangelical enthusiasm to engage with activism towards moral reform with the aim of achieving societal regeneration. They were not alone in seeking to fulfil their 'woman's mission' through work for the improvement of society. The proliferation of philanthropy, aligned with religious perspectives, frequently undertaken by women, was evident at congress, not just on the platform, but in fringe events such as the exhibition where numerous societies and topical causes were represented.

By 1913 women were a conspicuous presence at congress and women's issues including their contribution to the Church came to the fore as momentum gathered towards the articulation of aspirations for women's civil rights. At the Southampton congress, women speakers presented to a range of audiences: in the main sessions, under the theme of the Kingdom of God and the Sexes; in the separate women's sections; and, for Royden, as noted earlier, in the separate men-only meeting.[106]

Although the First World War brought a temporary halt to congress, wartime activity offered opportunities for women to pursue their aspirations

Figure 2.1 Agnes Maude Royden by Underwood and Underwood, *c.* 1928.
Source: By permission National Portrait Gallery.

to active citizenships through demonstrating competence and leadership in tasks associated with war work. As part of the war effort, the patriotic Mother's Union urged mothers to encourage their sons to enlist whilst the GFS organized fundraising. In addition, the GFS allowed its hostels and other facilities to be used to provide accommodation and rest rooms for munitions workers.[107] Lilian C. Barker was a leading figure in the manufacture of munitions. Her appointment as Lady Superintendent of Woolwich arsenal made her responsible for the supervision and welfare of 30,000 female workers. Barker, a devout

Christian, was an invited speaker at the first post-war congress of 1919 where she addressed a meeting for young women and girls.[108] Edith Picton-Turbervill, who contributed to congress at Southend in 1920 in the session on 'Christ and Womanhood', was, despite her commitment to Women International League for Peace and Freedom, during the wartime period an officer of the Young Women's Christian Association (YWCA) and led a campaign to provide better facilities, canteens, hostels and clubs, for girls working in the munitions factories.[109]

Whilst those involved in the GFS and MU and, notably central president Beatrice Hudson Lyall who was decorated for her work for war savings, were actively supporting the war effort, other congress women utilized opportunities in the period to continue to lobby towards the realization of women's spiritual aspirations. The 1916 Church of England's 'National Mission of Repentance and Hope', a campaign for spiritual revival, extended women's access to sanctified spaces in providing the catalyst for 'women messengers' being permitted to speak in church to other women and girls from either the nave or the chancel steps. Maude Royden used this campaign and the 'wartime conditions' to encourage more women into speaking roles within the Anglican Church. However, there was opposition to her initiative, and Bishop Winnington-Ingram, under pressure from those against women having an authorized place to speak in church, withdrew his permission for women to preach in the churches in his London diocese.[110] In 1917, partially in response to the controversy over women preaching stimulated by the National Mission of Hope and Repentance, Edith Picton-Turbervill, collaborated with Canon B H Streeter, on *Woman and the Church*. Picton-Turbervill refuted the appropriation of St Paul by opponents of women's spiritual authority noting that 'if St. Paul is to be quoted he can be quoted on both sides'. Although Canon Streeter rejected ordination for women in this publication, he welcomed a much larger role for women within the Church and acknowledged the possibility of women's eventual admittance to the priesthood.[111]

Following the trauma of the First World War congress reconvened in 1919. In this period women were creating spaces outside the Church within educational, professional fields, political and judicial fields.[112] Despite women's 'progress' in these fields which was exemplified by their presence at and contribution to congress, within the Church there were still barriers to women gaining further spiritually authority. Some congress women had been involved in the League for Women's Suffrage which, following the franchise being granted to women over thirty, shifted its focus towards women's greater spiritual role and became the

League of the Church Militant. The League began arguing for the establishment of equal rights and opportunities in both the Church and State. The league's newspaper *The Church Militant* reported the council meeting resolution of 1919 that sought to 'challenge what has hitherto been the custom of the Church of confining the priesthood to men'.[113] Picton-Turbervill and Royden were not the only League members who were active at events associated with congress. Louie Marston Acres, who chaired the society, contributed to fringe meetings and Louisa Knight-Bruce, GFS activist and widow of a former Bishop of Mashonaland, spoke from congress platforms on several occasions taking the subject of consider Christianity and relations between nations in 1923.[114]

The first church congress after the First World War was held in Leicester in 1919 with *The Times* noting that women were to 'take a considerable part'. Women presented in the main sessions as well as in a separate meeting for women and girls thus carrying on the momentum from 1913. The congress included a focus on women's aspirations and role within the Church, a number of women speakers contributed either a paper or to the discussion in the main session on 'The church's equipment for corporate life and witness (iv) the ministry of women' including Deaconess Siddall and Dr Leticia Fairfield.[115] The following year, Dr Fairfield, 'a well-known female physician', church feminist and congress speaker, was invited to contribute to the Lambeth Conference and to 'comment privately on the medical aspects of "women and the lay ministries"'. Dr Fairfield produced a document stating preaching was no more difficult for women than some of their existing roles such as district visiting, or Sunday school teaching. She contended that the only reason why women were prevented from doing this was to do with the belief by 'some' of a woman's 'ceremonial uncleanliness' due to menstruation.[116] Despite Dr Fairfield's efforts, the Conference drew the line at sacramental functions. The Conference's ruling came after a few women had already decided to push against these constraints and break the rules. Edith Picton-Turbervill, who went on to speak at the Southend congress in 1920, had early in 1919 become 'the first woman to preach in the Church of England at a statutory service'.[117] The *Church League for Women's Suffrage* noted that the Rev. Samuel Proudfoot, vicar of the parish of North Somercotes in Lincolnshire, who had invited Picton-Turbervill after receiving permission from his diocesan Bishop, Edward Lee Hicks, was later summoned to an 'Archidiaconal Court' by the Archdeacon and was told to apologize to the court which he refused to do.[118] In the same year, Picton-Turbervill published *Christ and Woman's Power* drawing on women asserting spiritual aptitude from hearing the voice of God. The year also saw a report from the Archbishop of Canterbury committee on

'The ministry of women; A report by a Committee Appointed by His Grace the Archbishop of Canterbury'.[119] The report discussed the amount of good work achieved by women within the church. This 'good work' was achieved, the report stated, by the MU and GFS and through the work of deaconesses, those in the sisterhood, foreign missionaries alongside wives and daughters of clergymen. The report also noted that by 1919 there were ten training homes for deaconesses. This demonstrates the continuing differing views in regard to women's role in the church with views on spiritual aspirations varying and with those women who aspired to preach continuously facing resistance from some within the church.

The following year at Southend there were nine women speakers. The *Falkirk Herald* commented on the novelty of women speakers especially on such various subjects as 'The Relation of Physical to Spiritual Development'.[120] Miss Lily Dougall presented a paper in the section on Spiritualism, the only woman presenter/discussant in the session. The session chaired by the Bishop of Barking on 'Christ and Womanhood' included papers from Gertrude Tuckwell, Mrs Cyril Bailey, Edith Picton-Turbervill with discussion contributions from Tuckwell and Picton-Turbervill as well as Louie Marston Acres and Head Deaconess Banks.[121] Members of the League of Church Militant who spoke at this congress included Maude Royden who presented a paper on 'Christ and the Evangelistic message of the church' in the main session whilst Louisa Knight Bruce spoke in the session for women. One meeting arranged by the League to coincide with congress, a debate on 'Women and the Priesthood' featuring Royden, proved so popular that crowds queued down the street and hundreds had to be turned away.[122]

The *Exeter and Plymouth Gazette*, reporting on the 1921 Birmingham congress, noted: 'There was considerable debate on women's position in the ministry of the Church and sharp division of opinion was expressed particularly in regard to different interpretations of the doctrine of difference'.[123] Arch conservative Canon Sparrow Simpson opened the section of the programme on 'Women's Position in the Ministry of the Church'. He argued that the principle of subordination existed in the Church as well as in the home. Sparrow Simpson drew on the presumed character of the Virgin Mary to assert the appropriateness of women's subordination: 'She certainly never preached; still less did she celebrate the Eucharist. She must have thought that in this restraint she was acting in accordance with the mind of her Son.'[124] Emma Paget followed Sparrow Simpson on the platform. Although Mrs Paget did not support ordination for women, she did make a strong case for women's greater spiritual authority with the Church. Her paper noted the popularity of sisterhoods and she commented that: 'of all whole-time groups [in which women worked for the church] ... [sisterhoods were] the most attractive to women, although ... least encouraged by authority'.[125]

After 1920 the number of women presenting at congress started to decline and for the following three years the more fervent advocates of women's ordination including Maude Royden and Edith Picton-Turbervill were notable absentees. *The Yorkshire Post and Leeds Intelligencer* in its coverage of the Sheffield congress reported on the unofficial meeting featuring Miss Maude Royden, speaking on 'the Churchwoman of the future'. It remarked that no official congress session was held that afternoon 'so that Maude Royden had a large audience'. The Dean of Worcester, speaking at the same event, argued that debarring women from the priesthood was 'driving large numbers of women from the Church, because they felt that the Church was against women'.[126] 1924 saw the return of Maude Royden to congress. The *Western Morning News* announced in its congress report that Maude Royden 'appears to have returned to the bosom of the church of England'. Royden, joining forces with congress stalwart Louise Creighton, spoke of the 'revision of the marriage service'.[127] The following year at Eastbourne, *The Vote* noted that although there were women speakers, they were not given prominent places in the sections: 'it can only be by design that in every case the name of the woman speaker was placed last on the programme – the alphabetical order was not followed even in the preliminary announcement – and that the woman, at four of the five sessions when there was a woman speaker, should be called upon last'.[128] The reduction in prominence of the place allocated to women on the platform at congress coincided with a greater increase in the use of alternative spaces by women, amongst them, previous congress speakers, to push for women's greater spiritual role within the church.

The League of Church Militant continued to organize meetings to run parallel to congress events in the same towns and cities with the intention of attracting congress members and attendees. The *International Woman Suffrage News* in 1926 noted that 'In October, during Church Congress week, held this year at Eastbourne in the Chichester Diocese, the League ran a successful campaign. The Pier music pavilion was crowded to hear Miss Maude Royden speak on "Christianity, Psychology, and Some Problems of To-day," one of the problems to be dealt with being the position of women in the Church'.[129] In the following years 1927 and 1928, the year women gained the franchise on the same terms as men, few women appeared on the congress platform. The year after that, logistic challenges meant that congress was not held, *The Yorkshire Post* noting that 'it is clear however that there is less enthusiasm for the Church congress than has been shown in the past'.[130] However, in 1935 Miss Evelyn Underhill, who lectured to clergy and conducted spiritual retreats, broke new ground as the first woman theologian to address congress. Whilst the topic of women's ordination attracted attention, there was little enthusiasm for the ordination of women amongst Church hierarchy and the Archbishops commission of the same year examined the case for women priests but ruled it out.[131]

Conclusion

Official roles conceded to women within the Church were slowly and modestly enlarged in the period between the inception of congress and the outbreak of war in 1914. The Southampton congress in 1913 was a turning point; however, it was not until the period following the 1914–18 war that more radical questioning of the status and sacramental authority of women in the Church was reflected at congress. Congress is a space in which this process can be seen to play out. The aspiration of women towards official roles in the Church, particularly with regard to sisterhoods and the deaconess movement, resonates with the analytical category of institution building suggested by Linda Eisenmann. Eisenmann envisages two strategies towards institution building: one being for women to seek space with existing institutions, and the other involving the instigation of separate institutions. Although Eisenmann conceived this categorization with women's activism in the field of education in mind, she also identified religion as a conduit through which women pursued self-realization, both categories come together in the women who sought officially designated roles in the Anglican Church. Deploying the thinking tools of Bourdieu that were referred to in the introductory chapter (themes which will be unpicked further in the concluding chapter) provides a further way of conceptualizing the means deployed by these women towards fuller inclusion in religious life, and the context of belief and social practice against which this occurred. Religion is, according to Bourdieu's understanding of areas of cultural engagement and competition for advantage, a field.[132] The institution of the Anglican Church is a subfield within the greater religious field. According to Bourdieu fields establish, validate and prioritize varieties of knowledge and desirable attributes. It is these assets designated by Bourdieu as capital that are recognized within the field and may be transacted to secure higher field position. Women seeking recognition, legitimization and authority within the Church had to acknowledge and negotiate within the notions of desirable capital framed by the Anglican religious field. A key point for reflection is the extent to which the dominant doxa of subordination was recognized as legitimate by women collectively or individually seeking space in the Anglican field.

Churchmen were having to come to terms with women as a presence in the Church. Women were strongly represented in congregations, and also a conspicuous presence at congress, whether on the platform in later years, or in the audience. At a time when defence of the Church was perceived as important it made sense to exploit women's appetite for social activism and utilize their contribution to the cause of sustaining Anglican religion. Clergy were uninhibited and even vociferous in asserting their views on women. Two key strands that relate to prioritized knowledge in the Anglican field and desirable capital assets underpin the discourse and run through debate on women's space and place in relation to official church roles. They concern the supposed divinely ordained 'nature' of woman and the contingent question of how much, if any, authority should be conceded to them. Both relate to the interpretation of scripture and the embedded prioritization of religiously framed notions of desirable capital in social practice. The Anglican interpretation of biblical authority saw women as secondary in creation and presented them in terms of binary opposites, the 'Eve type', a suggestive sinner, temptress and scapegoat for the fall, contrasted with the self-restrained, sexually continent, maternal helpmeet, subject under God to the patriarchal authority of the family. Claims in relation to Church roles for women whether favourable or adverse drew on the religiously endorsed notion and contingent arbitrary assumption that good women were chaste, caring and domesticated. Bishop of Southwark Edward Talbot, who may be considered a progressive voice amongst clergy, speaking from the chair at the 1910 Cambridge congress women's meeting, nevertheless endorsed his approval of women's Church work by saying: 'its activities broaden out from the home and from woman's first duty; it is still the wifeliness and the motherliness which she has to carry out into the world'.[133]

If motherhood was a sentimentalized popular trope, so too was the lady missionary, who added the capital of bravery and endurance, and a hint of excitement to the womanly attributes of piety, self-restraint and service. Her role was lauded, and as an activist in distant places and in some cases, spaces exclusively allocated to women, the lady missionary offered no challenge to authority in the Church. Moreover, accounts of the British imperial periphery and contact zones from missionaries and travellers featured at congress, conjured a narrative of difference which aligned Christianity with 'civilization' and, by drawing on the well-worn alignment of the zenana with restriction, and seclusion with imprisonment constructed for Christian women 'at home' in the imperial metropole, an identity of superiority and privilege drawn from preferences in religion, and culture, mediated by assumptions accruing around 'race', which masked the constraints of their own gendered horizons of possibility delineated according to biblical authority.

The Deaconess movement represented women with a serious commitment to a religious vocation, but also ultimately proved acceptable to the Anglican hierarchy as it was clear that the vocation of the deaconess closely aligned with traditions of philanthropy, and was largely realized through practical intervention towards promoting Christian conduct and spiritual welfare. Organized under parochial and episcopal authority deaconesses did not impinge on the sacramental role allocated to the male cleric. However, this is not to underestimate their aspirations towards spiritual authority.

Sisterhoods were most problematic because they were associated with the contest for denominational ascendancy in the wider religious field. There is some resonance between the perception of the zenana and convent as places of incarceration. Women living in segregated communities as sisters moved them away from the paternal governance of the family. Sisterhoods were tainted by association with Roman Catholic practice which gave extra familial intimate male access to women via the confessional and chimed with anxieties fed by highly coloured gothic fiction.

Women activists represented at congress in the field of mission, as moral evangelists and in official church roles were largely drawn from a middle class, that informed dispositions of group and individual habitus that prioritized Anglican religious knowledge. United in Anglican allegiance several overtly articulated their complicity with the Anglican doctrine of subordination. In several cases these women drew not only on their symbolic capital as pious Christian women but also mobilized the advantages accruing from clerical connections and the support of figures of distinction within the Church.

Prior to 1913, despite divergence in interpretations of appropriate spheres of activity, no congress contributors (perhaps unsurprisingly) challenged biblical authority, nor at this point did women's advocacy for their aims overtly confront the patriarchal authority vested in the Church hierarchy and family. This changed after 1919 when congresses provided a focus for the articulation of aspirations for a greater spiritual role for women within the Church that demanded a more radical confrontation of gendered assumption of difference.

This reflected a wider pattern highlighted by Timothy Jones who points to 'a vibrant and active campaign for the ordination of women as priests' existing with the Church from 1910 onwards. However, these attempts by women to be able to preach and perform liturgical roles which challenged the existing 'gendered ordering of the sacred space' within the Church continued to be vehemently opposed.[134]

3

The Mothers' Union and the Girls' Friendly Society

Wives and helpmeets

As Eileen Janes Yeo has noted, the religious role of the wife and mother in the Christian home became a 'hegemonic and a dominant discourse'.[1] Numerous speakers, many of them women, throughout the congress period, reiterated the primary importance of women's work in the home, despite following differing agendas. As the previous chapter has noted, the Anglican doctrine of subordination drew on biblical authority to frame and legitimize notions of women's purpose, nature and appropriate position, assumptions that were reflected in social conventions, and the status accorded to women in law. Churchmen, imbued with patriarchal notions of authority and drawing on scripture, envisaged womanhood in terms of marriage and motherhood, and found the notion of woman as helpmeet to her husband attractive.[2] The Bishop of Bedford, William Walsham How, speaking to working women at the Wolverhampton Church congress in 1887, encapsulated wifely duties in this exhortation: 'Ah dear sisters – make homes where husbands can love to come and sit.'[3] The implication being that husbands at home would not be in the public house frittering domestic resources on drink and thereby increasing the likelihood of anti-social and immoral behaviour.

Three years later, Archdeacon Emery, speaking in the context of a discussion on women's work in the Church, claimed that: 'What they wanted was the clergyman's wife to feel she was one with her husband'.[4] His aspiration not only suggested that wives should offer spiritual support to their spouses through comforting and caring, but also signalled the need for wives to offer concrete support to enable their husbands to fulfil their duties as clergymen. It was during the congress period that the Girls' Friendly Society and the Mothers' Union emerged. These two most prominent Anglican organizations for women drew strongly for organizational support and expansion on the wives and daughters of clergy. Both organizations were well represented on congress platforms.

It was through kinship or social affiliation with clergy that women became involved in the congresses, initially as members of the audience, platform companions or in the role of hostesses. It was a family affair, George Sumner and Mary shared a platform at Hull and another husband and wife team, George and Laura Ridding also shared a platform four years later at Exeter. The daughter of the long-serving congress permanent secretary Archdeacon Emery also contributed to congress in her role as advocate for the GFS.[5] With the introduction of women's meetings from 1881, 'ladies' distinguished by social position or affiliation to high-status clerics were called upon to chair meetings. Amongst several examples of this practice is Beatrice Temple who took the chair at Exeter in 1894, her husband's former diocese, where she had served as the first diocesan president of the GFS in 1880. Margaret Sheepshanks took the chair in her husband's diocese of Norwich the following year, and Fanny Legge, wife of the Bishop of Lichfield did chairing duty at Shrewsbury in 1896. Augusta Maclagan was obliged to do double duty in the chair at Derby and Wolverhampton.[6] Chairing of meetings was not the only obligation of the spouse of a bishop, like other clergy wives, they ran the household, entertained and assisted with administration.

Laura Ridding who gave five congress speeches between 1887 and 1898, took her role as a Bishop's wife seriously. Her diary records, amongst numerous other commitments in the years between 1890 and 1903, workhouse visiting as a poor law guardian, work for the Church of England Temperance Society, Education Committee meetings and a visit to Colney Hatch mental asylum. Her commitment to her husband's career was also demonstrated in the memoir she wrote following his death in 1904.[7] Louise Creighton, who took a leading role in the organization of the 1899 London Congress, relished the introduction to intellectual activity and significant affairs allowed by the role of Bishop's wife.[8] Creighton was a prolific author in her own right, and, like her friend Laura Riding, published a memorial to her husband in the *Life and Letters of Mandell Creighton*.[9] Whilst she accepted the public obligations that fell to her in the role of bishop's wife such as instigating Mothers' Union and GFS branches, and in the diocese of London, enjoyed 'garden parties at Buckingham palace' and 'brilliant' Foreign Office parties, she was grudging with regard to some other social obligations such as entertaining 'the rather tiresome Australian Bishop. The Bishop of Ballarat I think', and she refused from the outset to open Church bazaars.[10] In her memoirs she commented on the challenge of the role, noting that the wife of a public man can never really be herself as far as the outward world is concerned and may be called upon to let some of her powers lie dormant. A few pages further on she returned to the theme:

> I do not think it is easy to be a good bishop's wife. Of course her position gives her special opportunities and special duties, but she cannot fulfil them as an individual. She must always think of how what she does may affect her husband's position and reputation.[11]

Mary Sumner, too, relished the social opportunities her husband's career presented both before and after his investiture as Suffragan Bishop of Guildford, but was more consistently appreciative of the role and social opportunities it allowed, noting that Lambeth place under Archbishop and Mrs Benson was 'a clever and delightful house to be in, for they were both so clever and agreeable'.[12]

It was the convention in congress reports to give a place of affiliation after the name of speakers and many women's names are followed by 'the Vicarage' or 'the Rectory'. In 1898, at Bradford, Mrs Rogers of Littleport Vicarage, Ely, spoke on 'Holy' Sunday and the Rhyl women's meeting of 1891 was addressed by Mrs Walter Thomas of St Ann's Vicarage near Bangor, whose theme was the importance of mothers in influencing daughters. The congress report noted that she spoke in Welsh 'as requested by the congress committee'.[13] The subject of being a clerical spouse featured as an agenda item at Shrewsbury in 1896. Mrs Louisa Herbert spoke on the work of the clergyman's wife, and Louise Creighton, who would later contribute 'The work of Women in the Parish' to the 1901 publication *Laity in Council Essays in Ecclesiastical and Social Problems*, also considered the subject.[14] She recalled her speech in her memoirs but was mistaken in claiming that she took this subject at Exeter, where she had spoken on 'What women can do to raise the Moral Life of the Church'.[15]

> I said that her first duty was to her home and family, that she had no official position that gave her special opportunities. I recommend that in the parish she should make the Mothers' Union her main work, as all that she had to do in her own home and for her own family fitted in so well with what she should try to do for other homes through the Mothers' Union.[16]

Laura Ridding too aired her views on the subject in an article for *Woman and Home Magazine* in May 1901. In 'The Girl who Should Marry a Clergyman' she referred to Creighton's Shrewsbury speech and reiterated that home duties should come first. She also claimed that the clergy wife should be compassionate, have sympathy and 'a deep longing to be in touch with the restless, suffering passionate world of human nature in its struggles and aspirations'. Living as clergy wife was not a '"Business" or a "profession" but a life'.[17]

Being a clergyman, particularly in the established Anglican Church which was a bastion of state temporal power as well as a spiritual institution, was an identity as much as an occupation. Clergy were assumed to be gentlemen aligned with the interests of the ruling class. There were practical obligations and tasks attendant on living in the vicarage or the Bishop's palace that fell to female clerical kin. They ran the clergy household, entertained and assisted with administration. This involved keeping up social dignity, demonstrating (at least in public) behaviour in accordance with Christian proscription on morality and discharging obligations towards the poor and less socially advantaged. Despite the popular trope of separate spheres the family was a public institution. The constraints noted by Louise Creighton as a Bishop's wife also applied to less exalted clergy wives. Female kin in the vicarage or rectory were situated in the workplace and their conduct was under the public scrutiny of parishioners, so it was in their power to make or mar the career pursued by their husbands, fathers of brothers. The discharge of home duties such as childrearing, was, as Creighton also noted, woman's first responsibility and the activism of Mary Sumner took place after her children were grown up. The female relatives of clerics of whatever status formed a constituency who were also likely to have leading roles in philanthropic organizations.[18] In the following the alignment of women speakers with clerical kin is not intended to diminish their stature and contribution or present these women as mere adjuncts to their menfolk; however, it is relevant to illustrate the constituency of women who were in positions likely to engender participation in congress and Church outreach notably via the MU and GFS.

The requirements of upholding clerical family life were not confined to the performance of piety, modesty, chastity and charity. The obligation to maintain the style and appearance of gentility placed a strain on clergy families with slender resources. This issue, which received press coverage in national and regional newspapers, was treated in literature, engendered charitable organizations, and was tackled repeatedly on congress agendas.[19] The Oxford congress of 1862 discussed payment of clergy, and two years later at Bristol, 'Associations for aiding poor, enfeebled, and disabled clergymen, and the widows and children of the clergy' was an agenda item.[20] Further attention to clergy finance was given in 1874, 1877, 1895, 1909 and 1911. The subject was clearly close to the heart of Miss Florence Moore, a worker on behalf of the Queen Victoria Clergy Fund. She addressed the audience in the session on the supply of clergy at the 1902

Northampton congress with an appeal against 'the starvation wage' that clergy who lacked private means were forced to subsist upon. The following year she repeated this message and also asserted that women should demonstrate their views on matters of Church finance because they were well informed and should be taken seriously.[21]

The Mothers' Union

A key development for Anglican women, which grew out of the association of women with clerical kin and friends, and one that is evident at congress, was the emergence of Church-endorsed organizations, not only aimed at a membership of women, but under their direction. Whilst there had been societies that focused on special categories of problem cases such as in 'rescue work' as exemplified by Jane Ellice Hopkins' Ladies' Association for the Care of Friendless Girls, and other associations with religious affiliation such as the Young Women's Christian Association, and the Anglican Girls Diocesan Association and Women's League would emerge later, the Girls' Friendly Society and Mothers' Union are significant as the first and most prominent Church-endorsed organizations for women that, through having a mass transnational membership, could claim to articulate a collective women's perspective in the Church. The instigation of the MU, which by 1921 had grown to a worldwide membership of almost 400,000, is directly attributable to the opportunity the congress provided as a forum for the discussion of women's issues, and, more significantly, for women to speak to, and for, women. The adoption of the MU as a diocesan organization exemplifies both the typical means through which women gained access to the platform as speakers, and the discourse of self-restraint, sexual continence and domesticated womanhood that dominated sections of the conference programme dedicated to women. It also illustrates the acknowledgement that women as 'helpmeets and handmaids' (to their male relatives) drawing on traditions of social patronage and philanthropy had a pastoral role in the Church.[22] MU 'foundress' Mary Sumner's initial access to the platform was as the consort of her husband. George Sumner was well connected to the Anglican elite, his uncle John Bird Sumner was Archbishop of Canterbury from 1848 to 1862 and his father Charles preceded family friend Samuel Wilberforce as Bishop of Winchester between 1827 and 1869. At the time of the Portsmouth congress George was serving as Archdeacon under Bishop of Winchester Harold Browne and bonds of patronage were reinforced by the marriage of the Sumners' daughter Louisa to a son of the bishop.

Figure 3.1 Mary Sumner, *c.* 1910. Source: By permission Hampshire Record Office.

A position amongst the dignitaries on the platform did not signify a speaking role for either men or women, for platform seats were available by ticket and were occupied by guest spectators as well as speakers. Mary Sumner's invitation to speak to an audience of working-class women at Portsmouth came from her friend Ernest Wilberforce, then Bishop of Newcastle, and the subsequent adoption of the MU as diocesan organization was under the patronage of Bishop

Edward Harold Browne.[23] Sumner's speech was an extemporized harangue about parental responsibility, and an advocacy for temperance, rather than the visionary call to start a union of mothers recounted in her 1921 official Mothers' Union biography. However, as the catalyst for Church endorsement of the MU and its future expansion, it is understandable that the society lauded the event in its first official history.[24] Whilst Mary Sumner was not the first woman to address a congress audience, nor was she the only female speaker at Portsmouth, addresses by women, especially those who were married, were still a novelty, and Mary Sumner's debut and the consequent adoption of the MU as an official diocesan organization contributed to the normalization of women as platform speakers. MU officials were frequently, like Mary Sumner, the wives of high-status clerics, and publicized their organization regularly at congress. Sumner, who was recognized as the 'foundress' of the society and then president, after the MU was given a formal constitution and central organization after 1896, spoke at Hull in 1890, Liverpool in 1904 and Southampton in 1913.

The MU vision of woman's mission, rooted in scripture and submission to patriarchal authority, upheld the Anglican doctrine of subordination but used the contingent understanding of good womanhood to assert the importance of mothering for the benefit of community and nation. In her debut speech at Portsmouth in 1885, Mary Sumner asserted that 'It is the mothers that can work the reformation of the country'. Sumner, who remained a dominant force in the organization until her death in 1921, conflated womanhood with motherhood, and identified with the succouring domesticity drawn from Wilberforce and Ruskin which was in accord with notions of women's talents and duties as articulated at congress by Archdeacon Emery and other clerics. Whilst women lacked temporal power and positions of authority, their role was 'influence' as the Rev. C. J. Atherton summed up at the Wakefield congress of 1886, men were 'made to govern and women made to guide'.[25] A view embedded in the 'Objects' of the Mothers' Union stated that mothers should: 'seek by their own example to lead their families in purity and holiness of life'.[26] Mary Sumner was careful not to challenge the paternal authority vested in Church and family; speaking at the Hull Congress of 1890, where her husband George also contributed, she said:

> It must be self-evident that the Mothers' Union is a work of women to women, of mothers to mothers and that we could hardly summon fathers of all ranks and classes, as well as mothers to our meetings we should be considered presumptuous and impertinent if we were to do so. It would be outside our province as women.[27]

As the speech by the Dowager Countess of Chichester, Mary Sumner's successor as MU central president in 1910, noted in the previous chapter, made clear, the MU sought to align its members on the side of the 'angels in the house' and to distance themselves from the 'Eve type', that is, women with unbridled appetites or tainted by sexual incontinence.[28] To this end the MU, which until its centralization in 1896 operated on a diocesan basis, was stringent in only admitting respectable married women. The rationale of the MU was to promote 'purity', a concept that encompassed self-restraint through the exercise of temperance, and the avoidance of blasphemy, but prioritized chastity as the foremost indicator of a woman's Christian capital. According to Mary Sumner, the initiator of the original MU membership card, and whose views on marriage, childrearing and morality were publicized in numerous pamphlets and through the MU magazines: 'no person should be admitted, who is known to be living in open sin, or causing gossip'.[29] The minutes of the Winchester Diocesan MU confirmed this stance:

> In many branches an excellent rule has been made that no mother can be admitted who has only been married to her husband before a registrar[…] and it is needless to say that no unmarried mother could ever be a Member of the Society.[30]

The exhortations contained in Sumner's congress speeches towards upholding the highest moral standards were a means to validate her claims of the significant work done by mothers, in the tradition of Hannah More, as religious educators and in training 'the future fathers and mothers of England'. However, her contributions at congress do not capture the sympathetic voice and practical advice contained in her 1895 volume *Home Life*, a collection of addresses aimed at working-class mothers, originally published in the *Mothers Union Journal*, nor do they represent her belief that mothers needed pedagogic expertise: 'the training of children is a profession'.[31] Her congress speeches also do not reveal her sympathy for the feelings of children, concern for fair treatment of boys and girls and advocacy for progressive methods in education as articulated in her 1888 publication *To Mothers of the Higher Classes*.[32] However, the consistent presence of representatives of the MU at congress signalled the importance of mothers as a category and given the rapid expansion of the society from the instigation of parish branches, diocesan adoption and the establishment of branches in colonies and contact zones, the MU could claim to represent a collective voice for significant numbers of women.[33] MU Associates, those women from the middle/upper middle classes who acted as branch organizers, and rank-and-file members were likely to have been present in congress audiences. Congress women's meetings may have served as a means of attracting adherents to the organization.

Mary Sumner and the Dowager Countess of Chichester were not the only MU presidents to address congress. Mrs Noel Hubert Barclay, unusually neither the wife nor daughter of a clergyman, was MU Central President between 1920 and 1927. At Birmingham in 1921 she spoke in a discussion session for women on 'the new responsibilities in Church and State' and at the Ipswich Congress of 1927, she spoke on the less weighty subject of Holiday Resorts.[34] Mrs Nina Theodore Woods served the MU as Central President between 1933 and 1944. Prior to this she had been Diocesan President of Peterborough (1916–23) and Winchester (1924–32), dates that coincided with her husband's episcopal appointments. She made platform appearances at three congresses. In 1919, at Leicester, a location within her husband's diocese, she took the chair and gave an address at the 'Meeting for Young Women and Girls'.[35] She again addressed 'Young Women and Girls' in an unofficial meeting at the Ipswich congress of 1927.[36] In 1935, at the Bournemouth congress, her speech advocating parental responsibility and the religious role of Christian parents was coloured by the context of world events: speaking on the Christian Ideal, she warned that in Russia the influence of family was threatened by the soviet state, even in England, family influence was being eroded. She urged her audience to beware lest the state encroach on things that are God's. She went on to aver that marriage was a vocation for life and to condemn contraception as a grave evil amongst the unmarried, and threatening to the intuition of marriage. It was her view that those who refuse parenthood were not only selfish but also losers.[37]

Several congress contributors who did not speak directly on behalf of the MU at congress did have roles within it. Louise Creighton had been obliged to instigate the MU in her husband's diocese when he was Bishop of Lincoln but was not enthusiastic about it. She considered the MU work 'by no means interesting' and she 'did not like some things in it as organized by Mrs Sumner … Specially I disliked the idea of Associates' on the grounds that it reinforced class divisions.[38] Laura Ridding, an acquaintance of Mary Sumner from her days in Winchester, was given a dispensation to use the MU prayer for the Women's League that she established in her husband's Southwell diocese, and later in 1908, reported on MU branches in South Africa.[39] In 1912 she instigated the MU 'Watch Committee' that reported to the MU central committee on legislative initiatives of interest to the society.[40] Perhaps a more typical representative of MU supporters and wives of distinguished clergy at congress was Mary Sumner's friend The Hon. Augusta

Maclagan (née Barrington). Her husband William was Bishop of Lichfield from 1878 (the year of their marriage) until 1891 when he was translated to the Archbishopric of York. Lichfield was one of the first dioceses after Winchester to adopt the Mothers' Union and under Bishop Maclagan's presidency hosted two congresses.[41] It was at Derby that Augusta Maclagan made her congress debut by taking the chair at the Women's Meeting.[42] At Wolverhampton she spoke at a meeting for 'working girls and young women'. She had also been engaged in the hospitality and organization of the congress for which she was given a vote of thanks noted by the *York Herald* in its congress coverage.[43] However, her contributions to congress were not always well received. After hearing Augusta Maclagan's speech to an audience of women at the 1896 Shrewsbury congress, Laura Ridding confided to her diary that: 'Mrs Maclagan was so prosy'.[44] Reporting on the proceedings of the Newcastle Congress of 1900, the *London Daily News* was equally unimpressed, commenting that: Mrs Maclagan read 'a thoroughly safe, thoroughly conventional, and appallingly dull paper'.[45] The topic of this paper, as in the case of her 1887 offering, was advocacy for the Girls' Friendly Society an organization founded in 1875, that Mary Sumner was also involved in, and which had the distinction of being the first organization run by women to be officially sanctioned by the Church.[46]

The Girls' Friendly Society

The Girls' Friendly Society had started as a result of social contact between its founder Mrs Mary Townsend and Bishop Samuel Wilberforce. It was endorsed from its inception by the Anglican Church under the patronage of the Archbishop of Canterbury, Archibald Campbell Tait. The founding committee included Mrs Catherine Tait, Mrs Elizabeth Harold Browne, wife of the Bishop of Winchester, philanthropist Mrs Nassau Senior and the Rev T. V. Fosbery, Vicar of St Giles, Reading.[47] GFS organization mirrored the administrative structure of the Church of England with parish branches, and diocesan presidents under a Central Council headed by the president of the society. By 1913 the society had achieved is greatest size with 197,494 members and 39,926 Associates in England and Wales.[48] The GFS focused on fostering the spiritual and material well-being of unmarried girls and working women by 'the preservation of purity', and the 'promotion of friendship'.[49] To qualify for membership the 'girls' had to be unmarried and 'of good character'. The desirable attributes advocated by the society included sexual continence, modesty, temperance, obedience to authority and an ethos of service. Members of the GFS could gather together for social activities such as music making, dance and drama in safe spaces supervised by a 'lady' Associate. The GFS also promoted its values and kept members in touch through its publications, notably the magazine *Friendly Leaves*, which appeared from 1876.[50] It also provided more structured activities focused on employment training, bible study and 'good literature', a topic under the supervision of well-known novelist Charlotte Yonge, in her role as GFS literature correspondent.

The organization expanded through the exploitation of the social and clerical networks in which Mary Townsend was located, initially in the dioceses of Winchester and Worcester. As in the case of the MU, GFS leadership at diocesan and parish level was assumed by clergy wives or socially distinguished women who often were active in both organizations and high office in both the GFS and MU was something of an occupational hazard for the wife of bishop.[51] At the 1885 Portsmouth congress, at which Mary Townsend's paper was delivered on her behalf by her husband, all the other women contributors in the section 'The work of women in the Church' were GFS Associates: in addition to Mary Sumner, there was a contribution from Mrs Grant 'of the Vicarage Portsmouth' 'Head of the Portsmouth GFS' and The Hon. Ellen Joyce (widow and mother of clergymen) who advocated emigration.[52] This was not the first time the GFS had been promoted at congress. The paper by Charlotte Yonge read at Stoke on Trent had advocated the society in its inaugural year. Mrs Jerome Mercier, the editor of the GFS magazine *Friendly Leaves*, joined fellow GFS supporter Augusta Maclagan on the platform of the 1882 Newcastle congress.[53] The following year at Reading, Dr George Ridding, the Bishop of Southwell and husband of Laura Ridding, advocated the GFS as a means to combat the degradation of women.[54] Following the saturation of the women's meeting at Portsmouth the GFS continued to have a high profile and a consistent presence on congress platforms. In 1886, at Wakefield, Mrs Pigou, wife of the Rev Francis Pigou, and the diocesan president of the Bristol GFS took the platform, and the congress also featured a contribution advocating the society from philanthropist Lord Brabazon, a trustee and benefactor of the Society.[55] Amongst other prominent speakers from the GFS was Mrs Eleanor Challoner Chute, the diocesan president for Winchester 1889–1900 and central president 1901–1916, who spoke at Norwich in 1895 on the dangers of popular entertainment, and Northampton in 1902 where she pursued the themes of purity, respectability and abstinence from drinking, before an audience of young women. She also contributed to discussion on 'Women in the Church' at the Swansea Congress where she was accompanied by Mrs Leonard Burrows, her successor as Winchester diocesan president.⁵⁶ Christabel Coleridge, the friend and biographer of her literary mentor Charlotte Yonge, represented the society at the 1898 congress 'Meeting for Young Women' where, talking the topic of true honesty, she encouraged her audience to get involved with Church work.⁵⁷ Also on the platform at Bradford was Mrs Emeline Francis Steinthal, who exemplifies the multiple allegiances and activism on behalf of philanthropic organizations typical of many congress women. At this time, Emeline Francis Steinthal was Secretary to the Yorkshire Association of Ladies for the Care of Friendless Girls.⁵⁸ She went on to serve the MU as Diocesan Secretary for Ripon from 1909, and to present evidence on behalf of the MU opposing divorce to the Gorell commission, and in 1914 she served the Ripon GFS as diocesan president.⁵⁹ However, her most significant initiative was as the joint founder of the 1887 Parent's Educational Union, the genesis of her friend Charlotte Mason's Parents National Education Union.⁶⁰

The GFS like the MU upheld a religiously sanctioned domestic ideology and the notions of self-restraint and service underpinned its objects. The possession of religiously framed notions of women's capital was claimed by the society in order to assert its authority and the significance of the work of the society and its members towards the betterment of society. Moreover the GFS, again in accord with the MU, envisaged the destiny of its members in marriage and motherhood and was dedicated to aligning its members with an elevated standard of womanhood which would make them desirable wives and upright citizens. Mary Townsend, the founder of the GFS, in a paper read on her behalf by her husband, to an audience at Portsmouth congress, claimed:

> As we begin with the home, so we end with it. The daughters of the present generation are the wives and mothers of the next. If we can early teach them that a brave and noble purity is possible to every women, whatever her rank in life, if we can show them that woman's unbounded influence over men is a gift from God to be used in HIS service, it is not difficult to see that such a Society as ours may become a great power in our nation, though always a quiet and silent one as woman's power should be.⁶¹

Through the GFS, Mary Townsend sought 'To prevent, tales of shame and misery, of wasted lives spent in the service of sin or vanity instead of in the service of Christ'.⁶² Central Rule Three (1875) stated: 'No girl who has not borne a virtuous character to be admitted; such a character being lost, the Member to forfeit her Card.' This was not entirely uncontested. At the Hull congress of 1890 Mrs Papillon took the platform to advocate what she referred to as a Women's Help Society. Her suggestion was for: 'a larger society which she thought might take in the GFS' which would cater for childless wives, unmarried women and, most provocatively, those who 'were lost but were now found'.[63] There was a proliferation of philanthropic societies as Mrs Papillon had rightly pointed out. Her proposal represented a threat to the autonomy of existing societies which drew resentment from their leaders whose authority was threatened. Mary Sumner resisted suggestions that the MU should join with other societies and defence of the MU as a distinctive organization illustrates the possessive attitude of a leader towards her society.

> How does the Mothers' Union affect the success of other societies and organizations- it is at the root of every one of them – if home life is good and the mother is a Christian woman – cruelty to children will be checked, morality will be taught (girls self-respect, boys chivalry and self-control) – kindness to animals inculcated.[64]

Opponents of Mrs Papillon's views (who included Mary Sumner) articulated their objections as moral rather than political ones. Ten years before the Hull congress, the GFS's insistence on purity as a requisite for membership had been the focus for dispute. Opinion polarized: whilst some took the pragmatic view that the insistence on purity in the GFS excluded women who might otherwise be brought into the Church, others were insistent that the moral absolute of purity underpinned the society's religious identity, status and authority.[65] The society's founder Mary Townsend took this latter view, and sought and achieved, episcopal sanction for the preservation of the contentious 'Rule III' in the constitution.[66] Mrs Papillon favoured the opposing view and, as a result, instigated the Women's Help Society which did not insist on purity as a condition of membership. A decade later, feelings were still running high. Archdeacon Emery, who was chairing the session to which Mrs Papillon contributed, was alert to the potential for disagreement and attempted to ameliorate discord by acknowledging the perspectives of both 'pragmatists' and 'absolutists':

> We have heard of various agencies supplementary to the most valuable Girls' Friendly Society. Mrs Papillon has spoken to you very admirably of the larger society that she thinks might take in the Girls' Friendly Society. Well it does seem to me that all the different agencies that have been mentioned, The Mothers' Union, The Girls Friendly Society, The Women's Help Society, and others may form different regiments in the Christian church, an army of women workers which may to some extent do valuable work independently, though with a common object, and to mutual subordination and agreement. The Girls' Friendly Society has a special rule, and I do think it is a most important rule. The society is helping to raise a higher standard throughout the land.[67]

However, the Archdeacon went on to concede that there were places where no girl who got married was pure: 'That is the evil which has to be somehow met, and that is the reason why you cannot get the Girls' Friendly Society established universally.'[68]

Archdeacon Emery's efforts were not enough to mollify Miss Marianne Mason, HMs inspector of boarded out pauper children, who was so offended by Mrs Papillon's suggestion that she abandoned her prepared speech to vigorously uphold the GFS public 'witness for purity' which she saw as a means towards the reform of society.[69] As she noted the following year at Rhyl: 'Woman's duties do not end at her home … her influence reaches much further'.[70] Having shown her prepared paper to the panel Marianne Mason then proceeded to read 'from a paper that I have already published'. The fact that she revealed that this was a paper that she had bought with her suggests that having seen Mrs Papillon's name on the list of speakers, she was already aware of her views and, like the Archdeacon, braced for an argument.

Spatial reach of the MU and GFS

The GFS and the MU both identified with the trope of women's mission which encapsulated the belief that their members, through Christian witness, would act as a civilizing and improving 'influence' on those around them. Whilst prioritizing domestic roles both organizations were outward-looking and saw women's interests in the context of politics, citizenship and patriotism, they also positioned themselves as participants in a worldwide Anglican communion, and, as organizations endorsed by Royal patronage, they encouraged their members to be patriotic supporters of the British empire. Both societies had keen imperialists in leadership positions who saw empire building and Christian evangelizing as bound together, and they established a transnational presence in dominions, colonies and contact zones.[71] The transnational presence of the MU and GFS was evident in their support of missionary workers and in the establishment of branches for expatriate and later indigenous members, both societies established committees to deal with overseas interests and linked home branches with those overseas.[72] The wives, daughters and sisters of army officers, colonial administrators, missionaries and churchmen were the type of women likely to take on the role of Associates. New branches depended on the initiative of these committed individuals, and 1888 saw the instigation of

Mothers' Union branches in Canada and New Zealand.[73] In 1902, branches were instigated in several overseas locations including China, Japan and Persia. The same year a branch started in Madagascar by SPG missionary Miss Gertrude King, sister of the Anglican bishop, had the distinction of being the first branch for indigenous members.[74] It was a project close to Mary Sumner's heart, and her correspondence with Miss King and her branch members was celebrated in MU publications.[75] It was also in 1902 that the MU second 'Object' was revised to read: 'To awaken in Mothers their sense of their great responsibility as mothers in the training of their boys and girls (the future fathers and mothers of Empire) empire having replaced England'.

Mary Sumner's enthusiasm for the work of overseas missions was expressed in her travel diary, *Our Holiday in the East*, in which she commended the Egyptian School run by 'the brave indomitable' Miss Whatley whose sister's paper advocating Church work for women had been read at the 1878 Sheffield congress. For Mary Sumner, the zenana condemned women to a life that was 'vacant and debilitating [...] dreary, useless, childish [and] inane'.[76] Women were 'kept in ignorance and practical imprisonment [...] employing their time in little else than idle gossip and the jealousies and inanities of their miserable life. We never saw a book or a bit of needle work in any harem we visited'.[77] Sumner's views on women in 'the East' and her assertion that: 'No religion treats women fairly but the Christian religion'[78] were in accord with the distinction drawn between the privileged life of the Christian woman, contrasted with her oppressed sister in heathen lands by Miss Mulvaney with whom she had shared the congress platform at Hull. Celebrated traveller and missionary advocate Isabella Bird Bishop, who also used the congress platform to disseminate a similar message, had her article 'Home Life in Foreign Countries' published in the MU magazine *Mothers in Council*, and was also an invited speaker at the MU central conference of 1899.[79] Mary Sumner also demonstrated a commitment to the practical support of missionary enterprise which was advocated in MU publications and articulated in a Winchester Diocesan Committee resolution of 1898:

> That it would be well to bring before members the duty of the Mothers' Union to help in sending women medical missionaries to try to raise home life in Zenanas and Harems – It is strongly agreed that Mothers' Union members support Mission Zenana work through the SPG or Church of England Zenana Society.[80]

Mary Sumner was not the only prominent official to be an advocate of positioning the MU as a missionary organization and seeing imperialism as a moral mission.

Mrs Phillp, who served the MU as organizing secretary for the Archdeaconry of Birmingham and also as a national organizing secretary, contributed to five congresses between 1896 and 1913. She made her debut at Shrewsbury where she advocated joining the Mothers' Union. She then spoke in the main section at Bristol in 1903 on the Responsibilities of Laymen.[81] The following year, four years before Laura Ridding's visit to South Africa Mrs Phillp and a colleague Mrs Braithwaite went out to the colony to represent the MU in its efforts to towards expansion of the society and reconciliation with the Dutch Boer population in the aftermath of the South African war.[82]

The GFS, too, positioned itself as a 'missionary society' and conflated mission, patriotism and legitimate empire building. It was leader Mary Townsend's view that: 'Helping to sustain the work of church and the GFS in distant lands [was] – a wide and most legitimate field' and according to the society's historian Mary Heath Stubbs, 'from the early days individual branches undertook the support of Missions' and these efforts and the achievement of missionaries were celebrated in the pages of *Friendly Leaves* as an example for GFS members to emulate.[83] The GFS collaborated with the MU in overseas projects. Mary Sumner fostered network contacts with 'GFS ladies who are speaking for the Mothers' Union in India, so that they might join the Mothers' Union as Associates'.[84] In 1907, Central President of the GFS Eleanor Chute, Beatrice E. Temple of the SPG and Mary Sumner signed a letter to *The Times* that explained the collaboration between the societies which had established a joint committee to promote evangelical work in India. The letter sought to recruit lady volunteers who would contribute to nurturing the faith of expatriate and converted women through their example: 'The uplifting of the tone of those who are representative of the Christian religion in a heathen country must tend to the spread of the Gospel of Christ'.[85]

The 'settler' destinations of South Africa, Australia and Canada were of particular interest to the GFS which saw emigration as both patriotic and a means for its members to better themselves. One of the membership benefits that the GFS offered was an emigration 'department' under the direction of the Hon. Ellen Joyce, one of the Winchester-based founding Associates of the Society.[86] Joyce was the driving force behind the Winchester Emigration Society, to which Mary Sumner, also a local resident, subscribed.[87] The WES later evolved to became part of the British Women's Emigration Association.[88] GFS members wishing to emigrate could apply to Mrs Joyce. Successful applicants could join one of what became known as the Joyce parties and travel in a group under the supervision of a matron to their chosen destination, where they were met by GFS contacts and assured employment and accommodation. Joyce took a personal interest in the progress of the emigrants she had selected as suitable and followed up on their ongoing welfare through correspondence with government officials, employers and network of GFS contacts. The GFS *Friendly Leaves* magazine, which reported on GFS branches overseas and encouraged members to raise funds for church building in the dominions, advertised the service. In June 1907, its column for members emigrating concluded with a warning in bold type: 'Caution – Agencies are not always to be depended on: trust your own society'.[89]

Ellen Joyce, who contributed evidence to the 1912 Royal Commission on the Dominions, and received a CBE in 1920, believed emigration to be: 'missionary work done by hundreds rather than units'.[90] This missionary work was to be achieved not just by professing the faith and upholding the implicitly 'civilized' culture of 'home'. In 1920, the year she received a CBE in recognition of her services to women's emigration, she wrote:

> If England believes herself and the English speaking people to be the power entrusted with the evangelization of that vast part of the globe that is entrusted to their jurisdiction, then the duty of fully populating the fringes of the huge Oversea [sic] Empire becomes paramount. If again, it is the exponent of Purity, it must focus its efforts to distribute its daughters under protection, where they can find their mates and help make homes pure, happy and Christian.[91]

The success of the imperial project required the physical reproduction of the 'race' in sufficient numbers. Speaking to the Winchester Diocesan GFS Committee she added her support to the campaign to 'keep Australia white'. She asserted:

> the absolute necessity in the cause of religion and morality, of stimulating the Protected Migration of members, to parts of the Empire where good women are really needed to preserve in those far parts of our possessions a high standard of morals, [and] in equalising the sexes, to multiply a race practising religious habits and in one part of our vast Dominions to keep for King and Empire a "White Australia".[92]

Ellen Joyce made two platform appearances at congress. At Portsmouth in 1885 she promoted the benefits of emigration in a meeting for women. It was an opportunity for individual social betterment and a means of patriotic service. She recommended that aspiring emigrants use the agency of the recently established GFS emigration department which, in addition to supplying practical advice, fellowship and security, also gave the would-be emigrant the endorsement of the society, and assured future employers and government administrators that she should be welcomed as 'the right sort of woman'.[93] Ellen Joyce was herself an experienced traveller and the previous year had escorted a party of eighty young women to destinations in Canada. Whilst there, she attended a GFS conference in Montreal where her emigration scheme secured the endorsement of the bishop.[94] In 1891, she returned to the platform at Rhyl where she gave a talk titled 'Footsteps' which advertised the United British Emigration Society, an organization that encompassed her own original Winchester Emigration Society. Her message on emigration was the same as that given at Portsmouth, but she also chastised girls for abandoning work in domestic service: whether at home or overseas as it was good preparation for married life.[95] A fellow GFS Associate and imperial enthusiast who participated in congress was Lady Louisa Knightley who edited the British Women's Emigration Society's magazine *The Imperial Colonist* from its inception in 1902. Knightley, like Joyce, also shared political affiliation, mutual links with other organizations and ties of acquaintance. These will be explored in the following chapter that locates congress women in social, organizational and political networks. Knightley served the GFS as Diocesan President for Peterborough between 1887 and 1905, the year she was sent by the GFS to South Africa.[96]

Joyce and Knightley were not the only well-travelled representatives of the GFS at congress. Miss Kathleen M. Townend made two appearances on the platform. At Bradford in 1898, speaking to an audience of women, she took the subject of temperance, an attribute advocated with purity, dutifulness to parents, faithfulness to employers and thrift in the second 'Object of the Society'.[97] At Swansea in 1909, the year following a tour to Canada and the United States as a representative of the GFS, she gave a paper in the main meeting section on the subject of women's work for the Church.[98] Six years previously, Kathleen Townend had been sent by the GFS on a six-month tour around India to gather support for the society and increase the number of branches for expatriate, Eurasian and indigenous members.[99] On her return she reported back to a meeting of Branch Secretaries and asserted the role of the society in the imperial project.

> In that great work which England today is doing for her Indian Empire, I have proud hopes that our GFS may play its part, helping to break down racial distinctions, binding together Anglo – Indian, Eurasian and Christian native with its chord of love and sympathy and prayer.[100]

GFS members working as servants or in childcare were also to be found in continental Europe. The GFS provided an overseas employment registry and lodges were established to cater for the needs of members whilst travelling or in need of respite care in illness. Agnes Money, in the 1902 edition of her *History of the Girls' Friendly Society*, wrote: 'A GFS member may now travel from Paris to Odessa, or from Biarritz to St Petersburg, and be safe in the care of the GFS all the way'.[101] Overseas, as at home, the society was organized under Diocesan Presidents. Lady Clara Vincent had represented the GFS from 1888 as Diocesan President for Northern and Western Europe. Based in Paris she had, according to the first historian of the GFS, Agnes Money, 'addressed public meetings at the British Embassy giving information on the working and progress of the GFS all over the world'. She had also 'addressed similar meetings in Biarritz, Lille, Rouen, Calais, Boulogne, The Hague, Brussels, Bruges, Düsseldorf, Cologne, Frankfort, Lausanne, Geneva, Dieppe, Bordeaux, Arcachon, Malaunay, Chantilly, Compiegne, Lyons, St Jean de luz, and Croix'.[102] Hard-working Lady Vincent represented the society at the 1892 Folkstone congress in the section 'The Church of England on the Continent'. She commended the GFS as a 'hand maid of the Church' and went on to explain the practical assistance it gave to those who were stranded or unwell, a prophetic remark given the role the society was to play in the repatriation of overseas workers on the outbreak of hostilities in 1914 and at the onset of the Russian Revolution.[103]

A significant event for the outward-looking MU and GFS which connected home identities with contact zones and the imperial was the Pan Anglican congress of 1908 which took place that summer between the 15th and 24th of June. The brainchild of former colonial Bishop Henry Montgomery, whose wife Maud, a former president of the MU for Tasmania was to address the Cambridge Church congress of 1910,[104] the Pan Anglican congress was a gathering of senior clergy representing the Anglican communion. Many were accompanied by their wives, and meetings as with the UK-based Church congress meeting were open to laymen and women. As with the UK congress the MU and GFS used the event to demonstrate their participation in the Anglican communion. The Pan Anglican Congress itself (like the UK congress) had a women's committee and women's meetings chaired by Louise Creighton and she was joined on the Women's General Committee of the conference by Mary Sumner, Maud Montgomery and Lady Chichester, the current MU president.[105] Both societies organized mass meeting of their members to coincide with the event. In the autumn following the Pan Anglican congress the GFS staged a meeting at London's Royal Albert Hall. The MU also capitalized on the assembly of Church people from overseas in their own Albert Hall gathering. Mary Sumner told her audience that the MU: 'covered the Empire with their number of over a quarter-of-a-million members and associates and 6000 branches [...]their objects and their rules had been translated into twelve different languages'. Amongst the thousands who gave a standing ovation were the wives of overseas clergy who had been specially invited. Mrs Olowole, the wife of the indigenous Bishop of Nigeria, took the platform to express:

> ... the deep appreciation felt by her fellow country women in Western Equatorial Africa for the Mothers' Union and of the help it brought to Christian mothers of every race and colour uniting them in an unbreakable bond of fellowship and prayer.[106]

Conclusion

The Church congress played a significant part in the endorsement and exposure of the GFS and the MU, the largest and most durable organizations run by and for women to be endorsed by the Anglican Church. In the case of the MU, congress was the catalyst for its adoption as a diocesan organization. The impromptu nature of Mary Sumner's debut speech to congress speech was an incident retold and elaborated on in official MU histories as a moment of spiritual inspirational that gave impetus towards the expansion of Mothers' Union branches across the country and transnationally. For the GFS too, although it had had the endorsement of clergy at the highest level from its inception, the 1885 provided an opportunity for publicizing its aims. All the women contributors to this congress including Mary Sumner were GFS Associates.

Women in positions of authority in the GFS and The Mothers' Union, and the activists at parochial level who ran branches as Associates, formed an overlapping category. Many congress women, notably Augusta Maclagan, Louise Creighton, Mary Sumner, Laura Ridding and Ellen Joyce served both organizations. GFS and MU activists were drawn from a catchment located in kinship and social networks that intersected with a clerical milieu. This informed a shared habitus in which assumptions of what constituted 'good' womanhood (and manhood too) were framed by biblical authority. Attributes such as piety, modesty, charitableness, chastity and attention to 'home duties', which were recognized and admired in women, in Bourdieu's terminology symbolic capital, informed women's horizons of possibility, that is, behaviours, activities and access to spaces likely to be favourably reviewed.[107] The social problems associated with rapid industrial and urban expansion throughout the nineteenth century stimulated philanthropic action which was an acceptable outlet for 'caring' women of conscience and religious conviction who sought to contribute to the betterment of society.[108] Mary Sumner and Mary Townsend clearly belong to this category and demonstrated the strength of their convictions by sustained personal effort to further the expansion and success of their organizations. The significant numbers of Associates and rank-and-file members in both the MU and GFS indicate the widespread appeal of the organizations across class divisions.

The clergy home, whether Bishop's palace or vicarage, was bound up with the discharge of the pastoral and social duties accruing to the clergyman and can be considered a work place. Clergy wives (or in some cases sisters or daughters) were aligned to an occupation and their family lives required the performance of behaviours and obligations, such as philanthropic engagement, in order to uphold the authority and effectiveness of their menfolk. Failure to conform to conventions of religious and social propriety could reflect poorly on husbands and impair career prospects.

At GFS and MU leadership level women activists were connected, often by marriage, to elite churchmen, in Bourdieu's terms figures of distinction in the Anglican field recognized for their pedagogic authority as speakers on behalf of the institution of the Church.[109] Mary Sumner's father-in-law was the Bishop of Winchester and her husband George was also the nephew of the Archbishop of Canterbury. Mary Townsend, although married to a layman, was friends with Samuel Wilberforce who held episcopal office in the diocese of Oxford and Winchester. This positioning imposed duties and obligations but also gave opportunity, and by association authority. The engagement of MU and GFs women at congress provides an illustration of this interplay.

Proximity to influential clergy an allowed GFS and MU women access to the platform and the opportunity, whether at first hand or by proxy, to disseminate a message in a public space. Having achieved this initial access the MU and GFS became a regular feature of congress. Diocesan MU and GFS organization provided a resource for conference organizers to draw on when seeking speakers for women's meetings, session chairwomen. In host dioceses those involved in organization and hospitality would have come from the same constituency as MU and GFS associates.

The MU and GFS after 1885 became firmly embedded and in congress and were consistently represented. Speakers affiliated to the MU and/or GFS almost invariably articulated notions of good womanhood in accordance with the prevailing religious doxa that assumed women's primary duties were to home and family. Yet for both societies their understanding of women's mission was to provide a model of moral behaviour that would civilize not just the domestic sphere but the community. Both societies demonstrated, through their engagement with expatriate communities, missionaries and emigration the presence of speakers with overseas experience such as Lady Clara Vincent, Kathleen Townend and emigration advocate Ellen Joyce, that the sphere of women's legitimate interests extended beyond the home to nation, empire and contact zones where their example as 'good women' served to demonstrate the superiority of the Christian doxa and validate efforts towards conversion of indigenous populations.[110] Both societies were resolute in distancing their members from the corrupt and corrupting 'fallen woman'. Positioning their members as part of a moral elite and upholders of the highest standards of womanly capital framed in the religious field was a means to claim authority. The GFS and MU took the opportunity provided by congress to publicize their organizations in a space sanctified by its association with the Church and thus make a space and assert their place and perspective within it.[111] Having exploited the opportunities provided by congress to establish themselves as public bodies both organizations went on to run separate events, notable amongst them being the 'mass meetings' staged in large-scale venues such as London's Albert Hall.[112] It would be wrong to regard the GFS and MU solely as beneficiaries of congress. From an alternative perspective the consistent presence of women and at congress and the acknowledgement of their perspective can be seen to forward its popularizing and inclusive agenda and to endorse the congress with the supposed civilizing influence of women.[113]

4
Networks – Organizations, Politics, Empire and Suffrage

Introduction

Women who engaged with congress as platform speakers, and as attending 'members', were linked by their allegiance to, or recognition of, Anglicanism as the established Church. In Chapter 2 the focus was on women who sought to realize a religious vocation in official roles endorsed by the Church as deaconesses and sisters, or through missionary service. The preceding chapter identified the unsurprising preponderance of women from a clerical milieu, notably the wives of bishops, amongst women congress participants. A category that was well represented in The Girls' Friendly Society and The Mothers' Union, the two largest and most durable church organizations run by laywomen, which were a consistent presence at congress from 1885, the year that, as a result of a congress platform appearance by its founder Mary Sumner, the MU achieved diocesan adoption. The educational affiliations and experience of congress women are developed in a following chapter on 'Education and Leisure'. Likewise the emergence of professional activity relating to congress women is addressed in a dedicated chapter on 'Public service and the world of work'.

For women who identified as 'churchwomen' and sought to promote social well-being on lines in accord with their religious principles, there were many other opportunities beyond formal Church roles or the MU and GFS. The nineteenth-century decades of congress coincided with a period in which there was a proliferation of philanthropy, much of it inspired or validated by religion, in which women were active.[1] Women participants at the Church congress exemplify engagement with philanthropic activism, and they also demonstrate the tendency towards simultaneous allegiance to several organizations. Louise Creighton provides an example: in addition to her obligation as the wife of a bishop, to serve the GFS and MU, she undertook work on behalf of foreign missions through the Society for the Propagation of the Gospel (SPG) and also served on royal commissions, notably the venereal disease commission of 1913.[2] Laura Ridding, likewise active in the GFS and MU, also demonstrates the voluntary principle merging into government-sponsored initiatives and administration through her service as a poor law guardian between 1895 and 1904, and as a rural district councillor.[3]

An audit of the known affiliations of the more prominent women contributors to congress reveals engagement with over fifty organizations. Their affiliations were not confined to charitable or religious groups. Individual speakers can be linked with organizations concerned with temperance, health promotion and eugenics. Educational bodies and those concerned with government service linked women with 'professional' expertise and are explored in other chapters respectively.[4] Women congress contributors can also be located in networks of political orientation, imperial and colonial advocacy, and orientation on suffrage. They were also linked by acquaintance, and in some cases, strong ties of friendship.[5] This chapter follows these diverse threads as they come together in the forum of the Church congress.

Philanthropy: Rescue and Preventive Work, Poverty and Health

Congress brought together women whose allegiances reflect the wide spectrum of philanthropic activity typical of the period and the themes of geographical expansion, collectivization beyond the local and the formalization of organizational structures, evident in the initiatives of women activists.[6] Women congress participants link to a spectrum of diverse organizations. Those with a moral and religious emphasis, and those oriented towards the alleviation of poverty were well represented at congress. These women's activist networks drew on shared notions of desirable conduct, notably self-restraint, self-help and service, which resonated with religiously endorsed notions of good womanhood, and drew on, but did not necessarily endorse, traditions of class patronage. Chastity was a priority, and although the rescue of 'fallen women' was an element in charitable work, the notion of preventing perceived sexual degradation also received substantial attention. 'Purity' advocate Jane Ellice Hopkins used congress as a platform to raise awareness of her campaign against the sexual exploitation of girls and canvas support for proposed legislation towards raising the age of consent.[7] Purity was not just an ideal for women, nor was organizing to promote a cause. After her congress appearance at Derby in 1882, Hopkins went on to initiate the White Cross Army, a society that committed its male members to upholding chastity.[8] Hopkins's activism to oppose female prostitution was realized through the instigation of Ladies' Associations for the Care of Friendless Girls. The Birmingham branch launched in 1887, but her initiative had been adopted in other locations including Bath (1879), and King's Lynn in 1880, where she had been invited to speak by local ladies who were appalled by their visits to 'dens of iniquity' and sought to counter the 'great moral degradation' of their town.[9] The commitment to 'preventive work', that is, strategies designed to preserve the chastity of members, was also upheld in the GFS although the emphasis there was on self-help, and the working-class target membership was not specifically categorized as vulnerable. The MU also prioritized sexual continence as requisite for membership and advised mothers on the preservation of their daughters' 'innocence'.[10]

The GFS, which originated in 1875, and the Mothers' Union emerged as the dominant women's church organizations, but they were not the only religious organizations for women, and there were groups with a local focus. The MU marks its foundation from the issuing of membership cards by Mary Sumner to her mothers' meeting in 1876. However, the mothers' meeting was conventional parochial practice and the MU had, despite Church endorsement in the dioceses in which it operated, had regional variations until a centralization in 1895. Evidence of this is supplied by Mary Sumner's fellow congress contributors Augusta Maclagan and Laura Ridding. Augusta Maclagan, who served as MU central vice president in 1903 and who was a long-standing friend of Mary Sumner, had organized mothers' meetings in Lichfield *c.* 1873/4, two years before Mary Sumner's initiative. The Southwell Women's League started by Laura Ridding, who had no children, aimed to include mothers and unmarried women in one society. However, Laura Ridding did secure Mary Sumner's permission to use the MU prayer, and in later years served the central administration of the MU.

The dominance of the MU was not uncontested and a sense of competition between societies for allegiance can be discerned. At Newcastle in 1881 Mrs Papillon advocated the Church of England Young Women's Help Society when she spoke in the congress section on the 'Care for the Young'.[11] Nine years later (as the previous chapter has noted) her challenge to what she felt to be the unrealistic insistence on chastity in the GFS, and her advocacy for 'a larger society which ... might take in the GFS' drew an impassioned response from GFS supporter Marianne Mason.[12] Louise Creighton, although obliged to endorse them as officially sanctioned Anglican organizations, was also somewhat disaffected with both the GFS and the MU. However, it was their organizational hierarchy rather than the prioritization of chastity that she objected to. It was her view that the division into 'Associates', drawn from the middle and upper classes and 'members' in the GFS, and 'Subscribing members', also from the middle and upper class, and 'members' in the MU, perpetuated traditions of class patronage that were outdated. Louise Creighton also objected to the inclusion of spinsters as organizing Associates in the MU.[13] However, she did feel that young women from the middle classes should contribute to Church work. At the London congress under the presidency of her husband Mandell, the Bishop of London, the women's events were organized by her own Women's Diocesan Committee. She used the platform as an opportunity to criticize young women for their lack of interest in church work.[14] It was from her diocesan initiative to engage women that the Girls' Diocesan Association emerged. The GDA, which recruited from the middle class, aimed to stimulate and coordinate young women's participation in a variety of church projects under the direction of the bishop. Its first president was Louise Creighton's daughter Beatrice who later, having trained as a deaconess, went on to pursue her vocation in India.[15] The GDA was not directly represented on the congress platform but was advocated along with the 'Lend a Hand Club' at Bristol in 1903 by Augusta Deane who had a strong association with the large transnational Young Women's Christian Association (YWCA).[16] Blanche Pigott, president of the YWCA for 1908, also appeared at congress. Ruth Rouse, who was also to become president of the YWCA in 1938, made four congress speeches in her capacity as a worker for the 'World's Student Christian Federation' twice at Southampton in 1913 and again in 1921 and 1922.[17] Another transnational youth organization, the Girl Guides, was represented on the congress platform two year later when Head Guide Lady Maud Warrender spoke to the Oxford congress on 'The Social Life of the Village'.[18] Developments in the field of leisure were also reflected at congress. The emergence of women's sporting associations was personified by Lilian Faithfull, who, in addition to her educational achievements as Headmistress of Cheltenham Ladies' College, had been president of the All England Women's Hockey Association. Interest in the promotion of well-being was not confined to human subjects. *The Church Times* report on the Birmingham Congress of 1893 noted that: 'Ladies took a considerable share in the papers and speeches at fringe meetings for the Church of England Society for the Promotion of Kindness to Animals.' The congress exhibitions described in Chapter 1 provide further evidence of the number and diversity of interest groups that sought the support of congress attendees.[19]

In addition to societies that put morality to the fore, congress included women affiliated to organizations that sought to promote health and hygiene for the benefit of society. Advocates of temperance were well represented. These women are given fuller treatment in a following chapter that traces trajectories of voluntary to professional expertise. Here the focus is on identifying the diversity of women's associational links. As with the MU, GFS and GDA, allegiances could be multiple. Henrietta Barnett, who spoke at congress advocating old-age pensions and wrote a paper for congress on the evils of gambling, was associated with the influential Charity Organization Society as well as being an advocate for decent housing and workers' cultural education.[20] The National Health Society, a voluntary organization, which, with the benefit of the poor in mind, sought to promote public health through providing informal education in hygiene and nutrition, was represented by Alice Ravenhill who addressed congress audiences on three occasions.[21] On her first platform appearance at Bradford in 1893, she took the theme of cleanliness, but although speaking from a 'scientific' perspective she had not relinquished a moral agenda. Speaking in 1906 at Barrow-in-Furness, she emphasized self-control as essential in avoiding activities injurious to health. Uppermost in her mind was the evil of drink, a topic she had addressed the previous year at the Weymouth congress.[22] A fellow enthusiast for temperance, gynaecologist Mary Scharleib, advocated joining the Women's Union, an auxiliary to the Church of England Temperance Society, in a speech to the Exeter congress of 1894. Scharleib was also linked to the eugenic agenda publicized by congress speaker Ellen Pinsent at the Cambridge and Stoke-in-Trent congresses in 1910 and 1911, respectively.[23] Pinsent, the joint founder with Mary Dendy of the 1889 National Association for the Care and Protection of the Feeble Minded, advocated the separate institutional care of 'imbeciles' and the 'feeble minded'. This was intended to promote their humane treatment but also reflected topical eugenic anxieties that accrued around passing on characteristics perceived as undesirable that might weaken 'the race'.[24]

Congress also represented organizations that engaged with economic self-help and working conditions. Once again women congress speakers have links with more than one area of interest. Miss Elizabeth A. Tournier, the president of the 'Women's Co-operative Guild', addressed congress in 1892, and another congress speaker Kathleen Lyttleton, the initiator of a branch of the Cooperative Women's Guild, spoke at the 1899 London Congress. Lyttelton was also involved in Trade Union work as chair of the executive committee of the Manchester and Salford Trade Union Council. Mrs Hicks, secretary of the London Rope Makers Union, had shared the platform with Miss Tournier at Folkestone.[25] Employment law expert and congress stalwart Gertrude Tuckwell exemplifies engagement with various and evolving organizations dedicated to promoting welfare at work. In 1898 she became president of the Women's Trade Union League (formerly the Women's Protective and Provident League) and was also active in its offshoot the Industrial Law Committee. She was also involved in the Anti-Sweating League, a non-party pressure group that campaigned against a variety of exploitative employment practices. Tuckwell, one of the first seven women justices of the peace to be appointed, further embodies women banding together to assert their claims to citizenship and civic participation as the founder of the founder of the 1919 Magistrates Association. The link between public service and emergent professional expertise is exemplified by the presence on congress platforms of members of the 1881 Society for Promoting the Return of Women as Poor Law Guardians or Women's Guardians Society Women's Local Government Society (WLGS) notably Marianne Mason and Mary Clifford, who receive fuller attention in the chapter on congress and aspirations towards women's professional status.[26]

National Union of Women Workers

Women activists recognized the diversity and scope of their collective endeavours, and it was from an understanding that cooperation and collaboration rather than competition (as seen in the rivalry between the GFS and the Women's League) would make for greater effectiveness in promoting women's interests and their efforts towards the improvement of society, that the National Union of Women Workers emerged. There was an overlap of congress women and leadership in the NUWW, notably Louise Creighton and Laura Ridding. Moreover the timing, organization, format of NUWW conferences and its publicity and record keeping exhibit parallels with the Church congress that suggest the experience of attendance at the Church congress served as a model and perhaps catalyst for the NUWW.

Laura Ridding, who served on the union's first executive committee, was president in 1910, and sustained a lifelong involvement with it, recalled 'The Early Days of The National Union of Women Workers' in a manuscript written in 1939, at the point when the NUWW evolved into the National Council of Women of Great Britain. She explained the genesis of the society from the recognition of the need to coordinate Jane Ellice Hopkins' regional Associations

Figure 4.1 Lady Laura Elizabeth Ridding and George Ridding by Schemboche, after 1876. Source: By permission National Portrait Gallery.

for the Care of Friendless Girls which by 1889 numbered 120. She noted the role played by Hopkins's secretary Emily Janes, who went on to serve as secretary of the NUWW and editor of its publication the quarterly *Occasional Paper* until 1917.[27] Laura Ridding also noted the involvement of author and educationalist Mariah Grey.[28] This initiative led to a programme of conferences for 'women workers', both professional and amateur, in philanthropy and other fields. These were organized very much along the lines of the Church congress. They took place over a period of three or four days in cities around the country and a detailed record of proceedings was published. *The Official Report of the Central Conference of Women Workers* was as detailed as the *Official Report of the Church Congress* in verbatim recording of speeches and noting agendas and officers of the union. Like the Church congress report, it was an annual publication that signalled the professional approach of its contributors and the permanence of the institution, and it enabled the messages of speakers to reach an audience beyond conference attendees.[29] By 1891 a central conference committee had been established. The conference held that year in Liverpool was, according to Laura Ridding:

> ... attended by women workers from every part of England. Poor Law Guardians, Teachers, Deaconesses, Prison Visitors, Settlement workers, District Nurses, Workers for the Girls Friendly Society, Church Army, Salvation Army and other lines of social welfare that demanded fuller development.[30]

Louise Creighton, who spoke on behalf of the union numerous occasions, recalled the growth of the NUWW beyond the annual conference. The intention 'was to bring the women who were doing social work more together than by merely an annual conference'. She noted in her memoirs that a working party comprising 'a very fine set' of women that included Laura Ridding, poor law guardian Mary Clifford and the domestic science education pioneer Fanny Calder, 'thrashed out a constitution' for the union which was finally drawn up in 1895. Louise Creighton was chosen by her peers to be the first president of the newly constituted NUWW and assumed her duties at their Nottingham conference the following year. It was a role she was to return to over a period of several years.[31] The Union established a national headquarters at Berners Street, London, and by 1912 it had over 7,000 members. In 1918 the union changed its name to the National Council of Women of Great Britain and Ireland and ten years later it became known as the National Council of Women of Great Britain.[32]

Laura Ridding recorded the 'objects' of the NUWW which included the promotion of women's social, civil and religious welfare, the gathering and distribution of serviceable information and the federation of women's organizations. As Andrea Geddes Poole notes this 'parliament of women' 'gave women a forum wherein they could speak to each other about how to affect policy'.[33] NUWW participants exhibited a similar range of interests and appetite for reform to that evident amongst women contributors at the Church congress. They were also predominantly middle class. Topics of debate included education, temperance, emigration, employment, poverty, social reform and suffrage. There was also an overlap of expert speakers such as Dr Kate Mitchell who followed up her 1891 appearance at the Church congress with an address the following year to the NUWW conference, where she explained her medical perspective on alcoholism as a disease in her paper on 'The Inebriate Woman'.[34]

Louise Creighton was exhilarated by her experience as NUWW president. Her recollections also give a sense of NUWW procedure and the ambition of its members. She wrote:

> My connexion to the NUWW brought me many new friends, opened my eyes to many different kinds of work that were going on and in general proved a most instructive and enlightening experience. It added greatly to my opportunities for public speaking of all kinds, and I developed my capacity for business and organisation. I discovered I could be a very good chairman. I could keep order, and get things to go briskly with plenty of life and go, and could keep people contented and amused. It was a pretty exacting task to chair one of the long executive committees, with a vast number of subjects coming up and many eager, clever women all anxious to speak. To preside at a big conference was in its way even more exacting but also more exciting. I enjoyed it and enjoyed the credit I won, and the praises and complements showered upon me ... [35]

The NUWW organization was structured with a central president supported by ten vice presidents. In 1896 these included Mary Benson, GFS diocesan president and wife of the Archbishop of Canterbury, The Hon. Lavinia Talbot, also wife of a bishop and her sister, the educationalist Lady Frederick Cavendish and Mary Clifford, all of whom spoke at the Church congress. Other notable vice presidents were suffragist Millicent Garret Fawcett and Eleanor Mildred Sidgwick. Eleanor Sidgwick, although not a Church congress speaker, provides an example of the overlapping kinship, political, educational and other networks that connected women associated with congress. She was distinguished in the field of psychic research and served as Vice Principal of Newnham College. Eleanor Sidgwick was also the sister of the future prime minister Arthur Balfour, and wife of moral philosopher Henry Sidgwick.[36] She had been a member of the Cambridge Ladies' Dining Society founded by Louise Creighton and Creighton's 'closest friend', another congress speaker and NUWW president in 1900 and 1901, Kathleen Lyttelton, who was sister-in-law to Lavinia Talbot and Lucy Cavendish.[37]

There was also an executive committee of sixteen members. Here too, Church congress speakers were represented. In addition to Laura Riding, members of the inaugural committee included Deaconess Isabella Gilmore and Kathleen Lyttelton. The overlap of allegiance continued in later years. Educationalist

Lucy Soulsby was active in both congress and the NUWW as a representative of the Mothers' Union, and Henrietta Barnett, well known for her association with the Toynbee Hall university settlement and as the pioneer of Hampstead Garden Suburb, was also a presence in the NUWW. Congress chairwoman and imperialist Lady Louisa Knightley of the Girls' Friendly Society and the Conservative Primrose League took a leading role in its congresses and conferences.[38]

Political affiliation to the left was also represented on the NUWW executive. Beatrice Webb, referred to as a friend by Louise Creighton, was well known for her socialist activism and role, with her husband Sidney, in founding the London School of Economics, joined the executive with the intention of familiarizing herself with the perspectives of what she saw as the middle-class, middle-aged and conservative membership.[39] She also commented that the Anglican allegiance of several members was in contrast to her own secular perspective. Ultimately this resulted in her withdrawal from the NUWW executive in 1896.[40] Beatrice Webb was not alone in identifying the association of The NUWW and the Church. The Ladies' Page of *The Illustrated London News* of 12 October 1907 remarked that: 'October is becoming the month of conferences ... The Church Congress had its women speakers and the National Union of Women Workers, which is practically also a Congress of Church women, follows.'[41] Despite this Anglican ascendancy, and what even stalwart churchwoman Mary Clifford who served as president in 1903, acknowledged as the 'churchiness' of the NUWW conferences which started with prayers, the NUWW included Jewish and nonconformist organizations. It also upheld its inclusive principles by appointing non-Anglicans to positions of authority as the presidencies of presbyterian Mrs Albert Booth in 1897, representative of the Jewish elite Constance de Rothschild, Lady Battersea in 1902, and Quaker philanthropist Elizabeth Cadbury in 1905, demonstrate.[42]

Political Networks, Alignment and Action

The unavailability of the parliamentary franchise for women prior to the reforms of 1919 and 1924 did not mean that women were not engaged in political matters. As Simon Morgan, Katherine Gleadle and Sarah Richardson have noted, despite, or indeed because of, gendered tropes concerning the supposed interests and qualities pertaining to women, they did engage in public affairs and were also aligned with political parties.[43]

Lobbying via ostensibly non-politically aligned organizations was not the only outlet for political engagement amongst women associated with the Church congress. Chapter 6 explores voluntary philanthropic service and trajectories towards professionalism, paid employment and the appointment to government bodies. At national level this occurred prior to women achieving the parliamentary franchise. The outbreak of war in 1914 provided a catalyst for the exploitation of women's talent in public institutions and congress provides examples of women in this category. Augusta Deane, who was known for her association with the YWCA, and was awarded an O.B.E. in 1918 for her wartime work for the Ministry of Labour and service on agricultural committees, spoke to a congress audience of young women at Leicester in 1919. Also on the platform was Lilian C. Barker C.B.E., the first British female assistant prison commissioner and wartime superintendent of Woolwich arsenal, where she was in charge of 30,000 female workers.[44] Similarly, Violet Markham, who addressed the 1930 Newport congress on 'Women's Place in the World of Today',[45] was distinguished as a Companion of Honour in 1917 in recognition of her service to the women's section of the National Service Department, a government body responsible for coordinating civilian and military recruitment, a position awarded to her as a result of her contacts amongst politicians.[46]

Prior to the (staggered) achievement of the franchise, local government also offered some categories of women opportunities for electoral participation and election to office. School boards between 1870 and 1902 were an early development in giving access for women to electoral office and several congress speakers including Laura Ridding had served on them. As well as her school board position she served as a rural district councillor between 1895 and 1904. Laura Ridding was also a member of the Nottinghamshire Country Education Committee in 1902.[47] Congress platform speaker and eugenicist Ellen Pinsent was not only a pioneer towards systematic state intervention in the management of, and provision for, the mentally incapacitated, she was also the first woman to be elected to the city council of Birmingham, and chaired its special schools subcommittee.[48] Constance Cochrane, a Cambridge County Councillor and member of its education committee, contributed to three congresses. She was an acknowledged expert on the rural housing of the poor having written a paper on 'Labourers Cottages' for the National Housing Conference of 1900.[49] At Cambridge in 1910 she advocated the value of women serving on Rural District Councils, including sanitary committees in a discussion on the Poor Law.[50] At Southampton in 1913 in the section on 'The kingdom of God and the social order' she took the theme of rural betterment in an address to the main section of congress, and in 1919 she contributed to two discussions on Christian ideals of Education and citizenship in rural life.[51] Another three times contributor to women's sections at congress, Blanche Pigott was also noted in the congress record as a member of the Norfolk Rural District Council.[52] London Diocesan Mothers' Union President Beatrice Hudson Lyall was announced as a speaker on 'Parents and Children' at the 1922 congress. In its article on the forthcoming congress, the local *Sheffield Telegraph* emphasized her qualifications as a public servant: 'Mrs. Hudson Lyall should carry the courage of conviction, having regard to the fact that she is a Justice of the Peace as well a member of the London County Council, and in these capacities has had a varied experience'.[53] Beatrix Hudson Lyall's appearance at the following year's Plymouth congress also attracted attention. *The Common Cause* of Friday, 5 October 1923, in an article that began by observing: 'It was fitting that in the town which sent the first woman member to Westminster, there should have been a marked increase in the number of women speakers to the Church Congress this week', also noted that in a talk on 'The Christian Ideal in Civic Life': 'Mrs. Hudson Lyall, C.B.E., J.P., gave her hearers a good drubbing down for their apathy towards the local civic life of their districts, and urged them to come forward for service as councillors, guardians'. *The Common Cause*, which as a pro-suffrage publication had an interest in promoting women's engagement in public political life, also focused on Clara Winterbottom, another speaker who had held political office as Mayor of Cheltenham, who 'pleaded with women to take more interest in the responsibilities' that resulted from the enlargement of the franchise and the accessibility of service to the judiciary.[54] Seven years later, when the franchise was fully available to women on the same terms as men, the congress platform included Mrs Caruthers better known as Violet Markham, who despite her former prominence as an anti-suffrage leader, had stood for parliamentary election as an independent Liberal for the constituency of Mansfield in 1918 and who had also served as Mayor of Chesterfield in 1927.[55]

Fifteen women congress contributors were the wives of bishops, three were siblings to bishops and six were bishops' daughters. Having an elite churchman in the family put these women adjacent to sites of Anglican power, but also given the established status of the Church with some bishops entitled to seats in the House of Lords there was an overlap with temporal authority and social status. However, congress women's relationships, whether through kinship or acquaintance, also located them adjacent to other sites of power in politics and government. Personal lobbying and patronage by women located in networks which included male politicians was also a conduit for women to express their political aspirations. There were also political organizations, notably the Conservative Primrose league that included women and made use of them in campaigning. These categories of women were a presence amongst both the NUWW and Congress women.

Louisa Knightley 1842–1913, diarist, Church congress chair, GFS National Vice President, supporter of the Working Ladies Guild and imperialist, was also well known for her political activism.[56] A former lady-in-waiting, she was acknowledged as a force in the political career of her husband Sir Rainald (1819–95), whose re-election as Conservative MP to his South Northamptonshire constituency (a seat he had held since 1852) in the elections of 1885 and 1886 was assisted by her canvassing. Louisa Knightley also pursued her aspirations for political activism as one of the original members of the Primrose League. The league, which had been founded in 1833, and was named in honour of Benjamin Disraeli's favourite flower, was organized in local branches known as 'habitations'. The league aimed to 'uphold God, Queen and Country and the Conservative cause': it included men on the same terms as women and referred to them as associates, those more socially distinguished being known as 'knights' and 'dames', respectively. The talents and enthusiasm of women members were drawn on to widen the popularity of the party through canvassing, and the organization of social events intended to appeal to working people. Louisa Knightley, who enrolled in the organization in 1885, was responsible for initiating the branch in her area. She went on to serve on the League's Ladies' Grand Council executive committee from 1885 to 1907.[57]

Louisa Knightley was not alone in being a member of a family with politicians in it. GFS founder Mary Townsend's husband was Conservative MP for Stratford-on-Avon between 1886 and 1892. She was in sympathy with the Conservative perspective and was suspicious of 'spreading liberalism', and although the GFS avoided public commitment to an overt political stance their patriotic advocacy for 'Church, Queen and Family' oriented them towards conservatism, the political stance that they regarded as aligned to upholding religion and the maintenance of traditional social order.[58] The same was true for the Mothers' Union and Mary Sumner associated socialism with the breakdown of society and feared the 'peril of Anti-Christian Socialist Sunday schools'.[59]

Other women congress participants had links with players of even higher distinction in the political field. Laura Ridding was a member of a politically active family whose members achieved high office in government. She exemplifies the intricacy and overlap of kinship, social and political networks. Her father, Roundell Palmer the first Earl of Selborne (1812–95), served in

Gladstone's government and was Lord Chancellor 1872–4 and 1880–5.[60] A committed Churchman, he had contributed a Lecture at the 1866 York congress on 'Hymnology', which according to the *Bury and Norwich Post* was 'illustrated by a choir under the direction of E.G Monk Esq, Mus.Doc'.[61] Laura Ridding was not the only member of the family to follow her father as a congress speaker. The Nottingham congress of 1897 was under the presidency of George Ridding bishop of the host diocese of Southwell. Laura Ridding played a leading role in hospitality and the organisation and chairing of women's meetings, and it was at this congress that her younger sister, Lady Sophia Palmer (1852–1915) later following her 1903 marriage, The Comtesse de Franqueville, contributed a talk on the duties as well as rights of citizenship, in which she urged her audience of young women to follow the example of Christ, noting that: 'a good life teaches more than any sermon'.[62]

Laura's and Sophia's brother, William Palmer, known between 1882 and 1895, as Viscount Wolmer, followed the paternal example of holding political office, and the family tradition of contribution to congress as a speaker at Southampton in 1913.[63] He was the Liberal Member of Parliament for East Hants but later became a Liberal Unionist when Gladstone proposed Home Rule for Ireland. His 1885 election campaign was actively supported (at his request) by his sister Lady Sophia, according to her biography: 'He needed strenuous help in canvassing, and Sophia's zeal and eloquence were of inestimable value to him.' Like Louisa Knightley, Sophia was instrumental in helping to secure the election of her relative who scraped in with a majority of 161.[64]

In 1883 William had married Beatrix Maud Gascoyne-Cecil (d. 1940) a member of the distinguished political family. They had three sons and a daughter. Their second son, the Hon. Robert Palmer who was killed on active service 1916 whilst serving as a Captain in the Hampshire Regiment, had his biography written by his aunt Laura Ridding.[65] Maud Countess of Selborne, a suffragist like her sister-in-law Laura, was also politically engaged as a member of the Primrose League. She succeeded fellow Primrose League activist Louisa Knightley as president of the Conservative and Unionist Women's Franchise Association which had been formed in 1908 to counteract anti-suffrage alignment in the party. Maud, a Justice of the Peace for Hampshire after 1918, followed Laura Ridding's path as president of the successor to the NUWW, the National Council of Women of Great Britain and Ireland in 1920/21.[66]

Laura Ridding's network included other figures distinguished in the world of politics as well as the Church, notably members of the numerous Lyttelton family with whom Louisa Knightley also had connections.[67] Laura was close friends with Lucy Cavendish (1841-1925), the second eldest daughter of George, 4th Baron Lyttelton, the advocate of elementary schooling and the education of girls whose most notable services to government were his contributions to the Clarendon and Taunton commissions on education. Lucy married Lord Frederick Cavendish, the second son of the Duke of Devonshire, in 1864. The following year Lord Frederick embarked on a political career that ended sensationally with his assassination in Phoenix Park, Dublin, on 6 May 1882, the same day he took office as Chief Secretary for Ireland. Lucy Cavendish, a founding member of the Girls' Public Day School Company, whose services to education are recalled in the eponymous Lucy Cavendish College, supported Laura in her home diocese at the Nottingham congress where she spoke to mothers on 'how to lead children without driving them' and made four other congress appearances between 1892 and 1904.[68]

The Lyttelton connections overlapped with the Gladstone family who were also represented at congress. Catherine Glynne, 1812-1900, known as Aunt Pussy, the sister of Mary Glynne (1813-57), first wife of George 4th Barron Lyttelton and mother to twelve of his children born between 1840 and 1857, was the wife of Prime Minister William Ewart Gladstone. The connection was further reinforced by the union of George's sister Lavinia (1821-50) and the Rev Henry Glynne, Rector of Hawarden and brother to Catherine and Mary. Helen, the unmarried sixth child of Catherine and William Gladstone, was vice principal of Newnham College between 1882 and 1896, and later warden of the Women's University Settlement at Nelson Square Blackfriars Road London, contributed a speech on 'problems of poverty' to the Liverpool congress of 1904 where her cousin Lucy Cavendish, also an advocate of women's education was also on the platform.[69]

Lucy was not the only Lyttelton sister to connect with congress. Lavinia Lyttelton followed the pattern set by her eldest sister Meriel who married John Talbot (son of Caroline Talbot the philanthropist and friend of the Glynne sisters) by marrying his younger brother Edward. Here, too, was a Church congress connection: Edward Talbot was warden of Keble College Oxford and later as Bishop of Winchester presided over the notably 'feminist' Southampton Congress of 1913 which featured suffragist and advocate of women clergy Maude Royden, amongst a number of women speakers. Other members of the family also participated in this congress. Lavinia addressed the women's meeting and younger daughter Lavinia Caroline took the chair at the meeting for girls.[70]

Laura Ridding had other friends amongst the Lyttelton family. Her 'dear, dear friend', Kathleen, neé Clive (1856-1907) author, fellow suffragist and president of the NUWW in 1900, was married in 1880 to Arthur Temple Lyttleton one of the several Lyttelton brothers. Kathleen was also a friend of Louise Creighton whom she had met at Cambridge in the early years of her marriage where Arthur, who later became Suffragan Bishop of Southampton in 1898, was master of Selwyn College. It was at Louise's home congress in London where Mandell Creighton was the presiding Bishop that Kathleen (the Hon. Mrs A.T Lyttelton) took the platform to support her friend, and advocate remuneration for trained women church workers.[71] The spouse of another Lyttelton, Alfred, youngest of the eight brothers, Edith Sophie Balfour Lyttelton, the imperialist, campaigner and playwright also, also contributed to congress with a speech to the Plymouth Congress of 1923 on the theme of 'The Christian Ideal in Industry and Business'.[72]

The 'Call of Empire'

Women's interest in, and participation in, political discourse extended to the overseas empire. The geographical extent of British power invited explanation, and the exercise of power over dominions and colonies raised questions concerning national identity, legitimacy of rule, 'race' and, not least amongst 'Church people', what constituted appropriate relations with, and conduct towards, indigenous populations.[73] Overseas interests offered opportunities for political office and government positions for men, and for women, the opportunity to demonstrate capability through activism in support of a cause, as with other topical issues this was evident in the interests of congress participants and on congress agendas.

Several men amongst Laura Ridding's Selborne relatives and Lyttelton connections served in colonial administration. George, 4th Baron Lyttelton's service to government included serving as undersecretary of state for the colonies under the administration of Prime Minister Robert Peel. In 1895 Laura's brother, William Palmer, now second Earl of Selborne, was appointed Undersecretary of State for the Colonies by his father-in-law, the Prime Minster Lord Salisbury. He then was appointed to the post of first Lord of The Admiralty with a seat in cabinet and retained the post when Arthur Balfour became prime minister in 1902. He then became the second High Commissioner to South Africa and held this office between 1905 and 1910 in the aftermath of the South African Boer War of 1898–1902. It was during this period that Laura visited Maud and William whilst they were resident in South Africa and recorded her impressions in writing.[74] William's invitation to contribute to the 1913 Church congress acknowledged this expertise, and his speech explored the topical agenda theme of 'The Kingdom of God and the Races – Relations between Civilized and Backward Races'.[75]

The Boer War had raised questions not only about the future of colonial rule but the treatment of civilians. The high mortality of Boer women in concentration camps, an embarrassment to the British Government, was the catalyst for women's direct participation in government intervention. Millicent Garrett Fawcett, who visited thirty-three concentration camps, illustrates the operation of networks of women located in a political milieu, with an anecdote referring to congress contributor Edith Lyttelton. She recalled in her memoir *What I Remember* that:

> The [British] Government ardently desired to check or prevent the great mortality in the camps, and the questions arose as to how to do it. All this was very much occupying people's minds, when one day, in mid July 1901, Mrs Alfred [Edith Balfour] Lyttelton came to see me, and asked me if I should be willing to go to South Africa, starting almost immediately and accompanied by other ladies with expert knowledge of infant welfare, to make recommendations to the Government with the view of improving the conditions, especially of child life in the camps. Mrs Lyttelton's husband Alfred Lyttelton was then a member of the Government. He was admired, beloved and trusted by all parties and all sections of the country as few me have ever been, and although his wife did not say so, I felt sure she came, in a sense, as a messenger from him and the Government.[76]

The Lytteltons has been in South Africa in 1900 where they had been impressed by the views of colonial administrator Alfred Milner. This led to Edith helping to establish in 1901, with Violet Markham and Violet Cecil (at that time wife of Lord Edward Cecil, youngest son of the PM and brother of Maud alleged lover of Milner who later became her husband) the Victoria League, an organization of pro imperial women. The same year the topical interest in the Boer was evident at the Brighton congress. Violet Brooke-Hunt, a campaigner for boys' morality, who had previously contributed a paper on 'Clubs for Boys' to the NUWW conference of 1896, reported on her work amongst soldiers in South Africa, who should neither be seen as 'drunken brutes' or sentimentalized as 'Dear Tommy' but were in need of the services of good chaplains.[77]

Seven years later, in 1908 Laura Ridding undertook an extended tour of South Africa. While there, she kept a notebook which included reflections on social and educational issues and 'the native problem'.[78] In her 1909 paper, 'The Call of the Empire', she asserted an aspirational vision of empire and explained the virtues of empire and women's role in it, an ideal not matched by the realities of colonial rule in the recent South African conflict, nor in other parts of the empire.[79] For Laura Ridding, the empire should be 'a federation of free peoples under one flag or crown governed by their willing consent' and she considered that: 'the British government was the only one which stands for freedom for native races'.[80] While subscribing to Christian notions of spiritual inclusiveness, she was less certain about temporal equality. She noted the failure of the MU to engage with 'coloured' and 'native' girls, a failure she attributed to the low standard of morals amongst the indigenous people and to the reluctance of whites to mix with them.[81] Her notion of what constituted 'freedom for the native races' did not mean a rejection of notions of racial, cultural and social hierarchy. Her vision was of humane improving trusteeship and did not challenge the higher status conferred by whiteness.[82] Laura Ridding also thought that the 'Call of the Empire' was 'to fulfil our special duty as women, to be guardians of the moral standard of the Empire'.[83]

Enthusiasts for an empire that reflected and disseminated what were perceived as superior religious (Christian, Anglican) values and cultural practices saw emigration as a tool for empire building. Prominent advocates for women's emigration to colonies and dominions were Louisa Knightley and the Hon. Ellen Joyce. Joyce was active in the MU, and like Knightley, was involved with The Primrose League and GFS, a patriotic organization that saw emigration as offering opportunities for social and material betterment to working women members.[84] Moreover, the 'right sort of woman' would contribute to the civilizing mission of the imperial project. Joyce, who saw emigration as: 'the most practical bit of religious work that anyone can do', was the founder of the Winchester Women's Emigration Society and GFS 'emigration correspondent'.[85] She spoke at Portsmouth in 1885, and Rhyl in 1891, where she publicized the United British Women's Emigration Society. Ellen Joyce preceded Louisa Knightley who took over as editor the organization's magazine *The Imperial Colonist* in 1902.[86] Louisa Knightley also served as the president of the South African Colonisation Society (SACS), an offshoot of the BWEA which was instigated in anticipation of increased emigration after the Boer War in 1903.[87]

Suffrage Diverse Positions

The franchise was only fully available to all women on the same terms as men in the period coinciding with the last four congresses which were held in 1928, 1939, 1935 and 1938, respectively. Congress women held diverse perspectives on the issue of female suffrage. Positions taken on this issue transcended religious commitment, political orientation and ties of friendship and could be subject to change. However, the rationale for concluding whether or not the parliamentary franchise was appropriate or desirable was frequently rooted in similar notions of, and valuing of a 'women's perspective'.

The issue of suffrage was not directly addressed by speakers from the official platforms of congress where explicit advocacy for any party or faction would have been considered contrary to the conciliatory spirit of congress as laid out in the objects and procedural etiquette. This also proved to be an issue for the NUWW which encompassed groups holding opposed views on the issue. Despite a commitment to avoid the overtly political and divisive topics, pro and anti-suffrage views were aired notably by Mary Ward and Millicent Garrett Fawcett, key protagonists in anti- and pro-suffrage campaigning, respectively. By 1913 feelings were running high, and in 1910 Laura Ridding the current NUWW president was forced to ban the distribution of leaflets on the subject, in the interests of keeping focus on issues where consensus could be achieved.[88] Whilst little overt advocacy for female suffrage was heard from the Church congress platform in the years before the suspension of congress in 1914, it was acknowledged, albeit somewhat obliquely, as a topical issue. Speaking at the Barrow-in-Furness congress of 1906, Miss Cropper took the subject of the citizenship of women but prefaced her address with the disclaimer that; 'no one need fear that I am going to speak of our citizenship from the point of view of the parliamentary franchise'.[89]

As references in the preceding sections suggest, congress women were engaged with the issues of female suffrage and some were aligned with diverse pro-suffrage organizations. Significant amongst these for the presence of congress women was the Conservative and Unionist Women's Franchise Association which had Louisa Knightley as its first president, Maud Selborne as her successor and Kathleen Lyttelton as one of its numerous vice presidents. The Association, which was instigated to counter the alignment of the party with an anti-female suffrage position, had as its motto 'Loyalty, Insistency, Moderation', articulated its aims as 'Objects'. The first was 'to form a bond of union between conservatives and unionists who are in favour of the sex disqualification and the extension of the franchise to all duly qualified women'. However, the party political perspective was to the fore and the key words duly qualified were significant. The fifth 'Object' of the association declared the intention to: 'oppose universal suffrage in any form'. Louisa Knightley articulated the feelings behind this objective. Like many in her social milieu she was in accord with the views held by members of the governing elite who 'still believed that society was hierarchical and that hierarchy was to be defended and asserted'.[90] As member of the strata of society that she deemed qualified to hold power and obliged to exercise responsibility for the welfare of others, she resented not having the vote. This was partly because she knew that women like her, educated and active in philanthropic endeavour for the benefit of society, had, from a gendered 'woman's perspective', much to contribute to national life. The extension of the franchise to include categories of working-class men sharpened her resentment. She was infuriated that the uneducated man had a voice whereas the educated women did not, and she attributed Conservative party losses in the 1880 election to 'Dizzy's reform Bill ... putting all the power in the hands of an uneducated unreasoning mob'.[91]

However, those aligned with a conservative perspective were not the only pro-suffrage contributors to congress. Trade unionist Clementina Black, a friend of the Marx family, and a non-militant suffragist, spoke at the Folkstone congress of 1892 advocating better employment conditions for the working woman. Women who were employed in the increasingly respectable theatre were also represented on the congress platform. Lena Ashwell and Sybil Thorndike, active members of the Actresses Franchise League whose members published and produced feminist plays and entertainments designed to spread the suffrage message, both contributed to congress where their message concerned the uplifting rather than degrading cultural experience of theatre.[92]

Stances taken on suffrage were informed by religious as well as political perspectives. As Brian Heeney notes, 'There were many ardent Anglicans in suffragist ranks including well known activist Maude Royden, and Edith Picton-Turbervill'.[93] Royden and Picton-Turbervill both made congress appearances and were prominent members of the Church League for Women's Suffrage. This was an organization founded in 1909 by the Reverend Claude Hinscliff and Mrs Gertrude Hinscliff which after 1917 became the League of the Church Militant. The League, which published a monthly newsletter between 1912 and 1917, was less averse to the participation of the lower classes in the electoral process than the CWFA and aimed: 'to secure the Parliamentary vote as it is or may be granted to men non-violently'.[94] It also sought to draw out what its founder in a letter to Archbishop Davidson called 'the deep religious significance of the women's movement'.[95]

The congress tradition of the exhibition, fringe meetings and other events provided an opportunity for the promoting the cause. The *Church Times*, reporting on the Cambridge congress, noted just such a meeting of the Church

League for Women's Suffrage which featured speakers Miss F. Sterling, Maude Royden and the Rev C. Hinscliff founder of the Society, under the Chairmanship of the Rev. A S Duncan Jones MA Dean of Caius College. The *Church Times* reporter commented: 'There are some who regard this women's movement as a serious task from their Master' [Jesus Christ].[96] Two years later the Church League for Women's Suffrage which in addition to 'corporate devotions', specified 'conferences, meetings and the distribution of literature' as its methods, announced details of activities planned to coincide with the forthcoming Middlesbrough congress. The August 1912 edition of *The Church League for Women's Suffrage* announced that 'The CLWS will be much in evidence as usual' and noted an exhibition stall, committee room, 'our Big meeting' and the intention to hold a procession.[97]

The Reverends Hinscliff and Duncan Jones were not the only Anglican male supporters of suffrage. Amongst others were Laura Ridding's brother Lord Selborne who, according to Millicent Garrett Fawcett, 'introduced an extremely mild Women's suffrage bill in the Lords in May 1914. We thought we had done well when it was only defeated by 104 to 60. We had other consolations; Lord Lytton's magnificent speech, the support of the Archbishop of Canterbury and of all the Bishops present and voting'.[98] Millicent Garret Fawcett also commended Lord Selborne's son and Laura Ridding's nephew, Robert Palmer, for his work for the suffrage cause.[99]

By 1913 the suffrage issue was becoming more pressing, and this was reflected at the 1913 Southampton congress where well-known suffragist and advocate of women clergy 'Miss Maude Royden the only representative of her sex in the hall ... occupied a seat of honour, on the right of the president, the Bishop of Winchester' (Alfred Lyttelton) to address an audience of men.[100] The congress was notable for what the *Official Record of Proceedings* noted as 'a large increase in number of women speakers' and the negotiation of gender roles was in focus.[101] Prominent on the main agenda was a section dedicated to 'The Kingdom of God and the Sexes – the ideals of Manhood and Womanhood'. Two further sessions on 'The Kingdom of God and The Sexes – Marriage' completed the second day's proceedings. James Weldon, the Dean of Manchester, opened the session on the 'Ideals of Manhood and Womanhood'. His view was that Jesus provided the exemplar of Christian Chivalry so upholding Christian manhood would eliminate the need for women's suffrage.[102] The contributions of Lucy Soulsby and Ruth Rouse also touched on the issues of suffrage. Headmistress and Mothers' Union representative, Lucy Soulsby, an executive member of the 1908 Women's

National Anti-Suffrage League, revealed her anti-suffrage perspective in her address on the 'Victorian Woman' which emphasized the virtues of adherence to duty and self-restraint:

> The Woman of Yesterday was content to be a spiritual (i.e. an unseen) force, and to inspire Man to carry out reforms on his own account, knowing that only so would he enforce them. She was content to be the leaven and knew that if she tried to be the flour as well, she would spoil the baking.

She went on to warn that 'the new ideal of "Rights"' would compromise spiritual and temporal harmony.[103] Ruth Rouse, the 'Travelling Secretary of the World's Student Christian Federation', represented a later generation and took a different view. She argued that suffrage for women was 'approximate to the ideals of the kingdom of God'. Her point was supported in the discussion session by Helen Sprott, a member of Mrs Pankhurst's WSPU, who claimed women were being unfairly criticized for taking up the Suffrage cause and emphasized that God created men and women equal.[104] Views held by women of suffrage could change and once again congress provides notable examples. Violet Markham, who despite an appetite for political engagement, had been a vocal opponent of women's suffrage, having taken the platform at the Albert Hall in February 1912 to speak against female enfranchisement:

> We believe that men and women are different – not similar – beings, with talents that are complementary, not identical, and that they therefore ought to have different shares in the management of the State, that they severally compose. We do not depreciate by one jot or tittle women's work and mission. We are concerned to find proper channels of expression for that work. We seek a fruitful diversity of political function, not a stultifying uniformity.[105]

However, after the 1914–18 war her position changed and she pragmatically exploited the newly available 'proper channels of expression' and stood for election as a liberal parliamentary candidate.

Louise Creighton's friendships encompassed women with both pro- and anti-women's suffrage views. Laura Ridding and dear friend Kathleen Lyttelton were keen suffragists whereas fellow NUWW activist, and well-known novelist Mary (Mrs Humphrey) Ward, was at the fore front of anti-suffrage campaigning. Louise Creighton had met Mary Ward in Oxford where they were members of the ladies' dining society that sought to provide access to the kind intellectual stimulation that their husbands enjoyed as members of the university. In 1889 Louise Creighton was one of the signatories to the petition headed by Mary Ward, titled an 'Appeal Against Female Suffrage' that was published in The

Nineteenth Century. The essential argument of the appeal rested on the notion of women's 'difference' which, it was argued, suited them for indirect engagement in political endeavours at a community level. It asserted that women had sufficient power through exerting influence on the conduct of affairs and it also suggested that engagement in the franchise would weaken women's moral force.[106] In her *Memoir* Louise Creighton positioned herself as a joint instigator of the petition but noted that:

> Mary Ward and I did not oppose female suffrage for exactly the same reasons. She held that in certain directions, especially in matters of foreign policy, women were not capable of forming a wise judgement. My opposition was based on the belief that it was a great advantage to the country to have a large body of intelligent and influential opinion which was outside party politics ... My opinions on this question were a source of many discussions with Kathleen Lyttelton who was strong suffrage enthusiast.[107]

However, in 1908, Louise Creighton announced her change of heart in the public forum of the NUWW conference and recorded her reasoning in the memoir:

> What was most decisive in leading me to change my opinion ... was the fact that women whether in, whether in the Primrose League or the Women's Liberal Association, increasingly took part in politics in a very decidedly party manner. I felt that if they were going to mix in party strife they had better have full responsibility.[108]

She was relieved to be able to move on from this controversy and her memoir, completed in 1936, gives a sense that she is distancing herself from views that had by that time become both unpopular and overtaken by events. She wrote:

> Now I was very glad to be in agreement with Kathleen. She and I felt alike on so many points especially in religious matters. Mary Ward and I had never agreed on religious questions; she, as I discovered over the suffrage question, really loved controversy and her spirit rose at the thought of a fight whilst I always wanted peace and loved discussion tho' not argument or controversy. I do not think that our differences on the suffrage question interfered at all with our friendship which was too deeply rooted, But it was trying to be working in different directions and in time it become rather a closed subject between us.[109]

Creighton's memoir distils the fracture of opinion on the question of suffrage amongst Church women interested in the improvement of society which accrued over whether 'influence' was sufficient to exert a women's perspective on the conduct of affairs or whether constitutional rights were the way forward. By the time of the post-First World War congresses women's constitutional civil rights in secular society were largely a fait accompli, it was logical for reflective churchwomen such as Louise Creighton, Kathleen Lyttelton and others to consider the nature of woman, 'influence' and 'rights', in relation to the institution that they served and advocated, a thread that is picked up in the following chapter that considers the latter years and legacy of congress.

Conclusion

If politics is understood to include matters affecting domestic economy, health, education, morality and public order and the aspiration to affect these issues, congress must be seen as a political institution and a space in which the negotiation of power played out. The congress can be seen as dynamic space both a physical and socio-cultural that offered possibilities that were exploited towards further 'territorial' expansion on the part of women seeking meaningful and effective engagement in the conduct of public affairs. Issues that impinged on home and family and accrued to the supposed caring sensibilities of women had served as a legitimizing rationale for philanthropy and an expanding sphere of action in the 'public' world which by the time of the instigation of congress were gathering momentum, congress itself and the NUWW instigation being significant markers of this trend. Adding religion as a delineator of 'womanly qualities' and a frame for women's desirable conduct had also made reference to religion a legitimizing factor in activism.

Banding together to forward collective aims is an attribute of advocacy networks. Such networks can be formal or informal, are conduits for communication and may facilitate access to sites of power and be instrumental in effecting change.[110] The formation of interest/pressure groups on a single issue was a significant means for women to work for action and to articulate a viewpoint. The numerous and multiple organizational alliances of congress women illustrate this trend. Congress not only offered a forum through the official agenda and spaces for women's sessions, but also served as a hub via peripheral activities of the kind discussed in Chapter 1 such as the social events and exhibition, for meeting, interacting and the exchange of ideas. Congress demonstrates Doreen Massey's understanding that the social interaction of networks is instrumental in the construction of space for women both metaphorically and literally.[111] The previous chapter identified congress as instrumental in the genesis of the diocesan Mothers' Union and in the endorsement of the other large women's Church society the GFS. It noted that having secured their place within the Church as an approved organization, through their regular visibility at congress, the MU and GFS out grew the congress space and has accrued sufficient authority to stage their own separate public events in large-scale prestigious venues such as London's Royal Albert Hall. This use of the congress space as means towards the establishment of an exclusive 'space' for women is even more notable in the case of the National Union of Women Workers. Key personnel closely involved in congress in notably Laura Riding and Louise Creighton amongst distinguished others congress were instrumental in the establishment of the NUWW as a formalized body, which in its protocols and practice followed the format of the Church Congress. The NUWW is particularly significant as it was an autonomous women's forum detached from any existing patriarchal institution such as the Church or political party. It illustrates what Linda Eisenmann has identified as a separatist strategy used by women seeking to realize their aims through institution building.[112] Despite the presence within the NUWW of women who aligned themselves as Anglican Church women and a procedural model drawn from congress, it was not aligned with any one denomination, and included representatives of nonconformists and Judaism at leadership level.

Despite its commitment to focus on consensus, 'the parliament of women' did include participants who were located close to sites of power though their kinship and social relations with holders of political office, some of whom actively engaged in the contested arena of party politics. The NUWW encompassed women with differing and strongly held views on the desirability or utility of the parliamentary franchise that transcended party political lines. All participants in the NUWW and contributors to the Church congress sought change that could be categorized as political and made use of the opportunity provided by congress whether through speaking opportunities or perhaps most significantly in the opportunities for sustained social networking reinforced though repeated contact and involvement in hospitality or planning, to address their aspirations towards change and reform.

In an age of imperial expansion and missionary endeavour, the horizons of women's activism widened to occupy overseas spaces, and engage with the conduct of colonial and transnational relations. This was certainly the case amongst women engaged at the Church congress for whom patriotism had a moral dimension. There was an overlap between religious, political and imperial interests and the Church congress, where agendas reflect engagement with diverse issues relevant to the conduct of public life at national and transnational level, and affirm that the interests of 'Church people' could not be detached from the political. The durable assumptions that women were 'different', which drew on biblical interpretation and the views articulated by notable authorities Wilberforce and Ruskin, to align women with caring and religious sensibility, provided not just a rationale for action but indicated that there was a 'woman's perspective'. Whatever conclusions were drawn from this in terms of delineating roles and actions or the participation in aspects of public life such as the parliamentary franchise, 'congress women' were united in the desire to have a voice in public affairs.

5

Widening Horizons – Education and Leisure

Introduction

The Church congress occurred at a time when education was in evolution. As with employment government was moving towards increasing legislative intervention. The field of education was a site of an ongoing struggle for authority, power and control of educational provision between state, Church and rival denominations. These struggles and their outcomes were reflected on congress main agendas and those sections addressed to, and by, women. The Anglican position on education may be seen within the wider context of attempts to maintain its spiritual authority and position in the face of challenge from other Christian denominations. The establishment of the British and Foreign Schools Society, which promoted a non-denominational curriculum by the Quaker, Joseph Lancaster, in 1808, had challenged the assumption that the Anglican Church should have a monopoly of educational provision.[1] The 'National Society for Promoting the Education of the Poor in the Principles of the Church of England', guided by a committee composed of bishops and archbishops of England and Wales, was the Anglican response to the threat presented by the nonconformist British and Foreign Schools Society. Its goal was to build on existing provision to establish a school in every parish staffed by communicant Anglican teachers.[2]

Later in the century government-sponsored commissions into education signalled increasing state concern over educational provision. The Clarendon Commission focused on existing elite public schools, and the Taunton Commission, which reported in 1868, addressed the provision of secondary education other than at the elite public schools. It highlighted, in particular, the scarcity of secondary provision for girls. Working-class education was the subject of scrutiny from the Newcastle Commission of 1858–61 which concluded by recommending a universal system of elementary education.[3] The 1870 Education Act, which initiated the systematic involvement of government in the provision of mass elementary working-class education, allowed for the establishment of Board Schools, funded by local ratepayers, to be established where voluntary schools (i.e. those funded by voluntary subscription such as the Anglican National Schools) were insufficient for the local population. The concern amongst Anglicans, and other denominations who favoured specific doctrinal teaching, was that Board Schools, which despite The Cowper-Temple amendment (secured by Episcopal pressure in the House of Lords) which preserved Christian religion in the curriculum, but of a non-denominational character, would lead to secularization. With the exception of 1889, education featured on every congress agenda between 1896 and 1903. 'Elementary Education' was considered at Shrewsbury in 1896 and the following year Nottingham tackled 'Primary and Secondary Education'. 'Lines of Future Progress in Elementary and Secondary Education' was the subject at London in 1899. The concern over encroaching educational secularization, raised by the introduction of non-denominational Board Schools, continued after legislation replaced them with Local Education Authority-controlled schools in 1902. That year's Northampton congress put 'Primary and Secondary Education' and 'Provision and Training of Teachers' on the agenda.[4] Six years later the Lambeth Conference also addressed concerns over secularization. Resolution 11 stated:

> In the judgement of the Conference it is our duty as Christians to make it clear to the world that purely secular systems of education are educationally as well as morally unsound, since they fail to co-ordinate the training of the whole nature of the child, and necessarily leave many children deficient in a most important factor for that formation of character which is the principal aim of education.

Resolution 12 continued the theme and claimed that: 'no teaching can be regarded as adequate religious teaching which limits itself to historical information and moral culture'. Further resolutions advocated the strengthening of the Sunday school system, provision for denominational teaching in state schools, the religious training of teachers and the quality of Sunday school provision.[5] Congress followed up: in 1909, at Manchester an agenda section on 'Secularist Propaganda' was chaired by the Bishop of Burnley, and 'The Church and the New Universities' were also considered. 'The Religious Training of Teachers' was picked up on the agenda of 1911 Stoke-on-Trent congress.[6]

In addition to the provision of mass elementary education via Board, and then Local Education Authority Schools, the education, and higher education, of middle- and upper-class girls was expanded and developed during the congress period. Here too, the Church played a part, following the instigation of the

Girls' Public Day School Company in 1872, which was non-denominational in allegiance, the Church of England followed in 1883 with the Church School Company, with the aim of redressing the shortage of Church of England Girls' Schools of an equivalent standard and status to public schools.[7] Opportunities for higher education also opened as institutions such as the Maria Grey Training College catered for the professional accreditation of women teachers. London's pioneering Bedford College for Women founded in 1849 had a non-vocationally specific focus. Some considerable time later new university colleges such as Girton (1869) and Newnham (1871) at Cambridge, and Lady Margaret Hall (1878) and St Hugh's (1886) at Oxford gave opportunities to upper- and middle-class women with an appetite for scholarship.[8]

Women's attempts to overcome restricted access to, and opportunities for, learning, and the durability of religiously framed notions of womanhood in mediating access to education and curricula are a recurring theme in scholarly investigations into the education of women and girls in the nineteenth century.[9] These themes play out at congress which engaged with the education of women and girls well before the instigation of women's meetings and women speakers. 'The Education of Women' was an agenda item at the Brighton Congress of 1874. The Reverend O. Biggs revealed his assumptions on the intellectual and emotional capacity of women in claiming that: 'Few people would doubt the right of women to the best culture of which their nature is capable'. His view was that the purpose of education for women was to 'make the wife a fitter companion and a better mother'. He was against colleges for women, and anti-competition. He insisted that girls should be kept under home influence and above all that 'there should be no mixed education'.[10] The following speaker, the Rev J. Llewelyn Davis, took a different view and advocated a collegiate experience for women. He noted that: 'having trained school mistresses has not compromised their femininity', and concluded his address with the following challenge:

> One question in conclusion; It must have occurred to many that the education of women is a subject you have heard that at other congresses of which this congress is a fellow; ladies have taken part in the meeting with universal approval. Why should those who are invited to speak on the education of women at this meeting be men only?[11]

Women did speak on education at congress and this chapter explores the transition and negotiation of education from home-centred learning to intellectually aspirational secondary schooling, the opening of higher education and employment opportunities for women educators as reflected in the topics, categories of audience and professional platform speakers. The educational experiences of 'first generation' congress speakers Ellice Hopkins, Mary Sumner and Louise Creighton exemplify the restricted access to curricula and opportunities for formal education experienced by women in the period preceding, and coinciding with, the earlier decades of congress. The chapter then considers educational experiences of 'second generation' speakers who had experience of formal secondary schooling or university life. The perspectives of 'congress women' including 'pioneering' women education professionals in relation to the purpose and practice of higher education for women are analysed. Another topical educational initiative that drew together philanthropy, aspirations for social improvement and higher education was the settlement movement, and the chapter gives attention to the women associated with the university settlement movement represented at congress.[12]

Expansion in institutional educational provision coincided with a trend towards expansion in the mass production of popular media that reflected the increasing literacy of those lower down (but not at the very bottom of) the social scale.[13] The 1876 Plymouth congress had 'Periodical Literature and the Press' on the agenda and Godfrey Thring's paper advocating a 'Weekly Church Newspaper' suggested an addition to the already crowded field of publication on religious themes.[14]

Disapproval of the 'wrong sort' of literature, as epitomized by the sensational 'penny dreadful' aimed at working-class youths, and the risqué 'French Novel', reflected concern amongst upholders of religion, or the social status quo, that reading had the power to corrupt morals and encourage anti-social behaviour.[15] Anxieties that were reflected in congress agendas featuring contributions of popular but respectable authors such as Charlotte Yonge, whose paper on 'Aspects of Leisure', which advocated good reading, commended cheap editions of wholesome books and asserted the importance of libraries, were read at the 1888 Wakefield congress.[16]

Other leisure pursuits were given attention. Concern over popular pastimes was articulated by speakers from the early years of congress. An article featuring the Liverpool congress of 1869 in *Aris's Birmingham Gazetteer* was pleased to see, in what it referred to as 'an age of reckless freedom', the 'important' topic of 'The Recreation of the People' being given attention. The article covered, in some detail, the address given by The Rev. Erskine Clarke, of Derby, who:

> spoke of dancing, of dramatic entertainments, of music, as pursuits for which Englishmen had always betrayed a taste, and he asked whether such proclivities,

accepted as we find them, might not to be turned to good account, and so stamped with the approval rather than the stigma of a Church of the People. The question of course is one of the towns, and it was here, where incitements to vice are so intimately connected with the recreations to which Mr. Clarke alluded as innocent in themselves, that the rev. speaker found his difficulty. Dancing round the May-pole in pastoral mode and joining in a "hop" in a pestilential saloon are two very different things, and while the parson might smile benignantly upon the former, he feels forced to leave the latter to the patronage of vice alone. The apparent impossibility of excluding drink, and the license allowed by parents, were deemed by the speaker insuperable objections to the utilizing of terpsichorean proclivities in our crowded cities to the fitting recreation of the people. As to the stage, Mr. Clarke, bemoaning of course the "blood and murder" scenes of the "penny gaff," had the praiseworthy boldness to hazard a suggestion as to starting the experiment of a cheap theatre, to be conducted under healthy supervision, such as is the Regent Street Polytechnic, in our great metropolis.[17]

The *Gazetteer*'s reporter concluded by noting that: 'two courses lie before social reformers in entering upon the task of promoting the due recreation of the masses. In the first place, we must work upon the tastes they have; in the second, we must create a taste for something better.'[18]

The second section of the chapter, in addition to noting attention given to reading, also considers responses to informal education via leisure activities and the advice given on suitable pastimes in the hope of guiding popular taste towards improvement rather than corruption. Here too evidence of increasing professional opportunities and the negotiation of what might be approved as respectable can be discerned. The chapter concludes by reflecting on congress platforms as a space that responded to enlarged possibilities for the systematic education of girls, and one where assumptions concerning women's intellectual capacity, appropriate roles and pedagogic authority were negotiated.

Home Education: The Experience of Congress Pioneers

Women from middle- and upper-class backgrounds, who appeared as platform speakers in the earlier decades of the congress, could, despite the systemic inconsistencies and the limitations in curricula available to girls, position themselves as educated women, and were justified in doing so. Social purity campaigner Jane Ellice Hopkins (1836–1904), who gave a paper titled 'The Legal and Social Position of our Girls', which tackled prostitution, before (segregated) audiences of men and women at Derby in 1882, fits both these categories.[19] Hopkins, although homeschooled by her parents, was brought up in the academic milieu of Cambridge university life, thanks to the position held by her father as mathematics tutor. As 'his pupil and constant companion', it was to him that Hopkins attributed her 'scientific bent and wide knowledge so unusual especially in those days for a woman'.[20] Driven by religious faith and a reforming agenda, her activism conforms to Linda Eisenmann's categories for the analysis of women's pursuit of educational objectives via institution building. Hopkins can also be positioned (like other speakers who used the congress platform to promote their views and modify behaviour with the reform of society in mind) as a popular educator.[21]

Prior to her platform appearance at Derby, Hopkins had a record of philanthropic activism as the founder of the 1876 Ladies' Association for the Care of Friendless Girls, and author of *A Plea for the Wider Action of the Church of England in the Prevention of the Degradation of Women* an essay submitted to the Church of England Convocation of Bishops in 1879. In addition to promoting her message through numerous public-speaking engagements, Hopkins made extensive use of publication. Significant amongst her educational output of forty titles were *Man and Woman: The Christian Ideal* and *True Manliness*, both published in 1883, and the 1902 *Story of Life*, which engaged with sex education.

Hopkins was not the only congress speaker to acknowledge a debt to the educational efforts of her parents. Mothers' Union 'foundress' Mary Sumner, who incorporated Hopkins's ideas in her own writing,[22] also exemplifies the home-educated woman who was the beneficiary of a relatively broad curriculum, thanks to the involvement of both her parents. She also illustrates the emphasis on women in the home as educators of their children, and the tradition of philanthropy as an educational exercise directed towards those less socially advantaged. The retrospective 'Account of Early Life at Hope End', a manuscript written to inform a proposed memoir of her life, when the MU had been long established, refers to the active engagement of her parents in their children's education, but does not mention that they were former members of the influential Unitarian Cross Street Chapel who had converted to Anglicanism.[23] The 'Account of Early Life' underscores Mary Sumner's advocacy for mothers as educators, by emphasizing the active role her own mother assumed in the religious education of her children. The 'Account of Early Life' also celebrated the educational and cultural credentials of Mary's father Thomas Heywood, a former partner in Heywood's Bank, who, as a member of Chetham's Society, was recognized as an art collector and antiquarian. Mary was included in daily lessons in his library, which included readings from Gibbon's *Decline and Fall of the Roman Empire*, when her brother was home from Eton. Travel abroad, which included visits to Germany and France, where 'French and German were spoken all the time' by the family, also contributed to Mary's education. Literature was taught by governess Miss Parker, and conventional lady-like accomplishments tutored by 'Masters' of various kinds in London.[24] A proficient church organist and singer in public amateur performances, Mary had trained in operatic singing whilst staying in Rome, a fashionable cultural destination given distinction by its classical associations.[25] Although clearly proud of her own and her family's cultural capital, this enumeration of cultural credentials also signalled a belief in education for improvement that was accessible to all though their own efforts within the family. Mary Sumner envisaged the MU as an educational project, and congress presented a 'good opportunity' to educate audiences in its message.[26] Her written output contained specific examples advocating parents' engagement in the cultural, as well as moral and religious dimension, of their children's education that echoed the 'generous' liberal curriculum advocated by Charlotte Mason in her 1886 publication *Home Education*.[27] Speaking at the Hull congress in 1890, Mary Sumner emphasized the educational responsibilities of parents and suggested that 'habits of obedience and self-control much be formed gently and lovingly', and averred that 'upon mothers, in the main rests the responsibly of training the young children, and that this training is a profession, and must be learned like any other profession'. She went on to describe the educational drawing room meetings for 'lady mothers', and the meetings for 'poorer mothers', which featured lectures 'not on the physical moral and religious education of children but also on the sanitary, medical and industrial subjects – on cooking and thrift'.[28]

Louise Hume Creighton née Von Glenn (1850–1936), a generation younger than Hopkins and Sumner, illustrates an extension of educational space beyond the individual and domestic, although not necessarily formally in school or university. Her reminiscences of early education also illustrate continuities of educational practice; like Sumner, she notes the prominence of family prayer and exposure to languages and music in the family circle. She also describes home education conducted by her mother, governess and older sisters, with French, German and comprehension on the curriculum: 'none of us girls were sent to school. I do not think that such an idea was ever entertained'.[29] Her memoirs communicate her aspiration for a robust education, and she appears to have felt her exclusion from systematic schooling and the possibility of university acutely. According to the editor of her memoirs, James Thayne Covert, she demonstrated a 'determination to expand her cerebral ... horizons', and in her late teens, made a conscious decision to study whenever she could, even retiring to the schoolroom whilst everyone else was at dinner.[30] Creighton attempted to assuage her appetite for education by attending public talks and recorded attending a programme of lectures held at the Crystal Palace.[31] Creighton records the impression made on her by John Ruskin, the art critic and author of the influential essay *Sesame and Lilies*, which not only asserted the moral elevation and distinctive feminine attributes of women but advocated their application beyond the home sphere to redress social ills.[32] She also acknowledged the intellectual influence exerted on her by the historian J. R. Green, a family friend.[33] Creighton participated in an essay society instigated by Green who asked the preacher and essayist Augustus Stopford Brooke to 'send us subjects and to criticize our essays'; the first title was 'The Advantages of Anonymous Journalism', and when he became busy, the academic 'Mr Humphry Ward reviewed our last set of essays'.[34] The essay society provided a form of 'distance learning' accessible to, and popular amongst, self-educators. It's most distinguished advocate, novelist and congress contributor, Charlotte Yonge, as 'Mother Goose' mentored aspiring writers, 'the Goslings' who submitted essays that were circulated amongst a private audience in *The Barnacle* between 1863 and 1867. *The Monthly Packet*, the journal edited by Yonge, also ran an essay society for its readers.[35] Creighton, however, found the essay society unsatisfying as it did not involve consecutive study, but she did gain satisfaction from passing the 1869 London University Higher Examination for Women. Eight women entered, six of them, including Creighton, passed with honours. Candidates were required to pass at least six papers across a wide range of subjects: Latin, English Language, English History, Geography, Mathematics, Natural Philosophy, Greek, French, German and Italian, and either Chemistry or Botany. Some questions included in these exams were: 'Draw a plan of the city of Rome', 'Extract the square root of 1245456' and 'Give a brief account of the Second Punic War, with the dates of the principal battles'. Creighton wrote: 'This was the only examination for which I ever went in, and I have always been rather pleased that I passed the first higher examination for women that was held'.[36]

Creighton, like Hopkins, enjoyed the academic university milieu that became available to her following her marriage to Mandell (Max) Creighton in 1871. As a fellow of Merton College his married status had to be accommodated by the passing of a special statute. Mandell was among the first of Oxford tutors to admit women to his lectures.[37] It was here that she encountered Laura Ridding who was to become a friend, fellow congress speaker and ally in the National Union of Women Workers. She also enjoyed the company of former Gosling, Mary Arnold, the prominent author (under her married name) Mrs. Humphry Ward, whose achievements as a social reformer have, until recently, been overshadowed by twentieth-century perspectives on her position as an opponent of women's suffrage.[38] A third contact at Oxford was future congress speaker Lavinia Talbot (née Lyttelton), the wife of Edward Talbot, the head of Keble College. She, like Creighton, was conscious of the defects of her own education, and together with Mary Ward they were members of a committee that organized lectures for ladies given by eminent scholars, an initiative that resulted in the formation of the 1878 Association for the Higher Education of Women and later the instigation of colleges for women.[39]

Creighton was also to achieve distinction as a writer. It was during her three years at Oxford, where she had access to the Bodleian Library, that she was able to demonstrate her academic ability as a linguist by translating Ranke's *History of England*. Also, amongst her prolific output of twenty-four titles, either written or edited, was a novel *The Bloom of the Peach* published under the pseudonym Lois Hume, a monograph on missions, biography, and a *Child's History of England*. She edited nine volumes of her husband's speeches, sermons, lectures and essays and published the acclaimed two-volume *Life and Letters of Mandell Creighton* in 1904. Although Creighton, like Ridding and Mary Ward, gained intellectual stimulation from the concessionary access to university that their relationships granted, it was to be the next generation of women who gained admittance to higher education as participants rather than onlookers. Creighton's regret at not having had access to formal educational institutions may well have been shared by other women. At the 1925 Eastbourne congress, Miss Shields, speaking on the subject of education, warned against intellectual snobbishness and offered consolation to women who had not had the opportunity to achieve a university place. Whilst college life was a worthwhile opportunity:

> Culture could not be forcibly administered. Older woman sometimes allowed themselves to be discouraged by their brilliant daughters and nieces without realising that mature judgment: discrimination, and aesthetic appreciation, as well as actual assimilation of new knowledge might be theirs almost without limit of age.[40]

Creighton's girls were amongst the brilliant daughters who did obtain university places, Lucia at Newnham, whilst Lucy entered the Slade School of Art to study drawing, and her younger sister Gemma, after schooling at Surbiton High School, went to Lady Margaret Hall.[41] However, access to spaces for higher learning continued to be largely mediated by gender with men as custodians of, and gate keepers to, intellectual knowledge.

For Creighton, congress speaking was a means to assert the intellectual seriousness of women and the value of the woman's perspective towards addressing the improvement of society both socially and morally. Hopkins and Sumner cannot be considered 'professional' by virtue of the achievement of formal qualifications, nor were they remunerated for their efforts, but like Creighton, who did seek to measure her intellectual attainment against institutional benchmarks, they all demonstrate sustained commitment, the power to communicate, a systematic approach to the acquisition and dissemination of information and the aspiration to be perceived as well as informed. Each achieved distinction in the public realm as informal educators through the medium of public speaking. They also reached a wider audience through publication, whilst Hopkins's and Sumner's work was largely focused on promoting their religious aims, Creighton's work as a historian, translator and, in later life, editor of her husband's *Life and Letters* is located in an intellectual, academic tradition. They were recognized for having, particularly in the case of Creighton, who was to serve on the government-sponsored Venereal Disease Commission, expertise in their fields. With authority vested in social capital, religious affiliation, cultural capital demonstrated by experience and creative output rather than endorsement from an educational institution, they represent the first wave of home and 'self-educated' activists at congress, who, by virtue of exclusion from formal/patriarchal educational structures, negotiated marginal spaces and made use of their relationships with men of distinction and pedagogic authority in order to achieve education. They also signal women's engagement with congress as a forum which reflected the aspiration for, justification of and, over time, change towards the realization of formal institutional schooling and higher education, and the emergence of women as educational professionals. For women such as Hopkins, Sumner and Creighton, the congress platform was simultaneously a way to assert women's inclusion in the institution of the Church and the field of education whilst simultaneously claiming a distinctive place of their own within them.[42]

Schooling, Higher Education and Distinguished Professionals

The negotiation of the obstacles and possibilities presented by a tradition of emphasis on women's education in relation to domesticity and mothering is addressed by Mary Hilton and Pam Hirsch, and by Jane Martin and Joyce Goodman in their attention to the achievements of women educators.[43] Sarah Delamont and Deborah Gorham both observe that despite the expansion of more intellectually challenging schooling for girls that developed from the 1860s, advocates of girls' education continued to promote it as preparation for women's mission as good wives and mothers.[44] These themes are evident at congress, where advocacy for the education of women was persistently articulated according to a tradition that acknowledged women as 'different', domesticated, caring and morally 'sensible' – notions in accord with Ruskin's ideal of femininity as articulated in *Sesame and Lilies*, and which harked back to the Wilberforcian assertion of the religious sensibility of women, and contingent constructions of good womanhood framed by the interpretation of biblical authority.[45] Congress speakers, whilst advocating education for women and girls, appeared to acknowledge the concerns that education might compromise femininity. Whilst education for service and citizenship was emphasized, intellectual aspiration was downplayed, nor was the Anglican doctrine of subordination and the notion of woman as domestic helpmeet overtly confronted.

Religion was also bound up with advocacy for working-class educational inclusion, and was regarded by congress speakers as an essential dimension of the curriculum. The perception of education on religious lines as a civilizing strategy is evident in the initiatives of religiously motivated philanthropists who sought to mediate behaviour and remedy social ills through the application of moral medicine. It underpinned the activism of congress contributors, notable amongst them Mary Townsend of the Girls' Friendly Society and Mary Sumner of the Mothers' Union. For Sumner, it was God-fearing mothers who could 'work the reformation of the country' by rearing their children in principles of temperance, thrift and sexual continence.[46] At Hull in 1890 she claimed that: 'Education the forming of habits of mind and conduct, which is the work of the home, is confused with instruction, of storing the mind with facts – head teaching with heart teaching. It is a cruel wrong to equip a child with intellectual culture, and leave him ignorant of the means of self-conquest.'[47]

The establishment of non-denominational schools, administered by locally elected boards, following the 1870 'Forster' Act, stimulated fears amongst 'Church people' that the education of the populace would become secularized.[48] Mary Sumner articulated this concern and considered that: 'Every effort is apparently being made to advance this [Board School] system and starve out the voluntary and denominational schools'. For her, secularization was associated with socialism, divorce and the breakdown of the family, it thus compromised the stability of society. She urged mothers to recognize and resist the 'dangerous wave of infidelity lying behind the whole question of secular education'.[49] Resistance to secularization in education was a recurring theme from MU speakers at congress. At Rhyl in 1891, Mrs Herbert deplored the absence of religious education in Welsh elementary schools and exhorted her audience to redress this deficit by home teaching: 'dear mothers take up the glorious duty, and make it your own'.[50] At Cardiff in 1889, Mrs Henry Kingsley followed a similar theme in expressing concern over the inadequacy of religious education for children in workhouses.[51] In 1904, at Liverpool, Mary Sumner reiterated the key Mothers' Union message when she emphasized the need for parents to take responsibility for teaching religion to their children.[52]

The anxieties expressed by congress speakers were articulated in the resolutions passed by the Lambeth Conference of 1908 which also endorsed the need for revitalized Sunday schools.[53] A topic addressed at congress by several speakers. At Liverpool in 1904, headmistress Lucy Soulsby, speaking to an audience of girls, exhorted them to volunteer as Sunday school workers.[54] The Stoke-on-Trent congress of 1911 had a section of the programme devoted to 'The opportunity of Sunday schools for systematic teaching'. The paper delivered by Miss Hetty Lee received a glowing report in the *Church Times* which acknowledged her expertise as an educator. It recorded that: 'It was by far the best paper, to the point, simple in delivery, clearly expressed, weighty by reason of the readers experience and graced by Miss Lee's delightful gifts of elocution and manner'.[55] Miss Lee, the author of *Talks to the Training Class: A Manual for Heads of Sunday Kindergartens and Primary Departments* and 'organizer in Sunday School work for the National Society', spoke again at Middlesbrough the following year in a section of the programme dedicated to 'The Education of the People'.[56] The systematic approach to Sunday schooling was still on the agenda in 1927. At the Ipswich congress 'The Sunday School' was tackled by Miss Phyllis Dent. The congress official programme described her as: 'One of the pioneers of "Modern Methods" in Sunday School work, which she introduced in a speech at the Pan-Anglican Conference, 1908.' Miss Dent had formerly been 'Organising Secretary of the Church of England Sunday School Institute'. She was now 'Organizer of

Sunday Religious Education for the Diocese of London' and 'Lecturer for St Christopher's College and Sunday School Institute Extension Work'.[57]

Congresses responded to the expansion in the provision of schooling for middle- and upper-class girls by having specific meetings for school girls, and 'women and girl students', 'young women' also became a recognized target audience for meetings. Speakers were drawn from the emerging categories of elite school mistresses and key figures in higher education. By the turn of the century increasing numbers of speakers had experienced university education or training in institutions such as the Bishop Otter teacher training college.[58] Other advocates of education for women and girls were also represented. Lucy, Lady Frederick Cavendish, who spoke on educational themes at five congresses between 1897 and 1904, exemplifies this latter category. Speaking to an audience of 'young women' at Bradford in 1898 she took the subject of 'true honesty'; two years later at Newcastle, her talk on the subject of 'entertaining' was again addressed to young women.[59] Cavendish and her father George William, fourth baron Lyttelton, a loyal Churchman and advocate of educational reform, were members of the Women's Education Union. Inaugurated in 1871, the society was also known as The National Union for Improving the Education of Women of all Classes. They were also founding members of the highly influential Girls' Public Day School Company (later Trust), a response to the findings of the Taunton Commission. Lyttelton had been responsible for drafting the chapter which had identified a lack of secondary provision for girls. Although religious in ethos, Girls' Public Day Schools were not exclusively Anglican.[60] A situation that stimulated the inauguration of the 1883 Anglican Girls' School Company.

At Exeter in 1894, the Girls' Public Day School Company was represented in the person of Lucy Soulsby (1856–1927) but her subject was education for the populace, and she spoke in favour of '*Night Schools for Working Women*' to a mixed audience in the programme section on 'Secondary Education and Public Schools'.[61] Soulsby had secured her reputation as the headmistress of Oxford High School. She was also the published author of advisory pamphlets on moral conduct and an 'Associate' of the Mothers' Union.[62] Her *Two Aspects of Education* (1899) *Self Control* and *Fortitude, Humility and Large Heartedness*, advocated notions of good womanly conduct in accord with those asserted in the writings of Mary Sumner and Charlotte Yonge, and the publications of the MU and GFS. In 1898 at Bradford, Soulsby, by then the head of the Manor House School Brondesbury, advised girls over sixteen who were engaging in educational philanthropic work to avoid overfamiliarity with those of lower social status: 'the young lady too often spoils the pupil teacher or the GFS member by ignoring class distinctions'.[63] She was joined on the platform by Constance Maynard, a representative of the generation who had been the beneficiaries of access to formal institutional education. The joint founder in 1882, and Head of Westfield College, a University of London residential college for women, Maynard was an alumna of the pioneering girls' school Cheltenham Ladies' College and the equally innovative Girton College, Cambridge. The audience was also addressed 'On the Use of Imagination in Religion and Life' by Elizabeth Wordsworth, Head of Lady Margaret Hall, who had made her congress debut at Exeter in 1894.[64]

In 1904 at Liverpool, Soulsby and Wordsworth, who spoke on eliminating bad habits through self-discipline and self-control, once again took the platform at a 'Meeting for Girls at Secondary School'.[65] The Manchester Congress of 1908 also featured the distinguished head of Manchester High School, Miss Sara Burstall, who took the chair at a meeting for girls and spoke on 'influences for good'.[66] A former scholar of Miss Frances Buss' North London Collegiate School, Burstall was at this point the published author of *High Schools for Girls* and a lecture titled the *Hallowing of Humanity* in the series *What Is Christianity*.[67] At the same congress, 'girls and women students' were again addressed by Elizabeth Wordsworth, who spoke on 'charitable work', and Constance Maynard who enumerated character, industry and honesty amongst the 'British values' addressed by her paper.[68]

Cheltenham Ladies' College was again represented at Great Yarmouth in 1907. Miss Lilian M. Faithfull (1865–1952) took the platform in a general section of the programme to speak on religious education and its importance.[69] She had recently been appointed, following the death of Dorothea Beale, to the 'high and holy office' of headmistress of an institution which, in addition to having 600 girl pupils, also provided training for teachers.[70] Faithfull, who had the unusual distinction of having her early education in her uncle's boys' prep school, had taught for a year at Oxford High School c. 1888–9 under the headship of Lucy Soulsby. Prior to her appointment as head of the Ladies' College, Faithfull had been the vice principal of the ladies' department of King's College London, where she introduced hockey, a sport in which she herself had excelled.[71] At the 1921 Birmingham congress, the laughter she elicited from her audience of girls as she claimed there was 'no romance in dusting' in her talk on seizing life's opportunities, was noted in both the *Gloucestershire Daily Echo* and *Western Daily Press*.[72] Miss Faithfull's ability to use humour to draw in her audience was once again evident in her talk on childhood discipline to a congress audience in 1925. The *Church Times* noted that she 'roused delighted laughter' when she invoked A.A. Milne's precocious character James Morrison Willoughby George Dupree to illustrate children ignoring parental authority.[73] The Ladies' College was once again represented when Faithfull's successor Miss Beatrice M. Sparks MA took the chair at the 1928 Cheltenham Congress in a 'Special meeting for Young Women and Girls'.[74]

Figure 5.1 Lilian Mary Faithfull by Eliot and Fry. Source: By permission National Portrait Gallery.

As schools were becoming accepted as a practical solution to educating girls of the middle- and upper class for the accomplishment of feminine duties, ultimately marriage and homemaking or, for the spinster, the need to make her own living, congress platforms were populated by speakers drawn from a network of elite headmistresses who were linked by institutional and personal allegiance. The younger generation of headmistresses, exemplified by Lilian Faithfull and Sarah Burstall, illustrate the participation of university women from the field of education at congress. However, claiming access to higher education could be problematic. The pervasive influence of a gendered domestic ideology that informed notions of appropriate curricula for school girls also had to be negotiated in the context of higher education.[75] Seeking university access not only trespassed on the intellectual territory of men, but also on the seclusion of male space, and furthermore, removed the girl from the paternal supervision of the home. There was an ambivalence amongst Anglican clergy towards women's aspirations for education which was shared amongst laymen and some women. Whilst it was seen as desirable for women to be educated to support the role of helpmeet so esteemed by some congress speakers, too much intellectual knowledge was thought to compromise femininity and challenge the paternal authority vested in Church and family.[76] The key issues accrued around the purpose of education for women which related to notions of women's spiritual, moral and intellectual nature and contingent assumptions of appropriate roles in society.[77]

The most eminent figure from the field of education to speak at congress was Elizabeth Wordsworth. Distinguished for her religious and social capital as the daughter of Christopher Wordsworth, headmaster of Harrow School (1836–44), and Bishop of Lincoln from 1869 until his death in 1885, she also possessed formidable intellectual capital as the author of devotional works and co-author, in 1888, of a biography of her father.[78] A lifelong friend of novelist Charlotte Yonge, she also published novels under the pseudonym Grant Lloyd. Recognition of her distinction in the educational field, and safe religious credentials, was marked by her appointment in 1879, as the first principal of Lady Margaret Hall, the Anglican Oxford College inaugurated by a committee under the leadership of Edward Talbot.[79] Talbot summed up the value of her capital assets towards overcoming potential resistance to collegiate life for women. He wrote:

> The appointment was extraordinarily fortunate, it brought us not only the lady's own distinction of intellect and character, but the cachet and warrant of a name second to none in the confidence of English Church people. None could

have been a greater protection against any charge of rashness in our attempt. Within the Hall she was quietly supreme; and outside her social and intellectual distinction won a place for the Hall in Oxford Society which might have been long coming to it.[80]

At Exeter in 1894, Miss Wordsworth gave a paper on 'First Principles in Women's Education' in which she referred to current developments in educational provision and engaged with the underlying question concerning its purpose:

> We are at a new and noticeable era in the history women, and nothing but a grasp of first principles, nothing but judging things on their own merits, and not by conventional standards, will save us from blunders on the side of over restriction on the one hand or excessive and mischievous concession on the other.[81]

Miss Wordsworth appeared to be very much her father's daughter in following his assertion, made a decade earlier, in a sermon on 'Christian Womanhood', that: 'woman was subsequent to Man and derived from him'.[82] However, she concluded that:

> with Genesis in our hands we are prepared to look upon woman not only as a mother or a wife, taking these hallowed words for once in their very simplest and most restricted sense but as a being every faculty of whose body, soul and spirit is directly derived from Almighty God and directly intended to be a helpmate for man.[83]

She added the qualification that this subordinate service was, 'Not merely one woman for one man, surely but all women for all men in just relation and degree' a quiet assertion of women's contribution as citizens and justification of the role and where necessary, financial and emotional autonomy of unmarried women.[84] For Wordsworth 'a well crammed woman who is not a lady by no means fulfils the requisite conditions' of what she considered to be a worthwhile education.[85] She went on to articulate notions of womanliness and how these could be nurtured in higher education, underpinning the regime she recommended was 'the absolute necessity of a religious element – if possible a chapel, certainly of daily prayers and if possible some religious training, in all places where women are educated'.[86] Her speech avoided discussion of an academic curriculum, a notable lack of reference to intellectual knowledge from a woman of formidable learning, who taught herself ancient Greek and Hebrew in order to study biblical texts. Furthermore, Wordsworth warned against intellectual over strain, 'a perpetual race for marks', and she presented college as an extension of the home. 'My own ideal is a college consisting of moderately sized groups of students, each of them small enough to have somewhat of a homelike character'.[87]

Whilst advocacy of university for girls was prevalent at congress, the issue of womanliness and its enhancement or compromise in higher education resulted in different interpretations of how the provision and practice of higher education should be realized. Key areas of difference in interpretation were over curricula and examinations, and concerned the question of whether women should participate in the existing system of university education as experienced by men or have separate provision. These views crystalized into 'separatist' and 'uncompromising' positions. The uncompromising stance, which held that women should participate in the existing university curriculum and scheme of examinations undertaken by men, despite its acknowledged archaic limitations, was exemplified by Emily Davis at Girton College, Cambridge. Her rationale was that differentiation of the curriculum for women would be seen as less intellectually rigorous and thus complicit with those who maintained that women were of inferior intellectual capacity to men. Newnham, the other pioneer Cambridge college for women lead from 1871 by Ann Jemima Clough, a candidate like Elizabeth Wordsworth, chosen for her moral stature as well as teaching credentials, represented the separatist perspective. Clough, who avoided controversy and confrontation, although an advocate of women taking examinations, was obliged to accommodate the views of her patron Professor Henry Sidgwick. A former Cambridge don, Sidgwick was convinced that the curriculum followed in men's colleges, with its emphasis on Latin and Greek, was outdated and saw the instigation of a new college for women as a way to exert influence towards reform of male institutions where tradition was firmly entrenched. It was his initiative to petition the University Syndicate to institute special examinations for women c. 1869.[88] At Oxford the separatist stance was represented by Lady Margaret Hall and the uncompromising position by the non-denominational Somerville College.

At congress, both separatist and uncompromising institutions were represented. Alumnae of Lady Margaret Hall included Maude Royden, the prominent evangelist and advocate for women's ordination, and Miss M. Orlidge Davies, who pursued a career in higher education as an Assistant Lecturer in the Training Department, University of Birmingham, 1913–15 and was the author of children's titles *The Story of England, Saints and Heroes* and *Joan of Arc*.[89] Prominent among advocates of university education at congress in addition to Elizabeth Wordsworth were Louise Creighton (1920) and Lucy Cavendish, both were to serve on the council of Lady Margaret Hall. Creighton and Cavendish, who had been nominated as a suitable principal of Girton in the 1880s, both accepted the primary alignment of women's roles as wives and mothers and, like Wordsworth, acknowledged a doctrine of gendered difference legitimized by biblical authority, and as Cavendish expressed it, saw higher education for women as a means for cultivating 'special strengths for their own special duties'.[90] Most firmly 'separatist' of all educationalists represented at congress was Lucy Soulsby, who also served on the council of Lady Margaret Hall. Soulsby was convinced that education for girls and young women required a different curriculum and atmosphere than that provided for men. Few girls from her own school at Brondesbury went on to university, and in 1895 she opposed girls' access to the Oxford degree, the only Girls' Public Day School Company headmistress to do so.[91]

Congress was not entirely dominated by associates of Lady Margaret Hall. Graduates and academics from other colleges for women were represented on the platform. Lilian Faithfull, who made four appearances at congress between 1907 and 1930, lectured at Royal Holloway College and was an alumna of Somerville College, Oxford. She started her studies in 1883, four years after it opened, but despite achieving first-class honours in English was, by virtue of her sex, not allowed to graduate. She was amongst the 700 so-called 'steamboat ladies' who travelled across the Irish Sea to claim the ad eundem degree offered by Trinity College Dublin to Oxbridge graduands.[92] Girton College Cambridge, another uncompromising institution, was represented by Constance Maynard, one of its first intake of students. Sara Burstall, also a 'steamboat lady', and one of the founding members of the 1907 British Federation of University Women, had achieved the London University general examination for women in 1878, and then won a scholarship to Girton where she was one of six students. Miss Ruth Rouse, a former missionary and evangelizing 'Travelling Secretary of the World's Student Christian Federation', was another Girton alumna. In 1913 she gave a paper in the main congress section in the programme section dedicated to 'The Kingdom of God and the Sexes – the Ideals of Manhood and Womanhood' and again took the platform in 1920 and 1921, when she addressed audiences of girls and young women.[93] By 1924, at the Oxford congress, the student voice was directly represented in a session on 'What Youth asks of the Church'. Undergraduate speakers were a novelty that drew attention from the press. *The Sheffield Telegraph* recorded that 'Two strikingly arresting addresses were given … Both in their different ways expressed the misgivings and, aspirations of youth and both were conspicuous for courageous thought and outspoken expression'.

Miss Highley of Somerville College suggested that to attract young women the Church needed to offer them meaningful occupation beyond needle work and district visiting. Mr Godfrey Nicholson, of Christ Church, Oxford, who was not circumspect in expressing his opinions, having averred that 'the Church had no attraction for youth as they were supremely self-satisfied' still asked 'to be saved from women in the pulpit'.[94]

University Settlements

The emphasis on education as a preparation for service was sustained and exemplified in the women's university settlement movement, which, like other educational initiatives of the period, was represented at congress. The movement drew together traditions of philanthropic initiatives to alleviate poverty, and the evocation of mission as venture into the moral darkness evoked by inner-city slum locations. The settlement movement also drew on Ruskin's influential advocacy for popular access to liberal education, the idealist philosophy of T. H. Green, and the Christian Socialist tradition of F. D. Maurice and Charles Kingsley, which envisaged Christian social action as an educational enterprise, towards not only the alleviation of distress, but social change.[95] Toynbee Hall, notable as the first settlement, a residential colony of university men, established in 1884 at Whitechapel in east London by congress speakers Samuel Barnett and his wife Henrietta, emphasized cultural enrichment rather than charity, through a programme of education that included art and music in a collegiate atmosphere offered by educated residents to the local population. The nearby Oxford House Settlement, established by Edward Talbot, similarly brought university men into the slums on an improving cultural mission, but was distinct from Toynbee Hall in having a more specifically Anglican identity.[96] Four years after the establishment of Toynbee Hall, Henrietta Barnett was instrumental in the genesis of the Women's University Settlement. In 1887 she, with Miss Alice Gruner, had addressed a meeting of the Ladies' Dining Society, a Cambridge discussion group established by congress contributors Louise Creighton and social activist Kathleen (Mrs Arthur) Lyttelton whose husbands at that time were Dixie Professor Ecclesiastical History and Master of Selwyn College, respectively. A site on the south bank of the River Thames was acquired to house the settlement which came to be known as the Blackfriars Settlement on account of this location. The committee consisting of two representatives from Girton, two from Newnham, two representatives from Lady Margaret Hall and Somerville plus representatives from London University colleges, was convened and Miss Gruner appointed first warden. Accommodation was provided for permanent resident fee-paying 'workers' and part-time residents, with extramural volunteers being also recruited and financial support elicited from sympathetic subscribers.[97] The aim was to 'promote the welfare of the people of the poorer districts of London and especially of the younger women and children, by devising and promoting schemes which tend to elevate them physically, intellectually, or morally, and by giving them additional opportunities for education and recreation'.[98]

The settlement movement was strongly represented on congress platforms by speakers of distinction, and the settlement ideal was also supported by congress women who did not speak on the subject. Notable amongst them were Lavinia Talbot, who, with her husband Edward, had been instrumental in instigating the Anglican Oxford House settlement, and Louise Creighton, who, as president of the National Union of Women Workers, saw the establishment of 'religious' settlements in Liverpool and Birmingham in 1896 and 1897, respectively.[99] Creighton also instigated the Bishop Creighton House settlement in 1908 as a memorial to her recently deceased husband Mandell the Bishop of London, also a supporter of the settlement ideal.[100] It is unsurprising that the London Congress of 1899 under his presidency, and the organizing participation of Louise on the ladies' committee, featured a special section devoted to 'Women's Settlements'. Miss Beatrice Harrington, warden of St. Margaret's House, Bethnal Green, a sister organization to the men's Oxford House Settlement, claimed her organization to be the first women's Church settlement. Miss Edith Argles, an alumna of Lady Margaret Hall, and vice principal to Elizabeth Wordsworth, who succeeded Miss Gruner as its Warden, spoke on the social and educational initiatives of the Women's University Settlement.[101] Despite the commitment to intellectual elevation, and their ideological roots in the ideas of Ruskin and Maurice, the women's settlements emphasized practical philanthropy as exemplified by Octavia Hill and the Charity Organisation Society (COS), and were more engaged with the promotion of physical well-being than the men's settlements. However, for some settlement residents who sought to take up social work professionally, the settlement served as a training institution.[102] Speakers associated with the settlement movement also appeared in sections of congress programmes dedicated to poverty and social issues. Helen Gladstone, formerly a student of Newham and secretary to the principal, addressed congress in her role of warden of the Women University Settlement, a position she occupied from 1901 to 1906. She took the platform at Liverpool in 1904 in the section on 'Problems of Poverty' where she was joined by Miss Brankler also of the women's university settlement at Blackfriars.[103] London was not the only region to have settlements, the programme for the 1913 congress noted in its biography of Maude Royden her work at the NUWW's Victoria Women's Settlement Liverpool, and three years taking classes for factory girls organized by the Worker's Educational Association (WEA).[104] Most distinguished of all amongst congress speakers associated with the settlement movement was Mrs Henrietta Barnett, who, in addition to her association with Toynbee Hall and the Whitechapel Gallery, was also distinguished for her association with Octavia Hill and initiatives for housing reform, which she realized as the instigator of the Hampstead Garden Suburb.[105] She spoke at three congresses in sections of the programme dedicated to social issues. At Great Yarmouth in 1907, in the section on 'The Church and Poor Relief', she advocated compassion for the poor, training for work, and celebrated the fact that thanks to the assistance of state pensions, the aged poor could remain in their own homes. She again took the platform at Cambridge in 1910 where she spoke on the Poor Law, and at Leicester in 1919, her talk was in the section dedicated to 'Christian ideals of citizenship and service in cooperation with public authorities'.

Popular Education and Leisure Pursuits

Concern over leisure activities reflected women's increasing access into public space, good girls had long been advised to avoid the public house and the repeated attention to given to temperance would have left congress audiences in no doubt as to the perils of drink. Gambling was disapproved of on similar grounds as it led to loss of self-control, undermined thrift and led to poverty; moreover, the gamblers' hope of 'something for nothing' went against a moral code that prioritized reward for effort whether practical of spiritual. A paper from Henrietta Barnett, read by the Dean of Ely at the 1906 Congress in Barrow-in-Furness, argued against gambling especially in relation to horse racing.[106] At the same congress, Miss Cropper, in an address that associated morality with thrift and self-restraint, berated 'a class of women already numerous and probably increasing' who she thought were 'a source of national weakness'. They were 'ignorant, idle extravagant, and self-indulgent. They neglect their homes and children, they drink they bet and they exist in all ranks of society'. She referred to the 'present fever of gambling and betting' as a 'rapid and insidious pestilence … It begins so harmlessly, and leads to such dire results'. Worse still:

> Women book makers are alas! by no means uncommon, and laws which make it impossible in the open street have led to illicit bookmaking carried on by tradesmen's boys at back doors. No one who is interested in the subject can fail to have heard pitiful tales of the misery and ruin which this evil is causing.[107]

There was no doubt about the perils of drink and gambling, but the stance taken by 'Church people' at congress towards other leisure pursuits was less unequivocal. Congress coincided with an expansion in literacy amongst the populace and an increase in the production of reading material both 'low brow' and with a moral purpose. The power of reading to influence ideas and conduct was acknowledged, and thus whilst 'improving' reading was commended, concern accrued over the potential for reading of the wrong sort to corrupt. Judith Rowbotham has identified the role of fiction in reinforcing gendered notions of 'good' womanhood.[108] Rebecca Styler has noted the use made by women writers of secular material to communicate their ideas on religious themes in a way which allowed them to circumvent the notion that authority in theological matters was the province of men and by so doing construct female religious identity.[109] These themes and women as both readers and writers were reflected at congress. Styler's observations are exemplified by professional author Charlotte Yonge whose work as a journalist, bestselling novelist and writer for children was motivated by her religious faith. Yonge's heroines who exemplify feminine piety in their moral scruples, self-restraint and self-sacrifice in the interest of home duty would have been familiar to congress audiences. Louise Creighton's memoir recorded her affection for Yonge's works: 'I was a happy girl one Christmas when my mother gave me a copy of *The Daisy Chain* for my very own.'[110] Although too retiring to address a large public meeting face to face, Miss Yonge, who had a long association with the educational work of the GFS, in addition to her other literary credentials, supplied a paper that was read by Canon Brooke at the 1886 Wakefield Congress. Her theme was the education of the populace through reading. In it she stressed the importance of good reading and the need for libraries to provide such material. Additionally, she commended the supply of cheap editions of wholesome books. 'Now more than at any previous time, have our people's hearts to be reached through their heads and their heads through their recreative reading'.[111]

Mrs R. S. De Courcy Laffan, professionally known as Mrs Leith Adams, the author of the 1887 volume *Aunt Hepsy's Foundling*, similarly demonstrates the use of writing to promote religious ends and exemplify laudable behaviour. At Cardiff in 1889, she tackled the subject of 'Literature of the day and its attitude towards Christianity'. She noted that:

> free libraries and cheap editions bring every popular book within the reach of all classes: *ergo* the influences of religion upon life and conduct may be brought home to the masses of the people, the spiritual power of love and trust in God be manifested to them by tender touches and beautiful suggestions so the pen of the novelist may become the teacher of the people in the highest and deepest things in life.[112]

Religious faith and reading were also the subject of a paper written by Elizabeth Wordsworth, who, in addition to her academic achievements, was also a published novelist, which was delivered on her behalf to an audience of women by Canon de Chair at Norwich in 1895.[113] Three years later, the literary field was again represented at congress when Christabel Coleridge addressed a meeting for young women in which she advocated the spiritual and civic rewards of undertaking the Church work.[114] This was an appropriate topic for the protégée of Charlotte Yonge, who, like her mentor, identified with Anglican beliefs and contributed to publications that engaged with faith, morality and the exercise of conscience. Miss Coleridge was a distinguished author in her own right, and in addition to being Yonge's successor as editor of the long-running Anglican magazine for girls *The Monthly Packet*, also edited *Friendly Leaves*, the magazine for members of the GFS. Both these publications offered religious education and appropriate models for good conduct amongst girls from the middle class and working class, respectively. Coleridge was also the author of the 1903 volume *Charlotte Mary Yonge: Her Life and Letters*. She was in accord with Yonge's conservative stance on the role of women in society and articulated her own views in the 1894 essay collection *The Daughters Who Have Not Revolted*.[115] Another novelist and biographer of Charlotte Yonge, Mrs Ethel Romaines, continued the theme of advocacy for service when she contrasted 'Self-indulgence and self-sacrifice' at a meeting for girls and young women at the 1904 Liverpool congress.[116]

Propriety and respectability were also issues of concern in relation to public entertainment and performance from the perspective of both spectators and performers. In addition to reading, congress engaged with theatre and the emerging phenomenon of cinema. At the 1924 Oxford congress Miss

Highley, addressing the problems of attracting youth to the Church, pointed out that the appeal of modern entertainment, notably cinema, needed to be acknowledged and accommodated by the Church rather than proscribed. 'Thou shalt not' [she said] 'immediately urges one to say, "I shall I want to."'[117] As with reading, concerns focused on the power of media to corrupt or instruct. Additionally, in the case of the stage, the negotiation of the status of performers and the growing respectability of the profession were reflected on congress platforms. According to Christopher Kent, the 1880s saw a well-publicized debate over the status of the profession.[118] Moves towards asserting respectability in the profession were marked by the founding, by Stuart Hadlam in 1870, of the Church and Stage Guild. The intention was to break down Church prejudice against the stage, but the association of the stage with moral perils persisted, particularly in relation to 'lowbrow' popular productions featuring ballet girls. Although Emily Faithfull's 1876 *Hand book of Women's Work* does not mention the stage, moves towards respectability were boosted by the raising of the social profile of the profession through royal patronage, and the marriage of actresses into the nobility. From 1890 to 1914, there was a striking growth in the artistic quality and explicit social significance of the English drama which accorded actresses in particular artistic and social opportunities, and even political importance, 'unparalleled before or since'.[119] Despite this, at Norwich in 1895, GFS President Mrs Challoner Chute, in a paper tackling the subject of 'Amusement' warned of low standards on the stage, too much socializing, and excesses in sport.[120] The generation of women theatre professionals epitomized by Mrs Patrick Campbell and Janet Achurch, the producer of the 1896 landmark production of Ibsen's *Little Eyolf*, were represented at congress by Sybil Thorndike and Lena Ashwell. Miss Ashwell, who had been encouraged to enter the profession by Ellen Terry, had established her reputation playing against the most prominent actors of the late nineteenth century, notably Sir Henry Irving. She had also been a pioneer as a theatre manager at the Savoy Theatre. Ashwell, who was honoured with an OBE for her war work providing entertainment for the troops, had, post war, devoted herself to the promotion of non-commercial serious theatre, and enabling access to it for the populace, by running a touring company. It was this agenda, the entitlement (in the spirit of Ruskin) of the populace to the elevating effect of good art, she promoted in her talk on drama at the 1921 Birmingham Congress in the 'Recreation' section of the programme in which, as *The Times* reported, the Church attempted 'to meet the requirements of modern times'.[121] Sybil Thorndike, an associate of

Ashwell in the 1908 Actresses' Franchise League, and like her, the daughter of a clergyman, had also spoken at the Southend congress the previous year in the section on 'Christ and Recreation'.[122] The *Falkirk Herald* noted not just the relative innovation of women addressing a mixed audience at congress, but in particular drew attention to the entry of the theatre to mainstream discussion at a religious gathering:

> Our "pastors and masters" of old days would have shown some astonishment at being addressed by women at all ... But most of all would they have opened their eyes to find a leading light of the stage speaking to them on the "Ministry of The Church to those who provide amusements". Miss Sybil Thorndike was the lady chosen to handle this particular subject, and she might well have been expected to speak from wide experience of both Church and Stage. Herself the daughter of a clergyman, she has had an almost unique experience of stage work from the puerilities of the modern "revue" to the most blood curdling and thrilling tragedies of ancient Greece'.[123]

The topic of physical recreation was addressed at congress in relation to both men and women. Enthusiastic advocates for physical recreation for women appeared on congress platforms. Lilian Faithfull, although not speaking on the subject, was herself an elite sportswoman, Captain of Hockey at Somerville, she upheld the sporting tradition of Cheltenham Ladies' College and had previously introduced hockey to the students of Royal Holloway College, as well as serving as president of the All England Ladies Hockey Association. Elizabeth Wordsworth, too, encouraged games at Lady Margaret Hall, an enthusiasm she attributed to the frustrating experience of decorous walks as a school girl.[124] It was a time when the new profession for women of gymnastics teacher was emerging. Not only did secondary schooling for girls look beyond traditional ladylike pursuits, and (emulating the sporting ethos of boys' public schools) see games as a means of instilling character building attributes such as teamwork and loyalty, but systematic regimes of exercise had gained popularity following the pioneering work of Madame Bergman-Osterberg in promoting Swedish gymnastics.[125] Miss Stuart Snell of The Gymnasium, Alexandra House, Kensington, a former member of the staff of Bedford High School between 1886 and 1898, took the platform at Folkestone in 1893 where 'Physical Recreation: Use and Abuse' was on the agenda. She followed Colonel Onslow, who, in his talk on 'Physical Recreation', proved himself an advocate of muscular Christianity in asserting sport as a means of dissipating energy that might otherwise be expended in less wholesome pursuits.[126] In an extensive advocacy for gymnastics, delivered to a mixed audience, Miss Snell claimed that 'parents and instructors of girls now realize that the more highly educated and distinguished in mental faculties a women is required to be the more certainly should a due proportion of physical exercise be included in her studies and employments'.[127]

Girls' physical activity was subject to differences of opinion on what was appropriate. As with academic endeavour, positions taken accrued around socially embedded assumptions concerning women's 'natural' intellectual and emotional capacity and contingent behaviour. Women's reproductive function and prioritized maternal role were also to be considered in relation to education both mental and physical. The latter had particular topicality in the light of eugenic concerns articulated from medical and scientific authorities who considered that physical exertion made women 'unwomanly' and dissipated the energy they should reserve for rearing healthy children.[128] Whilst these concerns were not overtly articulated on the congress platform, there was concern about over indulgence in physical activity. As in other pastimes, self-restraint should be the guiding principle. At Norwich in 1895, GFS President Mrs Challoner Chute, in a paper tackling the subject of 'Amusement', warned of excesses in sport not only from the standpoint of physical over-exertion but on the grounds of dereliction of other duties and responsibilities.[129] Another contributor to congress, gynaecologist Mary Scharlieb, although a keen advocate of gymnastics, also cautioned of the dangers of excessive exercise which might result in a 'neuter' type of girl who might thereby compromise her reproductive ability.[130] Miss Snell was clearly aware of these concerns and used them to advocate the role of professional, qualified teachers in the supervision of exercise, but she refuted claims that gymnastics might overtire the female frame by referring to:

> ... a voluntary statement made to me by one of the lecturers at a celebrated college for women who asserts that all her best papers are written on gymnasium day and a head mistress whom I could mention begins her day's work with a steady half hours exercise on the extension machine so highly advocated by Dr Swingier of Berlin.[131]

She also obliquely dealt with potential concerns over the effect of physical activity on women's reproductive fitness by noting the benefits of gymnastics for the abdominal muscles 'the most important in the frame of woman, it stands to reason that these especial muscles should be developed and kept in order';

she also noted that a large proportion of her pupils were married women. She concluded her talk by averring the benefits of gymnastics for not just women's bodily health but their happiness and spirit: 'in a word her capital'.[132]

Conclusion

The recurrence of education on congress agendas illustrates topical themes, notably the introduction of systemic state elementary schooling and the expansion of educational spaces for women and girls and the negotiation of appropriate curricula. The views expressed by congress speakers, agenda topics and the categories of targeted congress audiences illustrate the mediating effects of gender (as well as class) to access to knowledge.

First-generation 'pioneer' speakers exemplified by Jane Ellice Hopkins, although without formal qualifications, demonstrated high levels of cultural capital and attainment beyond what were traditionally considered 'feminine subjects'. They illustrate the possibility some women had of engaging with an enlarged curriculum informally in 'papa's study', given a sympathetic paternal mentor. However, that this was not typical also points to the restricted access to educational institutions and curricula experienced by the majority of girls including those from the middle class. Louise Creighton provides an example of the strategy highlighted by Linda Eisenmann of drawing on extra-institutional means to acquire education via associative networks, through her use of the essay society or in the public domain of the lecture theatre.[133] However, Creighton's aspiration was for women to have access to formal, intellectually rigorous educational institutions. The associative networks in which Creighton was positioned were aligned with elite educational institutions for men, and with sympathetic male figures of distinction in the field of education, this capital by association was drawn upon to help legitimize aspirations for women's higher education not only by Creighton but by other women seeking to open up the field.[134]

Hopkins, Sumner and Creighton demonstrate common dispositions of habitus including mutual recognition of indices of cultural capital, a commitment to self-improvement and above all the prioritization of Anglican faith. They may be positioned within a tradition of philanthropic service, frequently motivated and legitimized by religious commitment, which assumed social position and the possession of 'education' as not just a mandate for patronage but an obligation to contribute to society.[135] All three made use of congress as a means of publicizing their views, and appearances at congress, a space endorsed by its association with institutionalized religious capital, served to affirm their distinction and pedagogic authority as speakers for the Church. In a reciprocal transaction of capital, as speakers of distinction, with capital accrued from association with powerful clergy, and philanthropic activism in their own right they added to the dignity and appeal of congress.

This reciprocal endorsement between space and speaker also operated for emergent professionals in the education of women and girls. The recurring presence of headmistresses at congress illustrates women moving towards the exercise of power in the educational field. It also signals the transition from women achieving distinction in fields by virtue of social capital, affiliation with men of distinction such as senior clergy or academics for example, to the acquisition of field-specific knowledge and recognition for the possession of specific markers of professional capital such as institutional leadership or a university attendance. However, social and religious capital continued to be recognized and their mobilization had been instrumental in the instigation and recognition of higher education institutions. Yet, by featuring women recognized as experts, congress served as space that functioned towards the enlargement of assumptions concerning women's intellectual capacity, and endorsed the enlargement of the opportunities available to categories of girls and women in formal education. In informal education through leisure too, speakers at congress negotiated appropriate conduct and activities for women and girls as they gained access to a widening range of public spaces such as the gymnasium and cinema, with religion in mind.

Conventional notions of femininity, the doctrine of difference, a discourse of caring maternalism, the prioritization of religion in education and an ethos of service proved durable, and were drawn on to justify access to secondary and higher education for middle-class girls. Clearly, some congress speakers such as Lucy Soulsby and Elizabeth Wordsworth were convinced by the religiously framed doxa of difference that legitimized patriarchal authority in family Church and state. The contributions of other educational speakers such as Lilian Faithfull indicate a more ambivalent view towards the masculine hegemony of power. Yet even the most academic of educational advocates and congress platform speakers underplayed intellectual aspirations and did not confront patriarchal authority in the field of education, or men as the custodians of and gatekeepers to elite knowledge, seeking instead to make dedicated educational spaces for women in school and college and thereby secure position within the wider educational field. In addition to exemplifying gender and religion as mediators of educational and opportunities congress also points to class in relation to educational opportunity. Against a context of government commissions and resultant legislation, which saw education as a civilizing strategy, the prioritization of Anglican religion informed the views and concerns of congress speakers who engaged with the education of the working class where key concerns focused on the lack of doctrinal education. However, despite advocacy for working-class education, systemic social stratification, like conventional notions of femininity, remained largely unchallenged.

6

Public Service and the World of Work

Introduction: Social and Legislative Context

The congress period coincided with government enquiries and legislation on working conditions and health that reflected concerns on issues associated with industrialization, urbanization, population growth, class and poverty.[1] Notable amongst these was the Royal Commission on the Poor Laws and Relief of Distress which reported in 1909. The lives of women in particular were also affected as a series of legislative reforms, ongoing throughout the congress period, marked milestones on the long road towards women's achievement of full civil rights. The 1882 extension of the Married Women's Property Act, the 1888 Local Government Act and the 1928 Equality of Franchise Act provide key examples.[2] Aspirations for access to 'respectable' work and the professions were marked by Emily Janes's 1859 Society for the Employment of Women, the 1876 Medical Act which allowed all who were suitably qualified, regardless of gender to practice medicine and the 1919 Sex Disqualification (Removal) Act which allows women's participation in the machinery of the law. 'Congress women' speakers and categories of targeted audience, and topics on the agenda reflect these developments, and congress can be seen as a forum in which women's aspirations and place as citizens were represented, asserted and indirectly negotiated.

As the male franchise was enlarged, relations between labour and capital were topical. A concern reflected in Lambeth Conference resolutions which illustrate the changing perspectives of the Church towards socialism and workers' rights.[3] Issues accruing around poverty, class, labour relations and the world of work were embedded in congress agendas. Congresses were an exercise in outreach by an organization sensitive to claims of social exclusiveness and mindful of the underrepresentation of working men in its congregations.[4] Anglican Clergy, frequently the younger sons of landed gentry, educated in Latin and Greek unlike nonconformists, positioned themselves as gentlemen. The social attitudes of the Church were informed by, and representative of, ruling-class values. Senior clergy sought social reconciliation and the upholding of the existing order rather than its reconstruction.[5] Suffragan Bishop of Guildford, George Sumner's claim that: 'anything that tends to unite the classes together should certainly be welcomed by us who have the interests of society at stake', made in a speech advocating the Mothers' Union, substantiates this claim, and also accords with Susan Mumm's identification of rectifying social disorder as a motivating element in philanthropy. Lucy Bland has drawn attention to the application of a moral agenda to material aspects of social improvement in attempts to modify working-class culture, notably with regard to temperance, an interest reflected in Mary Sumner's debut congress speech.[6] Similarly Jessica Gerard interprets the exercise of philanthropy by the upper/middle 'landed classes', as legitimizing the inequality of a stratified society. Diana Kendall likewise sees a tradition of benevolence upholding social stratification.[7] However, Andrea Geddes Poole sees, in her comparative scrutiny of the lives of Lucy Cavendish and Emma Conns, philanthropic work as an assertion of women's citizenship and a means towards the creation of a woman's public sphere.[8] In *Ladies Elect* Patricia Hollis considers trajectories of transition from philanthropic activism to professional and political positions, and it is this dimension that is also the focus of this chapter.

The location of the 1885 Church congress at Portsmouth illustrates venture into an urban district in which the parochial structure and the personal, social and economic sway of squire and cleric was less robust than in its rural strongholds. Congress agendas also reflected unease over urbanization and the association of the physical dirt and darkness of the city with moral pollution.[9] The later years of the century coincided with the influential series of publications recording the findings of Charles Booth's enquiry in to the causes of pauperism, *Labour and Life of the People of London*.[10] At the London congress in 1899, 'Economics and Charity', 'Old Age Pensions' and 'Housing' were on the agenda. Housing also featured in the following years at Newcastle and Brighton. The 1903 congress agenda item titled 'The Social Problems of a Great City', which included a paper by philanthropist Canon Samuel Barnett of the Toynbee Hall University settlement, maintained that urban areas blighted by poverty, overcrowding in housing and ineffective sanitation were breeding grounds for corruption, godlessness and sin.[11]

Congress agendas responded to the 1904 Report of the Inter-departmental Committee on Physical deterioration, which had been commissioned in response to the rejection of significant numbers of military recruits on the ground of physical incapacity.[12] The commission took evidence on the declining birth rate but noted that the urban population now stood at 77 per cent, an increase of 27 per cent over the preceding fifty years. Poverty, housing, health, pollution, employment conditions and alcohol abuse were considered. It also engaged with eugenic concerns that moral depravity would be passed from generation to generation, but concluded that although some medical conditions were hereditary, this could not be proven. Alcohol, whilst exacerbating existing weakness, was not a cause per se. However, a paragraph headed 'The Hereditary Taint' noted that: 'it is suggested that the depressing effects of life struggle on parents may be, in some measure, transmitted to their offspring. The employment of mothers in late pregnancy and also soon after child birth is taken into consideration.'[13] Much of the report, which acknowledged Seebohm Rowntree's *Poverty a Study of Town Life*, concluded that the alleviation of poverty and the provision of good nutrition were the key means to address physical incapacity and failure to thrive, termed in the report, retardation or backwardness. The report had implications for the education of girls and those who were already mothers.[14] It also advocated physical activity and introduced drill at school. As a result of the report, school meals and health visiting were introduced, and tighter enforcement of the 1902 Midwives Act advocated, initiatives that created more jobs for women. Whilst poverty was recognized, the finger of blame for children's failure to thrive was pointed at bad parenting, a theme with moral overtones, echoed on the congress platform. Exhortations to good mothering were an ongoing feature of congress agendas where Mothers' Union speakers were present. Dr Collie of the London School Board stated: 'Physical infirmity is practically confined to the poorest and lowest strata of the population where children are improperly and insufficiently fed and inadequately housed, and where parents are improvident, idle and intemperate.' 'Culpable neglect and ignorance and laziness of the parent' was censured and blamed for inculcating poor habits. Similarly parental ignorance was highlighted as a cause of infant deaths from 'overlaying of infants caused by drunkenness most cases occurring between Friday and Monday morning', a theme taken up explicitly by Louise Creighton at the Barrow Congress in 1906.[15] Excessive drinking was perceived as a cause of poverty, another recurrent theme on the congress agendas in main sessions and meetings aimed at women. Thrift was the subject taken by Mrs Edith Barnett at Cardiff in 1889, thrift and the poor law were agenda items for the women's meeting at Folkestone in 1892, and 1896 Shrewsbury congress featured a discussion on women as poor law guardians, a role assumed by several platform speakers.[16] The Manchester congress of 1908 had a section on 'Methods of Dealing with Poverty', and two years later Cambridge tackled 'The Poor Law' where Mrs S. A. [Henrietta] Barnett, the social reformer, philanthropist and housing expert shared the platform with Cambridge County Council member and authority on public health, Miss Constance Cochrane.[17]

The engagement of congress in the world of work and labour relations took place against a context of increasing government legislation in the regulation of working conditions. The Factory Acts of 1874, 1878 and 1896, and the Shops Acts between 1906 and 1913, exemplify legislation that had particular relevance to the conditions of employment for women and children. With the extension of the male franchise, the political rights of the labouring man (and woman), socialist ideals and morality in relation to economic structure became topical. At Leeds in 1872, Bishop Fraser of Manchester received an ovation at the working men's meeting for defending the right of agricultural labourers to a union. This was not typical of bishops who tended to be aligned with the interests of landowners. The organizers of the Plymouth Church congress in 1876 kept the subject of labour off the agenda because it had led to fierce controversy the previous year. In 1895, Bishop Mandell Creighton declined to intervene in the boot and shoe strike.[18] The following year at Shrewsbury congress tackled 'The Morality of Strikes', next year Newcastle considered 'Trade Disputes'. Bradford followed by addressing 'Social and Trade Relations'.

There was some anxiety in the Church over political change and social cohesion. Socialists were accused of atheism, and socialism was associated by some, including Mary Sumner, who feared the 'peril of Anti-Christian Socialist Sunday schools', with secularization, lack of morality, divorce and family breakdown. Bishop Harold Browne was in no doubt on the dangers of socialism. His 1883, sermon 'Antichrist', claimed that 'beneath all government, and waiting to subvert and submerge all, lie hidden, or scarcely hidden, volcanic fires of communistic anarchy, joined in close affinity with agnosticism and atheism', concern was reflected in the proceedings of the Lambeth Conference which in 1888 received the report of the committee on Socialism.[19] According to Chadwick it 'was something if a Christian treated socialism with sympathy', but a key figure, as the Church engaged with the development of industrial society, was Christian Socialist, Frederick Denison Maurice who believed that his faith necessitated a socialist stance.[20] The realignment of views towards Christian Socialist perspectives can be tracked in congress agendas. 'Commercial Morality' was on the agenda in London in 1899, and Brighton (1901) considered 'Covetousness in Commerce, Employment and Chance'. In 1902, the year after Seebohm Rowntree published his report on poverty, in which he identified the concepts of primary and secondary poverty as a product of systemic economic conditions rather than improvidence, Northampton continued the theme with an agenda section titled 'Teaching of the Sermon on the Mount as to Social Obligations and Economics'.[21] By 1908, the official position of the Church was to focus on social reconciliation rather than scaremongering. That year the Lambeth Conference Resolution 44 stated that:

> The Conference recognises the ideals of brotherhood which underlie the democratic movement of this century; and, remembering our Master's example in proclaiming the inestimable value of every human being in the sight of God, calls upon the Church to show sympathy with the movement, in so far as it strives to procure just treatment for all and a real opportunity of living a true human life, and by its sympathy to commend to the movement the spirit of our Lord Jesus Christ, in whom all the hopes of human society are bound up.[22]

Resolution 45 had concluded that 'the social mission and social principles of Christianity should be given a more prominent place in the study and teaching of the Church, both for the clergy and the laity'.[23] The 1909 congress organizers responded by putting 'Socialism from the Standpoint of Christianity' on the agenda. The proceedings included an address by the Bishop of Lichfield on 'The responsibility of employers for the spiritual and temporal Welfare of the employed'.[24]

The Poor, Caring Voluntarism and Official Positions

The domination of congress platforms by women speakers aligned with clerical networks, who drew on traditions of philanthropy, and upheld a discourse of caring womanhood endorsed by paternal authority in the family and Church, to frame their activism, has been noted in a previous chapter. The emergence of organized voluntary activism by women, notably in the Church-sanctioned Mothers' Union and Girls' Friendly Society, and women's engagement in advocacy networks and multiple allegiances, signalled a shift from action by individual amateur 'good deed mongers', towards collective interventions by societies. The voluntary principle did not coincide with an amateurish approach. The influential Charity Organisation Society, with which several congress speakers had links, was founded in 1896 with the intention of rationalizing and professionalizing philanthropy. The training and experience offered by the COS, and in other organizations, provided opportunities for women to develop expertise in social issues, committee work and administration. Congress and National Union of Women Workers activist, Laura Ridding, who served as a poor law guardian from 1895 to 1904 and was also a rural district councillor for the Southwell union, exemplifies this pattern. In addition to administrative competence this kind of work required emotional residence. Ridding described a visit to the 'enormous barracks' that was the purpose-built Southwell workhouse which contained 'room after room of imbeciles' and 'one poor baby I can't forget, dying from deliberate starvation'.[25]

The trajectory of movement from caring voluntarism towards official appointments, political engagement and recognized expertise, is also evident in other congress speakers of distinction.[26] Marianne Harriet Mason, her friends Mary Clifford and Blanche Pigott, and her associate Mrs (later Dame) Ellen Pinsent, moved from philanthropic work into government service via school boards or Poor Law administration. Blanche Pigott and Ellen Pinsent both became local government councillors and served on the North Norfolk Rural District Council and Birmingham City Council, respectively. These pioneers had other characteristics in common. All were the daughters of clergymen, habituated into an ethos of Christian service, and in addition to appearances on the Church congress platforms they were linked through philanthropic networks, notably the National Union of Women Workers. Specific to the field of government welfare provision was the 1881 Society for Promoting the Return of Women as Poor Law Guardians or Women's Guardians Society.[27] The degree of networking and overlapping between organizations is indicated by the suggestion from Marianne Mason and Mary Clifford that committees of the WGS, NUWW and Women's Local Government Society (WLGS) should jointly 'cooperate in forming a machinery for the selection of suitable persons and Guardians'.[28]

The topic of the poor recurred on congress agendas and drew the attention of women speakers. Mrs Henry Kingsley, a Richmond Poor Law Guardian since 1887, addressed the Cardiff congress of 1889 and identified unsanitary, slum accommodation, as the root of not only physical but moral and spiritual degradation: 'I am quite sure everyone on this platform will agree with me that over-crowding is the root of immorality, the drunkenness and the poverty of the nation'. It was her view that moral reform and spiritual reform of slum dwellers were impossible without first securing decent living conditions for them: 'I ask you in the name of the Church to make your voices heard on the subject of over-crowding'.[29] Almost half a century later the issue was still topical. At the Southport congress of 1926: 'Dr Margaret Ormiston urged that alongside better housing we should work for better rooms, more playgrounds and more holiday camps for the young', and Miss Moss 'drew attention to the increase of criminal assaults upon children as a consequence of overcrowded housing and the resultant undermining of decency and self-restraint'.[30]

At Exeter in 1894, the year legislative change eliminated the property qualification, and removed a final impediment to women's election to local workhouse boards of guardians, Mrs Malkin spoke in the 'Care of the Poor' section.[31] Two years later Mary Clifford, described by *The Bristol Mercury* as 'The Guardian Angel of Bristol', and by her NUWW associate Laura Ridding as 'beautiful',[32] a Guardian of the Barton Regis Union, Redlands, Bristol, took the platform twice at Shrewsbury, where she spoke firstly on 'The Poor Law', and secondly on 'Women as Poor Law Guardians'. What Laura Ridding judged as her 'stirring' message was a wakeup call to (Anglican) churchwomen on their duty of service:[33] 'Churchmen and women have not at, least in towns come forward as they should to take their share in poor law work'. Mary Clifford drove her message home with an unflattering comparison to rival denominations: 'Nonconformist women have, it seems to me, been educated to feel a more definite responsibility in social and political subjects, and we Church women, notwithstanding the immense public spirit of the Prayer Book, have failed to take our due share in poor law administration'.[34]

Women identified in congress reports by their official position as guardians did not confine themselves to talking about the poor and chose topics relevant to the focus of congress agendas. At the Shrewsbury congress, 'The Church Law of Marriage in Relation to Divorce' was tackled in a session to which women were not admitted, an exclusion that *The Saturday Review* considered 'exceedingly prudish'.[35] Mrs. Hatton, Guardian of the Poor for the Union of Wolverhampton, in a separate meeting for women, discussed the importance of the sanctity of engagement before marriage.[36] Blanche Pigott, a guardian for Erpingham in Norfolk, who was well known in her home county as the convenor of the Norfolk Women's Armenian Refugee Fund and as a Bible missionary at county fairs,[37] also avoided the subject of the poor, and focused on modest Christian conduct in her talks to women at Wolverhampton in 1887, and Norwich in 1895. However, her connection with the YWCA, an organization that she served as UK president in 1908, was reflected in her address on 'How to Make Life Beautiful' to an audience of young women at Bradford in 1894.[38] At Nottingham the year following her congress debut, Mary Clifford gave a paper on 'Women in the Indian Zenana', and at the London congress of 1899, she again pursued her enthusiasm for missionary work in a talk on 'Women's Work for Missions'.[39] Four years later, in her home city of Bristol, where, according to the *Church Times* her appearance on the platform was greeted with cheers, she gave a talk to an audience of mothers on the subject of childrearing in which she advocated communication with teachers in the interests of promoting good moral conduct.[40]

Marianne Mason, a contributor to the Royal Commission on poverty that reported in 1909, addressed congress on four occasions. In addition to a clerical father, she had two clergy brothers and a younger sister Frances Agnes (1849–1941), the founder in 1898 of the Anglican Community of the Holy Family.[41] Mason witnessed her own faith through advocacy for the religious principles of the Girls' Friendly Society where she served as vice president for the Diocese of Southwell. She also undertook Christian service through work for the poor and had been appointed as a full-time paid Assistant Inspector for Boarded Out [Workhouse] Children by the Local Government Board at Bolton in 1885, the year following the publication of her pamphlet on *The Classification of Girls and Boys in Workhouses*. Her role, in what was a controversial area on account of suspicion of the potential for abuse offered by the 'farming out' of children, was to inspect the homes in which children under ten years old were placed.[42] She was appropriately qualified to speak on 'Domestic Arrangements and the Most Important Articles of Diet' in the main agenda section 'The Church in Relation to Social Questions', which covered social improvement and housing at Wakefield in 1886. Mason's was a pioneering appointment because, in most situations, inspection depended on the contribution of volunteers, or was delegated to voluntary organizations such as the GFS which had a special department for workhouse children.[43] Prior to her official appointment Mason had performed exactly this voluntary service as the vice president of the Southwell Diocesan GFS, where she had taken responsibility for workhouse girls. She had also been recruited by Mary Clifford, another advocate of preventive work, to encourage the wives of Bristol Poor Law Guardians to join the GFS as Associates and provide aftercare for 'painfully and cruelly unprotected' girls leaving the workhouse, in order to 'weld them into the rank and company of ordinary respectable young women'.[44] Her speech to a mixed audience was not just advocacy for hygiene and thrift but an encouragement for members of the audience to take up voluntary service.[45] Six years later, although now based in Nottinghamshire, she was still Her Majesty's Inspector of Boarded Out Pauper Children. Her message was still one of advocating thrift and the encouragement of active involvement in the improvement of society: not only should women influence males in their families, she averred that: 'women's duties do not end at her home, but that her influence reaches much further'.[46]

As Laura Ridding noted in her diary, a particular category of the vulnerable poor in the workhouse were what were termed the feeble-minded. Mary Clifford, who had voiced her concerns about the indiscriminate mixing of children with mental or physical impediments in *The Classification of Girls and Boys in Workhouses*, shared her concern with Ellen Pinsent who gave a paper to the 1911 congress in the section on 'Poor Law Problems: The Feeble Minded'.[47] Ellen Pinsent, whose pathway to public service, political engagement and acknowledged expertise had been via School Board service, was, at the time of her address, a newly elected member of the Birmingham County Council. Her area of expertise was the care of the mentally incapacitated, and she chaired the Special Schools subcommittee of Birmingham Education Committee.[48] She, with fellow eugenicist, Mary Dendy, the Hon. Secretary of the Lancashire and Cheshire Association for the Permanent Care of the Feeble Minded, had founded the National Association for the Care and Protection of the Feeble Minded in 1889. Pinsent served on both the 1904 and 1908 Royal Commissions into the subject. The resulting report of 1909 advocated specific provision for different categories of need, separate from penal or poor law institutions. It also suggested that Boards of Categorisation which would rule on allocating individual categories of mental incapacity and contingent provision should contain 'at least one woman'. Moreover, the current labels, 'Lunatics', 'Idiots and Imbeciles' and 'Feeble Minded', should be replaced by one category, because:

> these labels deter people from aiding their friends to obtain proper care … in future persons suffering from brain trouble will be regarded in the same light as persons suffering from physical disease and will be similarly treated for it in "Hospitals", "homes" or "colonies".[49]

Although it arose from a concern for the plight of the mentally vulnerable housed together with the sane and able bodied that Pinsent and Dendy publicized at conferences of poor law guardians with their acquaintance Mary Clifford, compassion became overlaid with eugenic anxieties. The National Association for the Care and Protection of the Feeble Minded and the Eugenic Education Society (who were in sympathy with the Charity Organisation Society in seeing physically and mentally degenerate paupers as an unredeemable category) jointly published an abstract of the report.[50] They believed that the character weakness that led to drunkenness, venereal disease, large families and thus pauperism was due to a hereditary physical defect. To eliminate these defects, they advocated the containment of the feeble-minded in institutions to prevent them reproducing.[51]

> There are at this moment some 150,000 persons in the country, who while not certifiably insane, are suffering from mental defect – unhappy in themselves, a sorrow and burden to their families and a growing source of expense and danger to the community. Under proper care, in surroundings adapted to their needs, the majority of them can be trained to do work which supplies a stimulus and an interest to their limited intelligences and provides a substantial share of the cost of their subsistence. Left unprotected, they suffer moral and physical degradation. Mental defects are hereditary; the feeble minded are prolific; and thus, the relative amount of feeble mindedness and insanity increases at an ever growing rate and threatens the race with progressive deterioration.[52]

This view chimed with topical anxieties concerning racial decline that had led to the 1903 report into Physical Degeneration. It was also influential towards shaping the Mental Deficiency Act of 1913 which legislated for the incarceration of those officially diagnosed as feeble-minded.

The focus on public health stimulated by the 1903 enquiry brought domestic standards of hygiene into focus and served to promote professionally informed perspectives into the running of the home. Miss Alice Ravenhill, who addressed congress on four occasions between 1898 and 1906, was distinguished for her expertise in hygiene and homemaking. Ravenhill's expertise was located across disciplinary fields in the emerging areas of local government, sanitary inspection, public health, welfare and higher and vocational education. Initially a self-educated woman, she had acquired her professional credentials through engagement with the National Health Society, a voluntary organization, which, with the benefit of the poor in mind, sought to promote public health through informal education in hygiene and nutrition, and the provision of formal training aimed at women, in household health, childcare, nursing and ambulance work.[53] A pioneer of domestic science education, Ravenhill's career included working for the Yorkshire West Riding County Council to educate teachers in the integration of health and hygiene into the school curriculum. She had lectured in hygiene at King's College London, where fellow congress speaker educationalist Lilian Faithfull was vice principal. Ravenhill was the author of reports for the Board of Education and the Royal Sanitary institute which elected her as its first woman fellow in 1904. In 1906-7 she accompanied gynaecologist Mary Scharlieb (also a congress contributor) on an inspection tour of physical training colleges for women.[54] At Bradford in 1898, Alice Ravenhill, who was described in the congress official report as 'Lecturer to the National Health Society', spoke on the '5Cs' essential for domestic happiness 'Cleanliness, Comfort, Cheerfulness,

Carefulness, Charity'. At Barrow-in-Furness her paper once again focused on the expert knowledge needed to ensure good parenting and she enumerated not just physical hygiene but also training in healthy character and self-control. At Weymouth her address engaged with the topical health-related issue of temperance. She advocated the virtue of self-control as a means to combat the physical and moral evils of drink.[55]

Temperance: From Sin to Scientific Perspectives

Ravenhill was not the only speaker to tackle drink: between 1885 and 1907, the subject of temperance featured no less than sixteen times in women's section meetings. The prominence given to the subject reflected a perception that, particularly amongst the poorest in urban areas, drunkenness was the primary cause of social problems.[56] Congress speakers sought to educate the populace about both the moral and physical dangers of alcohol. Here, too, there was concern over the potential for undesirable characteristics to be passed from generation to generation either by nature or nurture. The way the perceived problem of drinking was tackled, and by whom, also illustrates the shift of emphasis from voluntary and moral to professional scientific and medical perspectives. Drunkenness was initially condemned by congress speakers on the grounds that it squandered family resources, exacerbated poverty and compromised the proper discharge of parental duties. It was also condemned on the grounds that it engendered the loss of self-control which might lead to theft, sexual licence and violent crime. Over time, whilst the moral condemnation of drinking on these grounds (especially amongst women) was not abandoned, the anti-drink message was articulated by medical professionals who emphasized the detriment to health of drinking against a background of imperial patriotism and contingent eugenic concern on the degeneration of 'the race', and (as in the case of feeble mindedness), scientific preoccupation with genetic inheritance.

Mary Sumner, who, in addition to her GFS allegiance, was the president of the Winchester branch of the Church of England Juvenile Temperance League, saw alcohol as a source of corruption. Speaking to an audience of 'working women' at Portsmouth in 1885, she said:

> A reason why the tone of the women of England is not so high as it should be? This reason is intemperance; so many girls are lost through drink. The wide spread ruin of young lives from this cause is simply appalling. Would that

I could persuade everyone in this hall to be a total abstainer. Example is far more powerful than precept ... Be yourself what you wish your children to be.[57]

At the same congress the 'sailors' friend' Agnes Weston, publisher of the newsletter *'Ashore and Afloat'*, spoke of the efforts being made to encourage seamen in the Royal Navy to refrain from 'the grog'.[58] She explained her methods; the provision of coffee taverns and sailors' rest homes ashore, and 'the essentially woman's work' of befriending and corresponding 'to draw our blue jackets and marines from a life of sin and pleasures that debase and ruin them, to a sober and godly life, to the glory of God's holy name'.[59] Agnes Weston's enterprise was much more than a charitable pastime undertaken by ladies. She elaborated on the scale and structure of her work and noted that: 'A most important feature of this work is o*rganisation*, [italics as source] ... In connection with Temperance and other work, I have committees and agents, all volunteers, on board every ship and gun boat, as well as in all shore establishments, hospitals, barracks, etc'.[60] Sixteen years later Agnes Weston was still working for the welfare of seamen and was able to report on her 'successes' to the Brighton congress. The following year she also took the platform and suggested that taking up the grog ration should be discouraged by the substitution of a pay bonus.[61]

Temperance also attracted support from women medical professionals. Dr Kate Mitchell and gynaecologist Mary Scharlieb's advocacy for temperance reflected eugenic concern over the relationship of alcohol abuse to the physical as well as moral 'degradation of the race'.[62] Dr Mitchell, addressing the 1891 congress in Rhyl, noted that she was 'firmly of the belief that all children ought to be brought up without any knowledge of alcohol', both for reasons of health and in order to inculcate habits of sobriety.[63] Speaking at the NUWW conference the following year, where 'The Temperance Question' was also on the agenda, she addressed the 'treatment of inebriate women', and argued that drunkenness should be regarded as a disease, for some were born with a physiological disposition to alcoholism. However, despite her scientific perspective, she did not abandon a moral stance, 'there is [she claimed] no will so strong, so stubborn, so determined as the will to evil'. Her remedy was individual treatment in free homes to restore the inebriate to both physical and moral health. She also urged her audience to help 'save the womanhood of our land from the shame and disgrace of drunkenness' by supporting initiatives to promote total abstinence, and by personal example.[64]

Mary Scharlieb, speaking at the Exeter congress in 1894, acknowledged that doctors had a poor reputation amongst temperance advocates, but suggested that the prescription of alcohol was now approached with greater caution.[65] Despite her medical perspective, like Mitchell, she focused on the moral evil of drink, and saw the remedy in abstinence. She advocated joining the Women's Union, an auxiliary to the Church of England Temperance Society, which worked to promote temperance through meetings, the distribution of literature and the establishment of 'counter attractions to the beer shop' such as coffee taverns and reading rooms. Echoing sentiments expressed nine years previously by Mary Sumner, she urged the women of congress to lead by example as total abstainers. For her, abstinence should be regarded not as a negative restriction, but rather as 'the positive virtue of self-control'.[66] Scharlieb was aware of the attraction of alcohol for the hard-pressed working-class woman, and her speech contained a caution against self-righteousness on the part of the middle-class would-be reformer, referring to 'gin palaces', she said:

> Probably none of us really appreciate the temptations these offer to the over worked and underfed poor. We see these places as we pass knowing the awful sin and sorrow that flow from them, we shudder and recoil as from a moral pest house. It is good however that we try and realize what they represent to those who have no food, no fire, no light at home. To them the public house with its warmth, light, comfort, yes, and let us admit it, the temporary sense of bien être given for the moment by the stimulant, seem an oasis in their desert lives.[67]

Scharlieb went on to question (albeit implicitly) conventional assumptions by suggesting that drink was a symptom and not necessarily the cause of poverty. In order to alleviate the evils of drink, other issues such as employment, wages, housing and education needed addressing. She concluded her remarks on the attractions of the public house with a challenge: 'What do we offer in exchange for this seductive glamour? Good advice, bad coffee, and a promise of a happier future. We must make a better offer than this'.[68] Drink was not just an issue for the working-class woman. Scharlieb condemned the practice of 'secret drinking' in the home by middle-, as well as working-class women, who could obtain alcohol clandestinely from the grocer's shop, and she urged her audience to support a change in the licensing laws.[69] Neither were the upper classes exempt form censure. Speaking at the 1892 Folkestone Church congress, Lady Frederick Cavendish complained about young ladies 'accompanying gentlemen to the smoking room after dinner, and sharing, not only the cigars, but the spirits and water'.[70]

Realities of Working Life, Workplace Regulation and Wider Class Perspectives

Whilst speakers predominantly represented a middle-/upper-class philanthropic perspective which assumed both the duty, and the authority, to advise those less socially advantaged, particularly on the conduct of 'home duties' and, like Henrietta Barnett, were of the opinion that married women should not work on the grounds that 'the men ought to earn the money',[71] congress agendas began to acknowledge the significance of the workplace in the lives of unmarried women. Lucy Soulsby's 1894 Exeter speech, engaged with 'Night Schools for Working Women', and at the same congress, Louise Creighton advocated 'the same opportunities for education and self-development as working men have', so that young women were prepared for life and were able to make good decisions.[72]

Talks about suitable employment and the conditions of working life also reflected these changing perceptions. The theme of the working girl featured repeatedly in congress speeches, and speakers began to engage with working conditions. Several were affiliated to the GFS which catered for unmarried working women. A constituency which initially was assumed to consist largely of domestic servants. The Hon. Ellen Joyce, a founding Associate of the GFS, speaking at Rhyl in 1891, represented a traditional perspective on women's work as an interlude prior to, and preparation for, domestic married life. She regretted the fact that girls were abandoning domestic service even though it was good preparation for homemaking.[73] However, the GFS did recognize that their members engaged in factory, clerical and retail work, and its activities expanded to include the provision of 'industrial' training in various aspects of employment.[74]

Another GFS Associate, Laura Ridding, speaking at the Exeter Congress in 1894, saw in her paper *The Guardianship of Working Girls*, the physical and moral welfare of workers as the responsibility of the wife of the manufacturer. She noted that the responsibility of a woman for her household extended to the workplace, where ideally 'the girls look up with a happy smile of friendship as the owner's wife goes through the rooms where she watches with motherly Christian care'. Although this may be seen as an articulation of a traditional patronizing stance on social welfare, *The Guardianship of Working Girls* also advocated the need for safe and suitable places for working girls to meet with their 'lovers'.[75] A perspective that acknowledged the realities of life for young working women. Ridding's interest in, and commitment to, the improvement of working women's lives is also indicated by her private meetings with Trades Union activists and congress speakers Gertrude Tuckwell and Clementina Black.[76]

The Hon. Augusta Maclagan, a stalwart activist on behalf of the Mothers' Union and the GFS, speaking ten years later, recognized widening opportunities for women's paid work. Amongst the suitable employments she recommended to her audience of young women were the traditional roles of governess (for the genteel girl) and nursery nurse for those who really were fond of children. She also advocated learning shorthand and typing, and noted that: 'Journalism of late has made great strides as a profession for women'. She was alert to the entry of middle-class women to the workplace, and emphasized the view that middle-class women could venture into occupations such as school teaching without 'loss of caste which she, although the daughter of a peer, considered an outdated notion'.[77]

> Should it be suggested that I am advising encroachment on ground hitherto occupied by what are called "the working classes". I answer that in these days of eager competition there can be no restriction. Intelligent working men and women can reach (and have reached) the top of the tree in every profession, and brave women, however gently nurtured, have a right to claim their independence and earn their livelihood in in any way which is open to them in which they can serve their God.[78]

Augusta Maclagan might also have noted the pathway that her own GFS and other organizations concerned with youth work opened up for 'respectable' women to move from voluntary to paid work in government agencies and institutions. An example of this trajectory can be found in Miss Augusta Deane who made her debut congress speech in 1903. Speaking to an audience of girls and young women, she emphasized the importance of service to the community and advocated participation in Church work through the Girls Diocesan Association (GDA) and other societies.[79] Augusta Deane had a strong association with the Young Women's Christian Association (YWCA) and other clubs for girls in her native city of Bristol, but it was for her work for the Ministry of Labour and organization of wartime agricultural committees for which she was honoured with an OBE in 1918, the year before she made her second congress appearance at Leicester, when she again addressed an audience of young women and girls.[80]

Work for the Church had also begun to offer opportunities for the employment of women with a sense of vocation, but the assumption that work on behalf of a good cause should be done gratis needed to be overcome. Writer and journalist Kathleen Lyttleton, a former poor law guardian, chair of the executive committee of the Manchester and Salford Trade Union Council, and the initiator of a branch of the Cooperative Women's Guild, spoke at the 1899 London Congress.[81] In a meeting devoted to payment for Church work, she asserted the need for a decent wage for women Church workers, especially as the work required expertise that could not be accomplished without training: 'payment of the trained church worker is permissible and even desirable'. She refuted the notion that the acceptance of payment for work was demeaning, and like Augusta Maclagan, challenged the traditional assumption that gentility was incompatible with paid work.[82]

Congress demonstrated a growing engagement with the realities of working-class life and some widening of class perspective. Miss Edith A. Barnett, who addressed a congress audience at Cardiff in 1889, echoed Mary Scharlieb in offering a challenge to middle-class complacency when she spoke in the section of the programme dedicated to 'The Church's Duty to the Working Classes'. She articulated some discomfort with a traditional patronizing stance that assumed social status as the requisite qualification for instructing those less socially advantaged. In her discussion of thrift, she pointed out the hypocrisy of middle-class speakers who preached to the working classes about it without exercising thriftiness themselves.[83] The theme of leading by example was still seen as an issue more than thirty years later. Lilian Faithfull's speech at the Eastbourne Congress of 1925 was reported by the *Taunton Courier and Western Advertiser* under the headline 'Society Women Pilloried'; the report noted that 'Miss Faithfull ... insisted that reform must come from the top. From those leaders of Society who despise and ignore their responsibilities'.[84]

Against an ongoing context of widely disseminated social commentary provided by writers such as Dickens, Kinsley, Mayhew and later Booth and Rowntree, attention focused on the conditions experienced by workers. At Hull in 1890, the Reverend Goodwin illustrated the long hours and arduous conditions experienced by female retail workers, who were not covered by 1878 Factory Act. He elaborated on the plight of shop girls, who were 'kept at work until 9.30 and 10 pm on Saturdays until 11.30, and even midnight'. It was common practice to forbid shop assistants from sitting down whilst working:

> Imagine the distress of these poor girls at the end of a long day, their limbs aching, their feet swollen and sore through standing, their brows throbbing under the monotonous routine of business, whilst the atmosphere, foul with gas, becomes more asphyxiating as the long hours roll on.[85]

Goodwin went on to present statistics from the Early Closing Association which claimed that as a result of these unhealthy conditions 'as many as 1,000 lives are sacrificed annually in London alone'.[86] He alerted his audience to forthcoming proposals for legislation on weekly half holidays for shop assistants and the Early Closing Bill, and urged his female audience to raise awareness of the plight of shop assistants in the interests of shaping public opinion.

Just in case the physical suffering experienced by workers was not enough to stir the conscience of his audience, Goodwin also presented a moral argument for the improvement of shop girls' conditions with a reminder that responsibility for their plight might lie uncomfortably close to home. He argued that arduous conditions left shop girls too fatigued to attend Sunday Church services. Moreover, lack of leisure time until after dark made them vulnerable to sexual predators.

> It is a pastime for a man who calls himself a gentleman to talk to a pretty girl behind the counter, to meet her by appointment when her work is done, to take her to the music hall, to treat her to the Sunday excursion. We know too well what may be the sequel of the sad story.... What if your son, or your son's friend, or the agreeable person who took your daughter into dinner last night was the villain who worked her fall?[87]

Two years later, at Folkestone, the plight of working women was again on the agenda, but here the perspective had moved towards the representation of working women by those more closely aligned with their experience. There was a shift towards emphasis on self-help through the collective action and organization of working women. Amie Hicks, secretary of the London Rope Makers Union, discussed the problems of poor working conditions and called for 'Christian assemblage' to help.[88] Another well-known advocate for improving working women's conditions, Clementina Black, secretary in 1886 of the Women's Protective and Provident League, the precursor of the Women's Trade Union, shared the platform and also spoke on similar themes.[89] In a different section of the programme headed 'Thrift and The Poor Law', Amie Hicks returned to the platform to point out the hardship encountered by working women who were unable to afford compulsory subscriptions towards the Poor Law.[90] The theme of self-help was also exemplified by Miss Elizabeth A. Tournier, the current president of the 'Women's Co-operative Guild', who spoke about the aspirations of the co-operative movement for social and educational improvement. She emphasized the practical economic advantages of profit sharing, whereby the dividends accrued through purchases were a means of saving, and she encouraged her audience to join a cooperative branch.[91]

The regulation of working conditions and the field of employment, as with initiatives in social care, educational provision and local governance, offered opportunities for women to demonstrate professional expertise and move into public service. Author, trades unionist and campaigner for workers' protection Gertrude Tuckwell is a distinguished representative of this trajectory. Her appearances on the platform between 1902 and 1911 also illustrate congress as a showcase for women participants who demonstrated an increasing breadth of professional expertise.[92] Tuckwell's contributions also exemplify the congress ambience shifting towards a more inclusive and empathetic approach to poverty and social justice that was mindful of working-class voices and recognized the need for systematic legislative interventions.

Figure 6.1 Gertrude Mary Tuckwell by Bassano Ltd. Source: By permission National Portrait Gallery.

Tuckwell's activism and stance on social justice had been informed by her upbringing as the daughter of Rosa Strong, and William Tuckwell, a clergyman and school master, whose advocacy for Christian Socialist ideals and practice was described in *Memoirs of a Radical Parson*, the autobiography dedicated to his daughter. Her mother's sister Emilia, an art historian, writer and trade union activist, who from 1885 was married to the radical Liberal politician Sir Charles Dilke, was also a key figure in steering Tuckwell towards activism in the field of employment. Emilia, then Pattinson, had, from 1874, been active in the Women's Protective and Provident League, a forerunner of the Women's Trade Union League. In 1886 she took over as president of the league following the death of its founder Emma Smith Patterson. It was through her aunt that Tuckwell was introduced to women members of the London School Board, an occurrence which prompted her to train as an elementary school teacher, a role which gave her experience of slum life in Liverpool and with working-class children in Chelsea which affirmed her interest in the improvement of social conditions. She went on to serve as secretary to the Christian Social Union Research Committee between 1889 and 1911. From 1893 Tuckwell also acted as secretary to her aunt, a position that placed her in the political milieu of the Dilke household, and it was the following year that she published *The State and Its Children* which advocated the prohibition of part-time child labour 'the little half timer toiling in the mill'.[93] During this period Tuckwell served as Honorary Secretary of the Women's Trade Union League and edited its journal. Following the death of her aunt in 1904, Tuckwell took over as president of the League from January 1905. 1898 had seen the genesis of the Industrial Law Committee, an offshoot to the Women's Trade Union League, which given that factory inspectors were insufficient in numbers, aimed to highlight hazardous working conditions and raise awareness of workers' rights under legislation, enforce employment law and protect workers from intimidation by unscrupulous employers. Tuckwell served on the first management committee and was active in campaigns that exposed the perils of phosphorous for women match makers, and lead poisoning for pottery workers.

Like poor law guardians, Marianne Mason and Mary Clifford, Tuckwell saw working to improve conditions, and attempts towards the betterment of society as a Christian duty, and she used congress as a platform to disseminate her views. The Northampton congress of 1902, where the implications of scripture for the conduct of economic and social affairs were in the spotlight, provided an ideal opportunity to share her Christian concerns and the findings of research into working conditions. In her debut speech she spoke as a representative of the Industrial Law Committee on the need to enforce safety legislation in the workplace. After flattering her audience for their compassion for the lives of workers in sickness and death, she then worked to stir their consciences on the issue of working conditions. Like Revered Goodwin, she conjured a vivid picture of distress and sought to speak on behalf of workers:

> I will try to call up for you the voices which are always sounding in the ears of myself and those who work with me among the workers in our factories and laundries. First, the voices of those maimed and mutilated by machinery … Six accidents were brought to us from a laundry the other day. All of them mutilated and maimed so that their earning capacity was ever diminished. Not long ago our attention was called to a factory in which a woman had been crushed to death, and when the body was carried to the hospital in the hope that life was not extinct, we found that the name the factory went by among the medical students was "the slaughter house".[94]

Tuckwell continued with examples of workers 'suffering from insanitary conditions', 'ankle deep in water' and 'hidden in rooms working seventeen hours a day including holidays and even Christmas day'. Moreover, they were 'earning a wage below the level at which they can subsist and from it are taken deductions for water, for gas, for machinery, for the doctor, for the hospitals'.[95] For Christian Socialist Tuckwell, exploited workers were condemned by poverty to ill health, bad housing and exclusion from respectability. It was her view that workers' material deprivation needed to be addressed before moral and spiritual progress could be achieved.

> You might as well talk of purity to the women who have been reared in the indiscriminate indecency of our overcrowded towns as talk of a spiritual life, of thrift, and any other virtue to these victims of civilization. So we build penitentiaries for those who need never have been impure, hospitals for those who might never have been sick, and workhouses for those whom we have never enabled to earn a living wage.[96]

She drew on biblical authority to inform her audience of their responsibility to ensure that existing laws were enforced and that further legislation should be introduced for categories of worker or trades that were as yet unregulated.[97] The speech was well received in the *Church Times*, a paper that was not overly sympathetic to contributions from women speakers. However, the 'Special correspondent' commended Tuckwell for delivering 'a most effective paper on our social obligations … As an appeal to conscience it was one of the best things I have listened to for a long time'.[98]

In 1906, at Barrow-in-Furness, Tuckwell, who was now the president of the Women's Trade Union League and the Hon. Secretary of the Industrial Law Committee, took the platform on two occasions. The Church congress coincided with the Sweated Industries Exhibition at the Guildhall in London. The exhibition, which was opened by Princess Henry of Battenberg, featured women workers demonstrating their trades alongside documentation of their pay and conditions, attracted considerable public attention and resulted in the formation of the Anti-Sweating League, a non-party pressure group that campaigned against a variety of exploitative employment practices, typified by long hours, insanitary conditions and above all wages insufficient to sustain a minimum level of health and tolerable life.[99] Tuckwell, who two years later contributed a chapter on 'The regulation of women's work' to the volume *Women and Industry from Seven Points of View*, which catalogued varieties of sweated trades, used the congress platform to publicize the issues that the league sought to redress.[100] She spoke to a mixed audience in a main agenda session under the heading 'The Church and the People'. In a speech that, according to the *Church Times*, was 'warmly applauded', she focused on the 'Sweated Industries', typically, but not exclusively, trades such as sewing or matchbox making, that were pursued by home workers for minimal wages, calculated on the piecework system – that is, payment by amount of output.[101] She drew the attention of her audience to harrowing conditions experienced by home workers for whom one room served as 'the living room, the sleeping room, the kitchen, the nursery, the laundry, the hospital, often the mortuary as well'. Her intention was once again to rouse her audience to witness their faith by action: 'Any Christian revival must go hand in hand with social reform.'[102] Speaking to an audience of women, she again focused on the sweated trades and the hardship of inadequate wages. She recommended that her audience read the penny pamphlet on the report of the inspection of factories written by Miss Lucy Deane, one of the first women to be appointed HM Factory Inspector of factories.[103] Echoing the sentiment she had expressed in the main meeting and at Northampton, she claimed that: 'For those on whom the burden of work presses there is no leisure and no time to think of things spiritual or to live the life which is beautiful.'[104]

Congress was suspended for the duration of the 1914–18 war, but the outbreak of hostilities provided increased opportunities for women to demonstrate their capabilities in official positions. Post-war legislation reflected an acknowledgement of women's contribution to public life. The landmark Sex Disqualification (Removal) Act of 1919 allowed not only categories of mature women to vote in parliamentary elections but also permitted them to serve on juries and as Justices of the Peace. Congress stalwart Gertrude Tuckwell, one of first seven appointees to the bench, and founder of the magistrates association, is a prominent example of the association of this civic service with distinction in philanthropy and the voluntary sector. Tuckwell, whose contribution to civic life and public welfare was acknowledged with the award of Companion of Honour in 1930, was not alone amongst JPs at congress, nor was she the only speaker to have her achievement marked by the bestowal of a public honour. At the 1919 Leicester congress, women holding public honours were represented by housing expert Henrietta Barnett CBE, and youth worker Augusta Deane OBE who spoke in the meeting for 'Young Women and Girls', a session to which Lilian C. Barker also contributed.[105] Barker was at this time employed by the Training Department of the Ministry of Labour. She had also served the London County Council education department as the director of its Women's Institute. In 1915 Barker had been appointed to the post of Lady Superintendent of the Woolwich Arsenal, where she was responsible for the discipline, welfare and productivity of 30,000 women munitions workers. For this contribution to the war effort Barker had been honoured with the CBE in 1917. Although, like Tuckwell, Barker had begun her career as an elementary teacher and was a practising Christian, she differed from Tuckwell and other contributors to congress in having working-class origins. The daughter of a tobacconist, Barker's achievement of leadership in public service was remarkable at a time when authority was usually vested in those of higher class. This was also the case at congress where her appearance as a figure of authority signals her exceptional ability rather than a widening in perspective of congress and the Church towards social inclusion.[106]

In addition to demonstrating career trajectories from voluntarism to public service and professionalism, congress showcased women who were politically active. The obituary of Mrs Griffith, who addressed the 1923 congress on the inadequacy of rural housing, illustrates the breadth of activity typical of speakers. Under the heading 'Death of Lady J.P.' The *Lincolnshire Echo* noted that

> Mrs. Griffith was an expert educationist. She was at one time on the staff of Cheltenham Ladies' College. She was a member of the Council of Church Schools, governor of several public schools, and one of the Kesteven County Council representative governors of the Bourne Secondary School. A prominent churchwoman, she addressed the Church Congress at Plymouth last year, and had the distinction being the only lady to address the Lincoln Diocesan Conference. In politics she was an active supporter of the Conservative cause, and was an effective platform speaker. She was a member of the Executive of the Rutland and Stamford Division Conservative Council. During the war she

acted as a V.A.D. nurse at the Bourne Hospital, and subsequently at Devonshire House. In the spring of this year Mrs. Griffith appointed magistrate for the parts of Kesteven, and attended the Bourne Sessions. She was 61 years of age.[107]

Whilst it was clear progress had been made, speakers felt that more women should be active participants in the political process. At the Birmingham congress of 1921, Gertrude Tuckwell addressed delegates in the section devoted to 'New Responsibilities in Church and State'. According to the *Hartlepool Northern Daily Mail* she claimed that: 'women had become tired of being the power behind the throne. Now she had come into her own, and the more working women came forward to stand for local bodies and parliament the better it would be'.[108] Reporting on the Church congress at Exeter in 1923, *The Vote*, 'the non-party organ of the Women's Freedom League' which concerned itself with women's political activism and civil rights, noted not just that Exeter, the congress location, had a woman MP, but reported that Alderman Clara Winterbotham JP, the former Mayor of Cheltenham, was a speaker. She shared the platform with Mrs (later Dame) Beatrix Hudson Lyall CBE JP, who, in addition to work for the War Savings Committee and election (as a Conservative) to the London County Council, was a distinguished leader in the Mothers' Union. According to *The Vote*, both 'stirred up their hearers to do more for Municipal and Parliamentary Government'.[109] *The Common Cause* was more forthright and reported that: 'Mrs. Hudson Lyall, C.B.E., J.P., gave her hearers a good drubbing down for their apathy towards the local civic life of their districts, and urged them to come forward for service as councillors, guardians, etc'.[110]

Conclusion

The congress period up to, and immediately following the First World War, coincided with a period of change in which rights to citizenship were asserted, and incremental progress was made towards the achievement of civil rights for women, and thereby, the possibilities for (some) women to gain access to power were enlarged. Class, working life and social justice were also in focus. A key strand represented at congress in this period is the move from voluntarism to professionalism. The congress years between 1890 and 1913 saw the increase of women who could be considered 'professionals' gaining access to the platform. Professionalism is a contested concept that requires definition.[111] It is perhaps helpful to think in terms of attributes of professionalism for this circumvents the restriction of a definition based exclusively on payment. Acknowledging attributes of professionalism accords varieties of capital as conceptualized by that include social capital from association, symbolic capital derived from the possession of less tangible qualities and, relevant to the idea of professionalism, capital derived from the possession of knowledge delineated with the field, medical expertise for example. This conceptualization accommodates congress women, many of whom had expert knowledge and were recognized for possessing it, in ways that did not necessarily involve financial remuneration. It also allows the trajectory of individual agents and women collectively, from 'patronage' philanthropy via organized collective voluntarism to state-endorsed positions, to be conceived of in terms of the transaction and acquisition of capital towards field position. This trajectory of change towards women's engagement is bound up with the negotiation, modification or conservation of the doxa, that is, those assumptions about knowledge, values, categories of person, codes of behaviour, possibilities for action and 'truth'.[112]

Congress provides examples of women sharing dispositions of habitus, whose horizon of possibilities was informed by notions of symbolic capital recognized within their social and religious milieu which oriented them towards, and authorized action aimed to promote the improvement of society. The uniting characteristic of congress women speakers, despite some differences of interpretation regarding implications for action, was the assumption that Christian witness was bound up with social reform. Congress also illustrates the expansion of recognized forms of capital that could secure access to the platform as a speaker, beyond the social and religious, to include field-specific capital – the technical expertise of the medical field for example. This transition is illustrated by Mary Clifford, Marianne Mason and Ellen Pinsent whose recognition for possessing symbolic (religious) capital accruing around service, duty and the willingness to engage with the unpleasant allowed entry into the field of voluntary public service. This enabled them to acquire field-specific capital in the form of expert knowledge into (in this instance) workhouse conditions, and this being recognized, transacted into higher field position in the form of remunerated positions or service in official roles. They exemplify access to power through obtaining positions in local government bodies and government commissions.[113] These trajectories are illustrated by other congress women who were elected members in local government or appointed as magistrates so becoming insiders in the application of the law if not as yet lawmakers. Augusta Deane, who gained employment in the Ministry of Labour, and Louise Creighton, who contributed to the Royal Commission on Venereal Disease in 1913, provide further examples of the transition from service in philanthropic bodies at local level to official government-sponsored institutions or initiatives.

These trajectories from lower to higher field position coincide with spatial expansion from what Lofland conceives as the parochial sphere comprising networks of acquaintance and local activism outwards towards wider public exposure.[114] Congress can be perceived as a both parochial space in offering the 'seclusion' of dedicated spaces for women but also within the public sphere of bourgeois associational life – 'occasions where people meet together on the basis of their collective identities – as campaigners for a particular cause, for example'.[115] These circumstances were conducive to women who wished to advertise and validate their engagement with public affairs, without attracting controversy. Congress provided a space where their message was sanctified by association with the institutionally invested religious (and temporal) capital of the established Church. Congress speakers 'spoke for' the Church and thereby gained pedagogic authority and Church endorsement for their views. The enumeration of the official titles of speakers, 'Poor Law Guardian', School Board Member, was used to endorse their status and reciprocally demonstrate the power of congress to attract figures of authority and expertise. The presence of 'expert' women on the congress platform not only allowed them to exercise pedagogic action to persuade the audience of the validity of their individual views and causes but also served to educate the audience towards enlarged notions of the roles and capacities of women by normalizing the presentence of authoritative expert women.

Congress speakers were unequivocal in asserting a change in the doxa that allowed middle-class women (in particular the unmarried) to participation in the world of paid work, a perspective articulated by even the most conservative speakers such as Augusta Maclagan. However, whilst speakers included those distinguished for the possession of capital specific to fields such as medicine or employment, in the context of congress, they continued to draw on assertions of socially and religiously endorsed notions of capital pertaining to good womanhood. Doctors Mary Scharlieb and Kate Ravenhill drew on moral as much as medical knowledge; furthermore the subjects that they engaged with such as temperance and childcare were aligned with the traditional 'women's sphere', a stance that accords with Katherine Gleadle's observation that where women are focused on as a collective group and their contribution likely to be contested women's contributions tend to be 'more constrained.... even progressive women tended to replicate normative understandings of the masculine public sphere'.[116] Women's aspirations as articulated at congress were for inclusion and participation in public affairs. Traditional assumptions of good womanly capital accruing around piety, service and nurture were not confronted but drawn upon to endorse women's claims to entry into positions of official authority or distinction in areas of expertise associated with poverty, health and labour, overlapping categories that can be conceived of as components within a broader field of public welfare administration which as a branch of government sits within the wider field of power.

In addition to gender, the trajectory of women moving from traditions of philanthropy via organized voluntarism to official positions or 'professional' roles goes alongside some realignment of the doxa on issues accruing around work, poverty, class and social justice. Women at congress represented a diversity of perspectives, and it is wrong to homogenize them into a singular category. The shared habitus of congress women prioritized religiously motivated and authorized service towards the improvement of society. It informed assumptions about certain categories of person such as the mentally incapacitated, as in the case of Ellen Pinsent, or the rehabilitation of workhouse girls into respectable citizens advocated by Marianne Mason. Yet, speakers at congress exemplify changes in perspectives in relation to class from the somewhat authoritarian patronage exemplified by Mason, Clifford and Pinsent to the Christian compassion of Tuckwell. A perspective that emphasized systemic economic causes of poverty and realigned the association of poverty with the moral failings of the poor to the moral failings of those with power to 'influence' these conditions. Clearly Gertrude Tuckwell exemplifies pedagogic action towards raising awareness of unacceptable conditions and the presence of other speakers with similar perspectives such as Reverend Goodwin, Clementina Black and women aligned with the cooperative moment signals a shift in assumptions on class and poverty. However, working-class voices remained a rarity on congress platforms and, as with gender, direct confrontation of existing sites of power was avoided. There remained some vestiges of patronage towards the lower classes which envisaged power (rightly) vested the middle and upper class, who should justify their dominant position by the exercise responsibility for social cohesion and reform. A perspective as articulated by Lilian Faithfull, in her assertion that reform must come from the top.[117] Despite the opportunity provided by congress to showcase women's talents and disseminate their views, and the exploration of social responsibility engaged in by speakers, by the end of the congress period the achievement of gender equality and social justice remained aspirations.

7

The Legacy of Congress – Women, Space and Place

The six decades in which congresses took place coincided with changes in women's lives that affected their economic and legal status, educational opportunities, access to the professions and participation in public life and social institutions. This chapter considers the legacy of congress and draws on the spatial turn in scholarship, and the concepts suggested by Bourdieu, to reflect on congress as a space for women, both intimate and public, in which women's spatial aspirations in the Church, society, nation and empire played put.

Jürgen Habermas and Henri Lefebvre have influenced feminist geographers and historians interested in women's agency.[1] In the field of religion too the work of Kim Knott exemplifies the recognition that the examination of spatial practice is a potentially fruitful analytical strategy.[2] Lefebvre's conceptualization of space through the triad of actual spaces, spatial practice and representational spaces applies to the Church congress as a 'conceptualized' space both physical and symbolic, mediated by, and mediating of social and gender practice. This also resonates with Michel Foucault's notion of the heterotopia, a concept that has been used as an analytical lens in the study of religion and space by Carmen Mangion.[3] Kathryne Beebe, Angela Davis and Katherine Gleadle in their synthesis of trends in feminist scholarship conclude that: 'gendered and political meanings of space – be that space domestic or public, rural or urban, real or imagined, or a combination of all these and more – are fashioned through the historical actors as they negotiate through space and time'.[4]

According to Linda McDowell, 'places are made through power relations which construct the rules which define boundaries. These boundaries are both social and spatial – they define who belongs to a place and who may be excluded, as well as the location or site of the experience'.[5] Bourdieu uses the term field, a spatial metaphor, to conceptualize political, economic or cultural arenas in which identity is established, agency is enacted and competition for ascendancy on the part of individuals or groups takes place.[6] Religion fits the category of field as it defines forms of knowledge and asserts value. Within the field competition over what knowledge is most esteemed takes place in order to legitimize and uphold the ascendancy of its owners.[7] This analysis applies to the efforts of the Anglican Church to assert its doctrine and practice as superior to other denominations. The congress can be seen as an initiative towards this and thus accords with Lefebvre's understanding of the 'Production of Space' as a means towards control and domination and also to Doreen Massey's interpretation of spaces/place as a theatre of conflict.[8]

Competition for orthodoxy and the ascendancy of ideas and those professing them occurred not just between denominations but within Anglicanism itself. Congress was instigated under Archbishop John Bird Sumner to promote adherence to the Anglican Church as, what Bourdieu would term the 'ownership of the goods of salvation', was being contested by rival denominations in the religious field.[9] Congress was also intended to promote unity within the Anglican Church at a time when differences between High Church Tractarians and Low Church evangelicals on appropriate form of worship had engendered bitter division, resulting in legal disputes and at worst defections to Roman Catholicism. This conciliatory and cohesive aspiration is reflected in the stated intention to avoid theological topics and in the encouragement of the participation of laymen, and the attendance of laywomen and the working classes. The established status of Anglicanism aligned it with the apparatus of the state and had accorded it preferential treatment in law and hegemony in higher education. However, the relaxation of restrictions on other denominations and pressure towards disestablishment in Ireland and Wales stimulated the Church to assert and legitimize its embeddedness in the fabric of national life and civic and secular institutions. The organization of congress on an annual basis, its location in different towns, the occupation of significant public buildings, the involvement of local government dignitaries and the pageantry of the parade, a conspicuous visual presence on the streets which brought congress to non-attending members of the public, can be seen as a response to this concern. The topics for discussion on congress agendas demonstrated the intention to engage with, and air, the perspectives of 'church people' on social issues such as poverty, work, leisure, health and 'race'. The role of women was also of topical interest. Ideas concerning the role and capabilities of women both in religion and other fields were also tested and contested at congress by women seeking to improve their position in the Church, in professions, as citizens or in politics.

The reach of congress was extended spatially and temporally by the exploitation of publicity, encouragement of press coverage and the creation of an archive through the publication of the official congress record. Congress as a temporarily convened, moveable, symbolic yet physically located space, which sought to uphold the ascendancy of the Established Anglican Church, an institution aligned with temporal as well as spiritual power, accords with Lefebvre's interpretation of an aspect of the *'Production of Space'* as a means towards control and domination.[10] As an occasion that drew together people who considered themselves members of the Church of England and attracted numerous groups representing diverse but not necessarily religious interests, congress also has characteristics of what Katherine Gleadle terms 'the public sphere of bourgeois associational life – occasions where people meet together on the basis of their collective identities – as campaigners for a particular cause, for example'.[11]

Bourdieu conceptualizes spheres of activity and interest as fields a categorization that encompasses religion. The attributes that help secure the success or dominance achieved by individuals or interest groups in the field are conceived of as capital. Capital includes non-material symbolic properties that individuals (and groups) seek to acquire and which may accrue from, and be transacted for, a better position in the field and thus power, authority or advantage.[12] Most pertinent to unpicking the trajectories of women represented at congress through space and place are Bourdieu's categories of social capital, and cultural capital; however, economic and political capital should not be discounted. Social capital refers to lasting personal relations, and networks to which an individual connects. Cultural capital may be embodied in individual persons, institutionalized in organizations such as the established Anglican Church which can bestow advantage or prestige, or objectified in things or locations invested with meaning and value.[13] Recognized capital assets within the field such as religious piety may endow the individual pedagogic authority the right to speak with institutional endorsement in and for the field. Embodied attributes, such as 'race' and as in the case of women congress speakers (the impediment of) gender (and advantage of) class, mediate capital.

The concept of reproduction, Bourdieu's theoretical stance on how groups, institutions or individuals invested with power seek to uphold their position of advantage and to maintain dominance, is also relevant to analysing women's access to congress and the diverse fields associated with it. Reproduction seeks to legitimize the authority and advantage of the dominant group. It is achieved through pedagogic action by individuals, aligned with or speaking for a site of power, or ongoing pedagogic work by institutions such as the Church, or societal structures, such as the family. Both involve 'educational' action to normalize assumptions of what, according to the arbitrary cultural preferences of the dominant group, is of value or conversely unacceptable.[14]

The first of Bourdieu's triad of thinking tools, habitus, informs a sense of place and horizons of possibility. It relates both to individual agents and groups, and engages with durable dispositions and habits of mind informed by the pedagogic work not just of institutions, but of family and social interactions.[15] It informs assumptions of social reality and social practice.[16] A conceptualization that accords with Judith Butler's understanding that: 'identities become intelligible through the repetition of normalizing assertions made within discourse'.[17] The term 'doxa' refers to the social and cultural messages and practices within habitus which concern the apparent self-evidence of social reality which in its habitual familiarity goes unquestioned and frames notions of opportunity and worth. However, although the dispositions of habitus are durable, it may be subject to experiences that modify its structures and thereby mediate doxa.[18] Congress was a forum in which the negotiation of assumptions as to the capabilities of women played out towards mediating the gendered doxa and expanding women's horizons of opportunity.

Despite differences of opinion on 'correct' forms of worship and amongst other issues, the role of women, congress organizers and attendees from the middle classes shared dispositions of habitus in which notions of value were informed by religious affiliation, and social convention. Desirable capital assets (and conversely undesirable attributes) accruing to women were informed by the Anglican doctrine of subordination that drew on the biblical interpretation of St Paul to endorse the paternal authority of men over fallible women, rightly contained within the family and aligned to the domestic sphere. Notions of gendered difference were further elaborated by the assertion of women's heightened religious sensibility by William Wilberforce and endorsed by the cultural commentary of John Ruskin that emphasized women as nurturing moral exemplars. Popular sentimentalized tropes, described by Eileen Janes Yeo as the hegemonic discourse of motherhood, also served to reinforce a doxa of difference.[19]

Discourse about what women could or could not do, and the spaces they were entitled to occupy played out repeatedly at congress whether in allocated or informal places of assembly, explicit discussion or obliquely through the subjects taken by speakers or the fields and expertise that they represented. Weymouth provides an example: unsurprisingly Mary Sumner of the Mothers' Union spoke on 'Character Training' but Elizabeth Wordsworth, the principal of Oxford College Lady Margaret Hall, took the subject of 'Amusement', and Mary

Clifford, an expert in poor law administration, spoke on 'home life'.[20] Whatever conclusions were drawn from assumptions about the nature of women, and there is repeated evidence of this at congress, the preoccupation with difference was a persistent theme.

Notions of difference were evident in the allocation of space/access to space. Doreen Massey's analysis of spatial allocation as control is illustrated by the initial containment of women spectators in the gallery at the 1861 congress.[21] The introduction of meetings for women too, whilst offering opportunity, also reflected gendered notions of difference in the allocation of space. However, place was not fixed at congress, where over time women moved from peripheral social association to inclusion on official agendas as expert speakers and established their own exclusive spaces beyond congress.

Social collective identity was as much a part of congress for its middle-class members as religious affiliation. In addition to the official programme congress offered space for social interaction, which was inclusive of, and it could be argued dependent on, the presence of women. Organized events with social cachet, notably the mayor's conversatzione and informal events such as the congress exhibition and gatherings for church services, gave opportunities for meeting. Furthermore congress served as the focus for the reunion of friends and acquaintances. Women's presence may also suggest an acknowledgement that they were a significant presence in congregations and as supporters of the pastoral work of the Church. The visibility of women endorsed the appearance of the paternalistic Church as benign: an institution in which Christian men were protectors and providers rather than oppressors, chivalrous towards women, and kind husbands and fathers. Tropes evident in the writing of Mary Sumner and the initiatives of purity campaigner Jane Ellice Hopkins, whose White Cross army drew in men, pledged to chastity and respect for women.[22] Women's presence may also have served as what Simon Morgan would interpret as a civilizing influence,[23] an inhibitor to the articulation of dissent, a plausible application to congress given that differences on doctrine had engendered bitter controversy, exemplified in its most extreme form by the antics of John Kensit's Wycliffe crusaders. However, the lady so infuriated by a Wycliffe protester that she knocked off his top hat which was clearly not conforming to gendered expectations of decorum and restraint.[24]

For the first two decades of congress women remained largely a visible rather than an audible presence. It was through social and familial connections (frequently clerical) that women initially gained access to the platform. For spouses, unmarried daughters and sisters of clergy their role extended to the discharge of pastoral duties to support parochial ministry. These might include dispensing charity, Sunday school teaching or as in the case of MU founder Mary Sumner, who also served as church organist, running a mothers' meeting. Activities such as 'Church work' were recognized as laudable and accrued symbolic capital to their performers. The same principles applied to the wives of elite clergy as the diaries of Laura Ridding and Louise Creighton illustrate.[25]

Jane Rendall's view that spaces involving degrees of public exposure relate to gendered codes and behaviours applies to Victorian phenomenon of female philanthropy.[26] Philanthropic activity, which proliferated during the earlier decades of congress, was accessible because the supposed nurturing duties and exemplary qualities accruing to ladies were seen to extend beyond family and household staff into the public sphere particularly to groups perceived to be in deficit such as 'fallen women', the poor and 'pagan' unbelievers overseas. These 'Angels out of the house' were,[27] although doing public work, shielded from the glare of immodest exposure because they were performing a 'caring' role, frequently with religious endorsement. Moreover, in addressing those of perceived lesser status they were not exceeding boundaries of gendered authority.

Lyn H. Lofland's understanding of the parochial realm as a community space which comprises acquaintance and relationships regarded by contemporaries as less publicly exposed than the wider public sphere applies to congress, a space sheltered under the umbrella of the Church.[28] The pioneer women speakers at congress were recognized for embodying varieties of religious, cultural and social capital, such as association with figures of authority in the Church, or philanthropic activism. The congress of 1882 that introduced a meeting targeted at women was also innovative in featuring women platform speakers. Both were recognized for their philanthropic work: Agnes Weston for campaigning for sailors' welfare and Mrs Papillon as an advocate for the Church of England Young Women's Help Society. The women's meeting offered a less exposed space than the main agenda meetings. Even so Mary Sumner's debut as an impromptu speaker at the 1885 congress, which instigated the diocesan Mothers' Union, was reported as a valorous act of public exposure. Sumner made sure to point out that she had not transgressed the boundaries of feminine authority by noting that she had the approval of her friend Bishop Wilberforce and her husband the Archdeacon of Winchester.[29]

From the 1885 congress the MU and the GFS, an official Anglican women's organization since 1875, became a regular feature of congress, easy to accommodate in the concessionary space of the women's meeting as they offered no direct challenge and indeed appeared to endorse assumptions concerning women's role and the appropriate ways in which it should be performed. However, both organizations went on to expand their presence in spaces beyond the confines of congress. Demonstration and assertion of esteemed attributes framed within Church values, notably chastity and the notion of 'woman's mission' as caring moral exemplars transacted into pedagogic authority for leaders and by association their organizations whose members were obliged to conform to standards of behaviour perceived as exemplifying the highest standards of womanhood. This and the social capital of royal patronage and endorsement by distinguished churchmen helped the MU and GFS establish their own discrete institutional space and opened the way for occupying high-profile iconic spaces invested with the highest cultural capital, notably the Royal Albert Hall and St Paul's Cathedral.

The MU and GFS may have been complicit with the notion of a women's sphere but from the start their interests in issues that affected women's lives necessarily extended beyond the domestic into public affairs. Moreover, they were insistent that women as homemakers and 'mothers of empire' contributed as citizens to a well-ordered society. MU and GFG leaders drawing on the capital of their leaders as bishops' wives, and philanthropic activists within the shelter of the respectable institution of the Church, were able to enlarge their sphere of operations from parish drawing rooms to dioceses, the nation and then overseas, where they claimed pedagogic authority in colonies and contact zones.[30] The MU and GFS positioned themselves as imperial organizations and established branches in expatriate communities and regions where missionary work was undertaken.[31] Their publications celebrated overseas endeavour and used it to encourage members 'at home' to uphold the religious endeavour that they sought to promote.[32] This was reflected at congress where MU- and GFS-affiliated speakers with overseas interests such as Miss Kathleen Townend who visited India on behalf of the GFS and Lady Vincent Diocesan GFS President for northern and central Europe took the platform.[33]

Members of the MU and GFS were not the only women seeking to make space for themselves within the Church. Nor were they the only women with an interest in distant places. Congress provided spaces both official and unofficial in which women who sought a vocational role in the Church both at home and overseas communicated their views and sought to forward their aspirations. As with other spheres of women's activity this involved the negotiation of boundaries of authority, and here too doxic gendered notions of the capital accruing to 'good' women were utilized to support or restrict the extension of roles for women in the Church.

The imperial periphery and the spatial reach of the Church offered a legitimate sphere of interest for women interested in religious activism overseas. Congress attendees recognized the religious valour of the lady missionary whose symbolic capital was enhanced by gendered notions that assumed the heightened sensibilities and physical fragility of ladies. Preferences in religious belief and cultural practices, and racial prejudice aligned Anglicanism, assumed 'civilized behaviour' and whiteness with superior capital. Work for the Church performed by women regarded as exceptional in distant exotic spaces where the priority was conversion did not challenge the patriarchal hierarchy of the Church. Missionary work also offered exclusive opportunities for women missionaries as embodied by Editha Mulvany who spoke at congress on two occasions. As a member of the CEZMS her work was focused on women in the exclusionary space of the Zenana where her exercise of authority worked within gendered boundaries.[34] Mulvany presented Christianity as privileging women, a theme evident in the publications of the GFS and MU and expanded on in her congress speeches by celebrity traveller Isabella Bird Bishop whose pedagogic authority as an intrepid traveller and author was further enhanced by her advocacy for missionary activity.[35]

Closer to home where the institutional structure of the Church was more closely scrutinized the negotiation of authority was more complex. Congress featured several contributions from women who sought to pursue a religious vocation as deaconesses, notably Isabella Gilmore who repeatedly asserted the seriousness of her vocation and the need for training for it. Activism that focused on largely practical Church work did not contest gendered boundaries and deaconesses were clearly subject to masculine authority at parochial and diocesan level. However, it was not until 1920 that the deaconess as a universally endorsed, but still restricted in terms of spiritual authority, role in the pastoral ministry of the Church was affirmed at the Lambeth Conference.[36] The attention drawn to the work of deaconesses at congress by Gilmore and others may well have familiarized attendees with deaconesses as church workers and helped convince the bishops in conference at Lambeth that they had a useful role to perform within the Church.

The case of Anglican sisterhoods was more problematic. Here segregated space for women rather than being desirable was regarded with suspicion. Discussion at congress by clerics (not sisters who with one exception did not speak) focused on articulations of concern over women in seclusion in all female space devoid of paternal authority that in the earlier decades of congress were heightened by anti-Roman Catholic antipathy. Whilst congress provided a space for the airing of these anxieties it was time rather than discussion that alleviated concerns and allowed the Lambeth congress of 1897 to approve the revival of Anglican Brotherhoods and Sisterhoods.[37]

The 1913 congress brought women's spiritual aspirations to the fore but it was not until the period following the First World War that aspirations relating to preaching and ordination of women were articulated more overtly. However, these were in the peripheral spaces of congress rather than from the platform. Fringe meetings such as those organized by the League of the Church Militant addressed by notable campaigners Maude Royden, Edith Picton-Turbervill and E. Louie Marston Acres were a regular feature. Yet, despite the support of some clerics and sustained campaigning until the final congress of 1938 where Canon Shinwell said 'I think it is God's will that women as well as men should serve Him as priests ... Unless the difference in sexes implies some form of inferiority, I know no reason why women should not be admitted to the ministry of the Christian Church there was no movement to allow women a sacramental role'.[38] The sticking point appeared to centre around women's bodies and largely unvoiced taboos about them. Congress speaker Dr Leticia Fairfield, an invited contributor to the 1920 Lambeth Conference on women and ministry in the Church, commented privately that the barrier to women performing sacramental functions was due to prejudice relating to a perception of woman's 'ceremonial uncleanliness' due to menstruation.[39]

Ideas of gendered difference are also evident in the trajectories of women speakers who illustrate moves towards entry into professional space in education and beyond. However, what was voiced from the platform may not represent the full extent of women's aspirations. As Katherine Gleadle has noted women's contributions in a space where they are focused on as a collective group 'may be more constrained and more frequently contested', and she suggests that 'even progressive women tended to replicate normative understandings of the masculine public sphere'.[40] This can be seen in the way that developments in secondary and higher education were represented and asserted at congress. Advocacy for female educational space worked within embedded doxic notions of esteemed 'womanly' capital. Gender-exclusive girls' schools and women's colleges maintained an element of seclusion and their supporters insisted that curricula or the experience of communal association would not compromise the influence of family life and women's ability to perform the roles it demanded. It was of course helpful to secure the endorsement of patriarchal authority, especially if this was embodied in figures of social or religious distinction. The negotiation of university access for women was particularly delicate. Not only was it an encroachment into masculine space, the perceived dangers of women knowing too much and thereby overstepping the bounds of their authority resonated with traditional biblical interpretation and doxa that presumed intellectual activity overstretched women's 'natural' capacity and function for reproduction and childcare. A situation that explains both the appointment of Elizabeth Wordsworth, whose formidable scholarship was mediated by the capital of kinship with two distinguished bishops, and the religious rhetoric of obedience and submission she deployed in her platform speeches.[41]

It was in the field of education that women made early inroads into professionalization. This was achieved sooner than in other areas because authority operated within gendered boundaries, the power structure was women over girls. Elite headmistresses became a frequent adornment to congress platforms in a reciprocal exchange of capital whereby they as figures of distinction and as representatives of their institutions, repositories of cultural and social capital, such as Cheltenham Ladies' College and Lady Margaret Hall, enhanced the cultural claims of congress. Conversely they received the endorsement of the Church as institutions that upheld values agreeable to its members and which were therefore attractive as spaces for their daughters' education. The repeated exposure of headmistresses on congress platforms familiarized audiences with the presence of authoritative women speaking for the educational field and embedded the expectation that aspirational academic education for girls (albeit for the socially advantaged) was both normal and desirable.

The alignment of women with the domestic sphere and traditions of caring voluntarism can also be seen in the evolution of (remunerated) posts in welfare administration and roles in local government. Service towards reforming the poor, a recognized asset according to religiously framed notions of capital, was further enhanced by the acquisition of expertise in the field of welfare provision such as the knowledge of poor law administration or workhouse conditions exemplified by Marianne Mason and eugenicist and local government electee Ellen Pinsent. In the field of health too, women's contributions were coloured by moral concerns. Even Mary Scharleib, the eminent gynaecologist, focused on the perils of drinking alcohol.[42]

Interest in employment conditions, whilst still having a moral caring dimension, moved the sphere of operations of activists such as Gertrude Tuckwell into the public spaces of the factory and sweatshop. Moreover understanding the law, a field aligned with legislative power, gave Tuckwell the necessary pedagogic authority to address mixed audiences in main congress sessions and which later was transacted to secure access to the courtroom as a magistrate once the opportunity arose. Tuckwell was not alone in gaining access to spaces associated with power such as government commissions or the judiciary. Other women congress speakers endorsed with pedagogic authority from speaking in the sanctified space of congress moved into government service. Here Louise Creighton provides an example, a reputation gained in the voluntary sector as a contributor to congress and notably the NUWW qualified her for service in the 1913 Royal Commission on venereal disease. Her selection for a committee that was addressing such an unsavoury topic indicates how doxic assumption on appropriate subjects for women to address had enlarged since Jane Ellice Hopkins told her audience 'how much it pained her as a woman' to address the subject of prostitution although this was not the terminology she used.[43]

Congress was attended by women with allegiances to diverse philanthropic, political and religious organizations. These alliances were often multiple as in the case of Ellen Joyce active in the Primrose League, GFS, BWES and SACS or Mary Sumner of the GFS and MU. It provided formal spaces where advocacy for causes could be articulated by experts but also provided possibilities for contact points through committee work and social opportunities. In this way congress linked women in a communicative structure that facilitated the exchange of ideas.[44] The most striking example of the use of the congress as means towards the establishment of an exclusive 'space' for women is in the case of the National Union of Women Workers. Dubbed by the press the 'parliament of women',[45] the union, which lives on as the National Council of Women, sought to draw together diverse groups both voluntary and professional with the intention of coordinating and making more efficient the promotion of women's interests. There was an overlap of organizations attracted to the NUWW but the most significant correspondence between congress and the NUWW was in its personnel, notably Louise Creighton, the first president of the union, and Laura Ridding, who were instrumental in the establishment of the NUWW as a formalized body. The close correspondence between the format and protocols of NUWW conferences and the similar practice of recording and disseminating NUWW proceedings via publication suggests that the Church Congress provided a model if not a catalyst for the instigation of the NUWW.[46]

Whilst women participants at congress identifying as 'Churchwomen' may have been complicit in the will to perpetuate religious preferences, and uphold the ascendance of the Church in the social fabric and institutions of the nation, they could also simultaneously take different positions on the role of women in the Church, education and civil rights notably on the issue of suffrage. Congress contributors included, even before the achievement of the equal franchise, a late development in the history of congress, women engaged in party politics such as Laura Ridding and Lucy Cavendish whose male relatives held government posts, Louisa Knightley and Ellen Joyce of the Conservative Primrose League, and Ellen Pinsent who was elected as a Birmingham County Councillor. Amongst congress women were those whose position changed, notably Louise Creighton and Violet Markham who moved from vociferous anti-suffragist to MP. Whilst Markham's change of position can be attributed to pragmatism and circumstances, that is, being overtaken by legislative reform, Louise Creighton's change of heart appears, from her diary entries, to have come about through discourse with her friends amongst whom were congress contributors Kathleen Lyttelton and Laura Ridding.[47]

Whatever their views women speakers and activists associated with congress were politically engaged. Although political positions and views on suffrage were approached obliquely from the platform the peripheral spaces around congress such as the exhibition and fringe meetings timed and located to coincide with congress were used to promote various causes and were specifically targeted by the Church League for Women's Suffrage and League of the Church Militant where there was some overlap of membership.

One aspect of political engagement which did receive exposure on congress platforms was relations with other nations, dominions, colonies and contact zones. Missionary work in overseas locations had been a recurring feature at congress as the Church expanded its global horizons and in later congresses women speakers participated in sessions that engaged with the negotiation of relations with other nations and subject peoples.[48] Imperial advocacy was bound up with the prioritization of religious and cultural capital, and assumptions concerning 'race'. For keen patriotic imperialists such as Mary Sumner, Ellen Joyce and Louisa Knightley spreading the perceived benefits of Christianity legitimized imperial rule. Congress women were certainly invested in patriotism and the notion that their Christian country possessed not only the most desirable religious capital. They also regarded it as being most civilized notably in the treatment of women and possessing superior cultural capital.[49] Their beliefs in traditions of service and a duty to be outward-facing made it logical for them to answer what Laura Ridding articulated as 'The Call of Empire'.[50]

Women who were prominent at congress as speakers positioned themselves as stakeholders in society. They identified with Church and crown and sought inclusion into social institutions as respected contributing citizens, and an acknowledgement that their talents (even if gendered) were to be taken seriously. Largely conservative they were agents of what Bourdieu conceives of as reproduction in that they did not seek to overturn existing institutions but felt that an enlargement of participatory possibilities for them as women would help alleviate social problems such as poverty, intemperance, ill health and crime and thereby uphold family, nation and empire/the structures of society.[51]

Congresses both offered and reflected extended opportunities for women activists and professionals to assert their professional expertise towards a redefinition and expansion of 'woman's place'. The demise of dedicated women's sections and loss of impetus following the fracture of the First World War coincided with the achievement of significant progress towards participatory citizenship, if not full equality. Moreover, women working collectively had established their own spaces for articulation of their voices in public space at local, national and transnational scales through organizations, notably the MU, GFS and NUWW. Women speakers, despite their distinction, were of course a minority yet through the congress official record and consistent press coverage the views were disseminated to a wide audience both clerical and secular. Women in much greater numbers were a consistent presence in congress audience where dedicated sessions proved popular with working-class women as a respectable public space in which they could encounter authoritative women with professional expertise or other forms of distinction.[52]

At a time when opportunities for women were restricted congress served as a significant means for women activists and professionals to access the public sphere and demonstrate their competence in and commitment to civic like. In so doing they expanded doxic assumptions of what women might do and where they might do it. Yet despite the persistent efforts of women with an obvious vocation and a demonstrable record of service although stretched, the boundary to the ultimate pedagogic authority for women in the Church, that of priesthood, remained impermeable for many years. Despite the pioneering examples of other members of the worldwide Anglican communion, notably Canada which permitted the ordination of women in 1976 and women talking episcopal office in 1986, the Church of England ordained its first women priests in 1994 and consecrated its first woman bishop in 2015. Although this change was slow in coming a debt is owed to the women of congress who first articulated their spiritual aspirations and asserted with reason and restraint their credentials for service to the Church.

Notes

Introduction

1. Owen Chadwick, *The Victorian Church Part 2 1860–1901* (London: A. and C. Black, 1972), 241, 127, 361. Clergy Convocations were held at Canterbury from 1851 and York from 1860; See also Nigel Scotland, *John Bird Sumner: Evangelical Archbishop* (Leominster: Gracewing, 1995).
2. Charles Earle Raven, *The Eternal Spirit. An Account of the Church Congress Held at Southport, October, 1926* (London: Hodder and Stoughton, 1926).
3. *Jacksons Oxford Journal* 5 July 1862, 3.
4. *Yorkshire Post and Leeds Intelligencer* 15 October 1872, 7.
5. *Hampshire Advertiser* 11 October 1873, 7.
6. ARCC Stoke-Upon-Trent, 61–74.
7. ORCC Newcastle Upon Tyne.
8. ORCC Derby, 569–73. Sue Morgan, 'Faith Sex and Purity: The Religio-Feminist Theory of Ellice Hopkins', *Women's History Review* 1 (2000).
9. Janet Wootton, ed. *Women in Christianity in the Age of Empire: (1800–1920)* (London: Routledge, 2022); Sue Morgan and Jacqueline de Vries, eds. *Women, Gender and Religious Cultures in Britain, 1800–1940* (London: Routledge, 2010); Sean Gill, *Women and the Church of England: From the Eighteenth Century to the Present* (London: Society for Promoting Christian Knowledge, 1994); Gail Malmgreen, *Religion in the Lives of English Women, 1760–1930* (London: Croom Helm, 1986).
10. Susan Mumm, 'Women and Philanthropic Cultures', in *Women, Gender and Religious Cultures in Britain, 1800–1940* (London: Routledge, 2010), ed. Morgan and de Vries; A.G. Poole, *Philanthropy and the Construction of Victorian Women's Citizenship: Lady Frederick Cavendish and Miss Emma Cons* (Toronto: University of Toronto Press, 2014); Moira Martin, 'Single Women and Philanthropy: A Case Study of Women's Associational Life in Bristol, 1880–1914', *Women's History Review* 17, no. 3 (2008); Angela Woollacott, 'From Moral to Professional Authority: Secularism, Social Work, and Middle-Class Women's Self-Construction in World War I', *Journal of Women's History* 10, no. 2 (1988); Frank Prochaska, *The Angel out of the House: Philanthropy and Gender in Nineteenth-Century England* (Charlottesville and London: University of Virginia Press, 2002).

11 Brian Harrison, 'For Church Queen and Family; the Girls' Friendly Society 1874-1920', *Past and Present* 61 (1973); Cordelia Moyse, *A History of the Mothers' Union: Women Anglicanism and Globalisation, 1876-2008* (Woodbridge: Boydell Press, 2009); Mary Porter, Mary Woodward, and Horatia Erskine, *Mary Sumner Her Life and Work and a Short History of the Mothers' Union* (Winchester: Warren and Sons, 1921).

12 Serena Kelly, 'A Sisterhood of Service: The Records and Early History of the National Union of Women Workers', *Journal of the Society of Archivists* 14, no. 2 (1993).

13 Louise Creighton, 'What Women Can Do to Raise the Standard of Moral Life', *ORCC Exeter*, 245; Louise Creighton, *Memoir of a Victorian Woman: Reflections of Louise Creighton 1850-1936* (Bloomington and Indianapolis: Indiana University Press, 1994).

14 Lucy Bland, 'Purifying the Public World: Feminist Vigilantes in Late Victorian England', *Women's History Review* 1, no. 3 (1992).

15 Susan Mumm, *All Saints Sisters of the Poor an Anglican Sisterhood in the Nineteenth Century* (Woodbridge Suffolk: Church of England Record Society Boydell Press, 2001).

16 Brian Heeney, 'Women's Struggle for Professional Work and Status in the Church of England 1900-1930', *The Historical Journal* 26, no. 2 (1983); Jenny Daggers, 'The Victorian Female Civilising Mission and Women's Aspirations towards Priesthood in the Church of England', *Women's History Review* 10, no. 4 (2001); Janet Grierson, *The Deaconess* (London: CIO, 1981); Katharine Bentley Beauman, *Women and the Settlement Movement* (London: Radcliffe, 1996).

17 Brian Heeney, *The Women's Movement in the Church of England, 1850-1930* (Oxford: Clarendon, 1988); Sue Morgan, 'A "Feminist Conspiracy": Maude Royden, Women's Ministry and the British Press, 1916-1921', *Women's History Review* 22, no. 5 (2013); Timothy Willem Jones, '"Unduly Conscious of Her Sex": Priesthood, Female Bodies, and Sacred Space in the Church of England', *Women's History Review* 21, no. 4 (2012); Sheila Fletcher, *Maude Royden: A Life* (Oxford: Basil Blackwell, 1989).

18 Deirdre Raftery, 'Religions and the History of Education: A Historiography', *History of Education* 41, no. 1 (2012); Kristine Moruzi, *Constructing Girlhood through the Periodical Press, 1850-1915* (London: Routledge, 2012); James Albisetti, Joyce Goodman, and Rebecca Rogers, eds., *Girls' Secondary Education in the Western World from 18th to 20th Centuries*, 2014 ed. (New York: Palgrave, 2010); R. D. Anderson 'Women and Universities', in *European Universities from the Enlightenment to 1914* (Oxford Scholarship Online, [2004] 2010).

19 Anne Logan, 'Professionalism and the Impact of England's First Women Justices, 1920-1950', *The Historical Journal* 49, no. 3 (2006); Patricia Hollis, *Ladies Elect: Women in English Local Government, 1865-1914* (Oxford: Clarendon Press, 1989);

Helen Jones, *Women in British Public Life, 1914-1950: Gender, Power, and Social Policy* (Harlow: Longman, 2000).

20 Harold L. Smith, ed., *The British Women's Suffrage Campaign, 1866-1928* (Harlow: Longman, 2010).

21 Julia Bush, *Edwardian Ladies and Imperial Power* (London: Leicester University Press, 2000); Lisa Chilton, *Agents of Empire: British Female Migration to Canada and Australia, 1860s-1930* (Toronto and Buffalo: University of Toronto Press, 2007); Vron Ware, *Beyond the Pale: White Women, Racism and History* (London: Verso, 1992).

22 Sutapa Dutta, ed., *British Women Travellers: Empire and Beyond, 1770-1870* (London: Routledge, 2019); Mary Louise Pratt, *Imperial Eyes: Travel Writing and Transculturation* (London: Routledge, 1992); Billie Melman, *Women's Orients: English Women and the Middle East, 1718-1918: Sexuality, Religion and Work*, 2nd ed. (Basingstoke: Macmillan, 1995); Catherine Hall, *Civilising Subjects: Metropole and Colony in the English Imagination, 1830-1867* (Cambridge: Polity, 2002).

23 Martha Vicinus, *Independent Women: Work and Community for Single Women: 1850-1920* (London: Virago, 1985).

24 Lady Laura Ridding, 'The Early Days of the National Union of Women Workers', n.d, *Selborne Papers* (HRO); Serena Kelly, 'Ridding, Lady Laura Elizabeth', (Oxford Dictionary of National Biography, 2004); Sue Anderson-Faithful, *Mary Sumner, Mission, Education and Motherhood: Thinking a Life with Bourdieu* (Cambridge: Lutterworth, 2018).

25 Anna Davin, 'Imperialism and Motherhood', *History Workshop* 5 (1978); Lesley Hall, *Sex, Gender and Social Change in Britain since 1880* (Basingstoke: Macmillan, 2000); Lucy Bland, *Banishing the Beast: English Feminism and Sexual Morality 1885-1914* (London: Penguin, 1995); For a New Zealand/Aotearoa perspective see Angela Wanhalla, 'To "Better the Breed of Men": Women and Eugenics in New Zealand, 1900-1935', *Women's History Review* 16, no. 2 (2007).

26 Mary Scharlieb, *Womanhood and Race-Regeneration* (1912); Mary Scharlieb and I. Arthur Sibly, *Youth & Sex: Dangers and Safeguards for Girls & Boys* (London: T. C. & E. C. Jack Ltd., 1919); Greta Jones, 'Women and Eugenics in Britain: The Case of Mary Scharlieb, Elizabeth Sloan Chesser, and Stella Browne', *Annals of Science* 52, no. 5 (1995); Kate Mitchell, *The Drink Question: Its Social and Medical Aspects* (London: Swan Sonnenschein). http://anglicanhistory.org/bios/mscharlieb.html (Accessed 23 March 2022); Hollis, *Ladies Elect*, 276 and 145. Pinsent served on both the 1904 and 1908 Royal Commissions into the subject.

27 Katherine Gleadle, *Borderline Citizens: Women, Gender and Political Culture in Britain, 1815-1867* (Oxford: OUP/British Academy, 2009); Sarah May Richardson, *The Political Worlds of Women: Gender and Politics in Nineteenth Century Britain, Routledge Research in Gender and History* (New York: Routledge, 2013); Krista Cowman, *Women in British Politics, c.1689-1979* (London: Bloomsbury, 2010).

28 Poole, *Philanthropy and the Construction of Victorian Women's Citizenship*; Sheila Fletcher, *Victorian Girls: Lord Lyttelton's Daughters* (London: Phoenix, 2004); Serena Kelly, 'Lyttelton [Née Clive], (Mary) Kathleen', (*ODNB*, 2004).

29 Julia Bush, Edwardian Ladies and Imperial Power, '"The Right Sort of Woman": Female Emigrators and Emigration to the British Empire,1890–1910', *Women's History Review* 3, no. 3 (1994); 'Joyce, Ellen' (*ODNB*, 2006); Lisa Chilton, 'A New Class of Women for the Colonies: The Imperial Colonist and the Construction of Empire', *The Journal of Imperial and Commonwealth History* 31, no. 2 (2003).

30 Gertrude M. Tuckwell, Constance Isabella Stuart Smith, Mary R MacArthur, May Tennant, Nettie Adler, and Adelaide Mary Anderson, *Clementina Black, Women in Industry from Seven Points of View* (London: Duckworth and Co., 1908); Cathy Hunt, 'Gertrude Tuckwell and the British Labour Movement, 1891–1921: A Study in Motives and Influences', *Women's History Review* 22, no. 3 (2013); Liselotte Glage, *Clementina Black: A Study in Social History and Literature* (Heidelberg: Winter, 1981); Ruth Livesey, 'The Politics of Work: Feminism, Professionalisation and Women Inspectors of Factories and Workshops', *Women's History Review* 13, no. 2 (2004); Sheila Blackburn, '"No Necessary Connection with Homework": Gender and Sweated Labour, 1840–1909', *Social History* 22, no. 3 (1997).

31 Gillian Avery, 'Faithfull, Lilian Mary' (*ODNB*, 2004); Sara Delamont, 'Burstall, Sara Annie', (*ODNB*, 2011); Georgina Battiscombe, *Reluctant Pioneer: A Life of Elizabeth Wordsworth* (London: Constable, 1978).

32 John Sutherland, ed., *The Longman Companion to Victorian Fiction* (Harlow: Pearson Longman, 2009); Christopher Kent, 'Image and Reality: The Actress and Society', in *A Widening Sphere*, ed. Martha Vicinus (Indiana: Indiana University Press, 1977).

33 Margaret Keck and Kathryn A. Sikkink, *Advocacy Networks in International Politics Activists Beyond Borders* (Ithaca and London: Cornell University Press, 1998).

34 Barbara Bush, 'Feminising Empire: British Women's Activist Networks in Defending and Challenging Empire from 1918 to Decolonisation', *Women's History Review* 25, no. 4 (2016); Tanya Fitzgerald, 'Cartographies of Friendship: Mapping Missionary Women's Educational Networks in Aotearoa/New Zealand 1823–40', *History of Education* 32, no. 5 (2003).

35 Linda Eisenmann, 'Creating a Framework for Interpreting US Women's Educational History: Lessons from Historical Lexicography', *History of Education: Journal of the History of Education Society* 30, no. 5 (2001).

36 Agency is understood as the capacity to act towards the realization of aims within and across private and public space. Sue Anderson-Faithful, 'Aspects of Agency: Change and Constraint in the Activism of Mary Sumner, Founder of the Anglican Mothers' Union', *Women's History Review* (2017).

37. Joan Wallach Scott, 'Gender: Still a Useful Category of Analysis?', *Diogenes* (2010). http://dio.sagepub.com/content/57/1/7.refs.html (Accessed 20 October 2020); Sheila Rowbotham, 'The Trouble with Patriarchy', in *The Feminist History Reader*, ed. Sue Morgan (London: New York: Routledge, 2007); John Tosh, *Manliness and Masculinities in Nineteenth-Century Britain: Essays on Gender, Family, and Empire* (Harlow: Pearson Longman, 2005).
38. Sue Morgan, *Women, Religion, and Feminism in Britain, 1750–1900* (Basingstoke: Palgrave Macmillan, 2002), 11.
39. David Cannadine, *Class in Britain* (New Haven and London: Yale University Press, 1998).
40. Linda Kerber, 'Separate Spheres, Female Worlds, Woman's Place; the Rhetoric of Womens' History', *Journal of American History* 75, no. 1 (1988); Amanda Vickery, '"Golden Age to Separate Spheres" a Review of the Categories and Chronology of English Women's History', in *Gender and History in Western Europe*, ed. Robert Shoemaker and Mary Vincent (London: Addison-Wesley Longman, 1998); Sue Morgan, 'Theorising Feminist History: A Thirty Year Retrospective', *Women's History Review* 18, no. 3 (2009).
41. Linda McDowell, *Gender, Identity and Place: Understanding Feminist Geographies* (London: Polity Press, 1999); Doreen B. Massey, *Space, Place and Gender* (Cambridge: Polity, 1994). See also Henri Lefebvre, *The Production of Space* (Oxford: Basil Blackwell, 1991).
42. Kim Knott, *The Location of Religion: A Spatial Analysis* (London: Equinox Publishing, 2005).
43. Simon Morgan, *A Victorian Woman's Place: Public Culture in the Nineteenth Century* (London: Tauris Academic Studies, 2007).
44. Jane Rendall, 'Women and the Public Sphere', *Gender and History* 11 (1999); Morgan, *A Victorian Woman's Place*, 478–88; Lyn H. Lofland, *The Public Realm: Exploring the City's Quintessential Social Territory* (Hawthorne, NY: Aldine de Gruyter, 1998).
45. Kerber, 'Separate Spheres, Female Worlds, Woman's' Place; the Rhetoric of Womens' History'.
46. Massey, *Space, Place and Gender*.
47. Pierre Bourdieu, *The Field of Cultural Production: Essays on Art and Literature* (Cambridge: Polity Press, 1993), 78, 121; Pierre Bourdieu and Loic J.D. Wacquant, *An Invitation to Reflexive Sociology* (Cambridge: Polity Press, 1992), 108.

Chapter 1

1. 'Future of Church Congress', *The Yorkshire Post*, 18 June 1929, 9.
2. K.E.N Lamplugh, 'Bournemouth Church Congress', *Church Monthly Parish Magazine*, no 5. October 1935, 1. HRO 44MB/44/5.

3   Frances Knight, *The Nineteenth Century Church and English Society* (Cambridge: Cambridge University Press, 1995), 89, 92–4.
4   *London Quarterly Review*, January 1884, 313.
5   Lamplugh, *Church Monthly Parish Magazine*.
6   Cohesion within the Church was a concern and was articulated in 1867 Lambeth Conference resolutions, and in the 1874 Public Worship Regulation Act. https://www.anglicancommunion.org/media/127716/1867.pdf (Accessed 20 July 202).
7   *Cardiff Times*, 7 September 1867, 3.
8   *The Examiner*, 12 October 1878, 1, 294.
9   Establishment gave legal and financial privileges. Disestablishment in Ireland and later Wales removed these. Prior to the congress period legislation addressed the civic disadvantage of non Anglican communicants. Key legislation included the Repeal of the Test and Corporations Act 1828 and Catholic Emancipation Act 1829. See Scotland, *John Bird Sumner: Evangelical Archbishop*, 67–80, for details of other legislation. The Irish Church Act of 1869 disassociated the Anglican Church in Ireland from the state and repealed the law that required tithes to be paid to it. In 1884, extension of the male franchise gave impetus to the campaign for Welsh disestablishment. See Chadwick, *The Victorian Church Part 2*, 427–9.
10 *ORCC Shrewsbury*; *ORCC Swansea*; *ORCC Cambridge*; *ORCC Middlesbrough*, 36–8; *ORCC Southampton*, 42–4. No evidence has been found of ecumenical overtures to RC congregations.
11 E.g. 'Church Congress Civic Reception', *The Queen*, 15 October 1904, 34; 'Church Congress Official Welcome at Southport', *Lancashire Evening Post*, 5 October 1926, 4.
12 *North Wales Chronicle*, 17 October 1891, 3; *Yorkshire Post and Leeds Intelligencer*, 7 October 1891, 6.
13 Laura Lady Ridding, *George Ridding, Schoolmaster and Bishop, Forty-Third Head Master of Winchester, 1866–1884, First Bishop of Southwell, 1884–1904* (London: Edward Arnold, 1908), 302.
14 *Norfolk Chronicle*, 30 September 1865, 9.
15 *Morning Post*, 2 October 1885, 2.
16 *The Times*, 5 October 1891, 9. 'Church Congress at Rhyl, Letter to the Editor', *Irish Times*, 8 September 1891, 6.
17 'Church Congress Procession', *Sheffield Daily Telegraph*, 3 October 1907, 8.
18 Ridding, *George Ridding*, 303.
19 *The Times*, 1 October 1913, 7.
20 Raven, *The Eternal Spirit*, 65, 66; Owen Chadwick, 'Raven, Charles Earle', (*ODNB*, 2004).
21 *Handbook of the 65th Church Congress Bournemouth October 1935*, HRO 38M49/E7/129.

22. 'Plymouth Church Congress Proccession' [sic], British Pathé, 25 September 1923.
23. 'Church Congress Opens' British Pathé, 7 October 1926: Cuts/Out Takes For Church Congress Opening 1926, British Pathé.
24. *Bury Free Press*, 14 October 1865, 4.
25. *ORCC Leicester*, 1880, preface.
26. 'The Coming of Kensit', *Hull Daily Mail*, 21 October 1898, 4; 'Kensit Protest', *The People*, 2 October 1898, 11; 'Church Congress a Kensit Scene', *Cheltenham Examiner*, 3 October 1900, 5–6.
27. *The Times*, 26 September 1900, 5.
28. Martin Wellings, 'The First Protestant Martyr of the Twentieth Century: The Life and Significance of John Kensit (1853–1902)', *Studies in Church History* 30 (1993); John Howard, 'The Making of a Martyr Reactions to John Kensit's Death in 1902', *Theology* 105, no. 872 (2002).
29. 'Kensit Crusader in Evidence', *Leeds Mercury*, 3 October 1906, 6. For further photographs see 'Church Congress the Absurd Side', *The Tatler*, 10 October 1906, 3 and 'Kensitites Busy at Barrow', *The Bystander*, 10 October 1906, 13.
30. *London Daily News (London)*, 6 October 1909, 3.
31. *The Bystander*, 14 October 1908, 12.
32. *Yorkshire Post and Leeds Intelligencer*, 7 October 1891, 6.
33. *CT*. 9 October, 1896, 367.
34. *Pall Mall Gazette*, 10 October 1899, 7.
35. Annie Ravenhill-Johnson, *The Art and Ideology of the Trade Union Emblem 1850–1925* (London: Anthem Press, 2014); Elizabeth Crawford, *Art and Suffrage: A Biographical Dictionary of Suffrage Artists* (London: Francis Boutle, 2018).
36. 'The Church Congress Banner', *The Queen*, 9 October 1897, 65.
37. Lisa Tickner, 'Banners and Banner-Making', in *The Nineteenth-Century Visual Reader*, ed. Vanessa R. Schwartz and Jeannene M. Przyblyski (New York: Routledge, 2004). According to Tickner, banner making dignified womanly skills and was seen an acceptable expression of femininity.
38. 'Correspondence Church Congress Banner', *Yarmouth Independent*, 2 March 1907, 8. Mrs Worlledge noted that the design was based on a drawing of St Nicholas by Mrs Nevill of Norwich 'after a painting by Botticelli'.
39. *The Times*, 26 September 1900, 5.
40. *The Sphere*, 12 October 1901, 9.
41. 'The Jubilee Church Congress at Ely', *The Graphic*, 1 October 1910, 6. The main venue was Cambridge but congress opened with a simultaneous procession to Ely Catherdal.
42. *Bristol Times and Mirror*, 4 October 1909, 9; *Western Morning News*, 21 May 1923, 7.
43. 'Church Congress Banner', *Eastern Daily Press*, 25 September 1907, 8.
44. 'Church Congress Banner', *Cambridge Independent Press*, 26 September 1902, 3.
45. *Jacksons Oxford Journal*, 5 July 1862, 3.

46 *Saturday Review*, 16 October 1875, 1, 042.
47 George Sumner, 'Speech to the Annual G.F.S. Diocesan Conference at Winchester' *GFS Associates Journal*, January 1885, 17.
48 http://www.anglicancommunion.org/media/127728/1908.pdf resolutions 44, 45, 47, 49 and 50. (Accessed 20 July 2020).
49 'Scenes at the Church Congress Barrow', *The Penny Illustrated Paper*, 13 October 1906,5. For Suffragan Bishops see Chadwick, *The Victorian Church Part 2*, 345–5.
50 *Exeter and Plymouth Gazette*, 3 October 1887, 3.
51 *York Herald*, 5 October 1881, 5, 7.
52 'Notes', *North Devon Journal*, 6 October 1881, 6.
53 *London Evening Standard*, 8 October 1881, 2.
54 *CT*, 16 October 1885, 781.
55 *ORCC Wakefield*, 447. *York Herald*, 9 October 1886, 5. Lady Laura Ridding, *Diaries*, 28 September 1897, *Selborne Papers* (HRO).
56 *ORCC Wolverhampton*; *ORCC Shrewsbury*; *ORCC Bradford*.
57 *ORCC Liverpool*.
58 *Gloucestershire Echo*, 15 October 1921, 5.
59 *Saturday Review*, 24 September 1898, 398.
60 *ORCC Weymouth*, xi, xii.
61 *ORCC Southampton*; Raven, *The Eternal Spirit*; Maxwell Studdy Leigh, *Christianity in the Modern State. A Report of the Proceedings of the Sixty-Fifth Church Congress* (London: Hodder and Stoughton, 1936).
62 *ORCC Norwich*, viii.
63 'Players of the Period', *The Era*, 12 December 1903, 13. The article also noted Madame Beresford training Clifton [public] School boys in elocution.
64 *ORCC Weymouth*, xi–xiv. Greyladies College was a community of women who supported Anglican parochial ministry.
65 *ORCC Southampton*; *ORCC Leicester*; *ORCC Southend*.
66 Ridding, *George Ridding*, 303.
67 *Saturday Review* 24 September 1898, 398.
68 *ORCC Southampton*, 115. Suffragette hecklers interrupted one session; Summer 1913 saw the Suffrage Pilgrimage in which non militant suffragists marched to London. It culminated with a service at St Paul's Cathedral and a rally of 50,000 in Hyde Park. Jane Robinson, *Hearts and Minds the Untold Story of the Great Pilgrimage and How Women Got the Vote* (London: Doubleday, 2018); Millicent Garrett Fawcett, *What I Remember* (London: Fisher Unwin, 1924). https://blog.nationalarchives.gov.uk/the-1913-suffrage-pilgrimage-peaceful-protest-and-local-disorder/ (Accessed 20 March 2021).
69 *CT,* 10 October 1913, 485.
70 *ORCC Rhyl*. Emily Charlotte Seymour (1850–92) m. William Ormesby Gore 2nd Baron Harlech.

71 Peter Gordon, 'Knightley [Née Bowater], Louisa Mary, Lady Knightley' (*ODNB*, 2004); See also Bush, *Edwardian Ladies and Imperial Power*.
72 *ORCC Manchester*; Robinson, *Hearts and Minds*. Lady Beatrice Kemp, later Lady Rochdale (1871–1966), was third daughter of Francis Egerton, 3rd Earl of Ellesmere, her husband George Kemp was a Liberal Unionist MP, soldier and Lancashire cricketer. Lady Beatrice was president of the Manchester Federation of Women's Suffrage Societies and a participant in the 1913 Suffrage Pilgrimage. During WW1 she supported Syrian refugees in Cairo and received an MBE in 1920.
73 Chadwick, *The Victorian Church. Part 2*, 155.
74 *ORCC Hull*, 282; *ORCC Folkestone*, 251, 382.
75 *ORCC Norwich*, viii.
76 *ORCC Shrewsbury*.
77 *Saturday Review*, 24 September 1898, 398.
78 *OCCR Norwich*.
79 'Church Congress at Swansea Revised List of Visitors and Their Entertainers', *South Wales Daily News*, 11 October 1879, 2. The 'entertainers' can be distinguished as they are given as a local address for visitors, amongst them are women possibly landladies.
80 *Norfolk Chronicle*, 30 September 1865, 1.
81 *Hastings and St Leonards Observer*, 26 September 1925, 6.
82 *CC Bournemouth*, handbook.
83 Anderson-Faithful, *Mary Sumner*, 38.
84 Arthur Burns, 'Emery, William', (*ODNB*, 2004).
85 *ORCC Liverpool*, 181.
86 *ORCC Newcastle*, preface.
87 Executive Committee minutes for the 1935 congress contain details of the contract with Hodder and Stoughton, samples of artwork for the cover and chapter headings.
88 Dunkley delegated editions of 1877, and 9 for unspecified reasons.
89 *ORCC Norwich*, preface.
90 Raven, *The Eternal Spirit*, 10.
91 *Dundee Courier*, 4 December 1926, 8.
92 *ORCC Birmingham*, xxiv.
93 'Church Congress a Financial Success', *Exeter and Plymouth Gazette*, 9 November 1894, 9.
94 'Church Congress Finance', *Western Mail*, 28 October 1909, 7.
95 *ORCC Weymouth*, xxii.
96 *ORCC Hull*, xi–xv.
97 *Sheffield Daily Telegraph*, 6 October 1922, 2.
98 *Western Morning News*, 5 June 1923, 6.
99 Creighton, *Memoir*, 122.

100 *ORCC Weymouth*, xvi.
101 *ORCC Birmingham*, xvii.
102 *Ipswich Official CC Programme,* 15–17.
103 *Church League for Women's Suffrage,* 15 October 1926, 1.
104 Creighton, *Memoir,* 112.
105 *ORCC Hull*, vi.
106 'Church Congress Reception', *Bury Free Press*, 8 October 1927, 7.
107 *CT,* 12 October 1883, 725.
108 Ridding, *Diaries*, 30 September 1897, *Selborne Papers* (HRO).
109 Creighton, *Memoir,* 127.
110 *North Wales Chronicle,* 17 October 1891, 3.
111 *ORCC Newcastle*, preface.
112 *Yorkshire Post and Leeds Intelligencer,* 14 October 1921, 8.
113 Congress ticket, 1935 (HRO).
114 'Bristol Welcome at Art Gallery', *Western Daily Press,* 4 October 1938, 9.
115 'Barbara's Budget', *Western Daily Press,* 24 September 1938, 10.
116 *Illustrated London News*, 14 October 1899, 23.
117 *The Times,* 25 August 1900, 7.
118 *ORCC Weymouth*, xxii.
119 'Congress Exhibition' and 'The Bristol Church Congress', *CT,* 30 September 1938, 351; 'Church Congress Day by Day', *CT,* 7 October 1938, 356.
120 *IGCC Southampton.*
121 *Sheffield Daily Telegraph,* 6 October 1922, 2.
122 *IGCC Southampton.*
123 *Tewkesbury Register*, 17 October 1903.
124 'Some Treasures of a By Gone Age', *CT,* 30 September 1938, 351.
125 *IGCC Nottingham; IGCC Plymouth; IGCC Cheltenham*; The National Art Collection at The Victoria and Albert museum holds a collection of these volumes.
126 *IGCC Southampton.*
127 *IGCC Newport;* Helen Jones, 'Markham, Violet Rosa' (*ODNB*, 2004).
128 *Ipswich Official CC Programme,* 29, 65–6.
129 E.g., *IGCC Liverpool.*
130 *IGCC Newport.*
131 *IGCC Rhyl; The Times,* 5 October 1891, 13.
132 *IGCC Brighton.*
133 *IGCC Southampton.*
134 *IGCC Bournemouth*, 210, 32.
135 E.g. *The Orchestra and the Choir, The Queen,* and suffrage journal, *The Common Cause.*
136 Andrew Hobbs, *A Fleet Street in Every Town: The Provincial Press in England, 1855–1900* (Cambridge: Open Book Publishers, 2018).

137 Godfrey Thring was a hymn writer and younger brother of the headmaster of Uppingham School. J. C. Hadden and Sayoni Basu, 'Thring, Godfrey' (*ODNB*, 2004); *Norfolk Chronicle*, 5 August 1876, 3; *CT*, 13 October 1893, 1045.
138 *ORCC Weymouth*, xxii.
139 Ipswich Official CC Programme, 28.
140 'Minutes', Bournemouth Church Congress Executive Committee (HRO). *The Times*, 5 October 1935, 16. '4.50 The Church Congress - 1935 by the Rt. Rev. the Lord Bishop of Winchester'.
141 *The Times*, 3 October 1893, 3.
142 *The Times*, 7 October 1938, 9.
143 'Church Congress Women's Position in the Ministry of the Church', *Exeter and Plymouth Gazette*, 13 October 1921, 1.
144 *Daily Mirror*, 1 October 1907; 'Church Congress Swansea: Prominent Personalities at the Congress', *The Tatler*, 13 October 1909, 36. Lady Llewellyn's husband was a local politician. Mr Talbot Rice was the Vicar of Swansea and Mr Davison, the Archbishop of Canterbury.
145 *Western Daily Press*, 3 October 1893, 8.
146 *Daily News (London)*, 29 September 1900, 7.
147 'Women's Work amongst Women', *Sheffield Daily Telegraph*, 2 October 1890, 6.
148 *CT*, 10 October 1884, 762.
149 *Morning Post*, Tuesday 10 October 1899, 2.
150 *ORCC Newcastle*, 338.
151 *Daily News (London)*, 29 September 1900, 7.
152 'John Bull', *Yorkshire Post and Leeds Intelligencer*, 15 October 1872, 7.
153 *Shields Daily Gazette*, 6 October 1881, 4.
154 *Derbyshire Advertiser and Journal*, 13 October 1882, 6. The protection of minors was topical. The Criminal law Amendment Act 1885 raised the age of consent from thirteen to sixteen. Hopkins worked for moral reform through her 'Ladies' National Association' and in 1883 her White Cross Society attempted to combat sexual double standards by encouraging chastity in men.
155 *CT*, 16 October 1885, 781.
156 *CT*, 14 October 1892, 1070.
157 'Church Congress Meeting for Young Women', *CT*, 8 October 1897, 399.
158 *CT*, 13 October 1899, 414.
159 'Women in Church Congress', *Huddersfield Chronicle*, 2 August 1892, 4.
160 *Illustrated London News*, 13 October 1894, 20.
161 *The Sphere*, 7 October 1905, 3.
162 'Southampton Congress', *Church Family Newspaper*, October 1913, 1. (HRO).
163 *CT*, 3 October 1913, 439.
164 'Cheltenham Speakers at the Church Congress', *Gloucester Echo*, 15 October 1921; 'Youth and the Elders', *Gloucester Citizen*, 10 October 1913; *Daily News (London)*, 25 September 1900, 7; 'An Adventurous Woman', *Barnsley Chronicle*, 6 October 1900.

Chapter 2

1. Eisenmann, 'Creating a Framework for Interpreting US Women's Educational History'.
2. Gill, *Women and the Church of England*, 15, 25, 125. Heeney, *The Women's Movement in the Church of England*, 7–9.
3. Heeney, *The Women's Movement in the Church of England*, 9; Gill, *Women and the Church of England*, 91.
4. Christopher Wordsworth, 'Christian Womanhood and Christian Sovereignty' (London:1884) in Heeney, *The Women's Movement in the Church of England*, 7.
5. Charlotte Yonge, *Womankind*, 2nd ed. (London and New York: Macmillan, 1890 [1876]), 1. Adam was not deceived but the woman being deceived was in transgression (Timothy, 2.14).
6. *ORCC Birmingham*, 449.
7. 'Women's Meeting', *CT*, 7 October 1910, 472.
8. Daggers, 'The Victorian Female Civilising Mission and Women's Aspirations towards Priesthood in the Church of England'; Julie Melnyk, 'Theological Approaches to Women in the Age of Enlightenment', in *Women in Christianity in the Age of Empire: (1800–1920)*, ed. Janet Wootton (London: Routledge, 2022); See William Wilberforce, *A Practical View of the Prevailing Religious System of Professed Christians in the Higher and Middle Classes of This Country Contrasted with Real Christianity* (Dublin: Dugdale, 1797); John Ruskin, *Sesame and Lilies* (Nelson: Hendon, 2000 [1865]).
9. Patricia Grimshaw, 'In Pursuit of True Anglican Womanhood in Victoria, 1880–1914', *Women's History Review* 2, no. 3 (1993).
10. Yonge, *Womankind*; See also F. K. Prochaska, *Women and Philanthropy in Nineteenth Century England* (Oxford: Clarendon Press, 1980), 1–17.
11. *ORCC Hull*, 611.
12. *ORCC Swansea*, 477.
13. George Sumner, 'Speech to the Annual G.F.S. Diocesan Conference at Winchester', *GFS Associates Journal*, January 1885, 17. George was the husband of Mary Sumner GFS activist and founder of the MU. According to scripture, it was 'a shame for women to speak in the Church' (1 Cor. 14. 35), it was considered appropriate, like Dorcas, 'to be full of good works' (Acts. 9. 36).
14. *ARCC Stoke-upon-Trent*, 61–74.
15. *ORCC Sheffield*, 347. Elizabeth Jane Whatley (1822–93) was the author of religious works including *The Life and Correspondence of* [her father] *Richard Whatley Archbishop of Dublin* (1831–63) and *The Life and Work of Mary Louisa Whatley* [her missionary sister](London: Religious Tract Society, 1890). See Emma Jane Pitman, *Missionary Heroines in Foreign Lands Woman's Work in Mission Fields* (London: S. W. Partridge & Co., 1895).

16 *ORCC Exeter,* 355–60. See following chapter Education and Leisure.
17 Heeney, *The Women's Movement in the Church of England,* 13.
18 *Jacksons Oxford Journal,* 12 October 1862, 3.
19 Ibid.
20 *Birmingham Daily Post,* 10 July 1862, 1.
21 *Proceedings of the Church Congress 1862* (Oxford: John Henry & James Parker, 1862), 135–9. Caroline Jane Talbot (1809–76) was the mother of Bishop Edward and mother-in-law to congress speaker Lavinia. Another son John Gilbert spoke at congress the following year.
22 *ORCC Reading; The London Quarterly Review,* January 1884, 319. J. G. Talbot was Conservative MP for Mid Kent 1868–78 and Oxford University 1878–1910. *Whitaker's Almanack* of 1891, 243, lists him as a member of the house of laymen for the province of Canterbury chaired by Laura Ridding's brother the Earl of Selborne.
23 Helen Bosanquet, *Social Work in London, 1869–1912: A History of the Charity Organisation* ([S.l.]: Murray, 1914).
24 Heeney, *The Women's Movement in the Church of England,* 52–5.
25 Mumm, *All Saints Sisters of the Poor.* The first community the Park Village Sisterhood was founded in 1845. By 1900 there were ninety Anglican sisterhoods. See Susan Mumm, *Making Space, Taking Space: Spatial Discomfort, Gender, and Victorian Religion.* http://anglicanhistory.org/academic/mumm_space. (Accessed 17 August 2021).
26 See Owen Chadwick, *The Victorian Church Part I 1827–1859* (London: A. & C.Black, 1966) for controversy over doctrine accruing around the 'High Church' Tractarian and 'Low Church' interpretations and the defections of elite Anglican clergy to Roman Catholicism; D. Newsome, *The Parting of Friends: A Study of the Wilberforces and Henry Manning* (London: Murray, 1966).
27 George Henry Sumner, *Life of C. R. Sumner, D.D., Bishop of Winchester, during a Forty Years' Episcopate* (London: Wells Gardner Darton, 1876), 286–7.
28 Vicinus, *Independent Women,* 49; For the spiritual aspirations of RC women and revival of convents in the UK see Laurence Lux-Sterritt and Carmen M. Mangion, *Gender, Catholicism and Spirituality: Women and the Roman Catholic Church in Britain and Europe, 1200–1900* (Basingstoke: Palgrave Macmillan, 2010); Gloria McAdam, 'Willing Women and the Rise of Convents in Nineteenth Century England', *Women's History Review* 8, no. 3 (1999).
29 Gill, *Women and the Church of England,* 95, 152, 153, 158; Vicinus, *Independent Women,* 49.
30 Mumm, *All Saints Sisters of the Poor.*
31 *John Bull,* 2 August 1862, 489.
32 Mumm, *All Saints Sisters of the Poor.*
33 *ARCC Stoke-Upon-Trent,* 52–3.
34 *CT,* 5 October 1883, 122; *London Quarterly Review,* January 1884: 320.

35 http://www.anglicancommunion.org/media/127725/1897.pdf (Accessed 14 June 2021).
36 Mumm, 'Making Space, Taking Space: Spatial Discomfort, Gender, and Victorian Religion'.
37 Ethel Romaines, *Charlotte Mary Yonge an Appreciation* (London: Mowbray, 1908), 150.
38 *ORCC London* (Anne Elizabeth) Mary Anderson Morshead (1845/6–1928) was a GFS activist, missionary worker and contributor to *The Monthly Packet*. She wrote the *Universities Mission to Central Africa 1859–1896* (1897) and A *Pioneer and Founder … Robert Gray, first Bishop of Cape Town* (1905). She was matron at Marlborough St Giles Industrial School for Girls, Andover from 1881.
39 *ORCC Birmingham*, 231.
40 Grierson, *The Deaconess*, 1, 21, 29, 32. Bishops Lightfoot, Harold Browne, Davidson and Tait are advocated deaconesses; Heeney, 'Women's Struggle for Professional Work and Status in the Church of England'.
41 J.S. Howson, *Deaconesses; or, the Official Help of Women in Parochial Work and in Charitable Institutions: An Essay Reprinted, with Large Additions, from the Quarterly Review, Sept. 1860* (London: Longman, Green, Longman and Roberts, 1862). Howson aligned to neither High nor Low Church parties.
42 *Birmingham Daily Post*, 10 July 1862, 9.
43 Knight, *The Nineteenth Century Church and English Society*, 197. Knight quotes Harold Browne's 1869 'Charge to the Clergy of the Diocese of Ely', on his appointment of stipendiary deaconess Fanny Elizabeth Eagles who 'setting aside all unwomanly usurpation of authority in the Church, should seek to edify the souls of Christ's people in the faith'.
44 *ARCC Stoke-Upon-Trent*, 56.
45 *ORCC Reading*, 156.
46 Grierson, *The Deaconess*, 20. 'Roots and Precedents' gives the historical and theological context of deaconesses.
47 http://www.anglicancommunion.org/media/127725/1897.pdf (Accessed 14 June 2021).
48 http://www.anglicancommunion.org/media/127731/1920.pdf (Accessed 14 June 2021).
49 Elizabeth Robinson, *Deaconess Gilmore Memories Collected by Deaconess Elizabeth Robinson* (London: Society for the Promotion of Christian Knowledge, 1924). Project Canterbury. http://anglicanhistory.org/women/gilmore1924/ (Accessed May 15 2022).
50 *ORCC Folkestone*, 237.
51 *ORCC Exeter*, 249. Heads of Deaconesses' institutions were sometimes styled 'mother'. The Exeter Diocese was a significant centre for the Deaconess movement. Sister Emily Cheveley had been ordained Deaconess in 1890 by Bishop Temple. See Grierson, *The Deaconess*, 28.

52 *ORCC Exeter*, 249.
53 Ibid., 252.
54 Ibid.
55 Grierson, *The Deaconess*, 38.
56 *ORCC Swansea*, 493–4.
57 Grierson, *The Deaconess*, 45.
58 *ORCC Leicester*, 299.
59 *ORCC Southend-on-Sea*, 194, 365.
60 'The Greyladies', *The Review of Reviews* 46, no. 274 (October 1912), 451.
61 Sarah Tooley, 'The Greyladies' College For - Women Workers' *Everywoman's Encyclopaedia*, 1910, 430–1. https://archive.org/details/everywomansencyc01londuoft/page/430?q=Greyladies (Accessed 12 March 2022).
62 Ibid.
63 Ibid.
64 *ORCC Norwich*, 498.
65 *ORCC Northampton*, 421–4.
66 *ORCC Weymouth*, 496, 538.
67 'Lady Speakers at the Church Congress', *The Sphere*, 7 October 1905, 11.
68 Mary Elizabeth Sumner, *Our Holiday in the East* (London: Hurst & Blackett, 1881); See also Pratt, *Imperial Eyes*; Melman, *Women's Orients: English Women and the Middle East, 1718–1918*.
69 Charlotte Yonge, *Life of John Coleridge Patteson Missionary Bishop of the Melanesian Islands* (London: Macmillan, 1875); Talia Schaffer, 'Taming the Tropics: Charlotte Yonge Takes on Melanesia', *Victorian Studies* 47 (2005).
70 *Whitaker's Almanack* (London: Whitaker, 1891); See Susan Thorne, 'Religion and Empire at Home', in *At Home with the Empire Metropolitan Culture and the Imperial World*, ed. Catherine Hall and Sonia O. Rose (Cambridge: Cambridge University Press, 2006). 'Victorians learned much of what they knew about empire in church'.
71 F.V. Emery, 'Geography and Imperialism: The Role of Sir Bartle Frere (1815–84)', *The Geographical Journal* 150, no. 3 (1984); Bartle Frere, *Eastern Africa as a Field for Missionary Labour. Four Letters to the Archbishop of Canterbury, Etc* (London: John Murray, 1874).
72 See A.N. Porter, *The Imperial Horizons of British Protestant Missions, 1880–1914* (Grand Rapids, MI: Wm. B. Eerdmans, 2003).
73 *Derbyshire Advertiser and Journal*, 16 October 1903, 12.
74 Steven Maughan, 'Imperial Christianity: Bishop Montgomery and the Foreign Missions of the Church of England, 1895–1915', in *The Imperial Horizons of British Protestant Missions 1880–1914*, ed. Porter.
75 Melnyk, 'Theological Approaches to Women in the Age of Empire'; Elizabeth E. Prevost, *The Communion of Women Missions and Gender in Colonial Africa and the British Metropole* (Oxford: Oxford University Press, 2010); Judith Rowbotham,

'Ministering Angels, Not Ministers: Women's Involvement in the Foreign Missionary Movement, C.1860–1910', in *Women, Religon and Feminism in Britain, 1750–1900*, ed. Sue Morgan (Basingstoke: Palgrave Macmillan, 2002).

76 Pitman, *Missionary Heroines in Eastern Lands*; Charlotte Yonge, *The Daisy Chain* (London: Virago, 1988 [1856]), 566. Missionary Norman May is supported in his vocation by wife Meta. Ethel, the central character, says 'together they will make a noble missionary!'.
77 *ORCC Cardiff*, 538.
78 *ORCC Hull*, 261–7.
79 Ibid., 263.
80 Ibid., 261.
81 Ibid., 264–5.
82 Ibid., 267.
83 *ORCC Nottingham*, 178.
84 Ibid., 142, 166.
85 Ibid., 175; Schaffer, 'Taming the Tropics: Charlotte Yonge Takes on Melanesia'.
86 Amongst her works were *A Lady's Life in the Rocky Mountains* (London: John Murray, 1879); *Among the Tibetans* (London: Religious Tract Society, 1894); *Korea and Her Neighbours* (London: John Murray, 1898).
87 *ORCC London*, 138.
88 *Manchester Courier and Lancashire General Advertiser*, 28 September 1900, 3; *ORCC Newcastle-Upon-Tyne*, 266.
89 Ibid., 338.
90 *ORCC Weymouth*, 273; *ORCC Stoke on Trent*, 155.
91 *Belfast* Newsletter, 3 October 1913, 4. *ORCC Southampton*; Not all women at congress were as forward-thinking. Ellen Joyce who receives attention in the following chapter was a member of the keep Australia white movement. Vron Ware, *Beyond the Pale: White Women, Racism and History* (London: Verso, 1992).
92 *Church League for Women's Suffrage*, 15 October 1925, 174.
93 *ORCC Bradford*, xxii.
94 See Chapter 6.
95 Angela Georgina Burdett-Coutts, *Woman's Mission: A Series of Congress Papers on the Philanthropic Work of Women by Eminent Writers*, Facsimile reprint, Portrayer Publishers 2002 ed. (London: Sampson Low, Marston and Company, 1893). Amongst the eminent writers were Florence Nightingale, Emily Janes and Louisa Hubbard.
96 *ORCC Brighton*, 321.
97 See for example Josephine Butler's experiences campaigning against the Contagious Diseases Acts, *Personal Reminiscences of a Great Crusade* ([S.l.]: Marshall, 1896). According to the York Herald 2 September 1882, Hopkins delivered her address twice to sexually segregated audiences.

98 ORCC Derby, 569; See also Sue Morgan, *A Passion for Purity: Ellice Hopkins and the Politics of Gender in the Late-Victorian Church* (Bristol: Centre for Comparative Studies in Religion and Gender, University of Bristol, 1999).
99 ORCC Derby, 596.
100 Sue Morgan, 'Faith Sex and Purity: The Religio-Feminist Theory of Ellice Hopkins'.
101 Grierson, *The Deaconess*, 1.
102 Fletcher, *Maude Royden*. Royden had been a settlement worker in Liverpool was also the editor of the Suffragist magazine *The Common Cause*.
103 ORCC Southampton, 306, 320.
104 *Manchester Courier and Lancashire General Advertiser*, 30 September 1913, 8.
105 Agnes Maude Royden, *Sex and Common-Sense* (New York: G. P. Putnam's Sons, 1922); Sue Morgan, 'Sex and Common-Sense: Maude Royden, Religion, and Modern Sexuality', *Journal of British Studies* 52, no. 1 (2013).
106 ORCC Southampton, xxiii.
107 *To British Mothers: How They Can Help Enlistment* (London: Mothers' Union, 1914); *Brave Women* (London: Mothers' Union, 1914): Heath Stubbs, *Friendship's Highway* 96.
108 Harold Scott, revised D. Thom, 'Barker, Dame Lilian Charlotte' (*ODNB*, 2004); ORCC Leicester, 373.
109 Pat Pleasance, 'Edith Picton Turbervill', in *These Dangerous Women* (London: Women's International League for Peace and Freedom, 2015), 40–1.
110 Jones, '"Unduly conscious of her sex"', 642. Heeney, *The Women's Movement in the Church of England*, 108, 122.
111 Burnett Hillman Streeter and Edith Picton-Turbervill, *Woman and the Church* (London: T. Fisher Unwin, 1917), 59–60; Gill, *Women and the Church of England*, 267, footnote 1.
112 See Chapters 4, 5 and 6.
113 *The Church Militant*, 1 May 1919, 4.
114 *The Church Militant*, 1 August 1921, 2 and 1 April 1924, 11; 'Women at the Church Congress', *The Common Cause*, 5 October, 1923, 5.
115 *The Times*, 22 September 1919, 7; ORCC Leicester, 299–300.
116 Heeney, *The Women's Movement in the Church of England*, 124–5.
117 Ibid., 90.
118 *Church League for Women's Suffrage*, 1 September 1919, 3.
119 Heeney, *The Women's Movement in the Church of England*, 13, 72.
120 *Falkirk Herald*, 27 October 1920, 1.
121 ORCC Southend, 166, 177, 179, 182, 196, 194.
122 Ibid., 292, 364–5; Heeney, *The Women's Movement in the Church of England*, 138.
123 *Exeter and Plymouth Gazette*, 13 October 1921, 1.
124 ORCC Birmingham, 227.

125 Ibid., 230–1.
126 *Yorkshire Post and Leeds Intelligencer,* 12 October 1922, 9.
127 *Western Morning News,* 27 September 1924, 6; Creighton, *Memoir,* 147; *Western Daily News,* 2 October 1924, 10.
128 *The Vote,* 16 October 1925, 5.
129 *International Woman Suffrage News,* 1 January 1926, 7.
130 *The Yorkshire Post,* 5 June 1929, 9.
131 Underhill was related to the Bishop of Bath and Wells. Gill, *Women and the Church of England,* 239, 240.
132 Bourdieu and Wacquant, *An Invitation to Reflexive Sociology;* Pierre Bourdieu, 'Genesis and Structure of the Religious Field', *Comparative Social Research* 13, no. 1 (1991).
133 *ORCC Cambridge,* 322.
134 Jones, '"Unduly conscious of her sex"', 639–40, see also Heeney, *The Women's Movement in the Church of England,* 138.

Chapter 3

1 Eileen Janes Yeo, *Radical Femininity; Womens' Self Representation in the Public Sphere* (Manchester: Manchester University Press, 1998), 4.
2 Gill, *Women and the Church of England,* 103.
3 *ORCC Wolverhampton.*
4 Christopher Wordsworth, 'Christian Womanhood and Christian Sovereignty' (London:1884) in Heeney, *The Women's Movement in the Church of England,* 7.
5 *London Daily News,* 28 September 1900. 'Miss Emery, daughter of the Archdeacon, a deputation speaker for the GFS spoke about "friendship amongst girls"'.
6 *ORCC Exeter,* 236; *ORCC Norwich,* 485; *ORCC Shrewsbury,* 492; *ORCC Derby; ORCC Wolverhampton.*
7 Ridding, *Diaries, Selborne Papers* (HRO); Ridding, *George Ridding.*
8 Creighton, *Memoir,* 112, 113.
9 Louise Creighton, *Life and Letters of Mandell Creighton* ([S.l.]: Longmans, Green, 1904), 10.
10 Creighton, *Memoir,* 124, 119, 125. *The Illustrated London News,* 10 October 1896, 17, referred to 'That robust colonial prelate', which suggests Creighton was not alone in finding his social skills unrefined.
11 Ibid., 113, 118.
12 Mary Sumner, *Memoir of George Henry Sumner, D.D. Bishop of Guildford: Published for His Friends by Special Request* (Winchester: Warren and Sons, 1910), 70.

13 *ORCC Bradford*, 322; *ORCC Rhyl*, 392.
14 *ORCC Shrewsbury*, 513, 518; John Henry Burn, *Laity in Council. Essays on Ecclesiastical and Social Problems. By Lay Members of the Anglican Communion.* [Edited by J. H. Burn.] (London:1901).
15 *ORCC Exeter*, 240.
16 Creighton, *Memoir*, 112.
17 Laura Ridding, 'The Girl Who Should Marry a Clergyman', *Woman and Home* X, no. 92 (May 1901).
18 Creighton, *Memoir*, 122; *ORCC Exeter*, vi.
19 Alan Haig, *The Victorian Clergy* (London: Croom Helm, 1984). See for example; *The Spectator*, 18 February 1893, 8; 'Clergy in Poverty', *Western Gazette*, 8 September 1911, 11.
20 *Report of the Proceedings of the Church Congress of 1862* (Oxford: John Henry & James Parker, 1862); *ORCC Bristol* 1864.
21 *ORCC Northampton*, 405; *ORCC Bristol* 1903, 203.
22 Gill, *Women and the Church of England*, 131–45.
23 Porter, Woodward, and Erskine, *Mary Sumner*, 21.
24 Ibid. The report of congress and the account in the biography are markedly different; *ORCC Portsmouth*, 448–9.
25 *ORCC Wakefield*, 447. Sumner recognized that the unmarried woman or childless wife could also act in a motherly capacity. 'Mothers work often devolves on unmarried women; we have many married women without children in our Mothers' Union and good unmarried who are mothering children as Godmothers or Guardians'. Mary Sumner, 'Letter to Mrs Sharme', 1911 (MU, Lambeth Palace Library).
26 Mary Sumner, *Home Life* (Winchester: Warren and Son, 1895), 8.
27 *ORCC Hull*, 256.
28 'Women's Meeting', *CT*, 7 October 1910, 472.
29 Sumner, *Home Life*, 4–7.
30 'Minute Book 1886–1910', 21 November 1890, *Diocese of Winchester Mothers' Union* (HRO). 'In the case of immorality it would be best if the member resign her card'.
31 Porter, Woodward, and Erskine, *Mary Sumner*, 31.
32 Mary Sumner, *To Mothers of the Higher Classes* (Winchester: Warren & Son, 1888).
33 In 1887 there were fifty-seven branches in 1888. The *Mothers' Union Journal* had a circulation of 46,000. Membership figures were 60.000 in 1892, 391,406 in 1921 and 490,000 in 1926 worldwide see MU timeline in Anderson-Faithful, *Mary Sumner*, xiii–xviii.
34 'The Church Attempt to Meet the Requirements of Modern Times', *The Times*, October 8 1921, 5. *The Ipswich Official CC Programme*, 22.
35 *ORCC Leicester*, 366.
36 *Ipswich Official CC Programme*. 24.
37 Studdy Leigh, *Christianity in the Modern State*, 303–10.

38 Creighton, *Memoir*, 113.
39 'Minute Book 1886–1910', 26 November 1890, *Diocese of Winchester Mothers' Union* (HRO); Porter, Woodward, and Erskine, *Mary Sumner*, 36. Without children Ridding could not comfortably lead a MU. Her solution was the Southwell Women's League, which had similar religious aims to the MU.
40 Anderson-Faithful, *Mary Sumner*, 80.
41 A. W. Ward and Ian Machin, 'Maclagan, William Dalrymple' (*ODNB*, 2004).
42 *ORCC Derby*, 573.
43 *York Herald*, 8 October 1887.
44 Ridding, *Diaries*, 5 October 1896 (Selborne Papers, HRO).
45 *London Daily News*, 28 September 1900; *ORCC Newcastle*, 358.
46 Augusta Maclagan was President of the Lichfield Diocesan GFS between 1880 and 1892, then the York Diocesan GFS between 1892 and 1895. Sumner was President of the Winchester Diocesan GFS 1887 and 1888 (her Granddaughter Miss Gore Browne became president in 1911).
47 Agnes Louisa Money, *History of the Girls' Friendly Society* (London: Wells Gardner, Darton, 1902); Mary Heath-Stubbs, *Friendship's Highway; Being the History of the Girls' Friendly Society* (London: GFS, 1926).
48 Harrison, 'For Church Queen and Family'.
49 *ORCC Portsmouth*, 156.
50 Other magazines were *The Associates Journal* (1880), *Friendly Work for Friendly Workers* (1902) amalgamated with *Friendly Leaves* in 1917 and later *The Worker's Paper*.
51 Anderson-Faithful, *Mary Sumner*, 214–18. In addition to Augusta Maclagan, Nina Theodore Woods (Peterborough) and Beatrice Temple (Exeter) provide examples. Louise Creighton was president of the Newcastle GFS in 1883 although her husband Mandell was not yet a Bishop. The current incumbent Ernest Wilberforce was at that point unmarried.
52 *ORCC Portsmouth*, 156–9.
53 *ORCC Newcastle*, 573.
54 *ORCC Reading*, 165.
55 Lady Brabazon, later Countess of Meath, funded the 1885 Brabazon Home of Comfort which provided long-term care 'for GFS Members who require medical care and skilled nursing but are not suitable cases for hospitals' and the Meath Home for members with epilepsy opened in 1892. *Friendship's Highway*, 45, 211. See also John Springhall, 'Brabazon, Reginald, Twelfth Earl of Meath', (*ODNB*, 2004).
56 *ORCC Norwich*, 492; *ORCC Swansea*, 496; *ORCC Northampton*, 425.
57 *ORCC Bradford*, 331. Christabel was the daughter of Headmaster Derwent Coleridge, a son of the distinguished poet.
58 Ibid., 335–7.
59 Moyse, *A History of the Mothers' Union*, 118; Heath-Stubbs, *Friendship's Highway*, 204.

60 Margaret A. Coombs, *Charlotte Mason Hidden Heritage and Educational Influence* (Cambridge: Lutterworth, 2015).
61 *ORCC Portsmouth*, 137.
62 Money, *History of the GFS*, 4, 6.
63 *ORCC Hull*, 271. She also suggested incorporating the MU and also catering for unmarried women.
64 Mary Sumner, *What Is the Mothers Union?* (London: Gardner Darton and Co, n.d surmised after 1896).
65 Money, *History of the GFS*, 18,19; Vivienne Richmond, '"It Is Not a Society for Human Beings but for Virgins"; the Girls' Friendly Society Membership Eligibility Dispute 1875–1931', *Journal of Historical Sociology* 20, no. 3 (2007).
66 Heath-Stubbs, *Friendship's Highway*, 10–11.
67 *ORCC Hull*, 247.
68 Ibid.
69 Ibid., 271, 272.
70 *ORCC Rhyl*, 389.
71 Bush, *Edwardian Ladies and Imperial Power*, 142–3. In addition to Laura Ridding and Ellen Joyce as leading GFS Associates was Lady Louisa Knightly of Fawsley a member of the pro-Imperial Primrose league and editor of the BWEA's magazine *Imperial Colonist*.
72 Moyse, *History of the Mothers' Union*, 84. Following 1896 central organization, an Overseas Committee was established, the same year that the first branches for indigenous (rather than expatriate) members were initiated in Hong Kong and India. Mary Sumner, 'Letters to Mrs Maude', in *Mothers' Union* (Lambeth Palace Library). February 13th 1915.
73 Porter, Woodward, and Erskine, *Mary Sumner*, 111.
74 Elizabeth E. Prevost, *The Communion of Women Missions and Gender in Colonial Africa and the British Metropole* (Oxford: Oxford University Press, 2010); Elizabeth Prevost, 'King, Gertrude May' (*ODNB*, 2012).
75 Gertrude King, 'Reports from Miss King in Madagascar', *MIC*, October 1906, 253; January 1909, 49; January 1910, 58–9; October 1912, 248.
76 Sumner, *Our Holiday in the East*, 310, 128. Miss Stanhope's 'exhibition of first rate riding' to an Arab audience is used to indicate the freedom accorded to Christian women.
77 Ibid., 266.
78 Sumner, *Memoir of George Sumner*, 50.
79 *MIC*, January, 1893, 249.
80 'Minute Book 1886–1910', 24 February 1898; *Diocese of Winchester Mothers' Union* (HRO); *MIC* October 1898, 211–13.
81 *ORCC Shrewsbury*, 593; *ORCC Bristol*, 126, 127. Phillp attended Cambridge 1910, Stoke 1911, Middlesborough 1912 and Southampton 1913.

82 Moyse, *History of the MU*, 81–2, 91–2.
83 Heath-Stubbs, *Friendship's Highway*, 82. Amongst others the GFS supported SPG missionary in Japan Ruth Wordsworth, niece of Lady Margaret Hall's Elizabeth. Ruth survived the sinking of the Lusitania in 1915.
84 Mary Sumner, 'Letter to Lady Horatia Erskine', in *Mothers' Union* (Lambeth Palace Library).
85 Beatrice Temple, Mary Sumner and Eleanor Chute, 'Letters to the Editor – Women Workers for India', *The Times*, 27 September 1907, 16.
86 *Friendly Leaves*' column for members emigrating advocated travelling with Joyce's escorted parties. The column concluded with a warning in bold type: 'Caution – Agencies are not always to be depended on trust your own society'.
87 'Winchester Emigration Society Appeal for Funds', *Hampshire Chronicle*, 10 April 1886. The Sumners subscribed £5. Mary gave a further pound to the Ladies' clothing scheme.
88 Heath-Stubbs, *Friendship's Highway*, 219; Julia Bush, 'Joyce, Ellen' (*ODNB*, 2006).
89 *Friendly Leaves*, June 1907, 220.
90 Money, *History*, 57; Heath-Stubbs, *Friendship's Highway*, 70.
91 Heath-Stubbs, *Friendship's Highway*, 76; Katie Pickles, *Female Imperialism and National Identity: Imperial Order Daughters of the Empire* (Manchester: Manchester University Press, 2002). The IODE promoted of white emigration.
92 Ellen Joyce, 'Letter to President of Winchester Diocesan G.F.S. Council 5th November 1921', in *Winchester Diocesan Girls' Friendly Society* (HRO); See Julia Bush, 'Edwardian Ladies and the "Race" Dimensions of British Imperialism', *Womens Studies International Forum* 21, no. 3 (1998); Marilyn Lake and Henry Reynolds, 'White Australia Points the Way', in *Drawing the Global Colour Line: White Men's Countries and the International Challenge of Racial Equality* (Cambridge: CUP, 2008). This association with institutionalized racism has tainted Joyce's reputation and may account for her memorial being consigned to Winchester Cathedral's crypt.
93 *ORCC Portsmouth*, 447–8.
94 Heath-Stubbs, *Friendship's Highway*, 72.
95 *ORCC Rhyl*, 394–6.
96 Heath-Stubbs, *Friendship's Highway*, 160; *ORCC Nottingham*, 197, 425, 435; Bush, *Edwardian Ladies and Imperial Power*.
97 *ORCC Bradford*, 319.
98 Heath-Stubbs, *Friendship's Highway*, 222; *ORCC Swansea*, 486.
99 Money, *History of the GFS*, 68, 69; Heath-Stubbs, *Friendship's Highway*, 147–8. Miss Townend was Head of Candidates [younger members] 1903–1913 and Vice Chair of the War Emergency Committee 1916–19. The committee provided accommodation and welfare initiatives for women workers. Miss Townend was awarded an OBE in 1918 as recognition for her services. See FH 97–9, 225.

100 Money, *History of the GFS*, 70–1; See Elizabeth Buettner, '"Not Quite Pukka": Schooling in India and the Acquisition of Racial Status', in *Empire Families: Britons and Late Imperial India* (Oxford: OUP, 2004) for the status of Eurasians in India; Heath-Stubbs, *Friendship's Highway*, 142, 143.
101 Money, *History of the GFS*, 57.
102 Ibid., 56, 61.
103 *ORCC Folkestone*, 109,110; Heath-Stubbs, *Friendship's Highway*, 91–3.
104 *ORCC Cambridge*, 334.
105 MU members were strongly represented on the Women's Committee of the congress. Louise Creighton was in the chair, other members included Mary Sumner, Lady Chichester and other MU Associates. Moyse, *History of the MU*, 85.
106 Porter, Woodward, and Erskine, *Mary Sumner*, 114–15.
107 Bourdieu and Wacquant, *An Invitation to Reflexive Sociology*.
108 Prochaska, *The Angel out of the House*; Mumm, 'Women and Philanthropic Cultures'.
109 Bourdieu, 'Genesis and Structure of the Religious Field'; Pierre Bourdieu, Jean-Claude Passeron, and Richard Nice, *Reproduction in Education, Society and Culture* (London: Sage Publications, 1977), 11–31.
110 Anderson-Faithful, *Mary Sumner*. Chapters 4 and 5 for GFS and MU overseas; See Prevost, *Communion of Women*. For the MU and missionary activity in Madagascar.
111 Eisenmann, 'Creating a Framework for Interpreting US Women's Educational History'.
112 Heath-Stubbs, *Friendship's Highway*, 126; Porter, Woodward, and Erskine, *Mary Sumner*, 83.
113 Morgan, *A Victorian Woman's Place*.

Chapter 4

1 For example Prochaska, *Women and Philanthropy*; A.G. Poole, *Philanthropy and the Construction of Victorian Women's Citizenship*; Mumm, 'Women and Philanthropic Cultures'.
2 Creighton, *Memoir*, 122, 123, 124, 129, 143. The full title of the SPG was The Society for the Propagation of the Gospel in Foreign Parts. It had originally focused on British Colonies.
3 Hollis, *Ladies Elect*.
4 See chapters 'Education and Leisure'; 'Public Service and the World of Work'.
5 Bush, 'Feminising Empire: British Women's Activist Networks in Defending and Challenging Empire from 1918 to Decolonisation'.

6   It was not just adults who undertook philanthropic activity. At Brighton in 1901 Mrs Arthur Philp of The Worcester MU advocated encouraging children to join the Countess of Meath's 'Ministering Children's League' which had the motto 'To try to do at least one kind deed every day'. *ORCC Brighton*, 380.
7   The Criminal Law Amendment Act 1885 raised the age of consent from thirteen to sixteen and criminalized male homosexuality.
8   Sue Morgan, '"Knights of God": Ellice Hopkins and the White Cross Army, 1883–95', *Studies in Church History* 34 (1998).
9   Clara Sharpley, 'Friendless Girls in Lynn', *The Sentinel*, August 1880, 7.
10 Heath-Stubbs, *Friendship's Highway*.
11 *ORCC Newcastle*: The Church of England Young Women's Help Society had its headquarters at 29 Queen's Square Bloomsbury.
12 *ORCC Hull*, 276.
13 Creighton, *Memoir*, 113.
14 *ORCC London*, 127.
15 Creighton, *Memoir*, 122, 134.
16 *ORCC Bristol*, 416.
17 *ORCC Southampton*, 104, 337; *Aberdeen Journal*, 7 October 1921: *Sheffield Daily Telegraph*, 6 October 1922.
18 *Yorkshire Post and Leeds Intelligencer*, 24 September 1924, 3.
19 CT, 13 October 1893, 1045.
20 *ORCC Barrow*, 100; *ORCC Great Yarmouth*, 391; Micky Watkins, *Henrietta Barnett: Social Worker and Community Planner* (London: Micky Watkins and Hampstead Garden Suburb Archive Trust, 2011); Alison Creedon, *Only a Woman: Henrietta Barnett: Social Reformer and Founder of Hampstead Garden Suburb* (Chichester: Phillimore, 2006).
21 Nancy L. Blakestad, 'Ravenhill, Alice' (*ODNB*, 2004). The National Health Society was founded in 1871 by medical pioneer Elizabeth Blackwell. In 1900 it introduced a diploma in health visiting.
22 *ORCC Bradford*, 316; *ORCC Barrow*, 259; *ORCC Weymouth*, 97.
23 *ORCC Cambridge*, 151; *ORCC Stoke*, 90.
24 R. Thomas and H. Series, 'Pinsent [Née Parker], Dame Ellen Frances' (*ODNB*, 2004); Pauline M. H. Mazumdar, 'The Eugenists and the Residuum: The Problem of the Urban Poor', *Bulletin of the History of Medicine* 54, no. 2 (1980). Pinsent served on the 1904 and 1908 Royal Commissions on the Care and Control of the Feeble Minded. See Mrs Walter Salter, *The Problem of the Feeble-Minded: An Abstract of the Report of the Royal Commission on the Care and Control of the Feeble-Minded. With an Introduction by the Rt. Hon. Sir Edward Fry and Contributions by Sir Francis Galton F.R.S., Professor Pigou and Miss Mary Dendy* (London: King, 1909).
25 *ORCC Folkestone*, 252, 382; *ORCC London*, 132.

26 Hollis, *Ladies Elect*, 231–5. Founders included Miss Ward Andrews of the *English Woman's Review* and Mrs Ormiston Chant of the National Vigilance Association, the organization also had the approval of Mrs Fawcett and Louisa Twining.
27 Serena Kelly, 'Janes, Emily' (*ODNB*, 2004).
28 Philippa Levine, 'Grey [Née Shirreff], Maria Georgina' (*ODNB*, 2005).
29 Kelly, 'A Sisterhood of Service'.
30 Laura Ridding, 'The Early Days of The National Union of Women Workers', *Selborne Papers* (HRO).
31 Creighton, *Memoir*, 91, 143; Martin, 'Single Women and Philanthropy: A Case Study of Women's Associational Life in Bristol, 1880–1914; Annmarie Turnbull, 'Calder, Fanny Louisa' (*ODNB*, 2004). Liverpool John Moore's University holds the Calder Archive it includes cookery books, administrative records and photographs. In one of the letters in the collection Florence Nightingale refers to Miss Calder as the 'Saint of the Laundry, Cooking and Health'. https://www.ljmu.ac.uk/about-us/news/articles/2020/2/12/who-were-the-founding-fathers-and-mothers-of-ljmu (Accessed 12 November 2021).
32 Peter Gordon and David Doughan, *Dictionary of British Women's Organisations, 1825–1960* (London: Woburn Press, 2001), 110–11.
33 Poole, *Philanthropy and the Construction of Victorian Women's Citizenship*, 218.
34 Dr Kate Mitchell, 'The Treatment of Inebriate Women', The Temperance Question, *Women Workers: Official Report of the Conference of the National Union of Workers*, 1892, 85, 86.
35 Creighton, *Memoir*, 90.
36 Helen Fowler, 'Sidgwick [Née Balfour], Eleanor Mildred' (*ODNB*, 2004).
37 Creighton, *Memoir*, 82, 116. Sidgwick and Kathleen Lyttelton were linked by political affiliation and stance on suffrage and both were Vice Presidents of The Conservative and Unionist Women's Suffrage Association. *Conservative and Unionist Women's Franchise Review*, No. 1, November 1909.
38 Gordon, 'Knightley [Née Bowater], Louisa Mary, Lady Knightley'. Louisa Knightley, *The Journals of Lady Knightley of Fawsley*. https://archive.org/details/journalsofladykn00knigrich (Accessed 20 June 2021).
39 Kelly, 'A Sisterhood of Service', 167.
40 Julia Bush, 'The National Union of Women Workers and Women's Suffrage', in *Suffrage Outside Suffragism*, ed. M. Boussahba-Bravard (London: Palgrave Macmillan, 2007).
41 'Ladies' Page', *Illustrated London News,* 12 October 1907.
42 Bush, 'The National Union of Women Workers and Women's Suffrage', 112. Mrs Albert Booth was the sister-in-law of social researcher Charles Booth who was Beatrice Webb's cousin. The first edition of his survey was: Charles Booth, *Labour and Life of the People* ([S.l.]: Williams and Norgate, 1889); Anne Summers,

Christian and Jewish Women in Britain, 1880–1940: Living with Difference (London: Palgrave Macmillan, 2017), 38.
43 Morgan, *A Victorian Woman's Place*; Gleadle, *Borderline Citizens*; Richardson, *The Political Worlds of Women*.
44 *ORCC Leicester*, 368, 373.
45 *IGCC Newport*, 21. The guide included biographies, 44. Mrs Carruthers, J.P (Miss Violet Markham) 'Member of the Executive Committee National Relief Fund, and Central Committee Women's Employment 1914. Deputy Director Women's Section National Service Department, 1917. Member of Lord Chancellor's Advisory Committee for Women Justices, 1919–20. Member of Industrial Court. F.R. Hist. S.F.R.G/S. Author of *South Africa Past and Present; The New Era in South Africa; The South African Scene; A Women's Watch in the Rhine etc*'.
46 Jones, 'Markham, Violet Rosa'.
47 Kelly, 'Ridding [Née Palmer], Lady Laura Elizabeth' (*ODNB*, 2004).
48 Thomas and Series, 'Pinsent [Née Parker], Dame Ellen Frances' (*ODNB*, 2004).
49 Constance Cochrane, 'Labourers Cottages', in Henry R. Aldridge, *Proceedings of The National Housing Conference* March 1900 (London, 1901). Slums were a topical issue see https://api.parliament.uk/historic-hansard/lords/1901/mar/08/the-housing-problem-government-policy 8 March 1901 → Lords Sitting → PETITION. (Accessed 22 July 2021.)
50 *ORCC Cambridge*, 140.
51 *ORCC Southamption*, 245; *ORCC Leicester*, 133, 231.
52 *ORCC Bradford*, 338. Pigott also spoke at Wolverhampton in 1887 and Norwich in 1895.
53 *Sheffield Daily Telegraph*, 6 October 1922, 2.
54 *The Common Cause*, Friday 5 October 1923, 5.
55 *IGCC Newport*, 44.
56 Knightley, *Journals*. https://archive.org/details/journalsofladykn00knigrich (Accessed 20 June 2021). The journal reflects Knightley's engagement in political matters. The guild had been founded in 1877 by Lady Mary Feilding to 'Assist Unmarried or Widowed Gentlewomen in need of Employment or in temporary difficulty', see Jane Garnett, 'Feilding, Lady Mary' (*ODNB* 2004). The Working Ladies' Guild worked through personal recommendation it offered holiday respite and cultural opportunities but focussed on equipping women with employment skills.
57 Gordon, 'Knightley [Née Bowater], Louisa Mary, Lady Knightley'.
58 M.E. Townsend, *The Girls Friendly Society* (London: n.d.), 21; Harrison, 'For Church Queen and Family', 131–2.
59 Mary Sumner, 'Letter to Dearest Minnie, Lady Addingon Anti Christian Sunday Schools', n.d. (MU Lambeth Palace Library); 'Letters to Mrs Maude', 17 November 19? (MU, Lambeth Palace Library).

60 David Steele, 'Palmer, Roundell, First Earl of Selborne' (*ODNB*, 2021).
61 'Church Congress Hymnology' Lecture – Sir Roundell Palmer, Q.C., M.P. Illustrated by a Choir, under the direction of E. G. Monk, Esq., Mus. Doc., *Bury and Norwich Post*, 2 October 1866.
62 Laura Elizabeth Ridding and Sophia Matilda Palmer afterwards Comtesss De Franqueville, *Sophia Matilda Palmer, Comtesse De Franqueville, 1852–1915. A Memoir*. 2; ORCC Nottingham, 498. Sophia was a devout 'churchwoman' and her marriage to the Roman Catholic Comte happened after much heart searching. It was celebrated according to both Anglican and RC rites. See *Memoir* 265, 267, 269, 270.
63 *ORCC Southampton*, 195–8.
64 Ridding and Palmer, *Sophia Matilda Palmer*, 164.
65 Laura Ridding, *The Life of Robert Palmer 1888–1916* (London: Hodder and Stoughton, 1921).
66 Mitzi Auchterlonie, *Conservative Suffragists: The Women's Vote and the Tory Party* (London: Tauris Academic Studies, 2007). Martin Pugh, 'Palmer, (Beatrix) Maud [Née Lady (Beatrix) Maud Gascoyne-Cecil], Countess of Selborne', (*ODNB*, 2007).
67 Knightley, *Journals*. https://archive.org/details/journalsofladykn00knigrich, 247 (Accessed 20 June 2021).
68 *ORCC Nottingham*, 489.
69 *ORCC Liverpool*, 250, 457. Lucy Cavendish spoke on 'Religion in the Home'; Sheila Fletcher, 'Gladstone, Helen' (*ODNB*, 2006).
70 *ORCC Southampton*, 299, 328, 337.
71 *ORCC London*, 132, 137.
72 *Western Morning News*, 28 June 1923, 8.
73 See Bush, *Edwardian Ladies and Imperial Power*; A.N. Porter, *The Imperial Horizons of British Protestant Missions, 1880–1914* (Grand Rapids, MI: Wm. B. Eerdmans, 2003).
74 Lady Laura Ridding, 'South African Note Book', 1908–9, *Selborne Papers* (HRO).
75 *ORCC Southampton*, 165–7.
76 Millicent Garrett Fawcett, *What I Remember* (London: Fisher Unwin, 1924), 153. Millicent travelled with daughter Phillipa. Lady Knox wife of General Sir William Knox and Lucy Deane, a trained Factory Inspector and expert in Infant welfare were also members of the committee of enquiry they were joined in SA by Dr Jane Waterson, Dr Ella Scarlett and nurse Katherine Brereton.
77 *ORCC Brighton*, 321; Andrew S. Thompson, 'Hunt, Violet Edith Gwynllyn Brooke-' (*ODNB*, 2006); G.E. Maguire, 'The Party Mobilizes for Women', in *Conservative Women: A History of Women and the Conservative Party, 1874–1997* (London: Palgrave Macmillan UK, 1998). Brooke-Hunt was Secretary of the Conservative Women's Unionist and Tariff Reform Association which sought preferential trade terms for the empire.

78　Ridding, 'South African Note Book', December 1908, 33, *Selborne Papers* (HRO).
79　Ridding, 'The Call of Empire', 1909, *Selborne Papers* (HRO); A.N. Porter, *The Nineteenth Century*, The Oxford History of the British Empire (Oxford: OUP, 1999). See examples Imperial India, 422–46; Southern Africa 597–623; Australia and the Western Pacific 546–572. Chapter 25 Southern Islands: New Zealand and Polynesia details conflict, resistance and dispossession despite colonization and colonialism 'being less brutal than some', 573.
80　Ridding, 'The Call of Empire'.
81　Ridding, 'South African Note Book', 33; Bush, *Edwardian Ladies and Imperial Power*, 113–14. Bush locates Ridding's view and anecdotes relating to fear of Black men recorded in the note book in relation to a context of 'Black Peril scares' between 1893 and 1913.
82　Andrew Ross, 'Christian Missions and the Mid-Nineteenth Century Change in Attitudes to Race: The African Experience', in *The Imperial Horizons of British Protestant Missions*, ed. Andrew Porter (Grand Rapids, Michigan and Cambridge: Wm. B. Eerdmans, 2003). Ross notes trusteeship as acceptance of responsibility for perceived 'lower' races who should be treated humanely as in Kipling's poem 'The White Man's Burden'.
83　Ridding, 'The Call of Empire'; Ridding's view of trusteeship on behalf of 'natives' replicates her attitude to those of lower social class. See 'Home Duties and Relations of the Educated Woman', *York Herald*, 8 October 1887, 6.
84　The imperial stance of the MU, GFS, Joyce and Knightley are given fuller treatment in the chapter on the MU and the GFS.
85　Money, *History of the GFS*; 57; Heath-Stubbs, *Friendship's Highway*, 70.
86　ORCC Portsmouth, 447–8; ORCC Rhyl, 395–7; Julia Bush, '"The Right Sort of Woman": Female Emigrators and Emigration to the British Empire, 1890–1910', *Women's History Review* 3, no. 3 (1994); Bush, *Edwardian Ladies and Imperial Power*, 68, 79, 194.
87　See Cecillie Swaisland, *Servants and Gentlewomen to the Golden Land: The Emigration of Single Women from Britain to Southern Africa, 1820–1939* (Oxford: Berg, 1993).
88　For suffrage and the NUWW see Bush, 'The National Union of Women Workers and Women's Suffrage', 111, 122. In the NUWW, views on suffrage were openly articulated and it fell to Laura Ridding as president in 1910 to prevent the fracture of the union as a result of diverse positions on suffrage and what stance the union should take on it. For wider perspectives on suffrage see June Purvis and June Hannam, eds., *The British Women's Suffrage Campaign: National and International Perspectives* (London: Routledge, 2021). For the early twentieth century see also Alexandra Hughes-Johnson and Lyndsey Jenkins, eds., *The Politics of Women's Suffrage: Local, National and International Dimensions* (London: University of London Press, 2022).

89. *ORCC Barrow*, 417.
90. Cannadine, *Class in Britain*, 60, 87.
91. Knightley, *Journals*, 5 April 1880. https://archive.org/details/journalsofladykn00knigrich (Accessed 20 June 2021).
92. *ORCC Southend*, 271; *ORCC Birmingham*, 201; Kent, 'Image and Reality: The Actress and Society', in *A Widening Sphere*, ed. Vicinus, 114–16.
93. Heeney, *The Women's Movement in the Church of England*, 105.
94. *Church League for Women's Suffrage*, August 1912, 73.
95. Heeney, *The Women's Movement in the Church of England*, 105.
96. 'Church League for Women's Suffrage', *CT*, 7 October, 1910, 473.
97. *Church League for Women's Suffrage*, August 1912, 67.
98. Fawcett, *What I Remember*, 193, 213.
99. Ibid., 198.
100. *Manchester Courier and Lancashire General Advertiser*, 30 September 1913, 9.
101. *ORCC Southampton*, xxiii.
102. Ibid., 9.
103. *ORCC Southampton*, 107; Soulsby also published her paper separately. Lucy Soulsby, *The Victorian Woman a Paper Read at the Church Congress at Southampton, October, 1913* (London and New York: Longmans, Green, and Co, 1914).
104. *ORCC Southampton*, 104, 115.
105. 'Miss Violet Markham's Great Speech at the Albert Hall February 28th 1912', pamphlet published by The National League for Opposing Woman Suffrage.
106. Helen Loader, *Mrs Humphry Ward and Greenian Philosophy: Religion, Society and Politics* (Basingstoke: Palgrave Macmillan, 2019).
107. Creighton, *Memoir*, 89.
108. Ibid.
109. Ibid.
110. Keck and Sikkink, *Advocacy Networks in International Politics*; Joyce Goodman and Jane Martin, 'Networks after Bourdieu: Women, Education and Politics from the 1980s to the 1920s', *History of Education Researcher* 80, no. November (2007).
111. Massey, *Space, Place and Gender*, Introduction.
112. Eisenmann, 'Creating a Framework for Interpreting US Women's Educational History'.

Chapter 5

1. James Murphy, *Church, State and Schools in Britain 1800–1970* (London: Routledge and Kegan Paul, 1971), 4–6. There was a political dimension to the Society which drew support from Whigs. Religious hostility and political

opposition were frequently aligned. Anglicanism was aligned with the Tory land-owning class. The Church sought to educate the poor in its doxa through Sunday schools which served as an outlet for the philanthropic action of socially advantaged women such as congress contributors Mary Sumner and Charlotte Yonge; Mary Sumner, 'Account of Her Early Life at Hope End 1828-46', in *Mothers' Union* (Lambeth Palace Library); Austin Whitaker, 'Winchester Memories 20 Mrs Elliot Talks About Her Old Schoolteacher Charlotte Yonge', in *Winchester Memories Oral History Recordings* (Hampshire Record Office, 1970).

2 John Hurt, *Education in Evolution Church, State, Society and Popular Education 1800–1870* (London: Rupert Hart-Davis, 1971), 11–38. Chapter 1 'Schism and Cohesion' for the National Society's negotiation with the state and competition with the British and Foreign Schools; not all Anglican Schools were National Society schools. Murphy, *Church, State and Schools*, Chapter 1; Charles Sumner's 1839 Winchester Diocesan Training College can be seen as another act of resistance to non-Anglican encroachment in the field of elementary education. George Sumner, *Life of C. R. Sumner*.

3 For legislation see Derrek Gillard's http://www.educationengland.org.uk (Accessed 20 May 2019).

4 *ORCC Shrewsbury*; ORCC *Nottingham*; ORCC *London*; ORCC *Northampton*.

5 http://www.lambethconference.org/resolutions/1908/1908-14.cfm (Accessed 12 July 2020). Resolutions 11, 12 14, 16, 17 and 18.

6 *ORCC Manchester*; ORCC *Stoke*.

7 Archdeacon William Emery, the faithful secretary to the Church congress, was amongst its instigators. http://www.churchhigh.me.uk/school-history/background-of-the-church-schools-company-limited/ (Accessed 19 June 2020).

8 Deirdre Raftery, 'The Opening of Higher Education to Women in Nineteenth Century England: "Unexpected Revolution" or Inevitable Change?', *Higher Education Quarterly* 56, no. 4 (2002); Carol Dyhouse, *No Distinction of Sex?: Women in British Universities, 1870–1939* (London; Bristol, PA: UCL Press, 1995); Julia Bush, '"Special Strengths for Their Own Special Duties": Women, Higher Education and Gender Conservatism in Late Victorian Britain', *History of Education* 34, no. 4 (2005); Anderson 'Women and Universities', in *European Universities from the Enlightenment to 1914*.

9 Examples for the UK and Eire include, Angharad Eyre, 'Education' in *Women in Christianity in the Age of Empire: (1800–1920)*; Dale Spender, *The Education Papers: Women's Quest for Equality in Britain 1850–1912* (London: Routledge and Kegan Paul, 1987); Carol Dyhouse, *Girls Growing up in Late Victorian and Edwardian Britain* (London: Routledge, 1981); June Purvis, *Hard Lessons: The Lives and Education of Working-Class Women in Nineteenth-Century England* (Cambridge: Polity Press, 1989); W. Gareth Evans, *Education and Female Emancipation: The*

Welsh Experience, 1847–1914 (Cardiff: University of Wales Press, 1990); Deirdre Raftery and Susan M. Parkes, *Female Education in Ireland 1700–1900: Minerva or Madonna* (Dublin: Irish Academic Press, 2007). Jane McDermid, *The Schooling of Working-Class Girls in Victorian Scotland: Gender, Education and Identity* (London: Routledge, 2005).

10 *ARCC Brighton*, 500, 504.
11 Ibid., 510.
12 Beauman, *Women and the Settlement Movement*; Nigel Scotland, *Squires in the Slums: Settlements and Missions in Late Victorian Britain* (London: I.B. Tauris, 2007).
13 Richard D. Altick, *The English Common Reader: A Social History of the Mass Reading Public, 1800–1900* (Columbus: Ohio State University Press, 1998); David Vincent, *Literacy and Popular Culture: England 1750–1914* (Cambridge: CUP, 1989). Vincent suggests that there is no evidence to link directly formal schooling and the growth of literacy.
14 *Norfolk Chronicle*, 5 August 1876, 3; Religious publishing was profitable. Sarah C. Williams, '"Is There a Bible in the House?" Gender Religion and Family Culture', in *Women, Gender and Religious Cultures in Britain, 1800–1940* (London: Routledge 2010), ed. Morgan and de Vries.
15 Kelly Mayes, 'The Disease of Reading and Victorian Periodicals', in *Literature in the Marketplace: Nineteenth-Century British Publishing and Reading Practices Cambridge Studies in Nineteenth-Century Literature and Culture Series, No. 5.*, ed. John O. Jordan and Robert L. Patten (Cambridge: Cambridge UP, 1995); Kristine Moruzi, '"Never Read Anything That Can at All Unsettle Your Religious Faith": Reading and Writing in the Monthly Packet', *Women's Writing* 17, no. 2 (2010).
16 *ORCC Wakefield*, 305–9.
17 'The Church of the People', *Aris's Birmingham Gazetteer*, 9 October 1869, 4.
18 Ibid.
19 'The Legal and Social Position of Our Girls', *ORCC Derby*, 569–73.
20 Rosa Mary Barrett, *Ellice Hopkins: A Memoir … With Introduction by H. Scott Holland* (London: Wells Gardner & Co., 1907), 7, 9.
21 Eisenmann, 'Creating a Framework for Interpreting US Women's Educational History'; Lawrence Cremin, *Public Education* (New York: Basic Books, 1976); Sjaak Braster, 'The People, the Poor, and the Oppressed: The Concept of Popular Education through Time', *Paedagogica Historica* 47, nos. 1–2 (2011).
22 Anderson-Faithful, *Mary Sumner*, 193–4.
23 Louisa Gore Browne, Sumner's daughter instigated the memoir. As former Unitarians they came from a tradition that acknowledged women's intellect and valued their education. Thomas Heywood was educated at Manchester Grammar School when nonconformists were barred from taking degrees in England. His elder brother Benjamin the supporter of Mechanics' Institutes graduated

in Scotland. Younger brother James who remained a Unitarian, and attended Cambridge was a supporter of university reform and served on Emily Davies' committee for the advancement of women's higher education. M.C. Curthoys, 'Heywood, James' (ODNB, 2009).
24 Sumner, 'Early Life', in *Mothers' Union* (Lambeth Palace Library).
25 Porter, Woodward, and Erskine, *Mary Sumner*, 16–17.
26 Ibid., 20.
27 Mary Sumner, 'When and Why the Mothers' Union Started' (Winchester: Warren and Sons, n.d. surmised, 1888); Charlotte Maria Shaw Mason, *Home Education: A Course of Lectures to Ladies, Etc* (London: Kegan Paul & Co., 1886).
28 *ORCC Hull*, 258, 259, 260.
29 Louise Creighton and James Thayne Covert, *A Victorian Family: As Seen through the Letters of Louise Creighton to Her Mother, 1872–1880* (Lewiston, NY; Lampeter: Edwin Mellen, 1998), 4; Creighton, *Memoir*, 15.
30 Ibid., xii. Introduction.
31 Creighton and Covert, *A Victorian Family*, 4.
32 Ruskin, *Sesame and Lilies*. 'Of Queens' Gardens' was included in this larger essay and dealt with ideals of womanhood.
33 John R. Green and Roger Hudson, *A Short History of the English People* (London: Folio Society, 1992 [1874]); Anthony Brundage, 'Green, John Richard' (*ODNB*, 2004).
34 Creighton, *Memoir*, 27. From 1866 to 1874 Brooke preached at York Street Chapel in the fashionable London district of St James; R.K. Webb, 'Brooke, Stopford Augustus' (*ODNB*, 2003).
35 See Charlotte Yonge, 'Hints on Reading', *The Monthly Packet*, 30 August 1865, 221–2.
36 https://london.ac.uk/day-changed-womens-education (Accessed 24 March 2019). Creighton, *Memoir*, 29–30.
37 *Everywoman's Encyclopedia* Vol VI 1912, 4035–7.
38 For Mary Arnold as social reformer see Loader *Mrs Humphry Ward and Greenian Philosophy*.
39 Sheila Fletcher, 'Talbot [Née Lyttelton], Lavinia' (*ODNB*, 2006); *Victorian Girls: Lord Lyttelton's Daughters* (London: Hambledon, 1997); Beauman, *Women and the Settlement Movement*, 36–9. Lavinia Talbot spoke at the 1913 congress in Southampton, her husband then Bishop of Winchester and president of the congress, invited Maude Royden to speak to an audience of men on 'the white slave traffic'.
40 'Women Soon to be Bishops', *Daily Herald*, 9 October 1925, 7.
41 Creighton, *Memoir*, 134, 135; James Thane Covert, *A Victorian Marriage: Mandell and Louise Creighton* (London: Hambledon, 2000), 130, 238.

42 Eisenmann, 'Creating a Framework for Interpreting US Women's Educational History'; Sarah Jane Aiston, 'Women, Education and Agency 1600–2000 an Historical Perspective', in *Women, Education and Agency*, ed. Jean Spence, Sarah Jane Aiston, and Maureen Meikle (London and New York: Routledge, 2010).
43 Mary Hilton and Pam Hirsch, eds., *Practical Visionaries Women, Education and Social Progress 1790–1930* (Harlow: Pearson, 2000); Jane Martin and Joyce Goodman, *Women and Education, 1800–1980* (Basingstoke: Palgrave Macmillan, 2004).
44 Deborah Gorham, *The Victorian Girl and the Feminine Ideal* (London: Croom Helm, 1982), 105–9.
45 Wilberforce, *A Practical View of the Prevailing Religious System of Professed Christians*.
46 ORCC Portsmouth, 448.
47 ORCC Hull, 237.
48 Bishop Christopher Wordsworth spoke against the bill on the grounds that it promoted secular education and would lead to: 'a race of godless teachers and infidel scholars' (*Hansard 3*, 1170).
49 Mary Sumner, 'Secular Education', *MIC*, October 1894, 193–202.
50 ORCC Rhyl, 387–8.
51 ORCC Cardiff, 352.
52 ORCC Liverpool, 593–9.
53 Lambeth Conference 1908, resolutions 11, 12, 13 and 14. http://www.anglicancommunion.org/media/127728/1908.pdf (Accessed 20 July 2020).
54 ORCC Liverpool, 627.
55 Ibid.
56 Hetty Lee, *Talks to the Training Class: A Manual for Heads of Sunday Kindergartens and Primary Departments* (London: National Society's Depository, 1910); ORCC Middlesbrough, 254–65.
57 *Ipswich Official CC Programme*.
58 Congress contributor Employment Law expert Gertrude Tuckwell being a notable example.
59 ORCC Bradford, 329; ORCC Newcastle-Upon-Tyne, 367.
60 Lyttelton articulated his support for public elementary education in an 1855 address 'Thoughts on National Education' and prior to the Taunton Commission he served on the 1864 Clarendon Commission into elite boys' public schools. Peter Gordon, 'Lyttelton, George William, fourth Baron Lyttelton and fourth Baron Westcote', (*ODNB*, 2006). Joyce F. Goodman, 'Girls' Public Day School Company', (*ODNB*, 2005).
61 'Ecclesiastical', *Derby Mercury*, 17 October 1894, 5.
62 Soulsby, an MU Associate, published, *Stray Thoughts for Mothers and Teachers* (London: Longmans, 1897).

63 *ORCC Bradford*, 353.
64 Ibid., 347–54, 355–60.
65 *ORCC Liverpool*, 627–32, 619–26.
66 *ORCC Manchester*, 650.
67 Sara A. Burstall, *English High Schools for Girls* (London: Charles H. Kelly, 1907); *The Hallowing of Humanity in the Kingdom of Christ … Being the Twenty-Seventh of a Series of Lectures on What Is Christianity?* (London: Charles H. Kelly, 1905).
68 *ORCC Manchester*, 658–62, 663–8.
69 *ORCC Great Yarmouth*, 169–72.
70 Faithfull wrote a memoir of her experience at Cheltenham, *In the House of My Pilgrimage* ([S.l.]: Chalto and Windus, 1925), 131; She also published *You and I Saturday Talks at Cheltenham* (London: Chatto and Windus, 1927).
71 Avery, 'Faithfull, Lilian Mary' (*ODNB*, 2004). Faithfull was hockey captain at Somerville, president of the All-England Women's Hockey Association and a member of the Association of Headmistresses which was the response of Frances Buss and Dorothea Beale to the Headmasters' Conference.
72 *Gloucestershire Daily Echo*, 15 October 1921, 5; *Western Daily Press*, 15 October 1921, 9.
73 'The Church Congress, Discipline in Modern Life', *CT*, 16 October 1925, 441.
74 *Programme of the Cheltenham Church Congress* 1928, 18. (HRO).
75 See Dyhouse, *No Distinction of Sex?: Women in British Universities, 1870–1939*.
76 See Chapter 2 for Emery's advocacy for clergy wives to be at one with their husbands. *ORCC Portsmouth*, 274–5.
77 Joan Burstyn, *Victorian Education and the Ideal of Womanhood* (London: Croom Helm, 1980), 99; Sara Delamont, 'The Contradictions in Ladies' Education', in *The Nineteenth-Century Woman: Her Cultural and Physical World*, ed. Sara Delamont and Lorna Duffin (London: Croom Helm, 1978); See also Gorham, *The Victorian Girl*, 101–5.
78 John Henry Overton, Elizabeth Wordsworth, and Christopher Wordsworth, *Christopher Wordsworth, Bishop of Lincoln, 1807–1885* (London: Rivingtons, 1888).
79 Battiscombe, *Reluctant Pioneer: A Life of Elizabeth Wordsworth*.
80 Beauman, *Women and the Settlement Movement*, 39.
81 *ORCC Exeter*, 264.
82 Christopher Wordsworth, 'Christian Womanhood and Christian Sovereignty (London 1884) in Heeney, *The Women's Movement in the Church of England*, 7.
83 *ORCC Exeter*, 264.
84 Ibid.
85 Ibid., 266.
86 Ibid., 268.
87 Ibid., 264, 267.

88 Mary P. Gallant, 'Against the Odds: Anne Jemima Clough and Women's Education in England', *History of Education* 26, no. 2 (1997).

89 *IGCC Newport*, 44.

90 Letter from Cavendish to Mary Gladstone 1888, in Bush; "'Special Strengths for Their Own Special Duties'", 338.

91 Kate Flint, 'Soulsby, Lucy Helen Muriel', (*ODNB*, 2004).

92 Susan M. Parkes, 'Trinity College, Dublin and the "Steamboat Ladies", 1904–1907', in *Women and Higher Education: Past, Present and Future*, ed. M.R. Masson and D. Simonton (Aberdeen: Aberdeen University Press, 1996).

93 Rouse published several works starting in 1906 with 'Studies in the Epistle to the Philippians' and ending in 1954 with 'A History of the Ecumenical Movement, 1517–1948'. Ruth Franzen, 'The Legacy of Ruth Rouse', *International Bulletin of Missionary Research*, no. October (1993); ORCC Southampton, 104; ORCC Southend, 360; ORCC Birmingham, 362.

94 *Sheffield Daily Telegraph*, 2 October 1924, 5.

95 Beauman, *Women and the Settlement Movement*, introduction; See also Vicinus, *Independent Women*, 21–46; and Scotland, *Squires in the Slums*; See Loader, *Mrs Humphry Ward and Greenian Philosophy* for Green's philosophy and its implications for social action.

96 Beauman, *Women and the Settlement Movement*, xix.

97 Ibid., 55–76.

98 'Woman and Religion, Practical Christianity the Story of the Women's University Settlement', *Everywoman's Encyclopedia*, Vol. VI 1912, 4395–7.

99 Beauman, *Women and the Settlement Movement*, 189. Hennrietta Barnett addressed the inaugural meeting of the National Union of Women Workers in Manchester 1896.

100 Ibid., 32–4, 150, 152–3. Creighton's children Cuthbert and Beatrice, who served as president of the Girls' Diocesan Association were involved with this settlement.

101 *ORCC London*, 146–15, 151–5. 'Miss Harington', *The Times*, 8 October 1936, 16.

102 Beauman, *Women and the Settlement Movement*, xix–xx, 32.

103 *ORCC Liverpool*, 250.

104 'Who's Who at Congress', Southampton Church Congress Ecclesiastical Exhibition Catalogue, 1913, 38. (HRO).

105 The Whitechapel Gallery was founded circa 1905/6. Mrs Barnett was honoured as CBE in 1917 and DBE in 1927. She published *The Making of the Home* (1885); *How to Mind the Baby* (1887); *Destitute, Neglected, and Delinquent Children* (Pan-Anglican papers, 1908); *Canon Barnett: His Life, Work and Friends* (1918)'.

106 *ORCC Barrow*, 100–4.

107 Ibid., 418, 419, 420.

108 Judith Rowbotham, *Good Girls Make Good Wives: Guidance for Girls in Victorian Fiction* (Oxford: Basil Blackwell, 1989). See also Moruzi, '"Never Read Anything That Can at All Unsettle Your Religious Faith": Reading and Writing in the Monthly Packet'; Patrick A. Dunae, 'Penny Dreadfuls: Late Nineteenth-Century Boys' Literature and Crime', *Victorian Studies* 22, no. 2 (1979).

109 Rebecca Styler, *The Contexts of Women's Literary Theology in the Nineteenth Century, Literary Theology by Women Writers of the Nineteenth Century* (Farnham: Ashgate, 2010). Creighton's friend Mary, Mrs Humphry Ward wrote *Robert Elsmere* which tackles loss of faith.

110 Creighton, *Memoir*, 15.

111 *ORCC Wakefield*, 390.

112 *ORCC Cardiff*, 235; See Sutherland, *The Longman Companion to Victorian Fiction*.

113 *ORCC Norwich*, 485–91.

114 *ORCC Bradford*, 331–4.

115 Christabel R. Coleridge and Charlotte Mary Yonge, *Charlotte Mary Yonge: Her Life and Letters* (London and New York: Macmillan & Co., 1903); Christabel R. Coleridge, *The Daughters Who Have Not Revolted. [Essays.]* (London: Wells, Gardner and Co., 1894); See 'The Religious Girl: Girlhood in the Monthly Packet' in Moruzi, *Constructing Girlhood*.

116 Romaines, *Charlotte Mary Yonge an Appreciation*; *ORCC Liverpool*, 609–14.

117 *Sheffield Daily Telegraph*, 2 October 1924.

118 Kent, 'Image and Reality: The Actress and Society', in *A Widening Sphere* ed. Vicinus, 95.

119 Ibid.

120 *ORCC Norwich*, 493.

121 *ORCC Birmingham*, 201–4. *The Times*, 8 October 1921, 5.

122 The League produced feminist plays designed to support the cause. Kent, 'Image and Reality', in *A Widening Sphere* ed. Vicinus, 115–16; *ORCC Southend-on-Sea*, 271–4.

123 *Falkirk Herald*, 27 October 1920, 1.

124 Elizabeth Wordsworth, *Glimpses of the Past* (London: A. R. Mowbray, 1912), 36.

125 Sheila Fletcher, *Women First: The Female Tradition in English Physical Education 1880–1980* (London: Athlone, 1984), 22, 23.

126 *ORCC Folkestone*, 294–303.

127 Ibid., 304.

128 Fletcher, *Women First*, 25–9.

129 *ORCC Norwich*, 492.

130 Mary Scharlieb, 'Recreational Activities of Girls' during Adolescence', *Child Study* 4 (1911).

131 *ORCC Folkstone*, 307.

132 Ibid., 308, 309, 310.
133 Eisenmann, 'Creating a Framework for Interpreting US Women's Educational History'.
134 Anderson-Faithful, *Mary Sumner*. Chapters 6 and 7 apply Bourdieu's thinking tools to home education, popular education and schooling.
135 E.g. Mumm, 'Women and Philanthropic Cultures'.

Chapter 6

1. The Public Health Act 1875 (and other dates); Factory and Workshop Act 1878; Prevention of Cruelty to and Protection of Children Act 1899; Report of the Inter-Departmental Committee on Physical Degeneration 1904, Education Provision of Meals Act 1906 and Mental Deficiency Act 1913 provide examples.
2. For legislation relevant to local government and the franchise see Hollis, *Ladies Elect*, 488–92.
3. Resolutions 44, 45, 47, 49 and 50 of the 1908 Lambeth Conference asserted that greater attention be paid to social justice and pointed to the moral duties of property owners and capitalists towards workers. http://www.anglicancommunion.org/media/127728/1908.pdf (Accessed 20 July 2020).
4. Susan Mumm, 'The Feminization of Nineteenth-Century Anglicanism', in *The Oxford History of Anglicanism, Volume III: Partisan Anglicanism and Its Global Expansion 1829–c.1914*, ed. Rowan Strong (Oxford: Oxford University Press, 2017).
5. E.R. Norman, *Church and Society in England, 1770–1970: A Historical Study* (Oxford: Clarendon Press, 1976), 96.
6. George Sumner, 'Speech to the Annual G.F.S. Diocesan Conference at the George Hotel Winchester', *Girls' Friendly Society Associates Journal*, January 1885; Mumm, 'Women and Philanthropic Cultures'; Bland, 'Purifying the Public World'.
7. Jessica Gerard, 'Lady Bountiful Women of the Landed Classes and Rural Philanthropy', *Victorian Studies* 30, no. 2 (1987); Diana Kendall, *The Power of Good Deeds: Privileged Women and the Social Reproduction of the Upper Class* (Boston: Rowman Littlefield, 2002).
8. Poole, *Philanthropy and the Construction of Victorian Women's Citizenship*, 10.
9. The kind of territory subject to attention from university and public school missioners via the settlement movement. See Scotland, *Squires in the Slums*. See also; J.R. Walkowitz, *City of Dreadful Delight: Narratives of Sexual Danger in Late-Victorian London* (Chicago: University of Chicago Press, 1992).
10. Charles Booth, George H. Duckworth, and Beatrice Webb, *Labour and Life of the People* (London: Williams & Norgate, 1889). Numerous editions followed retitled Life and Labour. Booth's work inlcuded mapping areas of poverty.

11 *ORCC Bristol*, 221–45.
12 Almeric W. Fitzroy, *Report of the Inter-Departmental Committee on Physical Deterioration. Vol.1. Report and Appendix* ([S.l.]: Printed for H.M.S.O., 1904).
13 Ibid., 44.
14 Davin, 'Imperialism and Motherhood'.
15 In Fitzroy, *Report on Physical Deterioration*, 15, 130, 199, 144; ORCC *Barrow-in-Furness*, 467–71.
16 *ORCC Cardiff*; *ORCC Folkestone*; *ORCC Shrewsbury*.
17 *ORCC Manchester*, xvii; *ORCC Cambridge*, 127, 124, 134, 140, 141.
18 Chadwick, *The Victorian Church Part 2*, 155, 272–3, 284–5.
19 Mary Sumner, 'Letter to Dearest Minnie, Lady Addingon Anti Christian Sunday Schools', in *Mothers' Union* (Lambeth Palace Library); Edward Harold Browne, *Antichrist. A Sermon* (London, 1883), 7–10. http://www.anglicancommunion.org/media/127722/1888.pdf (Accessed 20 July 2020).
20 Chadwick, *The Victorian Church Part 2*, 272.
21 B. Seebohm Rowntree, *Poverty: A Study of Town Life* ([S.l.]: Macmillan, 1901).
22 http://www.anglicancommunion.org/media/127728/1908.pdf (Accessed 20 July 2020).
23 Ibid.
24 *ORCC Swansea*, xiii, 93–116.
25 The phrase 'good deed mongers' is used by Ridding in her evocation of life in Winchester where she encountered Mary Sumner and Ellen Joyce. Lady Laura Ridding, 'An Account Written by Laura E. Ridding of Her Married Life at Winchester 1876–1884', Diary 19 March 1894, Selborne Papers (HRO). See also 30 September 1896 Poor Law Conference at Nottingham and 16 May 1903 Nottinghamshire County Council Education Committee 'spoke for women being school managers'.
26 Poole, *Philanthropy and the Construction of Victorian Women's Citizenship*.
27 Hollis, *Ladies Elect*, 231–5. Founders included Miss Ward Andrews of the *English Woman's Review* and Mrs. Ormiston Chant of the National Vigilance Association, the organization also had the approval of Mrs Fawcett and Louisa Twining.
28 NUWW Central Committee Minutes 16 November 1900 in fn. Ibid., 237. The cross party WLGS was revived in 2005 for its origins see Hollis, *Ladies Elect*.
29 *ORCC Cardiff*, 444.
30 Raven, *The Eternal Spirit*, 170–1.
31 *Derby Mercury*, 10 October 1894, 7.
32 'The Guardian Angel of Bristol', *Bristol Mercury*, 5 January 1899, 2. Ridding, *Diaries*, 5 October 1896, Selborne Papers (HRO).
33 Ibid., 7 October 1896.
34 *ORCC Shrewsbury*, 520; Bristol, Clifford's home city had a strong tradition of nonconformist philanthropy. See Martin, 'Single Women and Philanthropy: A Case Study of Women's Associational Life in Bristol, 1880–1914'.

35 *Saturday Review*, 3 October 1896, 360.
36 *ORCC Shrewsbury*, 538.
37 'Norfolk Women's Armenian Refugee Fund', *Eastern Daily Press*, 26 January 1896, 5. Hollis, *Ladies Elect*, 240. Christian Armenians were fleeing the Ottoman Empire on account of systematic and sustained persecution. Between 1894 and 1896, 200,000 were killed, 30,000 died on 1906, attempted genocide by massacres and forced deputations continued through the 1914–18 war. See http://www.nationalarchives.gov.uk/pathways/firstworldwar/spotlights/armenian.htm (Accessed 9 August 2021). Pigott was also the biographer of artist and missionary Lilias Trotter. *Lilias Trotter Founder of the Algiers Mission Band* (London: Marshall Morgan Scott, 1930).
38 *ORCC Bradford*; See Woollacott, 'From Moral to Professional Authority: Secularism, Social Work, and Middle-Class Women's Self-Construction in World War I Britain' for an exploration of trajectories towards professionalization in the YWCA.
39 *ORCC Nottingham*, 166; *ORCC London*, 142.
40 'Women's Meeting, Church Congress', *CT*, 16 October 1903, 481; *ORCC Bristol*, 439.
41 Julia Bolton Holloway, 'Mason, (Frances) Agnes' (*ODNB*, 2004).
42 Notorious amongst abusers was infanticide Amelia Dyer whose exposure led to the passing of the 1897 Infant Life Protection Bill which legislated for female inspection of child care premises. Dyer was not the only abuser. David Burnham, *The Social Worker Speaks: A History of Social Workers through the Twentieth Century* (Farnham: Ashgate, 2012), 33, 34, 39. Mason was known for her systematic inspection and stringent vetting of placement families. Moral as well as physical welfare was her priority. See also Florence Davenport Hill's advocacy for placing workhouse children in foster homes, 'The Boarding Out System Distinguished from Baby Farming', National Association for the Promotion of Social Science, Bristol 1869.
43 The GFS instigated a 'Department for Help for Workhouse Girls' under Joanna Hill an expert on boarded out children and sister to Florence author of *The Children of the State 1868*; Heath-Stubbs, *Friendship's Highway*, 65. The 1874 Metropolitan Association for befriending Young Servants (MABYS) took charge of girls from Poor Law Schools. Both societies supported girls as they started work.
44 Clifford speaking on 'Women as Poor Law Guardians', *ORCC Shrewsbury*, 521; Hollis, *Ladies Elect*, 266.
45 *ORCC Wakefield*, 274–8.
46 *ORCC Rhyl*, 389.
47 *ORCC Stoke on Trent*, 90–101.
48 Thomas and Series, 'Pinsent [Née Parker], Dame Ellen Frances' (*ODNB*, 2004).
49 W.H. Dickinson, 'Royal Commission on the Care and Control of the Feeble-Minded, 1908', *Charity Organisation Review* 25, no. 149 (1909).

50 Salter, *The Problem of the Feeble-Minded*.
51 Pauline M.H. Mazumdar, 'The Eugenists and the Residuum: The Problem of the Urban Poor', *Bulletin of the History of Medicine* 54, no. 2 (1980).
52 Salter, *The Problem of the Feeble-Minded*, preface.
53 The National Health Society was founded in 1871 by Dr Elizabeth Blackwell in 1900. It introduced a diploma that qualified women to work as health visitors.
54 Blakestad, 'Ravenhill, Alice', (*ODNB*, 2004).
55 *ORCC Bradford*, 316; *ORCC Barrow*, 259–64; *ORCC Weymouth*, 97–9.
56 See Lilian L. Shiman, 'The Church of England Temperance Society in the Nineteenth Century', *Historical Magazine of the Protestant Episcopal Church* 41, no. 2 (1972); Brian Harrison, *Drink and the Victorians: The Temperance Question in England, 1815–1872* (London: Faber and Faber, 1971).
57 *ORCC Portsmouth*, 448.
58 *London Daily News*, 7 October 1885, 3. Agnes was the author of *My Life among the Blue Jackets*. See Royal Navy Information sheet no. 043 nmrn.portsmouth.org.uk and aggies.org.uk for her legacy of welfare work for sailors and their families.
59 *ORCC Portsmouth*, 80.
60 Ibid., 81.
61 *ORCC Brighton*, 329; *ORCC Northampton*, 288. The grog ration lasted until 1970.
62 Scharlieb published *The Mother's Guide to the Health and Care of Her Children* (1905), *A Woman's Words to Women on the Care of the Health in England and in India* (1895), *Womanhood and Race-Regeneration* (1912).
63 *ORCC Rhyl*, 399.
64 Mitchell, 'The Treatment of Inebriate Women', 85, 86.
65 *ORCC Exeter*, 247.
66 Ibid., 246, 247.
67 Ibid., 248.
68 Ibid.
69 Ibid.
70 *ORCC Folkstone*, 261.
71 *Hampshire Advertiser*, 12 October 1887, 4.
72 *ORCC Exeter*, 241.
73 *ORCC Rhyl*, 396.
74 Heath-Stubbs, *Friendship's Highway*, 33–41.
75 *Derby Mercury*, 17 October 1894, 5.
76 Ridding, *Diaries*, 18 April 1890, *Selborne Papers* (HRO).
77 *ORCC Shrewsbury*, 496.
78 Ibid., 497.
79 *ORCC Bristol*, 416.
80 'Striking Tribute to the Late Miss Augusta Deane', *Western Daily Press*, 21 August, 1936, 5. *ORCC Leicester*, 368–72.

81   Kelly, 'Lyttelton [Née Clive], (Mary) Kathleen'.
82   *ORCC London*, 137; See Gill, *Women and the Church of England*, 216; Fletcher, 'Talbot [Née Lyttelton], Lavinia'. Two years after the London Congress Kathleen Lyttelton published '*Women and Their Work*' which included advocacy for women's education and the franchise. She also served as president of the NUWW between 1900 and 1901.
83   *ORCC Cardiff*, 439.
84   'Society Women Pilloried', *Taunton Courier and Western Advertiser*, 14 October 1925, 1.
85   *ORCC Hull*, 283.
86   Ibid.
87   Ibid., 284.
88   *ORCC Folkstone*, 251.
89   Ibid., 252. Black edited *Women's Industrial News* from 1895 and wrote *Sweated Industry and the Minimum Wage* (1907), *Married Women's Work* (1915) and *A New Way of Housekeeping* (1918). Black was secretary of the Women's Protective and Provident League from 1886.
90   Ibid., 382.
91   Ibid., 256–60; See also Catherine Webb, *The Woman with the Basket: The History of the Women's Co-Operative Guild 1883–1927* (Manchester: Co-operative Wholesale Society, 1927).
92   *ORCC Northampton*, 151; *ORCC Barrow*, 205; *ORCC Stoke*, 71; *ORCC Manchester*, 199.
93   Hunt, 'Gertrude Tuckwell and the British Labour Movement'; Angela V. John, 'Tuckwell, Gertrude Mary' (*ODNB* 2004); Tuckwell's speech to congress under Christianity and Social Questions, *ORCC Northampton*, 153.
94   *ORCC Northampton*, 152.
95   Ibid.
96   Ibid.
97   Ibid.
98   Social Questions', *CT*, 10 October 1902, 410.
99   The exhibition was a stimulus towards the 1907 Select Committee on Homework, the 1909 Select Committee on the Sweating System and the Trades Board Act of 1909 which moved to alleviate sweating by legislating on wages. Sheila Blackburn, 'Ideology and Social Policy: The Origins of the Trade Boards Act', *The Historical Journal* 34, no. 1 (1991).
100 Gertrude M. Tuckwell, Constance Isabella Stuart Smith, Mary R. MacArthur, May Tennant, Nettie Adler, Adelaide Mary Anderson and Clementina Black, *Women in Industry from Seven Points of View* (London: Duckworth and Co., 1908); See Blackburn, '"No Necessary Connection with Homework"'; Clementina Black contributed to the report of the Sweated Trades Conference. Tuckwell was also on the author of an undated pamphlet on Sweating and in 1910 published *Women's*

Trades Unions (London: Christian Social Union). Alfred Lyttelton supported the Anti-Sweating league.
101 'The Church Congress at Barrow'; 'Socialism', *CT*, 5 October 1906, 415.
102 *ORCC Barrow*, 206.
103 Elaine Harrison, 'Streatfeild, Lucy Anne Evelyn Deane', (*ODNB*, 2004); See Livesey, 'The Politics of Work: Feminism, Professionalisation and Women Inspectors of Factories and Workshops'.
104 *ORCC Barrow*, 425.
105 *ORCC Leicester*, 373.
106 Jones, *Women in British Public Life*, 30.
107 'Death of Lady J.P'. *Lincolnshire Echo*, 2 October 1924.
108 *Hartlepool Northern Daily Mail*, 15 October 1921, 2.
109 Women's part at the Church Congress', *The Vote*, Friday 3 October 1923, 315.
110 'The Woman's Leader', *The Common Cause*, 5 October 1923, 5.
111 See Logan, 'Professionalism and the Impact of England's First Women Justices, 1920–1950'; Woollacott, 'From Moral to Professional Authority: Secularism, Social Work, and Middle-Class Women's Self-Construction in World War I'; Livesey, 'The Politics of Work: Feminism, Professionalisation and Women Inspectors of Factories and Workshops'.
112 Bourdieu and Wacquant, *An Invitation to Reflexive Sociology*, 118; Bourdieu and Passeron, *Reproduction in Education, Society and Culture*.
113 The field of power is understood to relate to the apparatus of government. Power implies political power in a broad sense but not exclusively so.
114 Lofland, *The Public Realm*, 17–18.
115 Gleadle, *Borderline Citizens*, 18.
116 Ibid.
117 'Society Women Pilloried', *Taunton Courier and Western Advertiser*, 14 October 1925, 1.

Chapter 7

1 Jurgen Habermas, *The Structural Transformation of the Public Sphere: An Inquiry into a Category of Bourgeois Society* (Cambridge, MA: MIT Press, 1989); Lefebvre, *The Production of Space*.
2 Kim Knott, *The Location of Religion: A Spatial Analysis*; Kim Knott, 'Spatial Theory and the Study of Religion', *Religion Compass* 2, no. 6 (2008).
3 Carmen M. Mangion, '"To Console, to Nurse, to Prepare for Eternity": The Catholic Sickroom in Late Nineteenth-Century England', *Women's History Review* 21, no. 4 (2012).

4   Kathryne Beebe, Angela Davis, and Kathryn Gleadle, 'Introduction: Space, Place and Gendered Identities: Feminist History and the Spatial Turn', *Women's History Review* 21, no. 4 (2012).
5   McDowell, *Gender, Identity and Place: Understanding Feminist Geographies*, 4.
6   Bourdieu, *The Field of Cultural Production*, 78, 121.
7   Pierre Bourdieu, *The Logic of Practice* (Cambridge: Polity, 1990), 68.
8   Lefebvre, *The Production of Space*, 26; Massey, *Space, Place and Gender*.
9   Terry Rey, 'Marketing the Goods of Salvation: Bourdieu on Religion', *Religion* 34, no. 4 (2004). Bourdieu, 'Genesis and Structure of the Religious Field'.
10 Lefebvre, *The Production of Space*, 26, 33.
11 Gleadle, *Borderline Citizens*, 18.
12 Bourdieu and Wacquant, *An Invitation to Reflexive Sociology*, 119.
13 Ibid.
14 Bourdieu and Passeron, *Reproduction in Education, Society and Culture*, 11–31.
15 Bourdieu, *The Logic of Practice*, 53, 54.
16 Ibid., 20.
17 Judith Butler, *Gender Trouble: Feminism and the Subversion of Identity* (New York and London: Routledge, 1990), 33.
18 Bourdieu, *The Logic of Practice*, 57; Bourdieu and Wacquant, *An Invitation to Reflexive Sociology*, 133.
19 Yeo, *Radical Femininity: Womens' Self Representation in the Public Sphere*, 4.
20 ORCC Weymouth 460, 463, 493.
21 Massey, *Space, Place and Gender*, 179.
22 Mary Sumner, 'To Fathers' and 'To Husbands' in *Home Life*, 141–50, 151–63; Sue Morgan, '"Knights of God": Ellice Hopkins and the White Cross Army'.
23 Morgan, *A Victorian Woman's Place*.
24 'Kensit Crusader in Evidence', *Leeds Mercury*, 3 October 1906, 6.
25 Ridding, *Diaries, Selborne Papers* (HRO); Creighton, *Memoir*.
26 Rendall, 'Women and the Public Sphere'.
27 Prochaska, *The Angel out of the House*.
28 Lofland, *The Public Realm*, 18.
29 Porter, Woodward, and Erskine, *Mary Sumner*, 21.
30 Second 'object' of the MU 1902, in 1904, Mary Sumner claimed at the MU Central Council that the organization was a presence in nearly every British colony. Violet Lancaster, *A Short History of the Mothers' Union* (London: Mothers Union, 1958), 115. Heath-Stubbs, *Friendship's Highway*, 146–52, 153–65.
31 See Elizabeth E. Prevost, *The Communion of Women Missions and Gender in Colonial Africa and the British Metropole* (Oxford: Oxford University Press, 2010) for the MU's first branch for indigenours members, *Friendship's Highway* 82–90.
32 See Catherine Hall and Sonya O. Rose, eds., *At Home with the Empire: Metropolitan Culture and the Imperial World* (Cambridge: Cambridge University Press, 2006);

Alison Twells, *The Civilising Mission and the English Middle Class, 1792–1850: The 'Heathen' at Home and Overseas* (Basingstoke: Palgrave Macmillan, 2009).

33 *ORCC Bradford*, 315: *ORCC Swansea*, 486; *ORCC Folkestone*, 109.
34 *ORCC Hull*, 261; *ORCC Nottingham*, 178.
35 *ORCC London*, 138: *ORCC Newcastle*, 266.
36 http://www.anglicancommunion.org/media/127731/1920.pdf (Accessed 14 June 2021).
37 http://www.anglicancommunion.org/media/127725/1897.pdf (Accessed 14 June 2021).
38 *Western Daily Press*, 5 October 1938, 8.
39 Heeney, *Women's Movement in the Church of England*, 124–5; Jones, '"Unduly Conscious of her Sex"', 640.
40 Gleadle, *Borderline Citizens*, 18.
41 *ORCC Exeter*, 264; *ORCC Bradford*, 355: *ORCC Liverpool*, 619; *ORCC Weymouth*, 463; *ORCC Manchester*, 658.
42 *ORCC Exeter*, 245.
43 Women were still a minority on the commission. See David Evans, 'Tackling the "Hideous Scourge": The Creation of the Venereal Disease Treatment Centres in Early Twentieth-Century Britain', *Social History of Medicine* 5, no. 3 (December 1992). https://doi.org/10.1093/shm/5.3.413 (Accessed 6 April 2022); *ORCC Derby*, 569.
44 Keck and Sikkink, *Advocacy Networks in International Politics*, 2–3.
45 'Parliament of Women', *Dundee Evening Telegraph*, 23 May 1892, 2.
46 Ridding, 'The Early Days of the National Union of Women Workers'.
47 Creighton, *Memoir*, 89.
48 *ORCC Southampton*, 188, 190; 'Women at the Church Congress', *The Common Cause*, 5 October 1923, 5.
49 Sumner, *Our Holiday in the East*.
50 Ridding, 'The Call of Empire,' *Selborne Papers* (HRO).
51 Bourdieu and Passeron, *Reproduction*, 5, 8, 9.
52 *CT*, 16 October 1885, 781. *ORCC Wakefield*, 447. *York Herald*, 9 October 1886, 5. Ridding. *Diaries*, 28 September 1897, *Selborne Papers* (HRO).

Bibliography

Aiston, Sarah Jane. 'Women, Education and Agency 1600–2000 an Historical Perspective'. In *Women, Education and Agency*, edited by Jean Spence, Sarah Jane Aiston and Maureen Meikle, 1–8. London and New York: Routledge, 2010.

Albisetti, James, Joyce Goodman, and Rebecca Rogers, eds. *Girls' Secondary Education in the Western World from 18th to 20th Centuries*. New York: Palgrave, 2010.

Altick, Richard D. *The English Common Reader: A Social History of the Mass Reading Public, 1800–1900*. Columbus: Ohio State University Press, 1998.

Anderson-Faithful, Sue. 'Aspects of Agency: Change and Constraint in the Activism of Mary Sumner, Founder of the Anglican Mothers' Union'. *Women's History Review* no. 6 (2017): 1–18.

Anderson-Faithful, Sue. *Mary Sumner, Mission, Education and Motherhood: Thinking a Life with Bourdieu*. Cambridge: Lutterworth, 2018.

Anderson, R. D. 'Women and Universities'. In *European Universities from the Enlightenment to 1914*, 1–23. Oxford University Press, 2004, 2010.

Auchterlonie, Mitzi. *Conservative Suffragists: The Women's Vote and the Tory Party*. London: Tauris Academic Studies, 2007.

Avery, Gillian. 'Faithfull, Lilian Mary (1865–1952), Headmistress'. *Oxford Dictionary of National Biography*, 2004.

Battiscombe, Georgina. *Reluctant Pioneer: A Life of Elizabeth Wordsworth*. London: Constable, 1978.

Beauman, Katharine Bentley. *Women and the Settlement Movement*. London: Radcliffe, 1996.

Beebe, Kathryne. Angela Davis, and Kathryn Gleadle, 'Introduction: Space, Place and Gendered Identities: Feminist History and the Spatial Turn'. *Women's History Review* 21, no. 4 (2012): 523–32.

Blackburn, Sheila. 'Ideology and Social Policy: The Origins of the Trade Boards Act'. *The Historical Journal* 34, no. 1 (1991): 43–64.

Blackburn, Sheila. '"No Necessary Connection with Homework": Gender and Sweated Labour, 1840–1909'. *Social History* 22, no. 3 (1997): 269–85.

Blakestad, Nancy L. 'Ravenhill, Alice (1859–1954)'. *Oxford Dictionary of National Biography*, 2004.

Bland, Lucy. 'Purifying the Public World: Feminist Vigilantes in Late Victorian England'. *Women's History Review* 1, no. 3 (1992): 377–412.

Bland, Lucy. *Banishing the Beast: English Feminism and Sexual Morality 1885–1914*. London: Penguin, 1995.

Bourdieu, Pierre, and Jean-Claude Passeron. *Reproduction in Education, Society and Culture* [in Translation of: La reproduction.]. Rev. ed./preface to the 1990 edition by Pierre Bourdieu. ed. London: Sage, 1990.

Bourdieu, Pierre. 'Genesis and Structure of the Religious Field'. *Comparative Social Research* 13, no. 1 (1991): 1–44.

Bourdieu, Pierre, and Loic J. D. Wacquant. *An Invitation to Reflexive Sociology*. Cambridge: Polity Press, 1992.

Bourdieu, Pierre. *The Field of Cultural Production: Essays on Art and Literature*. Cambridge: Polity Press, 1993.

Braster, Sjaak. 'The People, the Poor, and the Oppressed: The Concept of Popular Education through Time'. *Paedagogica Historica* 47, nos. 1–2 (2011): 1–14.

Brundage, Anthony. 'Green, John Richard (1837–1883), Historian'. *Oxford Dictionary of National Biography*, 2004.

Buettner, Elizabeth. *Empire Families: Britons and Late Imperial India*. Oxford: Oxford University Press, 2004.

Burnham, David. *The Social Worker Speaks: A History of Social Workers through the Twentieth Century*. Farnham: Ashgate, 2012.

Burns, Arthur. 'Emery, William (1825–1910), Church of England Clergyman'. *Oxford Dictionary of National Biography*, 2004.

Burstyn, Joan. *Victorian Education and the Ideal of Womanhood*. London: Croom Helm, 1980.

Bush, Barbara. 'Feminising Empire: British Women's Activist Networks in Defending and Challenging Empire from 1918 to Decolonisation'. *Women's History Review* 25, no. 4 (2016): 499–519.

Bush, Julia. '"The Right Sort of Woman": Female Emigrators and Emigration to the British Empire,1890–1910'. *Women's History Review* 3, no. 3 (1994): 385–409.

Bush, Julia. 'Edwardian Ladies and the "Race" Dimensions of British Imperialism'. *Womens Studies International Forum* 21, no. 3 (1998): 277–89.

Bush, Julia. *Edwardian Ladies and Imperial Power*. London: Leicester University Press, 2000.

Bush, Julia. '"Special Strengths for Their Own Special Duties": Women, Higher Education and Gender Conservatism in Late Victorian Britain'. *History of Education* 34, no. 4 (2005): 387–405.

Bush, Julia. 'Joyce, Ellen (1832–1924)'. *Oxford Dictionary of National Biography*, 2006.

Bush, Julia. 'The National Union of Women Workers and Women's Suffrage'. In *Suffrage Outside Suffragism*, edited by M. Boussahba-Bravard, 105–31. London: Palgrave Macmillan, 2007.

Butler, Judith. *Gender Trouble: Feminism and the Subversion of Identity*. New York and London: Routledge, 1990.

Cannadine, David. *Class in Britain*. New Haven and London: Yale University Press, 1998.

Chadwick, Owen. *The Victorian Church Part 2 1860–1901*. 2nd edn. London: A. and C. Black, 1972.

Chadwick, Owen. *The Victorian Church Part I 1827–1859*. London: A. and C. Black, 1966.

Chadwick, Owen. 'Raven, Charles Earle (1885–1964), Theologian'. *Oxford Dictionary of National Biography*, 2004.

Chilton, Lisa. 'A New Class of Women for the Colonies: The Imperial Colonist and the Construction of Empire'. *The Journal of Imperial and Commonwealth History* 31, no. 2 (2003): 36–56.

Chilton, Lisa. *Agents of Empire: British Female Migration to Canada and Australia, 1860s–1930*. Toronto and Buffalo: University of Toronto Press, 2007.

Coombs, Margaret A. *Charlotte Mason Hidden Heritage and Educational Influence*. Cambridge: Lutterworth, 2015.

Cowman, Krista. *Women in British Politics, c.1689–1979*. London: Bloomsbury, 2010.

Crawford, Elizabeth. *Art and Suffrage: A Biographical Dictionary of Suffrage Artists*. London: Francis Boutle, 2018.

Creedon, Alison. *Only a Woman: Henrietta Barnett: Social Reformer and Founder of Hampstead Garden Suburb*. Chichester: Phillimore, 2006.

Creighton, Louise. *Life and Letters of Mandell Creighton*. [S.l.]: London: Longmans, Green, 1904.

Creighton, Louise. *Memoir of a Victorian Woman: Reflections of Louise Creighton 1850–1936*. Bloomington and Indianapolis: Indiana University Press, 1994.

Creighton, Louise, and James Thayne Covert. *A Victorian Family: As Seen through the Letters of Louise Creighton to Her Mother, 1872–1880*. Lewiston, NY and Lampeter: Edwin Mellen, 1998.

Cremin, Lawrence. *Public Education*. New York: Basic Books, 1976.

Curthoys, M. C. 'Heywood, James (1810–1897), Politician, University Reformer, and Philanthropist'. *Oxford Dictionary of National Biography*, 2009.

Daggers, Jenny. 'The Victorian Female Civilising Mission and Women's Aspirations towards Priesthood in the Church of England'. *Women's History Review* 10, no. 4 (2001): 651–70.

Davin, Anna. 'Imperialism and Motherhood'. *History Workshop* 5 (1978): 9–65.

Delamont, Sara. 'The Contradictions in Ladies' Education'. In *The Nineteenth-Century Woman: Her Cultural and Physical World*, edited by Sara Delamont and Lorna Duffin, 134–63. London: Croom Helm, 1978.

Delamont, Sara. 'Burstall, Sara Annie (1859–1939), Headmistress'. *Oxford Dictionary of National Biography*, 2011.

Dunae, Patrick A. 'Penny Dreadfuls: Late Nineteenth-Century Boys' Literature and Crime'. *Victorian Studies* 22, no. 2 (1979): 133–50.

Dutta, Sutapa, ed. *British Women Travellers: Empire and beyond, 1770–1870*. London: Routledge, 2019.

Dyhouse, Carol. *Girls Growing up in Late Victorian and Edwardian Britain*. London: Routledge, 1981.

Dyhouse, Carol. *No Distinction of Sex?: Women in British Universities, 1870–1939*. London and Bristol, PA: UCL Press, 1995.

Eisenmann, Linda. 'Creating a Framework for Interpreting US Women's Educational History: Lessons from Historical Lexicography'. *History of Education* 30, no. 5 (2001): 453–70.

Emery, F. V. 'Geography and Imperialism: The Role of Sir Bartle Frere (1815–84)'. *The Geographical Journal* 150, no. 3 (1984): 342–60.

Evans, David. 'Tackling the "Hideous Scourge": The Creation of the Venereal Disease Treatment Centres in Early Twentieth-Century Britain'. *Social History of Medicine* 5, no. 3 (1992): 413–33.

Evans, W. Gareth. *Education and Female Emancipation: The Welsh Experience, 1847–1914*. Cardiff: University of Wales Press, 1990.

Eyre, Angharad. 'Education'. In *Women in Christianity in the Age of Empire: (1800–1920)*, edited by Janet Wootton, 130–53. London: Routledge, 2022.

Fawcett, Millicent Garrett. *What I Remember*. [S.l.]: London: Fisher Unwin, 1924.

Fitzgerald, Tanya. 'Cartographies of Friendship: Mapping Missionary Women's Educational Networks in Aotearoa/New Zealand 1823–40'. *History of Education* 32, no. 5 (2003): 513–27.

Fletcher, Sheila. *Women First: The Female Tradition in English Physical Education 1880–1980*. London: Athlone, 1984.

Fletcher, Sheila. *Maude Royden: A Life*. Oxford: Basil Blackwell, 1989.

Fletcher, Sheila. *Victorian Girls: Lord Lyttelton's Daughters*. London: Phoenix, 2004.

Fletcher, Sheila. 'Talbot [Née Lyttelton], Lavinia (1849–1939), Promoter of Women's Education'. *Oxford Dictionary of National Biography*, 2006.

Fletcher, Sheila. 'Gladstone, Helen (1849–1925), Educationist'. *Oxford Dictionary of National Biography*, 2006.

Flint, Kate. 'Soulsby, Lucy Helen Muriel (1856–1927)'. *Oxford Dictionary of National Biography*, 2004.

Fowler, Helen. 'Sidgwick [Née Balfour], Eleanor Mildred (1845–1936), College Head'. *Oxford Dictionary of National Biography*, 2004.

Franzen, Ruth. 'The Legacy of Ruth Rouse'. *International Bulletin of Missionary Research* 17, no. 4 (1993): 154–8.

Gallant, Mary P. 'Against the Odds: Anne Jemima Clough and Women's Education in England'. *History of Education* 26, no. 2 (1997): 145–64.

Garnett, Jane. 'Feilding, Lady Mary (1823–1896), Founder of the Working Ladies' Guild'. *Oxford Dictionary of National Biography*, 2004.

Gerard, Jessica. 'Lady Bountiful Women of the Landed Classes and Rural Philanthropy'. *Victorian Studies* 30, no. 2 (1987): 183–210.

Gill, Sean. *Women and the Church of England: From the Eighteenth Century to the Present*. London: Society for Promoting Christian Knowledge, 1994.

Glage, Liselotte. *Clementina Black: A Study in Social History and Literature*. Heidelberg: Winter, 1981.

Gleadle, Katherine. *Borderline Citizens: Women, Gender and Political Culture in Britain, 1815–1867*. Oxford: OUP/British Academy, 2009.

Goodman, Joyce F. 'Girls' Public Day School Company'. *Oxford Dictionary of National Biography*, 2005.

Goodman, Joyce, and Jane Martin. 'Networks after Bourdieu: Women, Education and Politics from the 1980s to the 1920s'. *History of Education Researcher* 80, November (2007): 65–75.

Gordon, Peter. 'Knightley [Née Bowater], Louisa Mary, Lady Knightley (1842–1913), Churchwoman and Women's Activist'. *Oxford Dictionary of National Biography*, 2004.

Gordon, Peter. 'Lyttelton, George William, Fourth Baron Lyttelton and Fourth Baron Westcote (1817–1876), Educationist'. *Oxford Dictionary of National Biography*, 2006.

Gordon, Peter and David Doughan. *Dictionary of British Women's Organisations, 1825–1960*. London: Woburn Press, 2001.

Gorham, Deborah. *The Victorian Girl and the Feminine Ideal*. London: Croom Helm, 1982.

Grimshaw, Patricia. 'In Pursuit of True Anglican Womanhood in Victoria, 1880–1914'. *Women's History Review* 2, no. 3 (1993): 331–47.

Grierson, Janet. *The Deaconess*. London: CIO, 1981.

Hadden, J. C., and Sayoni Basu. 'Thring, Godfrey (1823–1903), Hymn Writer'. *Oxford Dictionary of National Biography*, 2004.

Haig, Alan. *The Victorian Clergy*. London: Croom Helm, 1984.

Hall, Catherine. *Civilising Subjects: Metropole and Colony in the English Imagination, 1830–1867*. Cambridge: Polity, 2002.

Hall, Catherine and Sonya O. Rose, eds. *At Home with the Empire: Metropolitan Culture and the Imperial World*. Cambridge: Cambridge University Press, 2006.

Hall, Lesley. *Sex, Gender and Social Change in Britain since 1880*. Basingstoke: Macmillan, 2000.

Harrison, Brian. *Drink and the Victorians: The Temperance Question in England, 1815–1872*. London: Faber and Faber, 1971.

Harrison, Brian. 'For Church Queen and Family; the Girls' Friendly Society 1874–1920'. *Past and Present* 61 (1973): 107–38.

Harrison, Elaine. 'Streatfeild, Lucy Anne Evelyn Deane (1865–1950)'. *Oxford Dictionary of National Biography*, 2004.

Heath-Stubbs, Mary. *Friendships Highway; Being the History of the Girls' Friendly Society*. London: GFS, 1926.

Heeney, Brian. 'Women's Struggle for Professional Work and Status in the Church of England 1900–1930'. *The Historical Journal* 26, no. 2 (1983): 329–47.

Heeney, Brian. *The Women's Movement in the Church of England, 1850–1930*. Oxford: Clarendon, 1988.

Hilton, Mary, and Pam Hirsch, eds. *Practical Visionaries Women, Education and Social Progress 1790–1930*. Harlow: Pearson, 2000.

Hobbs, Andrew. *A Fleet Street in Every Town: The Provincial Press in England, 1855–1900*. Cambridge: Open Book Publishers, 2018.

Hollis, Patricia. *Ladies Elect: Women in English Local Government, 1865–1914*. Oxford: Clarendon Press, 1989.

Holloway, Julia Bolton. 'Mason, (Frances) Agnes'. *Oxford Dictionary of National Biography*, 2004.

Howard, John. 'The Making of a Martyr Reactions to John Kensit's Death in 1902'. *Theology* 105, no. 872 (2002): 348–56.

Hughes-Johnson, Alexandra and Lyndsey Jenkins, eds. *The Politics of Women's Suffrage: Local, National and International Dimensions*. London: University of London Press, 2022.

Hunt, Cathy. 'Gertrude Tuckwell and the British Labour Movement, 1891–1921: A Study in Motives and Influences'. *Women's History Review* 22, no. 3 (2013): 478–96.

Hurt, John. *Education in Evolution Church, State, Society and Popular Education 1800–1870*. London: Rupert Hart-Davis, 1971.

Jones, Greta. 'Women and Eugenics in Britain: The Case of Mary Scharlieb, Elizabeth Sloan Chesser, and Stella Browne'. *Annals of Science* 52, no. 5 (1995): 481–502.

Jones, Helen. *Women in British Public Life, 1914–1950: Gender, Power, and Social Policy*. Harlow: Longman, 2000.

Jones, Helen. 'Markham, Violet Rosa (1872–1959), Public Servant'. *Oxford Dictionary of National Biography*, 2004.

Jones, Timothy Willem. '"Unduly Conscious of Her Sex": Priesthood, Female Bodies, and Sacred Space in the Church of England'. *Women's History Review* 21, no. 4 (2012): 639–55.

Keck, Margaret and Kathryn A. Sikkink. *Advocacy Networks in International Politics Activists beyond Borders*. Ithaca and London: Cornell University Press, 1998.

Kelly, Serena. 'A Sisterhood of Service: The Records and Early History of the National Union of Women Workers'. *Journal of the Society of Archivists* 14, no. 2 (1993): 167–74.

Kelly, Serena. 'Lyttelton [Née Clive], (Mary) Kathleen (1856–1907), Women's Activist'. *Oxford Dictionary of National Biography*, 2004.

Kelly, Serena. 'Janes, Emily (1846–1928), Women's Welfare Activist'. *Oxford Dictionary of National Biography*, 2004.

Kelly, Serena. 'Ridding, Lady Laura Elizabeth (1849–1939)'. *Oxford Dictionary of National Biography*, 2004.

Kendall, Diana. *The Power of Good Deeds: Privileged Women and the Social Reproduction of the Upper Class*. Boston: Rowman Littlefield, 2002.

Kent, Christopher. 'Image and Reality: The Actress and Society'. In *A Widening Sphere* edited by Martha Vicinus, 94–116. Indiana: Indiana University Press, 1977.

Kerber, Linda. 'Separate Spheres, Female Worlds, Woman's Place; the Rhetoric of Womens' History'. *Journal of American History* 75, no. 1 (1988): 9–39.

Knight, Frances. *The Nineteenth Century Church and English Society*. Cambridge: Cambridge University Press, 1995.

Knott, Kim. *The Location of Religion: A Spatial Analysis*. London: Equinox Publishing, 2005.
Lake, Marilyn and Henry Reynolds. 'White Australia Points the Way'. In *Drawing the Global Colour Line: White Men's Countries and the International Challenge of Racial Equality*, 137–65. Cambridge: Cambridge University Press, 2008.
Lancaster, Violet. *A Short History of the Mothers' Union*. London: Mothers' Union, 1958.
Lefebvre, Henri. *The Production of Space* [in Translation of: La production de l'espace.]. Oxford: Basil Blackwell, 1991.
Leigh, Maxwell Studdy, ed. *Christianity in the Modern State. A Report of the Proceedings of the Sixty-Fifth Church Congress*. London: Hodder and Stoughton, 1936.
Levine, Philippa. 'Grey [Née Shirreff], Maria Georgina (1816–1906), Educationist and Writer'. *Oxford Dictionary of National Biography*, 2005.
Livesey, Ruth. 'The Politics of Work: Feminism, Professionalisation and Women Inspectors of Factories and Workshops'. *Women's History Review* 13, no. 2 (2004): 233–62.
Loader, Helen. *Mrs Humphry Ward and Greenian Philosophy: Religion, Society and Politics*. Cham: Palgrave Macmillan, 2019.
Lofland, Lyn H. *The Public Realm: Exploring the City's Quintessential Social Territory*. Hawthorne, NY: Aldine de Gruyter, 1998.
Logan, Anne. 'Professionalism and the Impact of England's First Women Justices, 1920–1950'. *The Historical Journal* 49, no. 3 (2006): 833–50.
Lux-Sterritt, Laurence, and Carmen M. Mangion. *Gender, Catholicism and Spirituality: Women and the Roman Catholic Church in Britain and Europe, 1200–1900*. Basingstoke: Palgrave Macmillan, 2010.
Maguire, G. E. 'The Party Mobilizes for Women'. In *Conservative Women: A History of Women and the Conservative Party, 1874–1997*. London: Palgrave Macmillan UK, 1998.
Malmgreen, Gail. *Religion in the Lives of English Women, 1760–1930*. London: Croom Helm, 1986.
Mangion, Carmen M. '"To Console, to Nurse, to Prepare for Eternity": The Catholic Sickroom in Late Nineteenth-century England'. *Women's History Review* 21, no. 4 (2012): 657–72.
Martin, Jane, and Joyce Goodman. *Women and Education, 1800–1980*. Basingstoke: Palgrave Macmillan, 2004.
Martin, Moira. 'Single Women and Philanthropy: A Case Study of Women's Associational Life in Bristol, 1880–1914.' *Women's History Review* 17, no. 3 (2008): 395–417.
Massey, Doreen B. *Space, Place and Gender*. Cambridge: Polity, 1994.
Maughan, Steven. 'Imperial Christianity: Bishop Montgomery and the Foreign Missions of the Church of England, 1895–1915'. In *The Imperial Horizons of British Protestant Missions 1880–1914*, edited by A. N. Porter, 32–57. Grand Rapids MI: Wm. B. Eerdmans, 2003.

Mayes, Kelly. 'The Disease of Reading and Victorian Periodicals.' In *Literature in the Marketplace: Nineteenth-Century British Publishing and Reading Practices Cambridge Studies in Nineteenth-Century Literature and Culture Series, No. 5.*, edited by John O. Jordan and Robert L. Patten, 165–94. Cambridge: Cambridge UP, 1995.

Mazumdar, Pauline M. H. 'The Eugenists and the Residuum: The Problem of the Urban Poor'. *Bulletin of the History of Medicine* 54, no. 2 (1980): 204–15.

McAdam, Gloria. 'Willing Women and the Rise of Convents in Nineteenth-century England'. *Women's History Review* 8, no. 3 (1999): 422–41.

McDermid, Jane. *The Schooling of Working-Class Girls in Victorian Scotland: Gender, Education and Identity*. London: Routledge, 2005.

McDowell, Linda. *Gender, Identity and Place: Understanding Feminist Geographies*. London: Polity Press, 1999.

Melman, Billie. *Women's Orients: English Women and the Middle East, 1718-1918: Sexuality, Religion and Work* [in English]. 2nd ed. Basingstoke: Macmillan, 1995.

Melnyk, Julie. 'Theological Approaches to Women in the Age of Enlightenment'. In *Women in Christianity in the Age of Empire: (1800–1920)*, edited by Janet Wootton, 34–53. London: Routledge, 2022.

Money, Agnes Louisa. *History of the Girls' Friendly Society*. London: Wells Gardner, Darton, 1902.

Morgan, Simon. *A Victorian Woman's Place: Public Culture in the Nineteenth Century*. London: Tauris Academic Studies, 2007.

Morgan, Sue. *A Passion for Purity: Ellice Hopkins and the Politics of Gender in the Late-Victorian Church*. Bristol: Centre for Comparative Studies in Religion and Gender, University of Bristol, 1999.

Morgan, Sue. '"Knights of God": Ellice Hopkins and the White Cross Army, 1883-95'. *Studies in Church History* 34 (1998): 431–45.

Morgan, Sue. 'Faith Sex and Purity: The Religio-Feminist Theory of Ellice Hopkins'. *Women's History Review* 1 (2000): 13–34.

Morgan, Sue. *Women, Religion, and Feminism in Britain, 1750–1900*. Basingstoke: Palgrave Macmillan, 2002.

Morgan, Sue. 'Theorising Feminist History: A Thirty Year Retrospective'. *Women's History Review* 18, no. 3 (2009): 381–407.

Morgan, Sue and Jacqueline de Vries, eds. *Women, Gender and Religious Cultures in Britain, 1800–1940*. London: Routledge, 2010.

Morgan, Sue. 'A "Feminist Conspiracy": Maude Royden, Women's Ministry and the British Press, 1916–1921'. *Women's History Review* 22, no. 5 (2013): 777–800.

Morgan, Sue. 'Sex and Common-Sense: Maude Royden, Religion, and Modern Sexuality'. *Journal of British Studies* 52, no. 1 (2013): 153–78.

Moruzi, Kristine '"Never Read Anything That Can at All Unsettle Your Religious Faith": Reading and Writing in the Monthly Packet'. *Women's Writing* 17, no. 2 (2010): 288–304.

Moruzi, Kristine. *Constructing Girlhood through the Periodical Press, 1850–1915*. London: Routledge, 2012.

Moyse, Cordelia. *A History of the Mothers' Union: Women Anglicanism and Globalisation, 1876–2008*. Woodbridge: Boydell Press, 2009.

Mumm, Susan. *All Saints Sisters of the Poor an Anglican Sisterhood in the Nineteenth Century*. Woodbridge Suffolk: Church of England Record Society Boydell Press, 2001.

Mumm, Susan. 'Women and Philanthropic Cultures'. In *Women, Gender and Religious Cultures in Britain, 1800–1940*, edited by Sue Morgan and Jacqueline de Vries, 54–71. London: Routledge, 2010.

Mumm, Susan. 'Making Space, Taking Space: Spatial Discomfort, Gender,and Victorian Religion'. Project Canterbury, accessed 25 September 2021. http://anglicanhistory.org.

Murphy, James. *Church, State and Schools in Britain 1800–1970*. London: Routledge and Kegan Paul, 1971.

Newsome, D. *The Parting of Friends: A Study of the Wilberforces and Henry Manning*. London: Murray, 1966.

Norman, E. R. *Church and Society in England, 1770–1970: A Historical Study*. Oxford: Clarendon Press, 1976.

Parkes, Susan M. 'Trinity College, Dublin and the "Steamboat Ladies", 1904–1907'. In *Women and Higher Education: Past, Present and Future*, edited by M. R. Masson and D. Simonton, 244–50. Aberdeen: Aberdeen University Press, 1996.

Pickles, Katie. *Female Imperialism and National Identity: Imperial Order Daughters of the Empire*. Manchester: Manchester University Press, 2002.

Pleasance, Pat. 'Edith Picton-Turbervill'. In *These Dangerous Women*, 40–1. London: Women's International League for Peace and Freedom, 2015.

Poole, A. G. *Philanthropy and the Construction of Victorian Women's Citizenship: Lady Frederick Cavendish and Miss Emma Cons*. Toronto: University of Toronto Press, Scholarly Publishing Division, 2014.

Porter, A. N. *The Nineteenth Century, The Oxford History of the British Empire*. Oxford: Oxford University Press, 1999.

Porter, A. N. *The Imperial Horizons of British Protestant Missions, 1880–1914*. Grand Rapids, MI: Wm. B. Eerdmans, 2003.

Porter, Mary, Mary Woodward, and Horatia Erskine. *Mary Sumner Her Life and Work and a Short History of the Mothers' Union*. Winchester: Warren and Sons, 1921.

Pratt, Mary Louise. *Imperial Eyes: Travel Writing and Transculturation*. London: Routledge, 1992.

Prevost, Elizabeth E. *The Communion of Women Missions and Gender in Colonial Africa and the British Metropole*. Oxford: Oxford University Press, 2010.

Prochaska, F. K. *Women and Philanthropy in Nineteenth Century England*. Oxford: Clarendon Press, 1980.

Prochaska, Frank. *The Angel out of the House: Philanthropy and Gender in Nineteenth-Century England*. Charlottesville and London: University of Virginia Press, 2002.

Pugh, Martin. 'Palmer, (Beatrix) Maud [Née Lady (Beatrix) Maud Gascoyne-Cecil], Countess of Selborne (1858–1950), Suffragist and Political Wife'. *Oxford Dictionary of National Biography*, 2007.

Purvis, June. *Hard Lessons: The Lives and Education of Working-Class Women in Nineteenth-Century England*. Cambridge: Polity Press, 1989.
Purvis, June and June Hannam, eds. *The British Women's Suffrage Campaign: National and International Perspectives*. London: Routledge, 2021.
Raftery, Deirdre. 'The Opening of Higher Education to Women in Nineteenth Century England: "Unexpected Revolution" or Inevitable Change?'. *Higher Education Quarterly* 56, no. 4 (2002): 331–46.
Raftery, Deirdre. 'Religions and the History of Education: A Historiography'. *History of Education* 41, no. 1 (2012): 41–56.
Raftery, Deirdre, and Susan M. Parkes. *Female Education in Ireland 1700–1900: Minerva or Madonna* [in English]. Dublin: Irish Academic Press, 2007.
Raven, Charles Earle. *The Eternal Spirit. An Account of the Church Congress Held at Southport, October, 1926*. London: Hodder and Stoughton, 1926.
Ravenhill-Johnson, Annie. *The Art and Ideology of the Trade Union Emblem 1850–1925*. London: Anthem Press, 2014.
Rendall, Jane. 'Women and the Public Sphere'. *Gender and History* 11 (1999): 476–99.
Rey, Terry. 'Marketing the Goods of Salvation: Bourdieu on Religion'. *Religion* 34, no. 4 (2004): 331–43.
Richardson, Sarah May. *The Political Worlds of Women: Gender and Politics in Nineteenth Century Britain*. Routledge Research in Gender and History. New York: Routledge, 2013.
Richmond, Vivienne. '"It Is Not a Society for Human Beings but for Virgins"; the Girls Friendly Society Membership Eligibility Dispute 1875–1931'. *Journal of Historical Sociology* 20, no. 3 (2007): 304–27.
Ridding, Laura Elizabeth and Sophia Matilda Palmer afterwards Comtesss De Franqueville, *Sophia Matilda Palmer, Comtesse De Franqueville, 1852–1915. A Memoir*. London: John Murray, 1919.
Ridding, Laura Lady. *George Ridding, Schoolmaster and Bishop, Forty-Third Headmaster of Winchester, 1866–1884, First Bishop of Southwell, 1884–1904*. London: Edward Arnold, 1908.
Robinson, Elizabeth. *Deaconess Gilmore Memories Collected by Deaconess Elizabeth Robinson*. London: Society for the Promotion of Christian Knowledge, 1924.
Robinson, Jane. *Hearts and Minds the Untold Story of the Great Pilgrimage and How Women Got the Vote*. London: Doubleday, 2018.
Romaines, Ethel. *Charlotte Mary Yonge an Appreciation*. London: Mowbray, 1908.
Ross, Andrew. 'Christian Missions and the Mid- Nineteenth Century Change in Attitudes to Race: The African Experience'. In *The Imperial Horizons of British Protestant Missions*, edited by Andrew Porter, 85–103. Grand Rapids, Michigan and Cambridge: Wm. B. Eerdmans, 2003.
Rowbotham, Judith. *Good Girls Make Good Wives: Guidance for Girls in Victorian Fiction*. Oxford: Basil Blackwell, 1989.
Rowbotham, Judith. 'Ministering Angels, Not Ministers: Women's Involvement in the Foreign Missionary Movement, C.1860–1910'. In *Women, Religion and Feminism*

in Britain, 1750–1900, edited by Sue Morgan, 179–95. Basingstoke: Palgrave Macmillan, 2002.

Rowbotham, Sheila. 'The Trouble with Patriarchy.' In *The Feminist History Reader*, edited by Sue Morgan, 51–6. London and New York: Routledge, 2007.

Ruskin, John. *Sesame and Lilies*. Nelson: Hendon, 2000 [1865].

Schaffer, Talia. 'Taming the Tropics: Charlotte Yonge Takes on Melanesia.' *Victorian Studies* 47 (2005): 204–14.

Scotland, Nigel. *John Bird Sumner: Evangelical Archbishop*. Leominster: Gracewing, 1995.

Scott, Harold. revised D. Thom. 'Barker, Dame Lilian Charlotte (1874–1955).' *Oxford Dictionary of National Biography*, 2004.

Scott, Joan Wallach. 'Gender: Still a Useful Category of Analysis?' *Diogenes* (2010). accessed 5 August 2019. http://dio.sagepub.com/content/57/1/7.refs.html.

Shiman, Lilian L. 'The Church of England Temperance Society in the Nineteenth Century.' *Historical Magazine of the Protestant Episcopal Church* 41, no. 2 (1972): 179–95.

Smith, Harold L. *The British Women's Suffrage Campaign, 1866–1928*. 2nd rev. edn. Harlow: Longman, 2010.

Spender, Dale. *The Education Papers: Women's Quest for Equality in Britain 1850–1912*. London: Routledge and Kegan Paul, 1987.

Springhall, John. 'Brabazon, Reginald, Twelfth Earl of Meath (1841–1928).' *Oxford Dictionary of National Biography*, 2004.

Steele, David. 'Palmer, Roundell, First Earl of Selborne (1812–1895), Lord Chancellor.' *Oxford Dictionary of National Biography*, 2021.

Styler, Rebecca. *The Contexts of Women's Literary Theology in the Nineteenth Century. Literary Theology by Women Writers of the Nineteenth Century*. Farnham: Ashgate, 2010.

Sumner, George Henry. *Life of C. R. Sumner, D.D., Bishop of Winchester, during a Forty Years' Episcopate*. London: Wells, Gardner, 1876.

Sumner, Mary Elizabeth. *Our Holiday in the East*. London: Hurst & Blackett, 1881.

Sumner, Mary. *To Mothers of the Higher Classes*. Winchester: Warren and Son, 1888.

Sumner, Mary. *Home Life*. Winchester: Warren and Son, 1896.

Sumner, Mary. *Memoir of George Henry Sumner, D.D. Bishop of Guildford: Published for His Friends by Special Request*. Winchester: Warren and Sons, 1910.

Sutherland, John. *The Longman Companion to Victorian Fiction*. 2nd edn. Harlow: Pearson Longman, 2009.

Swaisland, Cecillie. *Servants and Gentlewomen to the Golden Land: The Emigration of Single Women from Britain to Southern Africa, 1820–1939*. Oxford: Providence; Berg; Pietermaritzburg, South Africa: University of Natal, 1993.

Thomas, R. and H. Series. 'Pinsent [Née Parker], Dame Ellen Frances (1866–1949) Promoter of the Mental Health Services.' *Oxford Dictionary of National Biography*, 2004.

Thompson, Andrew S. 'Hunt, Violet Edith Gwynllyn Brooke- (1870–1910), Writer, Social Worker, and Political Activist.' *Oxford Dictionary of National Biography*, 2006.

Thorne, Susan. 'Religion and Empire at Home'. In *At Home with the Empire Metropolitan Culture and the Imperial World*, edited by Catherine Hall and Sonia O. Rose, 143–65. Cambridge: Cambridge University Press, 2006.

Tickner, Lisa. 'Banners and Banner-Making'. In *The Nineteenth-Century Visual Reader*, edited by Vanessa R. Schwartz and Jeannene M. Przyblyski, 341–7. New York: Routledge, 2004.

Tosh, John. *Manliness and Masculinities in Nineteenth-Century Britain: Essays on Gender, Family, and Empire*. Harlow: Pearson Longman, 2005.

Turnbull, Annmarie. 'Calder, Fanny Louisa (1838–1923), Promoter of Education in Domestic Subjects'. *Oxford Dictionary of National Biography*, 2004.

Twells, Alison. *The Civilising Mission and the English Middle Class, 1792–1850: The 'Heathen' at Home and Overseas*. Basingstoke: Palgrave Macmillan, 2009.

Vicinus, Martha. *Independent Women: Work and Community for Single Women: 1850–1920*. London: Virago, 1985.

Vickery, Amanda. '"Golden Age to Separate Spheres" a Review of the Categories and Chronology of English Women's History'. In *Gender and History in Western Europe*, edited by Robert Shoemaker and Mary Vincent, 197–225. London: Addison-Wesley Longman, 1998.

Vincent, David. *Literacy and Popular Culture: England 1750–1914*. Cambridge: Cambridge University Press, 1989.

Walkowitz, J. R. *City of Dreadful Delight: Narratives of Sexual Danger in Late-Victorian London*. Chicago: University of Chicago Press, 1992.

Wanhalla, Angela. 'To "Better the Breed of Men": Women and Eugenics in New Zealand, 1900–1935'. *Women's History Review* 16, no. 2 (2007): 163–82.

Ward, A. W. and Ian Machin. 'Maclagan, William Dalrymple (1826–1910), Archbishop of York'. *Oxford Dictionary of National Biography*, 2004.

Ware, Vron. *Beyond the Pale: White Women, Racism and History*. London: Verso, 1992.

Watkins, Micky. *Henrietta Barnett: Social Worker and Community Planner*. London: Micky Watkins and Hampstead Garden Suburb Archive Trust, 2011.

Webb, R. K. 'Brooke, Stopford Augustus (1832–1916)'. *Oxford Dictionary of National Biography*, 2003.

Wellings, Martin. 'The First Protestant Martyr of the Twentieth Century: The Life and Significance of John Kensit (1853–1902)'. *Studies in Church History* 30 (1993): 347–58.

Wilberforce, William. *A Practical View of the Prevailing Religious System of Professed Christians in the Higher and Middle Classes of This Country Contrasted with Real Christianity*. Dublin: Dugdale, 1797.

Williams, Sarah C. '"Is There a Bible in the House?" Gender Religion and Family Culture'. In *Women, Gender and Religious Cultures in Britain, 1800–1940*, edited by Sue Morgan and Jacqueline de Vries, 11–31. London: Routledge, 2011.

Woollacott, Angela. 'From Moral to Professional Authority: Secularism, Social Work, and Middle-Class Women's Self-Construction in World War I'. *Journal of Women's History* 10, no. 2 (1988): 85–111.

Wootton, Janet, ed. *Women in Christianity in the Age of Empire: (1800–1920)*. London: Routledge, 2022.

Yeo, Eileen Janes. *Radical Femininity; Womens' Self Representation in the Public Sphere*. Manchester: Manchester University Press, 1998.

Yonge, Charlotte. *Womankind*. 2nd edn. London and New York: Macmillan, 1890 [1876].

Yonge, Charlotte. *The Daisy Chain, or, Aspirations: A Family Chronicle*. London: Virago, 1988 [1856].

Index

Acres, Louie Marston 68–9, 187
  Church League for Women's Suffrage 63
Actresses Franchise League 116, 148
Albert Booth, Mrs. 106
Alford, Mrs. 36
Alfred, Mrs. 113
All England Ladies Hockey Association 148
All England Women's Hockey Association 100
Ambulance Brigade for Women and Girls 39
Anderson Morshead, Miss. 53
Angel in the House 63
Anglican Brotherhoods and Sisterhoods 187
Anglican Girls' Diocesan Association 79
Anglicanism 13, 53, 56
  education 123–4, 128, 133–5, 138, 142–3, 146, 150
  political network and suffrage 97, 99–100, 106, 108, 114, 116–17, 121
  public service 153, 159–60
  segregation 51
  social cohesion 1, 16
  subordination 47–8, 75
  suffragist ranks 116
  views on education 123
  women's alliance 97
  women's space 180–2, 184, 186–7, 191
anti-Roman Catholic antipathy 57, 186–7
anti-suffrage views 38, 108, 110, 115, 118
Anti-Sweating League 102, 173
Argles, Edith 143
Arnold, Mary 131
Arsenal, Woolwich 19, 66, 107, 174
Arthur (Suffragan Bishop of Southampton) 112
Ashwell, Lena 116, 147–8

Associations for the Care of Friendless Girls 99, 102–3
Atherton, Rev. C. J. 81
audience 2
  church congress 1–2, 5, 10, 12–13, 16–20, 24–9, 31, 33, 37, 40–5
  congress legacy 188–9, 191
  educational development 128–30, 132, 134–6, 141, 144–6, 148–50
  Mothers' Union and the Girls' Friendly Society 76, 78, 80–1, 83–6, 92–3
  political networks 101, 104, 107, 110, 117
  public service 159–60, 163–5, 167–9, 172–3, 177
  spiritual aspirations 49–50, 52, 55–6, 58–9, 61–5, 70, 72
Avins, Eliza 32

Bailey, Mrs. Cyril 69
Banks, Edith 57
Banner Committee 33
Barker, Lilian C. 19, 66, 107, 174
Barnes, Miss. 33
Barnett, Edith A. 155, 168
Barnett, Henrietta 20–1, 101, 106, 142, 144, 154–6, 166, 168, 174
Barnett, Samuel 142, 154
Barrow congress 155
Barrow-in-Furness congress 29, 101, 115, 144, 163
Barton Regis Union Redlands Bristol 62, 159
Bath congress 1, 59
Battenberg, Princess Henry of 173
Bedford College for Women 125
Beebe, Kathryne 179
Bennett, Mrs. P. D. 31
Bennitt, Miss. E.G. 23
Benson, Mary 77, 105
Beresford, Madame Isabelle 18

Bergman-Osterberg, Madame 148
Bevan, Mrs. Frank 16
Biggs, Rev. O. 125
Bird, Bishop. Isabella 3, 41–2, 44, 62, 89, 186
   Ladies Life in the Rocky Mountains, A 62
Birmingham City Council 158
Birmingham congress 35, 40–1, 48, 69, 100, 136, 147, 175
Bishop Creighton House settlement 143
Bishop Otter Teacher Training College 135
Black, Clementina 4, 116, 167, 169, 178
Blackfriars Settlement 142
Bland, Lucy 154
Blunt, R. F. L. 49
Boards of Categorisation 161
Bodley, RA, Mr. G. F. 15
Boer War 60, 112–14
Boer women, mortality 113
Bond, Rev. C. W. 1, 49
Booth, Charles 154, 168
Boulter, Mrs. 33
Bourdieu, Pierre 6–7, 71, 94–5, 179–82, 190
Bournemouth congress 10, 12, 27, 36, 40, 83
Bradford congress 26, 63
Brankler, Miss. 144
Brighton congress 64, 113, 125, 164
Bristol congress 36–7
British and Foreign Schools Society 123
British Broadcasting Corporation (BBC) 40
British Women's Emigration Association/Society 4, 24, 90, 92, 114
Bromley, Mrs. 33
Brooke, Augustus Stopford 130
Brooke-Hunt, Violet 64, 113
Burrows, Captain 50
Burstall, Sara 5, 136, 138, 141
Buss, Frances 136

Cadbury, Elizabeth 106
Cadbury, Mrs. George 35
Caius College 117
Calder, Fanny 104
Cambridge congress 14, 36, 72, 93, 116

Cambridge Ladies' Dining Society 105
Cardiff congress 61, 158
Carr-Glynn, Alice 33
Carruthers, Mrs. 38
Carter, Father T. T. 19, 52
Carter Sturge, Mrs. 19
Cavendish, Lord Frederick 111
Cavendish, Lucy, Lady Frederick 4, 105, 135, 140–1, 154, 165, 190
Cecil, Lord Edward 113
Cecil, Violet 113
Central Committee Women's Employment 38
Challoner Chute, Mrs. 85, 147, 149
Charity Organisation Society (COS) 50, 58, 101, 143, 157, 161
Mason, Charlotte 16, 86, 129
chastity 48, 53, 65, 78, 82, 94, 98–100, 183, 185
Cheltenham Ladies' College 31, 100, 136, 188
Chetham's Society 129
Cheveley, Emily 55–6
Christian Ideal in Industry and Business, The 112
Christian Socialist perspectives 156–7
Christian Social Union Research Committee 171
Church. *See also* Church congress; Girls' Friendly Society; Mothers' Union
   creation of new dioceses 16
   women's work 75
Church congress
   ceremonial parade/procession 11–14
   educational initiatives 123–52
   frequent contributors 21–3, 32–3
   host towns 11
   legacy on women's space and place 179–91
   logistic challenges 11
   members and audiences 25–9
   in nonconformists region 10–11
   objectives 9–10
   organization and committees 29–39
   political networks 97–122
   programme and women participants 15–25
   public service 153–78
   publicity and press 40–4

Index

sociability 34–40
thematic sessions 18–24
ticket sales 26–32
working-class perspectives 25–6
Church League for Women's Suffrage 63, 68, 116–17, 190
Churchmen 1, 64, 72, 88, 95, 159, 185
patriarchal notions of authority 75
Church Nursing 39
Church of England 5, 14, 26
Account of Early Life at Hope End 128
Convocation of Bishops in 1879 64, 128
Girls' Schools, shortage of 125
Juvenile Temperance League 163
National Mission of Repentance and Hope 1916 67
Society for the Promotion of Kindness to Animals 100
Temperance Society, Education Committee 39, 76, 101
Women's Union 101
Young Women's Help Society 17, 39, 99, 184
Zenana Mission Society (CEZMS) 61–2
Church School Company 125
citizenship negotiations 2, 49, 66, 88, 102, 108, 110, 115, 133, 144, 154, 175, 191
Clapcott, Miss. 33
Clarendon and Taunton commissions on education 111
Clarendon Commission 123
clergymen 18, 41–2, 69, 75, 85, 158
practical obligation and task 78
social affiliation of women 76–8
Clifford, Mary 19, 21, 23, 44, 62, 102, 104–6, 158–61, 171, 176, 178, 183
Women in the Indian Zenana 62
Clive, Kathleen, neé 111
Clough, Ann Jemima 140
Clubs for Boys 64, 113
Cochrane, Constance 107, 156
Colenso, Bishop's persecution 10
Coleridge, Christabel 5, 62, 86, 146
Collie, Dr. 155
Comber, Mrs. 23
Conns, Emma 154

Conservative and Unionist Women's Franchise Association 24, 110, 115
Conservative Primrose League 3, 106, 109, 190
Cooperative Women's Guild 101, 168
Coutts, Angela Burdett, *Woman's Mission: A Series of Congress Papers on the Philanthropic Work of Women by Eminent Writers* 63
Covert, James Thayne 130
Cowman, Krista 4
Cowper-Temple amendment 124
Creighton, Louise 3–4, 19–21, 24, 33–5, 43–4, 70, 76–8, 83, 93–4
congress legacy 184, 189–90
educational activism 126, 129–32, 140–3, 150
Laity in Council essays in Ecclesiastical and Social Problems 77
Life and Letters of Mandell Creighton 76
philanthropic activism 97
public service 155–6, 166, 176
role in organizational network 97, 99–100, 102, 104–6, 112, 118–21
Sesame and Lilies 130
Creighton, Mandell (Bishop of London) 100, 112, 130–1, 143, 156
Cropper, Miss. 115, 144

Daggers, Jenny 48
Davidson, Archbishop, Randall 56–7, 116
Davidson, Mrs. 41
Davis, Angela 179
Davis, Emily 140
Day, Emma Marrat, *Church's Equipment for Corporate Life and Witness, The* 57
deaconesses 3, 7, 24, 47, 51, 60, 69, 73, 97, 114, 186
congress agenda 49–59
costumes 54
Deane, Augusta 19, 100, 107, 167, 174, 176
Deane, Lucy 173
De Courcy Laffan, Mrs. R. S. 146
Delamont, Sarah 133
Dendy, Mary 101, 161
Dent, Phyllis 39, 134
Denton Thompson, Canon 49
Derby congress 2, 17, 64

Dilke, Sir Charles 171
Dougall, Lily 69
Dowager Countess of Chichester 48, 82–3
Duncan Jones, Rev. A S 117
Dunkley, Charles 30–1, 34
Dwelly, Canon 12
Dynevor, Lady 27

Early Closing Association 169
Eastbourne congress 27, 131, 168
education 2, 4–5, 49
   distinguished professionals 133–42
   home-centred learning 125
   legislative intervention 123–4
   and leisure pursuits 144–50
   middle- and upper-class girls 135
   non-denominational schools 133–4
   secondary schooling 125–6
   secular education 133–4
   social improvement and higher education 126
   working-class 133
Education Act 1870 123
Edwards, Mrs. 34
Eisenmann, Linda 71, 128, 150
Emma Yeatman 19, 22, 25, 33, 44, 57–9
Emery, William 29–30, 75–6, 81, 87–8
employment 2, 4, 16, 23, 25, 38, 45, 64, 85, 90, 92
   congress agenda 49–59, 176–7, 188
   education and 123, 145, 149
   organizational network 102, 104, 107, 116
   world of work 153, 155–6, 165–7, 170–1, 173
enfranchisement 4
Erskine Clarke, Rev. 126–7
Equality of Franchise Act 153
Eucharist 9, 51, 69
Executive Committee National Relief Fund 38
Exeter congress 32, 101, 165–6

Factory Acts of 1874, 1878 and 1896 156
Fairfield, Dr. Leticia 68, 187
Faithfull, Lilian M. 5, 44, 100, 136–8, 141, 148, 151, 162, 168
   Hand book of Women's Work 147
Fawcett, Millicent Garrett 105, 113, 115, 117
female participants 2

female suffrage, diverse perspectives 114–20
First World War 3, 9, 18, 44, 47, 59, 65, 68, 119, 175, 187, 191
Flavel, Edith 31
Fletcher, Mrs. W. E. 33
Folkestone congress 43, 55, 93
Forster Act 133
Fosbery, Rev. T. V. 84
Foucault, Michel 179
Francis, Emeline 86
Francis Petrie, Mrs. 61
Franqueville, Comtesse de 110
Fraser of Manchester, Bishop 25, 156
Frere, Sir Bartle, *Eastern Africa as a field for Missionary Labour Four letters to the Archbishop of Canterbury* 60
Friendly Leaves 85, 90–1, 146

Garbett, Cyril, Bishop of Winchester 36, 40
Garbet, Miss. 36
Gascoyne-Cecil, Beatrix Maud 110
Gerard, Jessica 154
Gibbon, *Decline and Fall of the Roman Empire* 129
Gilchrist, Mrs. 23
Gilmore, Isabella 55–7, 105, 186
Girls' Diocesan Association (GDA) 100, 167
Girls' Friendly Society 2, 4, 16, 20, 39, 41, 64, 66–7, 69, 75. *See also* Mrs. Mary Townsend
   administrative structure 84–5
   congress legacy 184–6, 189, 191
   domestic ideology/home identities 85–6, 93
   insistence on purity 87
   philanthropic activism 97–102, 105, 109, 114, 120–1
   public service 160, 163, 166–7
   role in education and leisure 135, 145–7, 149
   social and clerical networks 85
   spatial reach 88–94
Girls' Public Day School Company 111, 125, 135, 141
Girton College Cambridge 125, 136, 140–1, 143
Gladstone, Helen 4, 111, 143
Gladstone, William Ewart 4, 110–11

Gleadle, Katherine 4, 106, 177, 179, 181, 187
Glyn, Mary 15
Glynne, Catherine 111
Glynne, Rev. Henry 111
Glynne, Mary 111
Goodman, Joyce 133
Goodwin, Rev. 172
Gorell Commission 86
Gorham Case controversy 10
Gorham, Deborah 133
Grant, Mrs. 17, 85
Green, Bethnal 143
Green, J. R. 130
Green, T. H. 142
Greene, Mrs. J. W. 33
Grey, Mariah 103
Greyladies College 57–8
Griffith, Mrs. 174–5
Grubbe, Mrs. 23
Gruner, Miss. Alice 142–3

Habermas, Jürgen 179
Hampstead Garden Suburb 20, 106, 144
Harold, Browne, Edward (Bishop of Winchester) 54, 79–81, 84, 156
Harold, Browne Elizabeth 84
Harrington, Beatrice 143
Harlech, Lady 24
Hatton, Mrs. 159
Heath, Stubbs, Mary 90
Herbert, Mrs. 77, 134
Heywood, Sir Arthur Percival 27
Heywood, Thomas 128–9
Hicks, Mrs. Amie 25, 101, 169
Hicks, Bishop Edward Lee 68
High Church Tractarians 9, 13, 51–2, 180
High Church views 13, 52
    Tracts for the Times 51
Highley, Miss. 142, 146–7
Hilton, Mary 133
Hinscliff, Rev. Claude 116
Hinscliff, Gertrude 116–17
Hirsch, Pam 133
Hitchman, Robert 11
Hollis, Patricia 154
home education 127–32
Home Life 82
Home Rule for Ireland 110
House of Lords 108, 124

Hopkins, Jane Ellice 2, 17, 20, 42, 44, 64–5, 79, 99, 127–8
    academic tradition 128–32
    campaign against sexual exploitation 98
    congress legacy 183, 189
    educational activism 126–30, 132, 150
    Ladies' Association for the Care of Friendless Girls 79, 99, 128
    philanthropy 99, 102
    Plea for the Wider Action of the Church of England in the Prevention of the Degradation of Women, A 64, 128
Howson, Dean 52
    Deaconesses or, the Official Help of Women in Parochial Work and in Charitable Institutions 54
Hubert, Barclay, Noel 31, 39, 83
Hudson, Lyall Beatrice 67, 108, 175
Hull congress 32, 34, 49, 61, 81, 86–7, 129
Humphry Ward, Mrs. 130–1

indigenous populations 63, 88–9, 92, 94, 96, 112, 114
Industrial Law Committee 102, 171–3
Ingram, Miss. 15
Ipswich congress 38, 40, 83, 134
Ipswich Executive Committee 33
Irving, Sir Henry 147
Isaac, Mrs. 31

James, Miss. 23
Janes, Emily 103, 153, 182
Jerome Mercier, Mrs. 8
John Jones, Mrs. 23, 62
journalism 4
Joyce, Ellen 4, 17, 85, 90–2, 94, 96

Keble, John 53, 111
Keighly, Mabel 15
Kemp, Beatrice 24
Kendall, Diana 154
Kensit, John 13, 183
King, Gertrude 89
Kingsbury, Rev. 61
Kingsley, Charles 142

Kingsley, Mrs. Henry 134, 158
Knight-Bruce, Louisa 68
Knightley, Louisa 4, 24, 92, 106, 110, 114–15

Labourers Cottages (National Housing Conference) 107
Ladies' Association for the Care of Friendless Girls 64, 79, 86, 99, 103, 128
Ladies' Dining Society 105, 118, 142
Ladies of the Guild of Church Embroiderers 15
Lady Margaret Hall 5, 48
Lambeth Conference 16, 55, 57, 68, 124, 134, 153, 156-7, 186–7
   Resolution 11 55
Lambeth congress 53, 187
Lamplugh, Rev. 9–10
Lancashire and Cheshire Association for the Permanent Care of the Feeble Minded 161
Lancaster, Joseph 123
League for Women's Suffrage 34, 39, 63, 67-8, 116-17, 190
League of the Church Militant 68, 116, 187, 190
Lee, Hetty 134
   Talks to the Training Class: A Manual for Heads of Sunday Kindergartens and Primary Departments 134
Leeds congress 25, 42
Lefebvre, Henri 179–81
   Production of Space 6
Legge, Mrs. (wife of Bishop Lichfield) 24, 76
legislative reforms/law 3–4, 16, 83, 123, 153-7, 159, 170, 188, 190
Leicester congress 19, 57, 174
Leigh, Maxwell Studdy 31
Leith Adams, Mrs. 5, 25, 146
leisure 5–7, 16, 97, 100, 169, 173, 180
   education and 123–52
   work and 2
Lend a Hand Club (Bristol) 100
Leonard Burrows, Mrs. 33, 85
Lightfoot, Joseph (Bishop of Durham) 17, 65
   Primary Charge of the Clergy of the diocese of Durham 65

Little, Mrs. 23, 63
Liverpool congress 27, 29, 111, 126, 146
Llewelyn Davis, Rev. J. 125
Llewellyn, Lady 41
Local Education Authority Schools 124
Local Government Act 1888 153
Lofland, Lyn H. 184
London congress 10, 33–4, 42, 53, 62, 76, 100–1, 143, 154, 159, 168
   Women's Work for Missions 62
London Diocesan Mothers' Union 108
London Rope Makers Union 25, 101, 169
London University Higher Examination for Women 130
Lord Chancellor's Advisory Committee for Women Justices 38
Low Church party/Evangelicals 9, 13, 51, 180
Lydia, Seldon 42
Lyttelton, Alfred, Bishop of Winchester 65, 112, 117
Lyttelton, Edith Sophie Balfour 112
Lyttelton, George 4th Barron 24, 30, 111–12, 135
Lyttelton, Kathleen 4, 105, 112118–20, 142, 190

Maclagan, Augusta 16, 41, 76, 84–5, 94, 99, 167-8, 177
   speeches 84
Magistrates Association 102, 174
Malkin, Mrs. 159
Manchester and Salford Blind Aid Society 27
Manchester and Salford Trade Union Council 101, 168
Manchester congress 136, 155
Manchester Federation of Women's Suffrage Societies 24
Mangion, Carmen 179
Maria Grey Training College 125
Markham, Violet (Mrs. Caruthers) 38, 107–8, 113, 118, 190
Married Women's Property Act 153
Martin. Rev. W. L 39
Martin, Jane 133
Mason, Charlotte 16, 86, 129
Mason, Marianne 24–5, 88, 99, 102, 158, 160, 171, 176, 178, 188
Massey, Doreen 6–7, 120, 180, 183

Maud Countess of Selborne 110, 115
  Sex and Common Sense 65
Maurice, Frederick Denison 142–3, 156
Maynard, Constance 136, 141
McDowell, Linda 6, 179
Medical Act 153
medical perspectives 25, 61, 68, 89, 105, 129, 149, 153, 155, 163–5, 172, 176–7
  morality and self-restraint 4
Melnyk, Julie, Theological Approaches to Women in the Age of Empire 48
Mental Deficiency Act of 1913 162
Methodist Assembly 10
Midwives Act 155
Milne, A. A. 137
Milner, Alfred 113
missionaries 7, 24, 59–63, 69, 73, 88–90, 96, 186
  philanthropic activism 63–4
  spiritual authority 63–71
Mitchell, Dr. Kate 104, 164
  Drink Question: Its Social and Medical Aspects, The 4
Money, Agnes 93
Monk, E.G. Esq., Mus.Doc. 110
Montgomery, Henry (Bishop of Tasmania) 60, 93
Moore, Florence 78
More, Hannah 82
Morgan, Simon 106, 183
Moss, Miss. 159
Mothers in Council 89
Mothers' Union 2, 4, 20, 39, 41, 64, 66–7, 69, 75. *See also* Sumner, Mary
  centralization in 1896 82
  Church endorsement 81
  collective women's perspective 79–81
  congress legacy 184–6, 189, 191
  diocesan adoption 97
  education and leisure activities 128–9, 134–5
  home identities 93
  key development 79
  new branches 88–9
  political network 97–101, 114, 121
  spatial reach 88–94
Mulvany, Editha 61–2, 186
Mumm, Susan 52, 154

Nassau Senior, Mrs. 84
National Association for the Care and Protection of the Feeble Minded 4, 23, 101, 161
National Council of Women of Great Britain 102, 104, 110, 189
National Health Society 19, 101, 162
National Service Department 38, 107
National Society for Promoting the Education of the Poor in the Principles of the Church of England 123
National Union of Women Workers (NUWW) 3, 102–6, 121, 131, 143, 158
National Union of Women's Suffrage Societies 38, 107, 189
Newcastle Commission of 1858–61 123
Newcastle congress 1, 14, 17, 84–5
Newport congress, Women's Place in the World of Today 107
New Testament 54
Nicholson, Godfrey 142
Norfolk Rural District Council 108
Northampton congress 15, 79, 124, 171
North Norfolk Rural District Council 158
Norwich Committee 25
Norwich congress 13, 26, 32, 58, 60
Nottingham congress 11, 17, 20, 59–60, 80, 110–11

Orlidge Davies, Miss. 140
Olowole, Mrs. 94
Ormiston, Dr. Margaret 158
Oxbridge graduands 141
Oxford congress 16, 53, 78, 100, 141, 146
Oxford House Settlement 142–3

Paget, Emma 53, 69
Palmer, Hon. Robert 110, 117
Palmer, Lady Sophia 43, 110
Palmer, Roundell (Earl of Selborne (1812–95)) 4, 43, 109
Palmer, William 110, 112
Pan Anglican Congress 56, 60, 93, 134
Pankhurst, Dame Christabel 41
Pankhurst, Emmeline 23, 118
Parent's Educational Union 86
Parents National Education Union 86
Parker, Miss. 129

Park Village West community 52
Patrick Campbell, Mrs. 19, 147
Patterson, Bishop of Melanesia 59
Patterson Develin, Mrs. T. 15
Patterson, Emma Smith 171
Patteson, John Coleridge 62
Patteson, Miss. 62
Peel, Robert 112
philanthropic activities 2–7, 20, 35, 45, 79, 84–7, 94
   congress legacy 184–5, 189
   deaconesses and missionaries 48, 50, 54, 58, 61, 73
   education and leisure 106–7, 111, 116, 120, 126, 128, 133, 135, 142–3, 145, 150–1
   public service 154, 156–8, 166, 174, 176–8
   religion and 63–5
   rescue and preventive works 98–102
   Victorian phenomenon 184
Phillimore, Lucy 23, 63
Philip, Papillon, Mrs. 17, 44, 86–8, 99, 184
   opponents 87
   Women's Help Society 86–7
Phillips, Miss. 23
Phillp, Mrs. 90
Picton-Turbervill, Edith 3, 67–70, 116, 187
   Christ and Woman's Power 68
Pigott, Blanche 100, 158–9
Pinsent, Ellen 4, 23, 101, 107, 158, 161, 176, 178, 188, 190
Pigou, Rev. Francis 85
Plymouth congress 15, 108, 112, 126, 156
political activism 4
political networks 106–12
Poor Law guardian 19, 23–4, 64, 76, 98, 102, 104, 155, 158–61, 168, 171, 177
Portsmouth congress 79, 85–6
pro-suffrage campaigning 115
Protestant Reformation 51
Protestant Truth Society 13
Proudfoot, Rev. Samuel 68
public service
   organized voluntary activism 157–63
   social and legislative context 153–7

   subject of temperance 163–5
   workplace regulation 166–75
Pusey, Dr. 52

Quaker philanthropists 35, 106, 123
Queen Victoria Clergy Fund 78

Rackham, Mrs. 23
Ranke, *History of England* 131
Raven, Charles Earle 12, 31
Ravenhill, Miss. Alice 19, 101, 162–3
Ravenhill, Kate 177
Reading congress 50, 53–4, 146
religion 1–2, 6–7, 71–3, 89–91, 97, 109, 120, 179–81
   education and 124, 126, 133–4, 136, 146, 151–2
   gendered difference 2, 47–9
Rendall, Jane 6, 184
Resolution 12 124
Richardson, Sarah 4, 106
Ridding, George, Bishop of Southwell 11, 85, 103, 110
Ridding, Laura 4, 11, 17, 20, 24, 34, 43, 83–5, 94, 99
   Call of the Empire 113
   congress legacy 184, 189–90
   educational activism 131
   'Girl who Should Marry a Clergyman, The' 77
   role in organizational network 98–9, 102–4, 107, 109–11, 113–15, 118
   voluntarism 98, 158–9, 161, 166
Rogers, Mrs. 77
Romaines, Ethel 146
Roman Catholicism 13, 51, 53–4, 56, 60, 73, 180, 186
Rouse, Ruth 38, 63, 100, 117–18, 137, 141, 173
Rowntree, Seebohm 156, 168
   Poverty a Study of Town Life 155
Royal Commission on the Dominions 91
Royal Commission on the Poor Laws and Relief of Distress 153
Royal Commission on Venereal Disease 176, 189
Royal Commissions 4, 98, 161
Royal Geographical Society 60
Royal Holloway College 141, 148

Royden, Maude, A. 3, 19–21, 25, 38, 44, 64–70, 111, 116, 140, 187
Rural District Councils 107
Ruskin, John 48, 81, 122, 130, 133, 142–3, 147, 182
  Sesame and Lilies 130, 133

Salisbury, Lord 33, 112
Scharlieb, Mary 4, 149, 164–5, 168, 177
  Womanhood and Race Regeneration 4
  Youth and Sex 4
Selborne, Earl of. *See* Palmer, Roundell (Earl of Selborne (1812–95))
Sellon, Lydia 52
Sex Disqualification (Removal) Act 115, 153, 173
Shields, Miss. 131
Sheepshanks, Margaret 76
Sheffield congress 7, 70, 89
Shops Acts between 1906 and 1913 156
Shrewsbury congress 43, 84, 155–6, 159
Siddall, Mary 57, 68
Sidgwick, Eleanor Mildred 105
Sidgwick, Henry 105, 140
Simpson, Canon Sparrow 48, 69
  Women's Position in the Ministry of the Church 69
Singleton Cooper, H. E. 33
sisterhoods 3, 51, 71, 73, 186–91
  attitudes towards deaconesses 54–5
  congress agenda 49–60
  revival 52
Sisters of Mercy 52
Snell, W. D. 15
Society for Promoting the Return of Women as Poor Law Guardians or Women's Guardians Society 102, 158
Society for the Employment of Women 153
Society for the Propagation of the Gospel (SPG) 89–90, 98
Soulsby, Lucy 24, 38, 106, 117, 134–6, 141, 151, 166
South African Colonisation Society (SACS) 24, 114, 189
Southam, Rev. Eric 12
Southampton congress 12, 23, 37, 44, 65, 71, 111, 117
Southend congress 15, 18–19, 57, 68, 148
Southport congress 12, 31, 34, 158

Southwark Diocesan Training School for Deaconesses 57
Sparks MA, Beatrice M. 31, 137
Sprott, Helen 23, 118
Steinthal, Emeline Francis 86
Sterling, F. 117
St Mary's Wantage community 53
Stoke on Trent congress 52, 101, 124, 134
Storrs, Monica 63
Strachan, Miss. 19
Strahan, Miss. 62
Streeter, B. H. 23, 67
Strong, Rosa 171
Stuart Snell, Miss. 25, 148–9
Suffragan Bishop of Guildford 77, 154
suffrage and political engagement 3–4, 24
Suffrage Pilgrimage of 1913 24
Sumner, Bishop Charles 51
Sumner, George 16, 49, 51, 76, 79
Sumner, John Bird 1, 79
Sumner, Margaret, Effie 27
Sumner, Mary 4, 77, 79–80, 97
  congress legacy 182–4, 189–90
  educational activism 126, 129, 133–5
  organizational network 97, 99, 109
  Our Holiday in the East 59, 89
  public service 156, 163, 165
  Responsibilities of Mothers, The 64
  speeches 81–2
  To Mothers of the Higher Classes 82
Sunday school workers 134
Swansea congress 10, 26, 32, 41, 85
Sweated Industries Exhibition 173

Tait, Archibald, Campbell (Archbishop of Canterbury) 84
Tait, Catherine 84
Talbot, Caroline 111
Talbot, Edward, Bishop of Southwark 72, 111, 131, 138, 142
Talbot, J.G. 50
Talbot, Lavinia 24, 105, 111, 131, 143
Talbot, Meriel 111
Talbot Rice, Mrs. 41
Talbot Rice, Rev. W. 10
Taunton Commission 123, 135
Temple, Beatrice 76, 90, 112, 124
Thorndike, Sybil 5, 116, 147–8
Thring, Godfrey 40, 126
Tidsall, Rev. Dr. 60

Townend, Kathleen M. 92, 96, 185
Townsend, Mary 17, 84–7, 90, 95, 109, 133
Tournier, Elizabeth. A. 101, 169
Toynbee Hall 142
Toynbee Hall University Settlement 20, 106, 154
Trinity College Dublin 141
Tuckwell, Gertrude 4, 21, 23–5, 45, 69, 102, 167, 170–5, 178, 188
Tuckwell, William 171

Underhill, Evelyn 71
Unitarian Cross Street Chapel 128
United British Emigration Society 92
United British Women's Emigration Society 114
university settlement movement 126, 142–4

Venereal Disease Commission 98, 132
Vicinus, Martha 4
Victoria League 113
Victoria Women's Settlement Liverpool 38, 144
Vincent, Clara 93, 96, 185
Vincent, Lady 185

Walsham Howe, William, Bishop of Bedford 75
Walter, Thomas, Mrs. 77
Wakefield congress 81, 126, 145
Ward, Mary 23, 115, 118–19
Warrender, Lady Maud 100
Weldon, James (Dean of Manchester) 117
Welsh School of Art Needlework 14
Weston, Agnes, Miss. 17, 25, 42, 64, 164, 184
Work amongst Sailors 64
Wellington, Furze, C. 50
Weymouth congress 23, 27, 32–3, 44, 59, 101
Whatley, Miss. 49, 89
Whitechapel Gallery 144
White Cross Army 64, 99, 183
Whytehead, Mrs. 33
Wilberforce, Ernest (Bishop of Newcastle) 80–1
Wilberforce, Samuel, (Bishop of Oxford) 29, 79, 84, 95, 122
Wilberforce, William 182
Wilkinson, George 64

William, Bishop of Lichfield 84, 157
William, George 135
Williams, Mrs. 33
Wilshere, Rev. A. R. M. 61
Winchester Women's Emigration Society 114
Winnington-Ingram, Bishop of London 67
Winterbotham, Alderman Clara 175
wives 4, 17, 24, 42, 51, 60, 62, 69, 81, 83, 85–6, 88, 93–5
  educational activism 133, 141
  religious role 75–9
  role in congress 97, 108, 184–5
  public service 155, 160
Wolmer, Viscount 110
Wolverhampton congress 15–18, 30, 75–6, 84, 159
women. *See also* public service; wives
  activist networks 98
  agency and activism 5
  as churchwomen 97
  citizenship 114–20
  conduct regulation 4
  congress agenda 49–59
  educators 125
  formal education 126
  home duties 3, 78
  marriage and motherhood 75
  religious role 3
  restricted access to learning 125
  right to property 3
Women as Poor Law Guardians 24, 102, 155, 158–9
Women in Industry from Seven Points of View 4
Women's International League for Peace and Freedom 67
Women's Co-operative Guild 101, 169
Women's Franchise League 3
Women's Freedom League 175
Women's Guardians Society Women's Local Government Society (WLGS) 102, 158
Women's League 79, 83, 99, 102
Women's National Anti-Suffrage League 117–18
Women's Protective and Provident League 169, 171
Women's Section National Service Department 38

women's spatial aspirations, legacy of congress 179–91
women speakers 2–4, 16–17, 19–20, 41, 44–6, 65, 68–70, 78, 106, 108, 111, 117, 125, 153, 157–8, 172, 176, 184, 187–8, 190–1
Women's Trade Union League 102, 169, 171–3
Women's University Settlement 111, 142–4
Woods, Mrs. Nina Theodore 19, 37, 83
Woods, Theodore, Bishop 37
Wordsworth, Christopher (Bishop of Lincoln) 48, 138
Wordsworth, Elizabeth 5, 23–4, 33, 43–4, 48–9, 57, 136, 138, 140, 143, 146, 148, 151, 182, 188
Wordsworth, Susan 57
Worker's Educational Association (WEA) 144
working-class
  audience 25, 68
  congress agenda 165, 168, 170–1, 178, 191
  education 123, 133, 152
  mothers 82
  women 42, 80, 99, 154, 165
Working Ladies Guild 109
World's Student Christian Federation 38, 100, 118, 141
Wycliffe Crusaders 13, 183

Yeatman, Bishop of Southwark 57
Yeo, Eileen Janes 75, 182
Yonge, Charlotte 1, 48–9, 53, 59, 62, 85–6, 126, 130, 135, 138, 145–6, 186
  Heir of Redcliffe, The 62
  Womankind 48
  Women's Work in the Church 1
Yorkshire Association of Ladies for the Care of Friendless Girls 86
Yorkshire West Riding County Council 162
Young Women's Christian Association (YWCA) 67, 79, 100, 107, 159, 167
Young Women's meeting on 'Work and Recreation' 24

Zenana 73, 89, 159, 186

www.ingramcontent.com/pod-product-compliance
Lightning Source LLC
Chambersburg PA
CBHW071816300426
44116CB00009B/1337